2

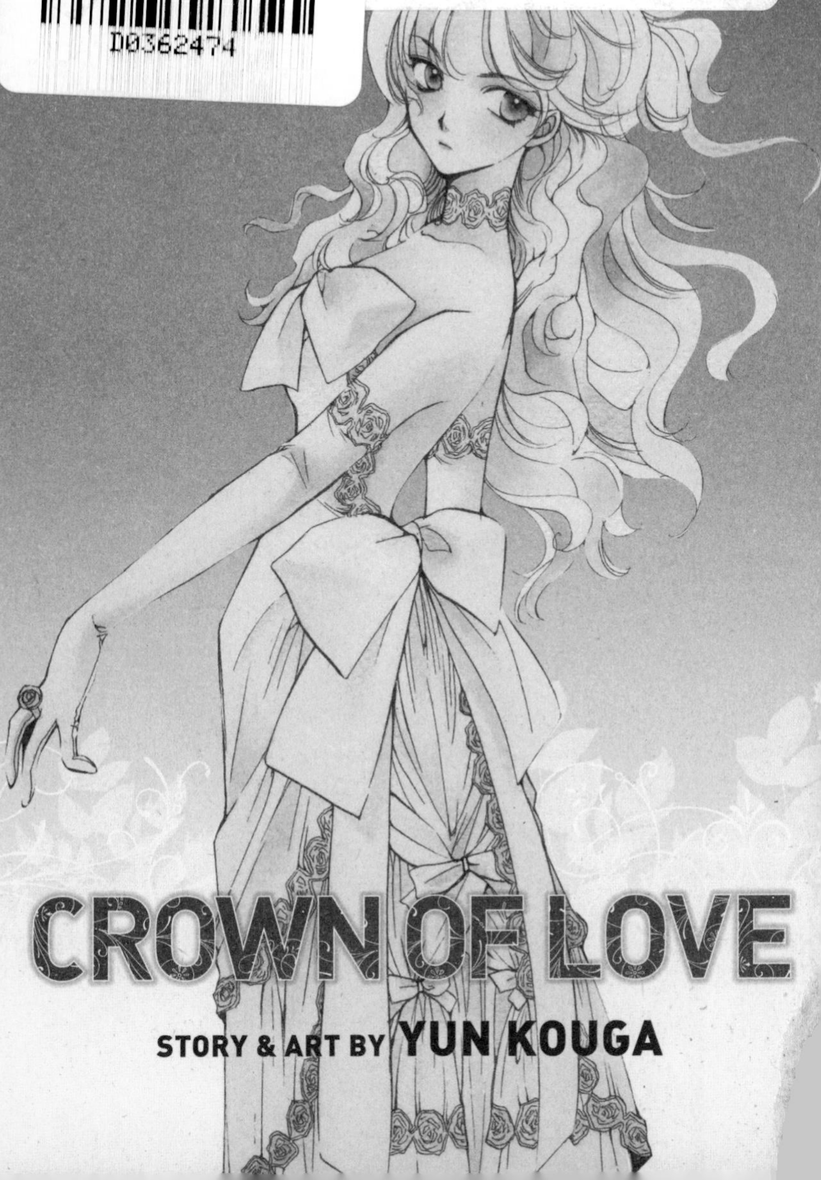

CROWN OF LOVE

STORY & ART BY **YUN KOUGA**

Table of Contents

Story Thus Far

When Hisayoshi Tajima, a 16-year-old high school student, runs into pop idol Rima Fujio, he falls head over heels in love. Constantly thinking of her, almost to the point of obsession, he can only watch her from afar as a fan. He even bonds with fellow fan Shingo Tachibana, a 10-year-old kid with money to spare. But when Rima's former manager Ikeshiba approaches Hisayoshi about becoming an idol himself, he gains entry into Rima's world. When Hisayoshi's father forbids him to become an idol, he runs away from home in desperation. But Rima agrees with his father—she doesn't want Hisayoshi in show-biz either! With Hisayoshi hogging all of Ikeshiba's attention, she can't hide her displeasure. But she'll have to suck it up if she wants Hisayoshi's help in passing the entrance exams to elite Hakuô High School...

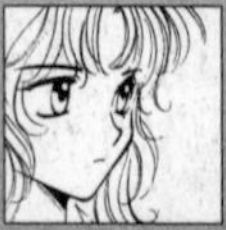

Rima Fujio

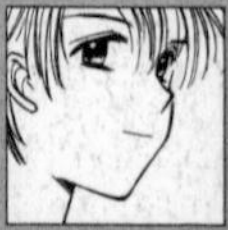

Hisayoshi "Kumi" Tajima

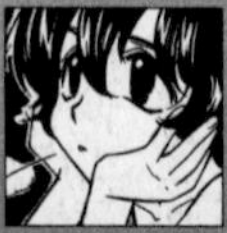

Shingo Tachibana

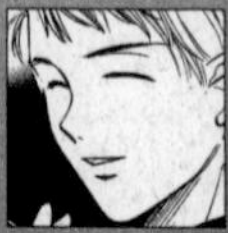

Ikeshiba

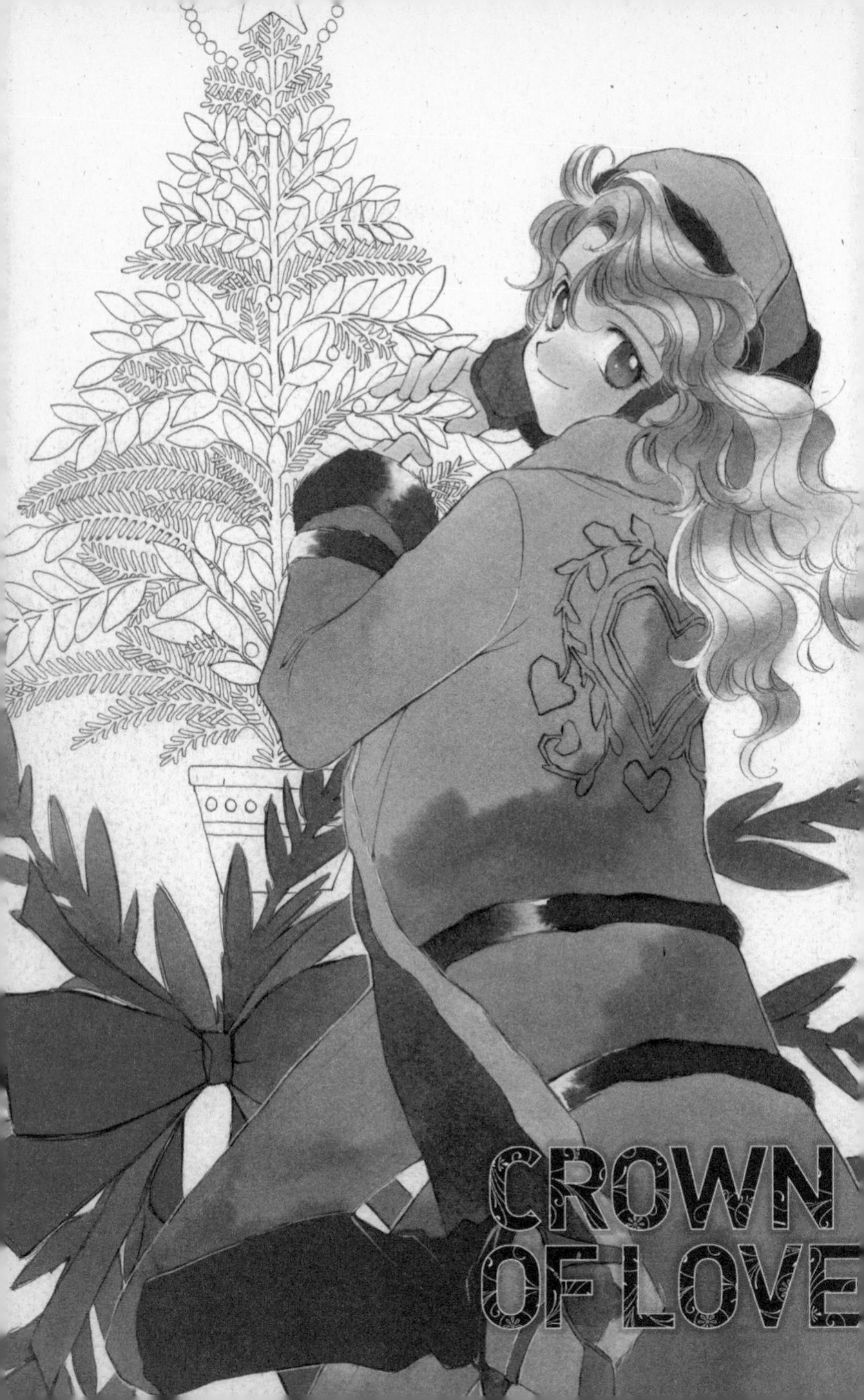
CROWN
OF LOVE

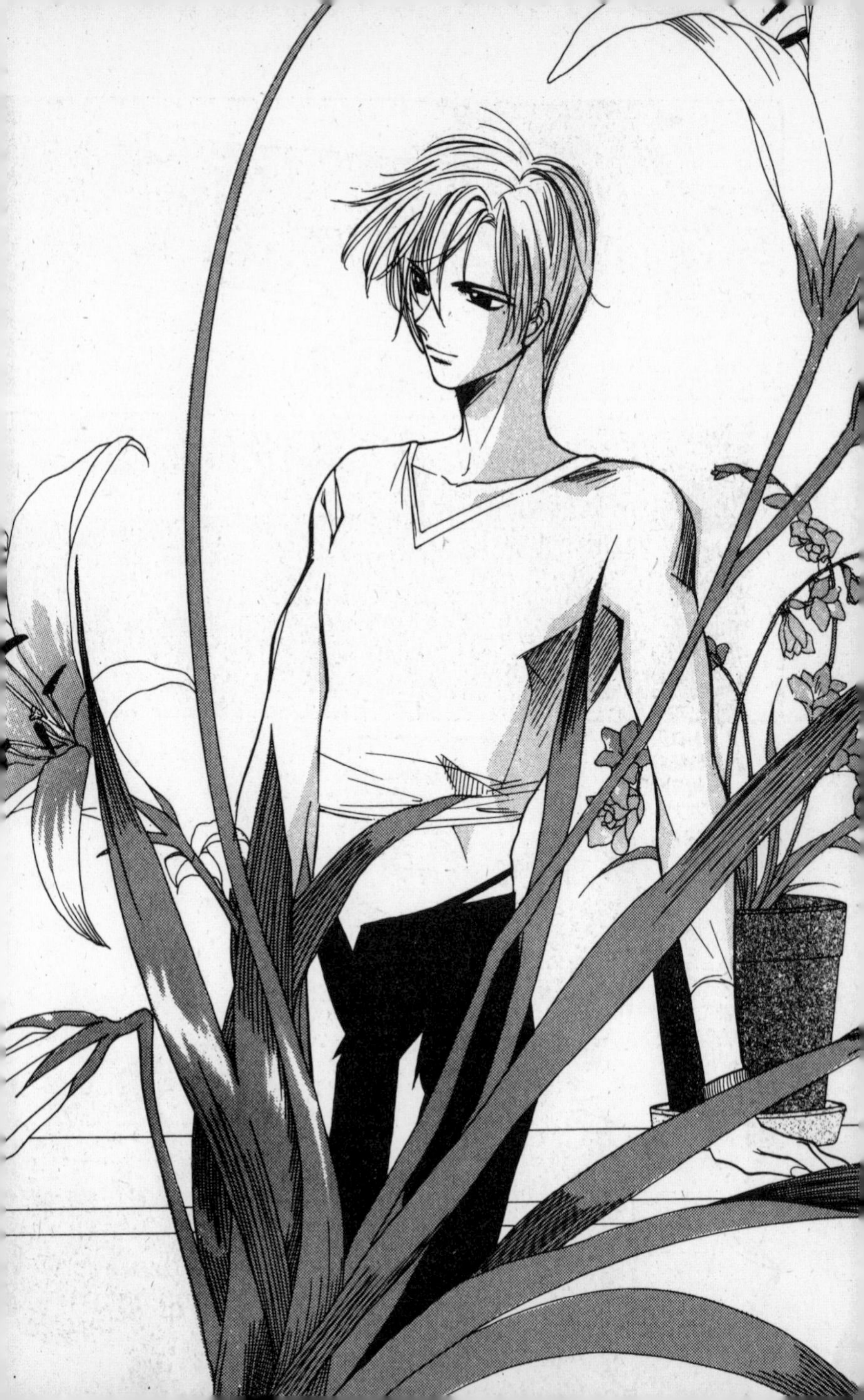

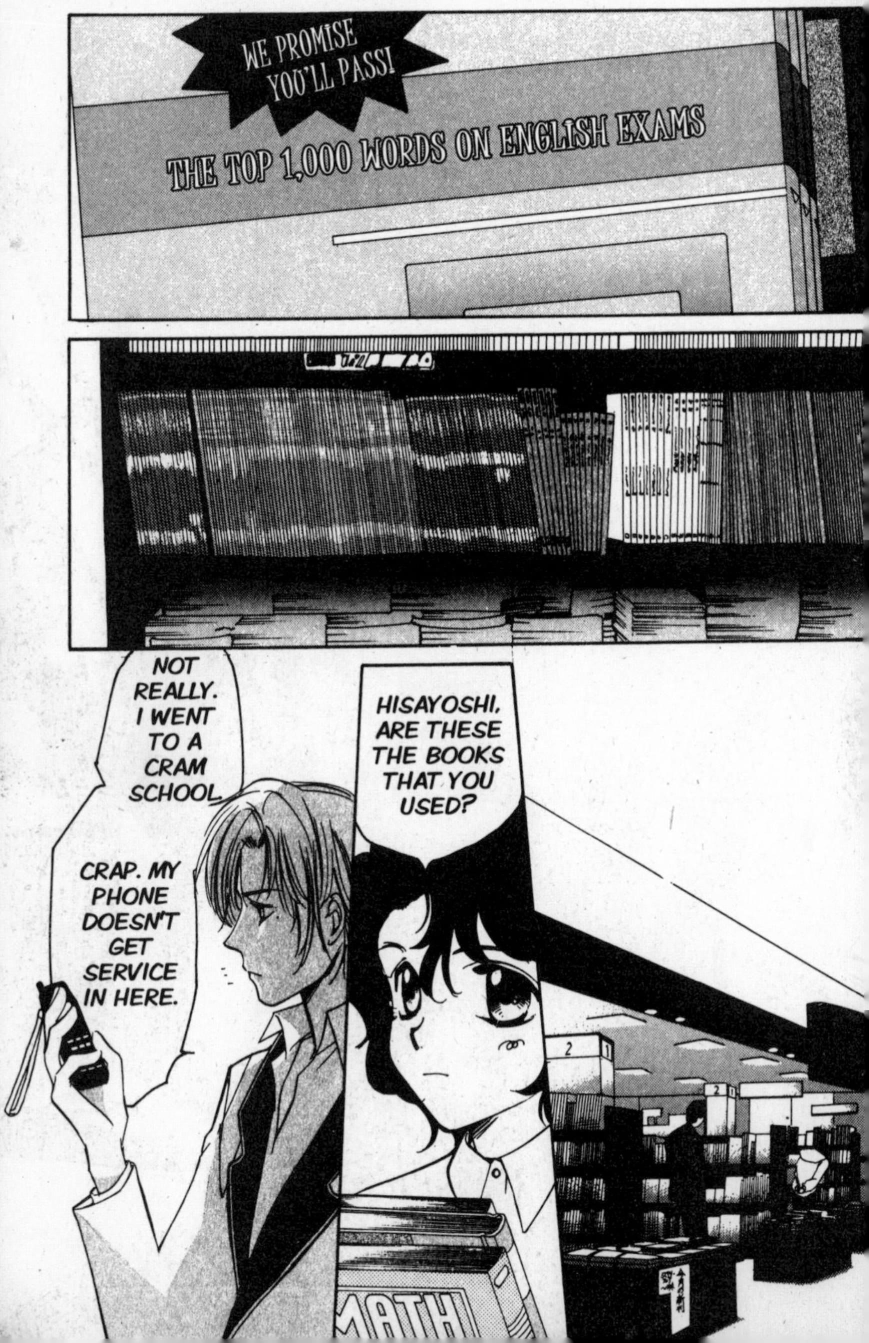
WE PROMISE YOU'LL PASS!
THE TOP 1,000 WORDS ON ENGLISH EXAMS
HISAYOSHI, ARE THESE THE BOOKS THAT YOU USED?
NOT REALLY. I WENT TO A CRAM SCHOOL.
CRAP. MY PHONE DOESN'T GET SERVICE IN HERE.
MATH

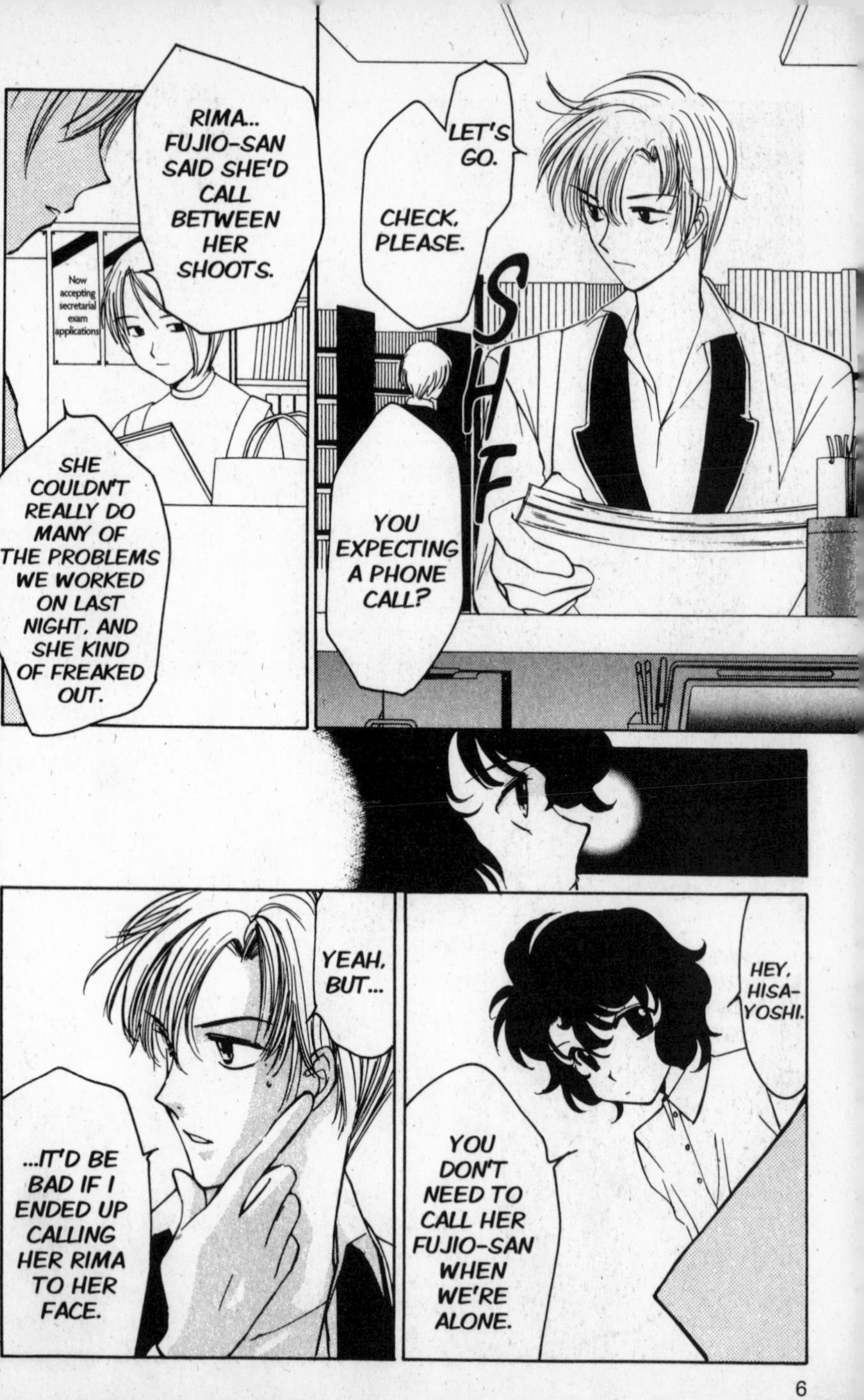
LET'S GO.
CHECK, PLEASE.
SHF
YOU EXPECTING A PHONE CALL?
RIMA... FUJIO-SAN SAID SHE'D CALL BETWEEN HER SHOOTS.
Now accepting secretarial exam applications
SHE COULDN'T REALLY DO MANY OF THE PROBLEMS WE WORKED ON LAST NIGHT, AND SHE KIND OF FREAKED OUT.
HEY, HISA-YOSHI.
YOU DON'T NEED TO CALL HER FUJIO-SAN WHEN WE'RE ALONE.
YEAH, BUT...
...IT'D BE BAD IF I ENDED UP CALLING HER RIMA TO HER FACE.

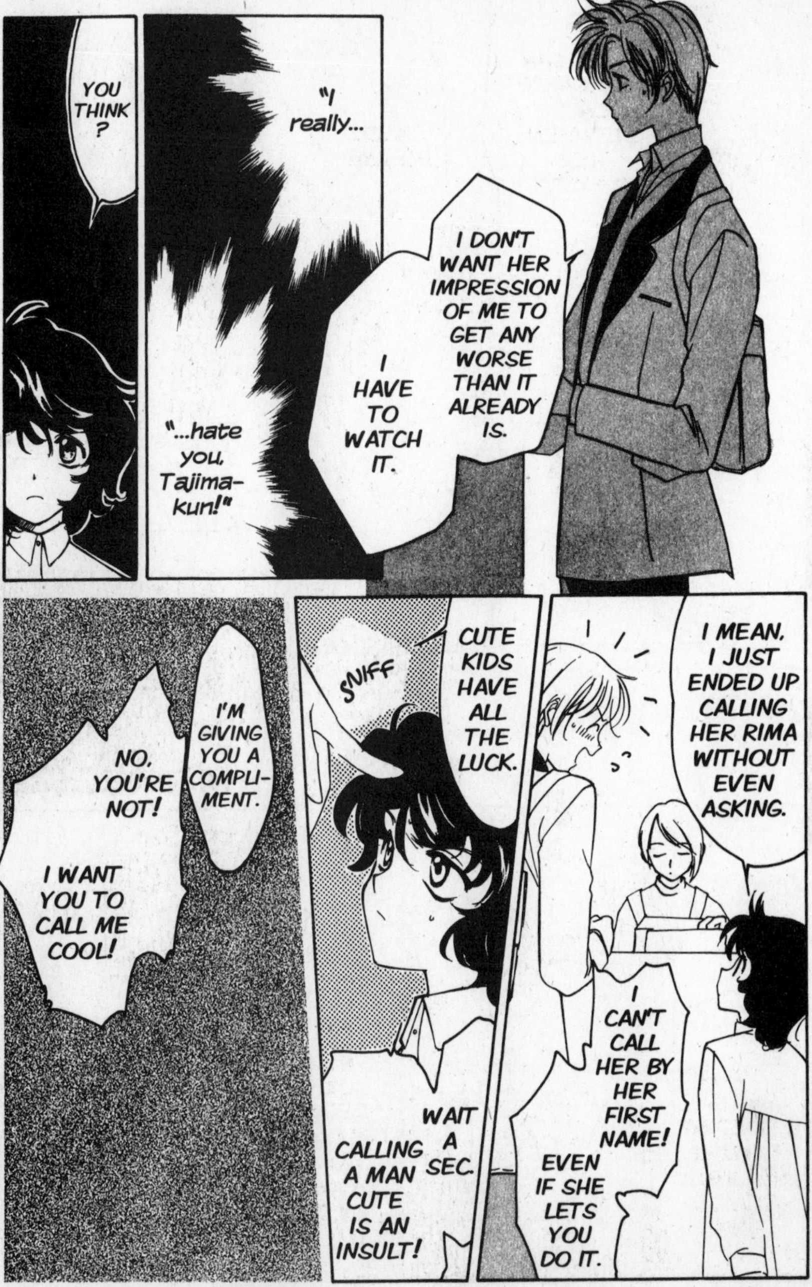
I DON'T WANT HER IMPRESSION OF ME TO GET ANY WORSE THAN IT ALREADY IS.
I HAVE TO WATCH IT.
"I really...
"...hate you, Tajima-kun!"
YOU THINK?
I MEAN, I JUST ENDED UP CALLING HER RIMA WITHOUT EVEN ASKING.
I CAN'T CALL HER BY HER FIRST NAME!
EVEN IF SHE LETS YOU DO IT.
CUTE KIDS HAVE ALL THE LUCK.
SNIFF
WAIT A SEC.
CALLING A MAN CUTE IS AN INSULT!
I'M GIVING YOU A COMPLIMENT.
NO, YOU'RE NOT!
I WANT YOU TO CALL ME COOL!

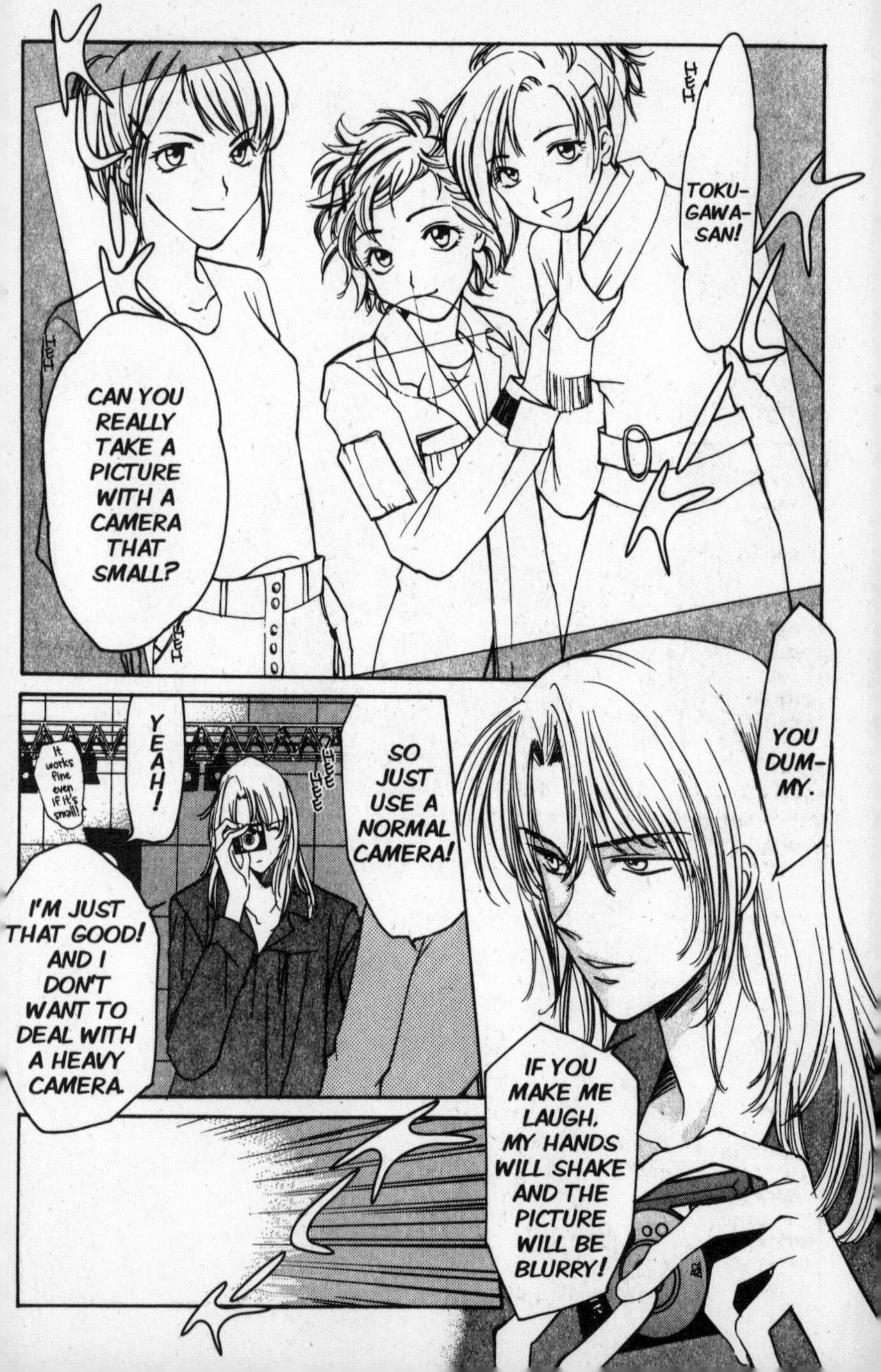

HEH
TOKU-GAWA-SAN!
HEH
CAN YOU REALLY TAKE A PICTURE WITH A CAMERA THAT SMALL?
HEH
YOU DUMMY.
IF YOU MAKE ME LAUGH, MY HANDS WILL SHAKE AND THE PICTURE WILL BE BLURRY!
SO JUST USE A NORMAL CAMERA!
YEAH!
It works fine even if it's small!
I'M JUST THAT GOOD! AND I DON'T WANT TO DEAL WITH A HEAVY CAMERA.

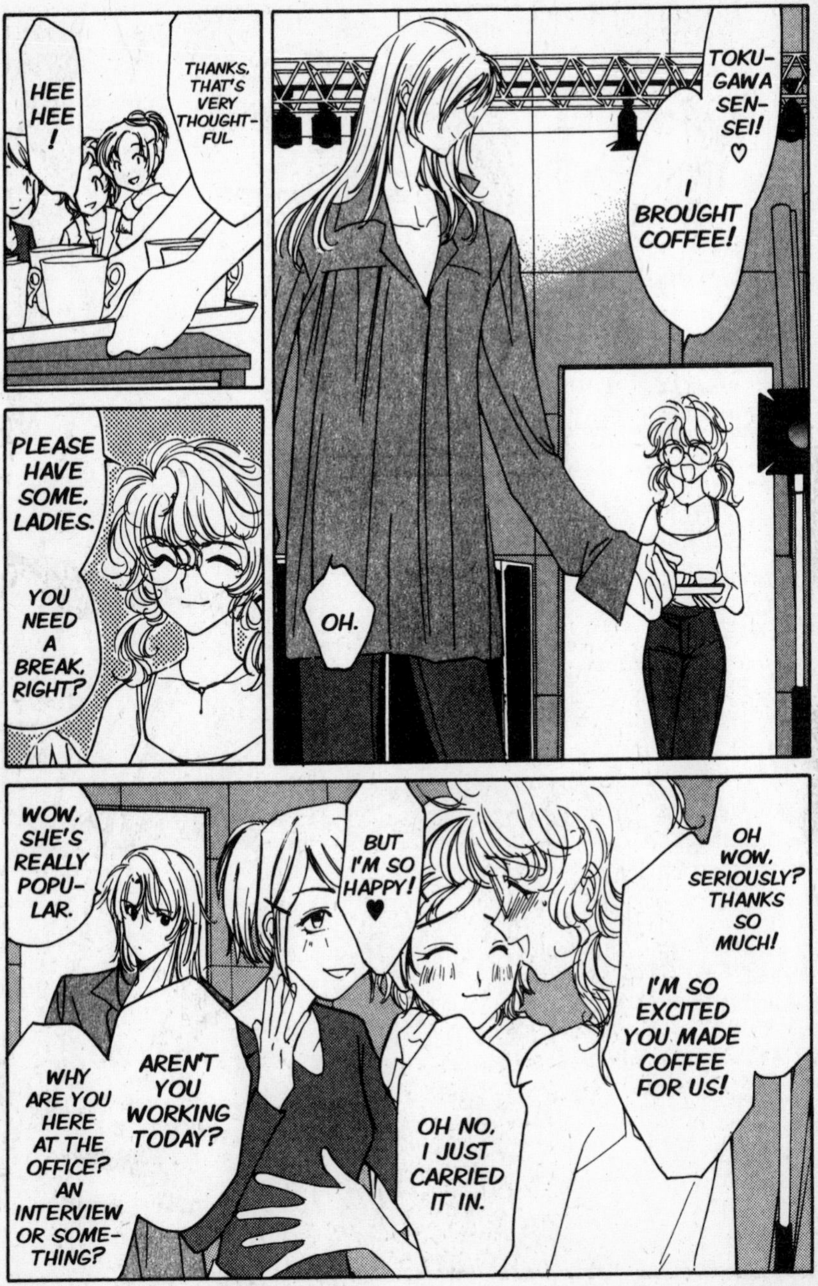
TOKUGAWA SENSEI! ♡
I BROUGHT COFFEE!
OH.
THANKS, THAT'S VERY THOUGHTFUL
HEE HEE!
PLEASE HAVE SOME, LADIES.
YOU NEED A BREAK, RIGHT?
OH WOW, SERIOUSLY? THANKS SO MUCH!
I'M SO EXCITED YOU MADE COFFEE FOR US!
OH NO. I JUST CARRIED IT IN.
BUT I'M SO HAPPY! ♥
WOW, SHE'S REALLY POPULAR.
AREN'T YOU WORKING TODAY?
WHY ARE YOU HERE AT THE OFFICE? AN INTERVIEW OR SOMETHING?

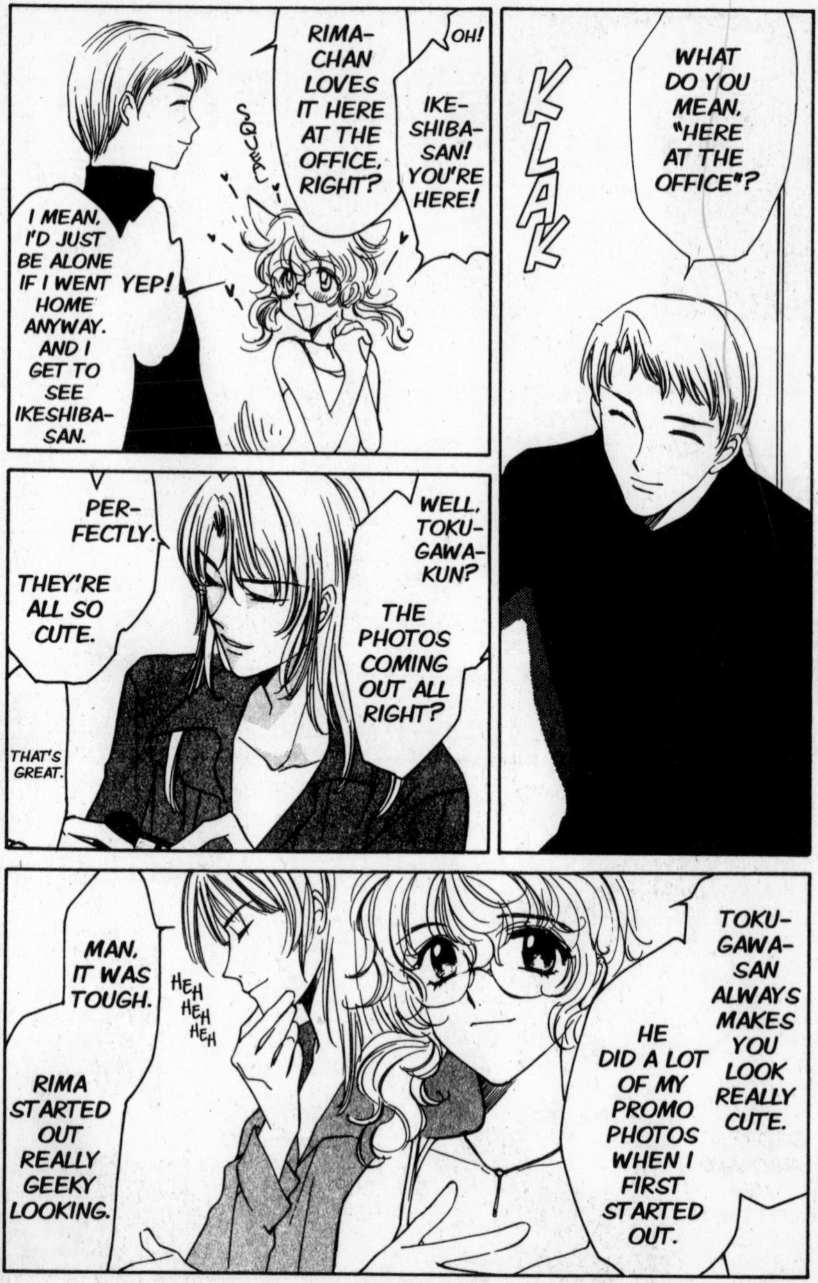
KLAK
WHAT DO YOU MEAN, "HERE AT THE OFFICE"?
OH!
IKE-SHIBA-SAN! YOU'RE HERE!
RIMA-CHAN LOVES IT HERE AT THE OFFICE, RIGHT?
YEP!
I MEAN, I'D JUST BE ALONE IF I WENT HOME ANYWAY. AND I GET TO SEE IKESHIBA-SAN.
WELL, TOKU-GAWA-KUN?
THE PHOTOS COMING OUT ALL RIGHT?
PER-FECTLY.
THEY'RE ALL SO CUTE.
THAT'S GREAT.
TOKU-GAWA-SAN ALWAYS MAKES YOU LOOK REALLY CUTE.
HE DID A LOT OF MY PROMO PHOTOS WHEN I FIRST STARTED OUT.
HEH HEH HEH
MAN, IT WAS TOUGH.
RIMA STARTED OUT REALLY GEEKY LOOKING.

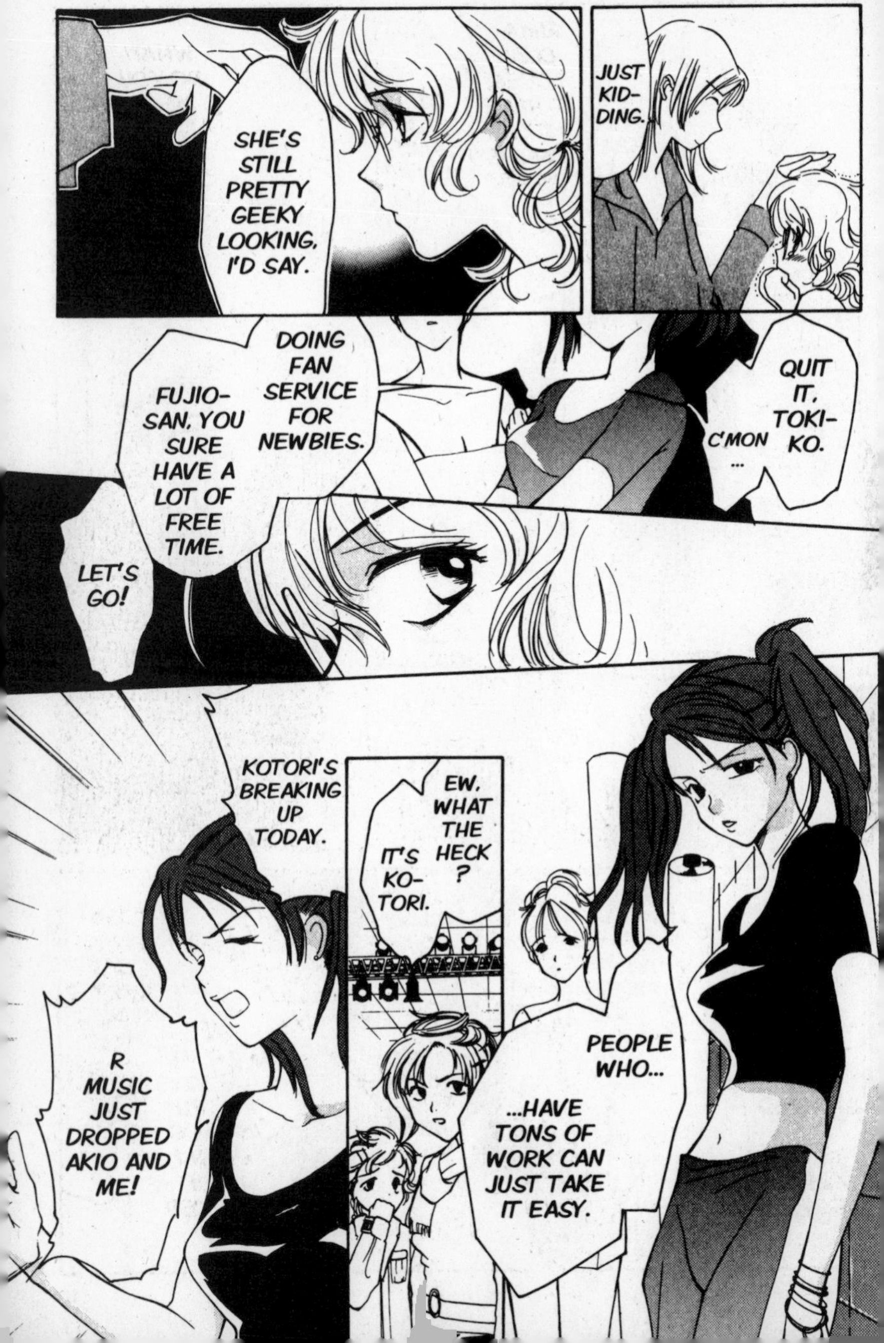
JUST KID-DING.
SHE'S STILL PRETTY GEEKY LOOKING, I'D SAY.
QUIT IT, TOKI-KO.
C'MON ...
DOING FAN SERVICE FOR NEWBIES.
FUJIO-SAN, YOU SURE HAVE A LOT OF FREE TIME.
LET'S GO!
EW, WHAT THE HECK ?
IT'S KO-TORI.
KOTORI'S BREAKING UP TODAY.
PEOPLE WHO...
...HAVE TONS OF WORK CAN JUST TAKE IT EASY.
R MUSIC JUST DROPPED AKIO AND ME!

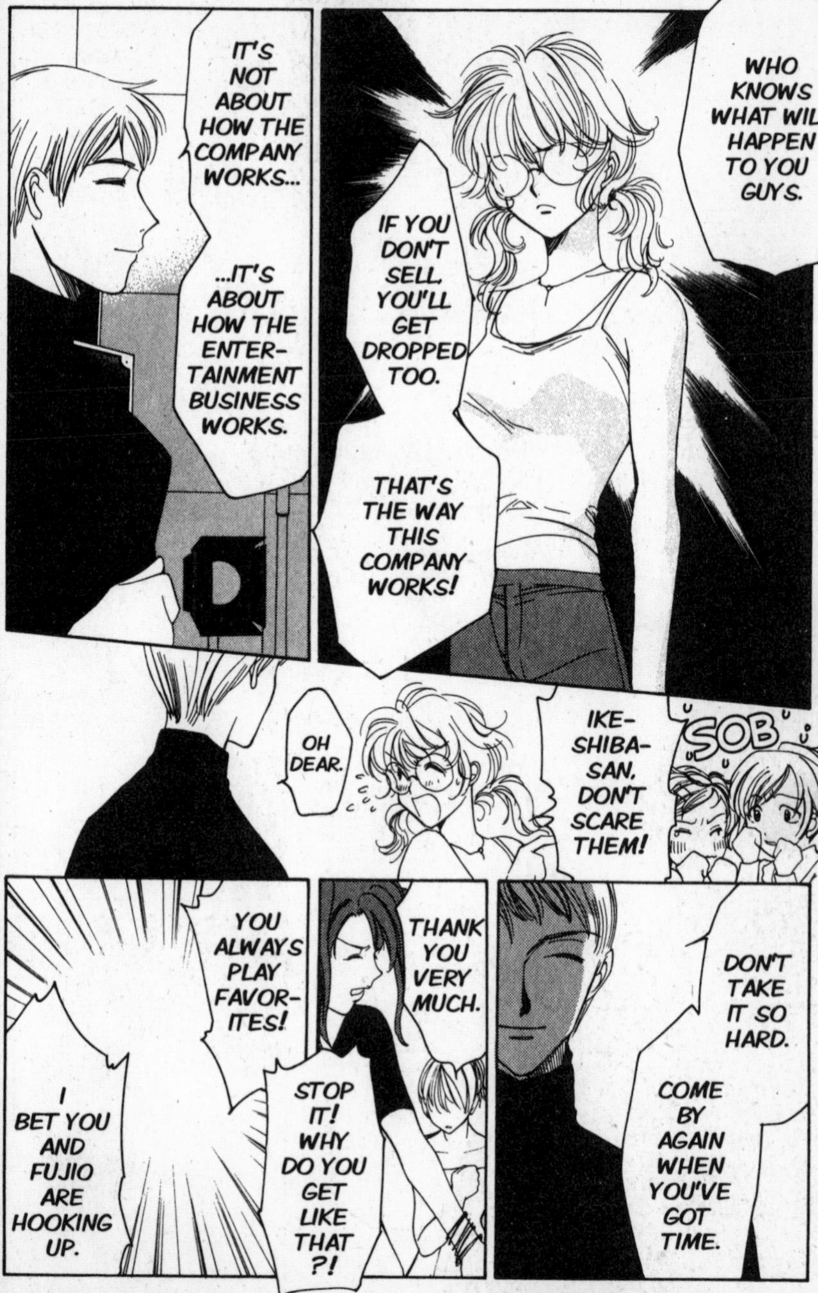
WHO KNOWS WHAT WILL HAPPEN TO YOU GUYS.
IF YOU DON'T SELL, YOU'LL GET DROPPED TOO.
THAT'S THE WAY THIS COMPANY WORKS!
IT'S NOT ABOUT HOW THE COMPANY WORKS...
...IT'S ABOUT HOW THE ENTER-TAINMENT BUSINESS WORKS.
SOB
IKE-SHIBA-SAN, DON'T SCARE THEM!
OH DEAR.
DON'T TAKE IT SO HARD.
COME BY AGAIN WHEN YOU'VE GOT TIME.
THANK YOU VERY MUCH.
YOU ALWAYS PLAY FAVOR-ITES!
I BET YOU AND FUJIO ARE HOOKING UP.
STOP IT! WHY DO YOU GET LIKE THAT?!

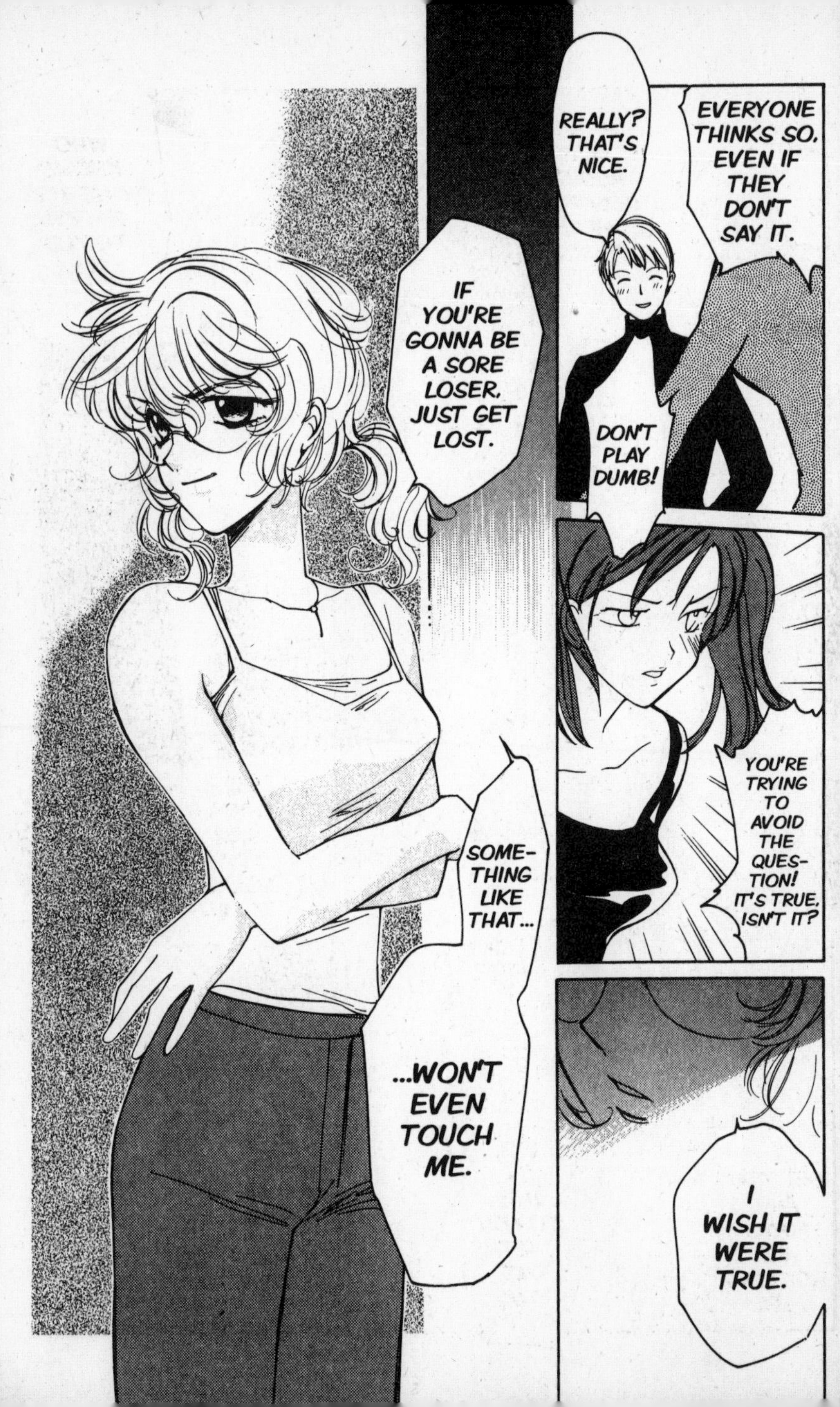
EVERYONE THINKS SO, EVEN IF THEY DON'T SAY IT.
REALLY? THAT'S NICE.
DON'T PLAY DUMB!
YOU'RE TRYING TO AVOID THE QUESTION! IT'S TRUE, ISN'T IT?
I WISH IT WERE TRUE.
IF YOU'RE GONNA BE A SORE LOSER, JUST GET LOST.
SOMETHING LIKE THAT...
...WON'T EVEN TOUCH ME.

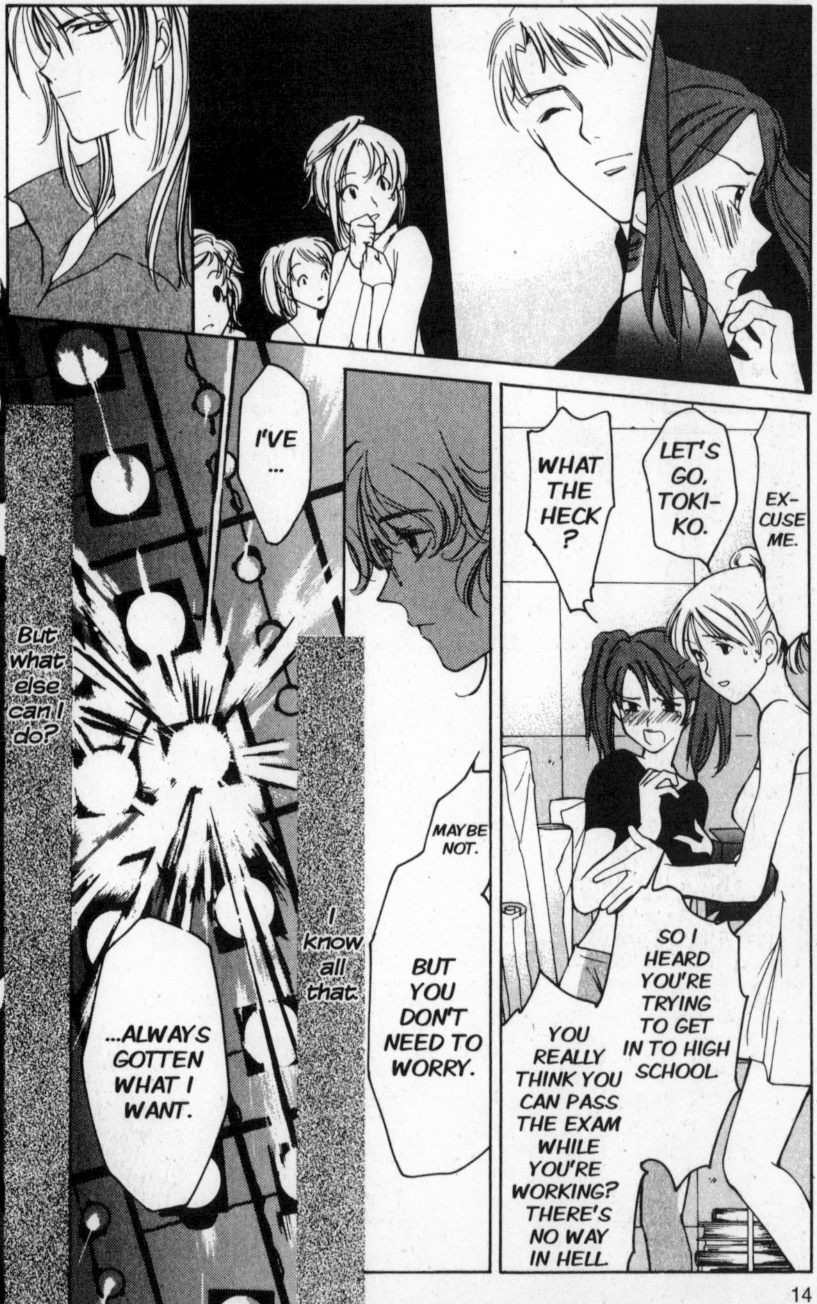
EX-CUSE ME.
LET'S GO, TOKI-KO.
WHAT THE HECK?
SO I HEARD YOU'RE TRYING TO GET IN TO HIGH SCHOOL.
YOU REALLY THINK YOU CAN PASS THE EXAM WHILE YOU'RE WORKING? THERE'S NO WAY IN HELL.
MAYBE NOT.
BUT YOU DON'T NEED TO WORRY.
I know all that.
I'VE ...
But what else can I do?
...ALWAYS GOTTEN WHAT I WANT.

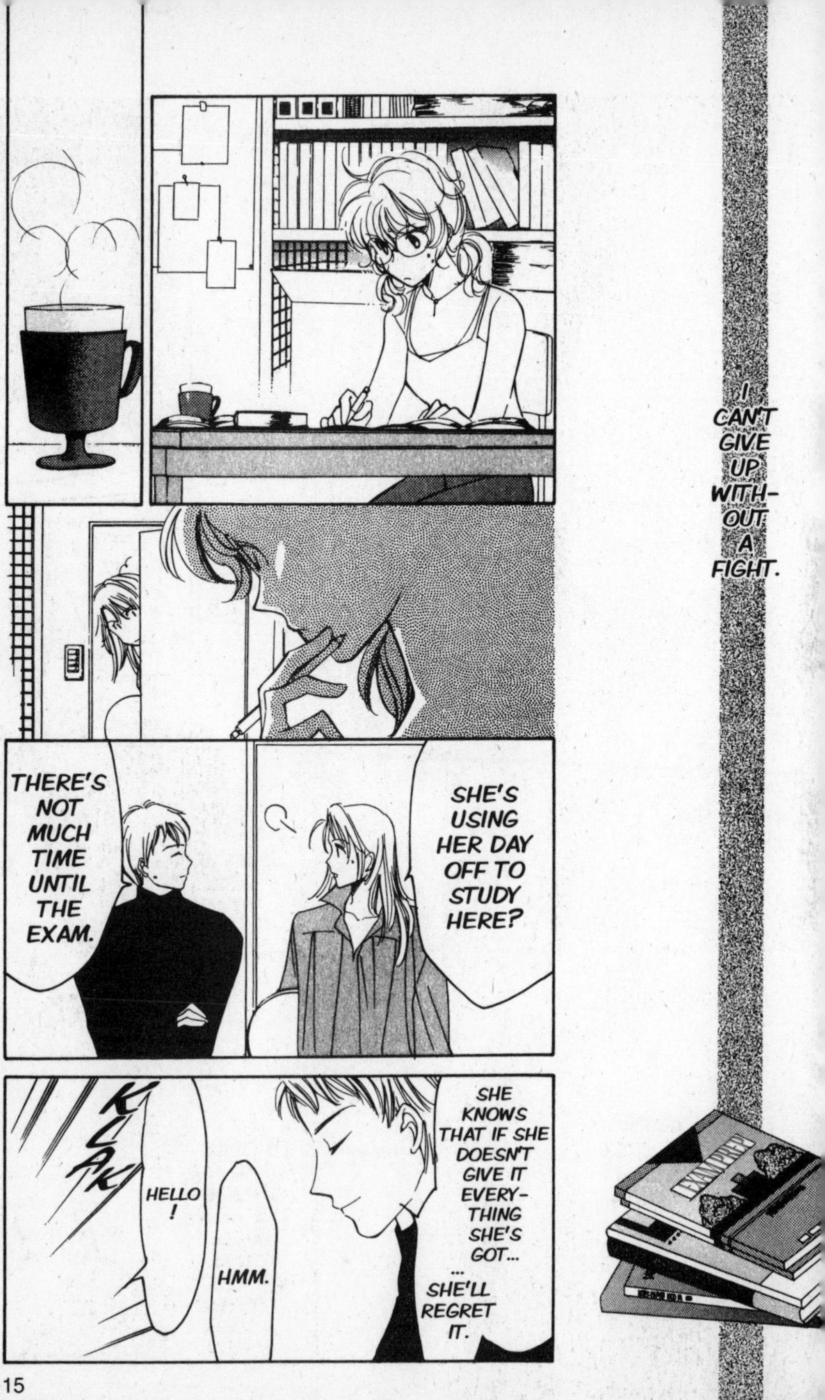
I CAN'T GIVE UP WITH-OUT A FIGHT.
SHE'S USING HER DAY OFF TO STUDY HERE?
THERE'S NOT MUCH TIME UNTIL THE EXAM.
SHE KNOWS THAT IF SHE DOESN'T GIVE IT EVERY-THING SHE'S GOT...
...SHE'LL REGRET IT.
KLAK!
HELLO!
HMM.
EXAM PREP

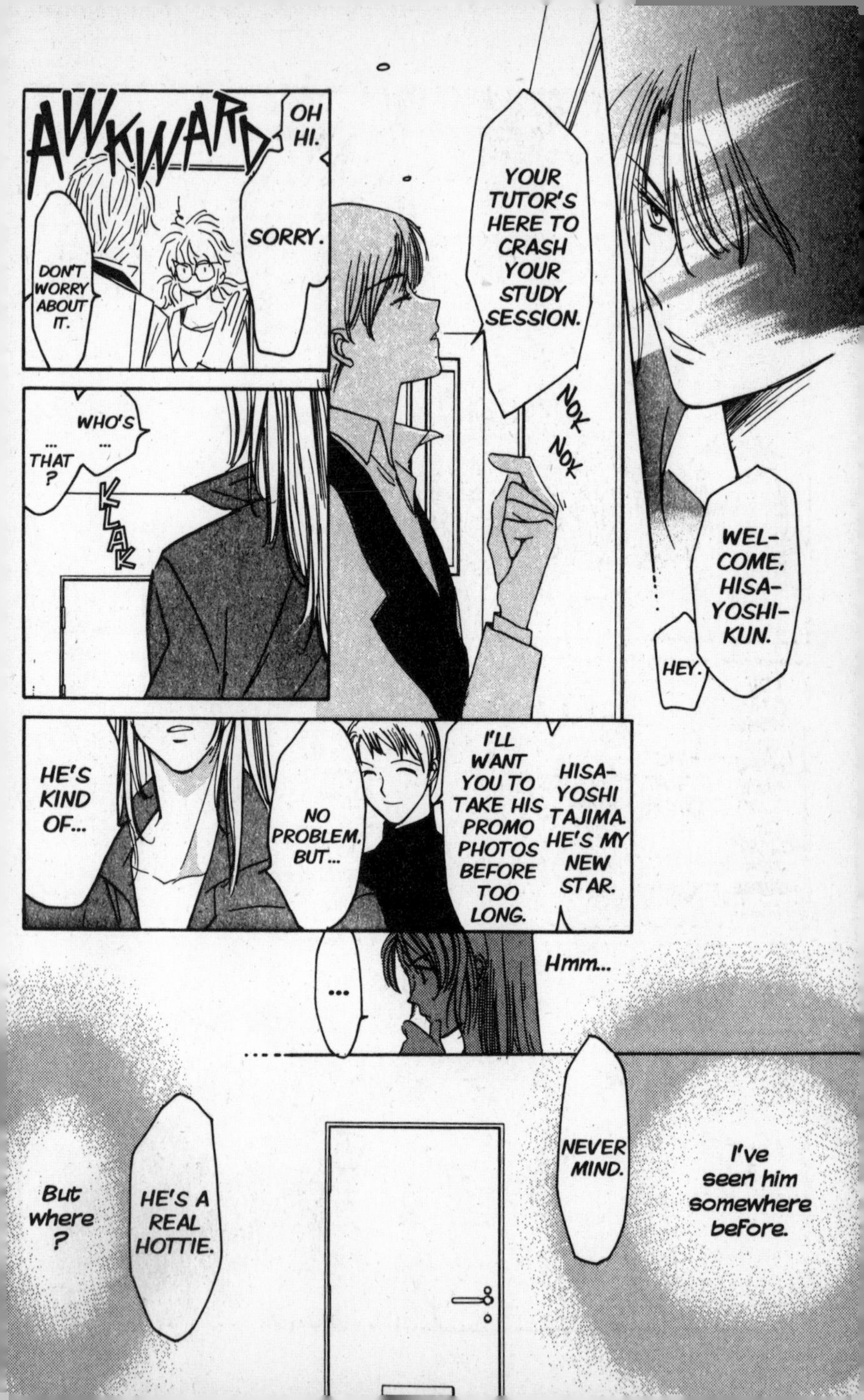

YOUR TUTOR'S HERE TO CRASH YOUR STUDY SESSION.
NOK NOK
WELCOME, HISAYOSHI-KUN.
HEY.
OH HI.
SORRY.
AWKWARD
DON'T WORRY ABOUT IT.
WHO'S ... ... THAT?
KLAK
HISAYOSHI TAJIMA. HE'S MY NEW STAR.
I'LL WANT YOU TO TAKE HIS PROMO PHOTOS BEFORE TOO LONG.
NO PROBLEM, BUT...
HE'S KIND OF...
Hmm...
...
I've seen him somewhere before.
NEVER MIND.
HE'S A REAL HOTTIE.
But where?

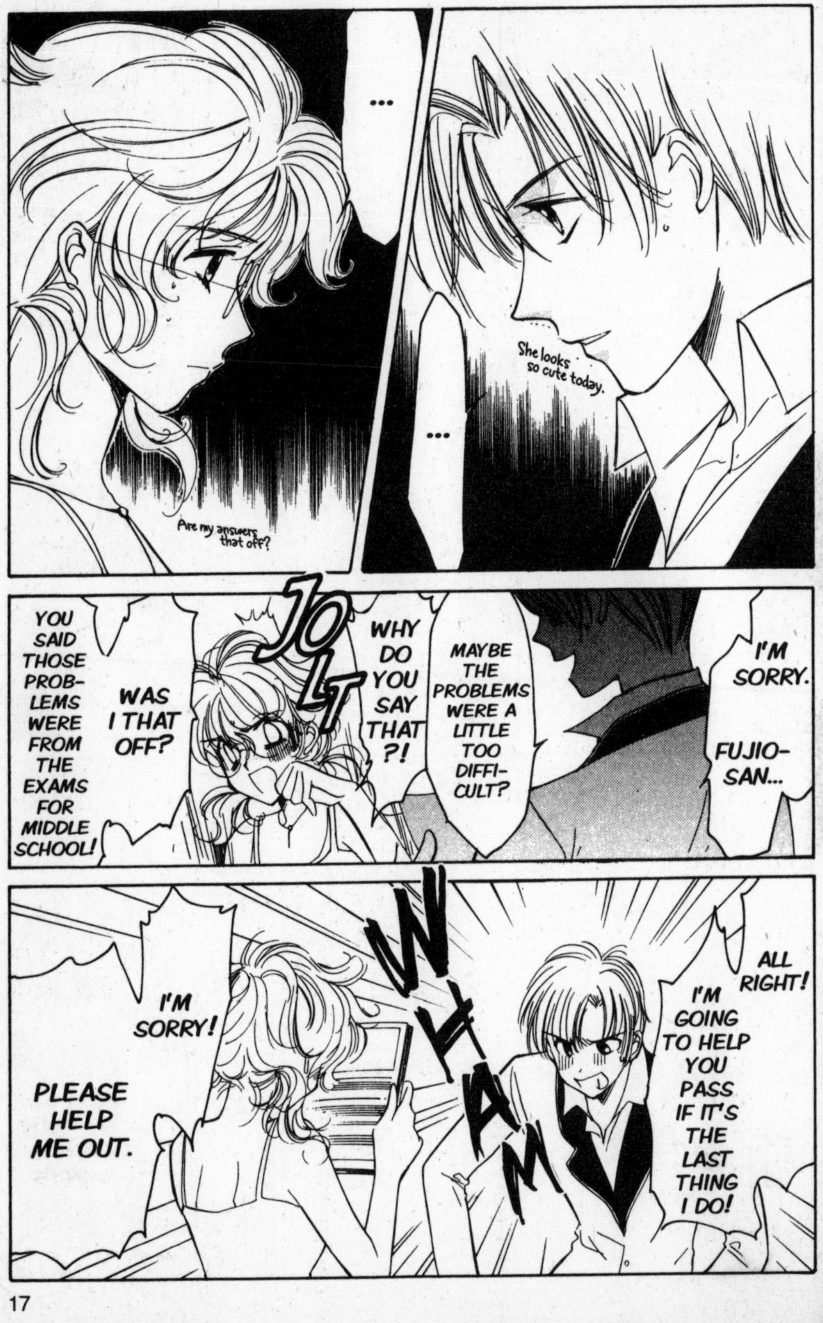
She looks so cute today.
...
...
Are my answers that off?
I'M SORRY.
FUJIO-SAN...
MAYBE THE PROBLEMS WERE A LITTLE TOO DIFFI-CULT?
WHY DO YOU SAY THAT?!
JOLT
WAS I THAT OFF?
YOU SAID THOSE PROB-LEMS WERE FROM THE EXAMS FOR MIDDLE SCHOOL!
ALL RIGHT!
I'M GOING TO HELP YOU PASS IF IT'S THE LAST THING I DO!
WHAM
I'M SORRY!
PLEASE HELP ME OUT.

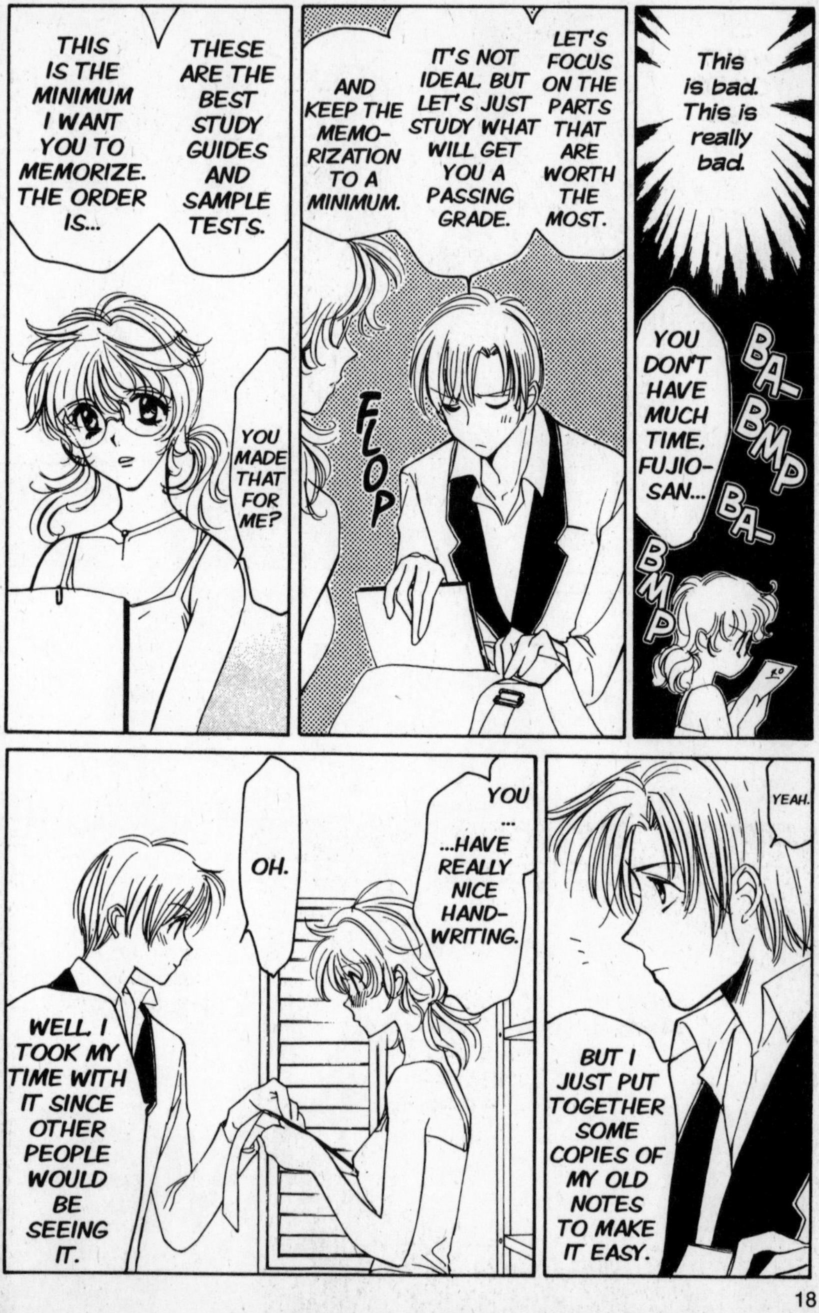
This is bad. This is really bad.
YOU DON'T HAVE MUCH TIME, FUJIO-SAN...
BA-BMP BA-BMP
LET'S FOCUS ON THE PARTS THAT ARE WORTH THE MOST.
IT'S NOT IDEAL, BUT LET'S JUST STUDY WHAT WILL GET YOU A PASSING GRADE.
AND KEEP THE MEMORIZATION TO A MINIMUM.
FLOP
THESE ARE THE BEST STUDY GUIDES AND SAMPLE TESTS.
THIS IS THE MINIMUM I WANT YOU TO MEMORIZE. THE ORDER IS...
YOU MADE THAT FOR ME?
YEAH.
BUT I JUST PUT TOGETHER SOME COPIES OF MY OLD NOTES TO MAKE IT EASY.
YOU ... ...HAVE REALLY NICE HANDWRITING.
OH.
WELL, I TOOK MY TIME WITH IT SINCE OTHER PEOPLE WOULD BE SEEING IT.

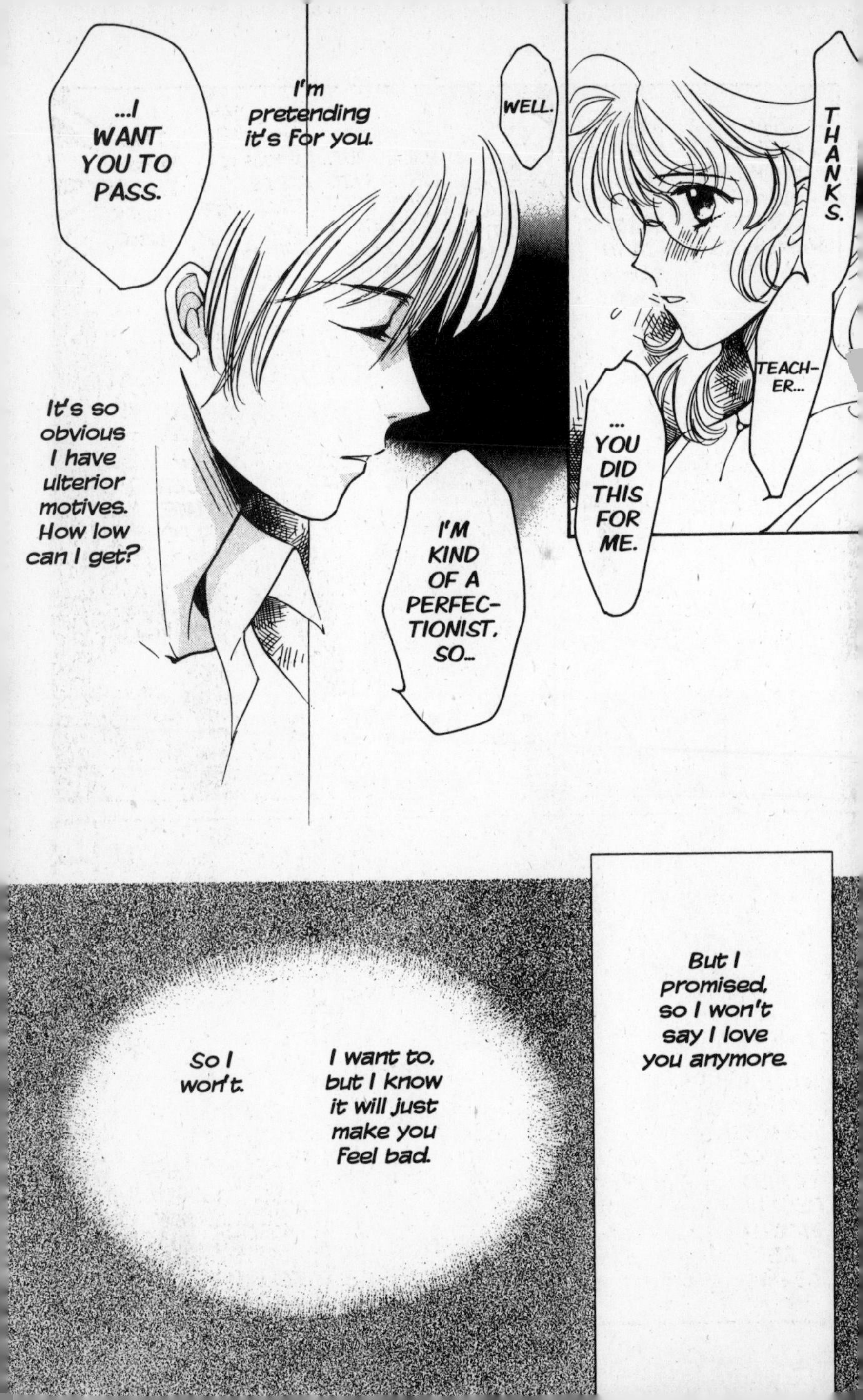
THANKS.
TEACHER...
...YOU DID THIS FOR ME.
WELL.
I'M KIND OF A PERFECTIONIST, SO...
I'm pretending it's for you.
...I WANT YOU TO PASS.
It's so obvious I have ulterior motives. How low can I get?
But I promised, so I won't say I love you anymore.
I want to, but I know it will just make you feel bad.
So I won't.

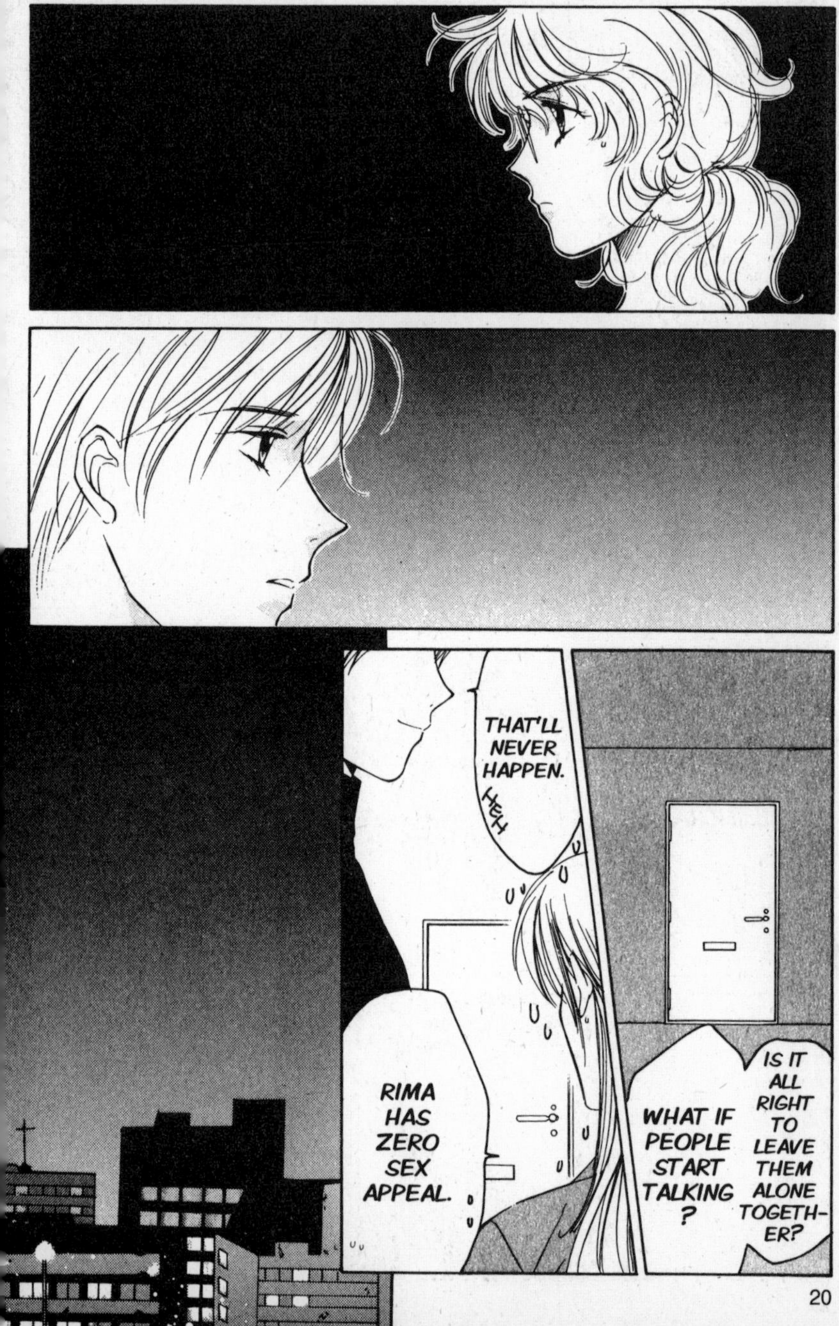
IS IT ALL RIGHT TO LEAVE THEM ALONE TOGETHER?
WHAT IF PEOPLE START TALKING?
THAT'LL NEVER HAPPEN.
HEH
RIMA HAS ZERO SEX APPEAL.

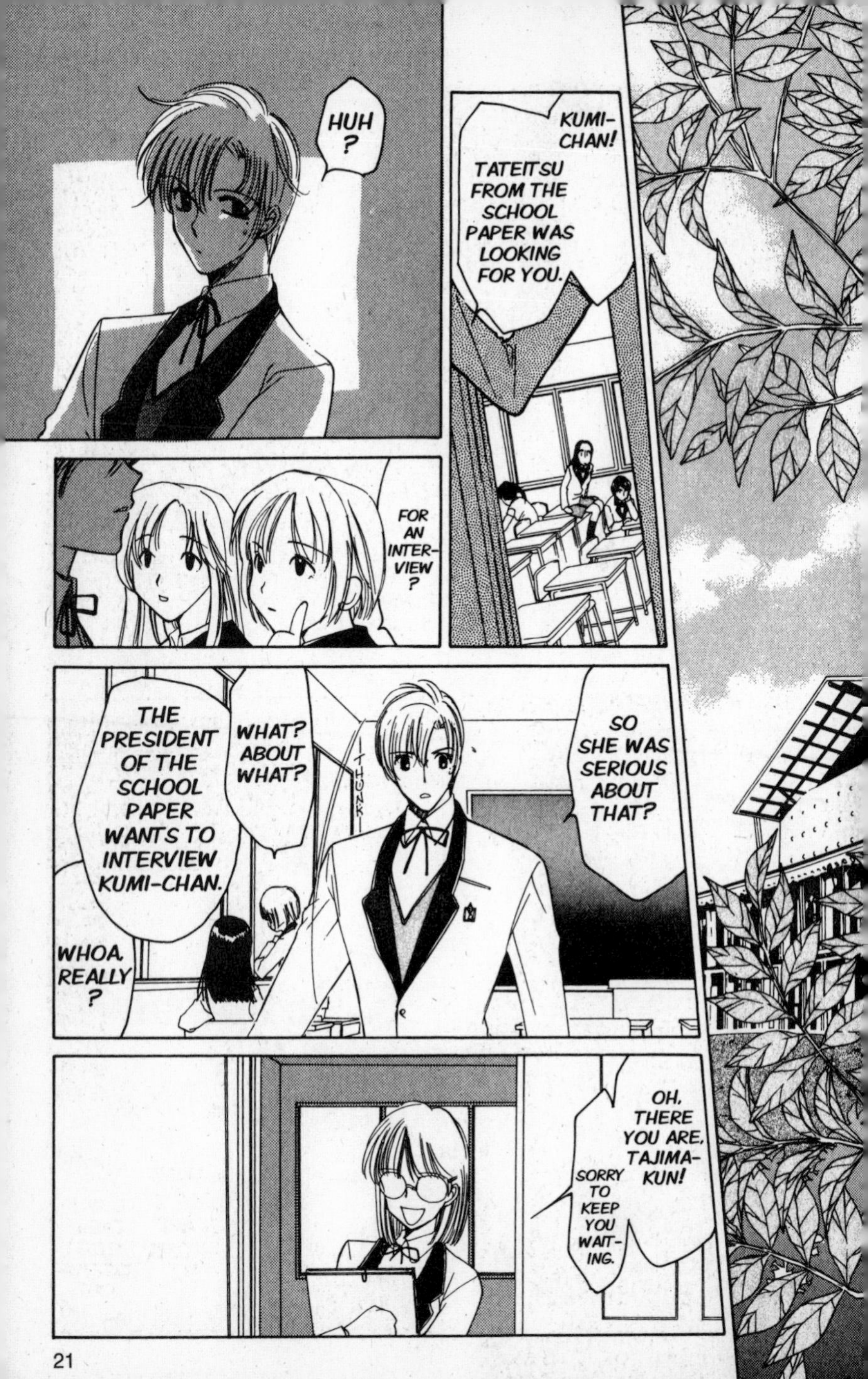
KUMI-CHAN!
TATEITSU FROM THE SCHOOL PAPER WAS LOOKING FOR YOU.
HUH?
FOR AN INTER-VIEW?
SO SHE WAS SERIOUS ABOUT THAT?
WHAT? ABOUT WHAT?
THE PRESIDENT OF THE SCHOOL PAPER WANTS TO INTERVIEW KUMI-CHAN.
THUNK
WHOA, REALLY?
OH, THERE YOU ARE, TAJIMA-KUN!
SORRY TO KEEP YOU WAIT-ING.

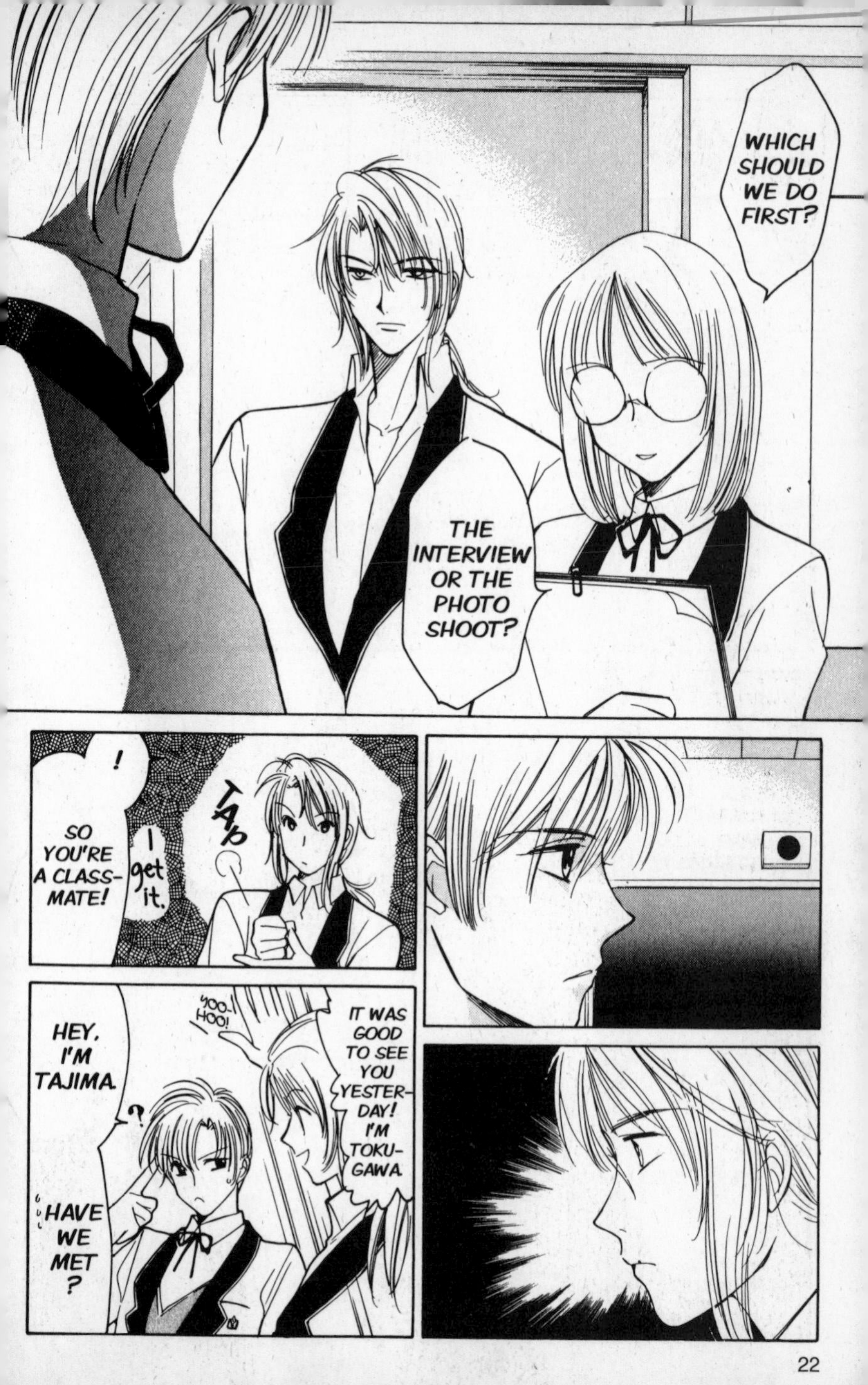
WHICH SHOULD WE DO FIRST?
THE INTERVIEW OR THE PHOTO SHOOT?
TAP
I get it.
!
SO YOU'RE A CLASS-MATE!
IT WAS GOOD TO SEE YOU YESTER-DAY! I'M TOKU-GAWA
YOO-HOO!
HEY, I'M TAJIMA.
?
HAVE WE MET ?

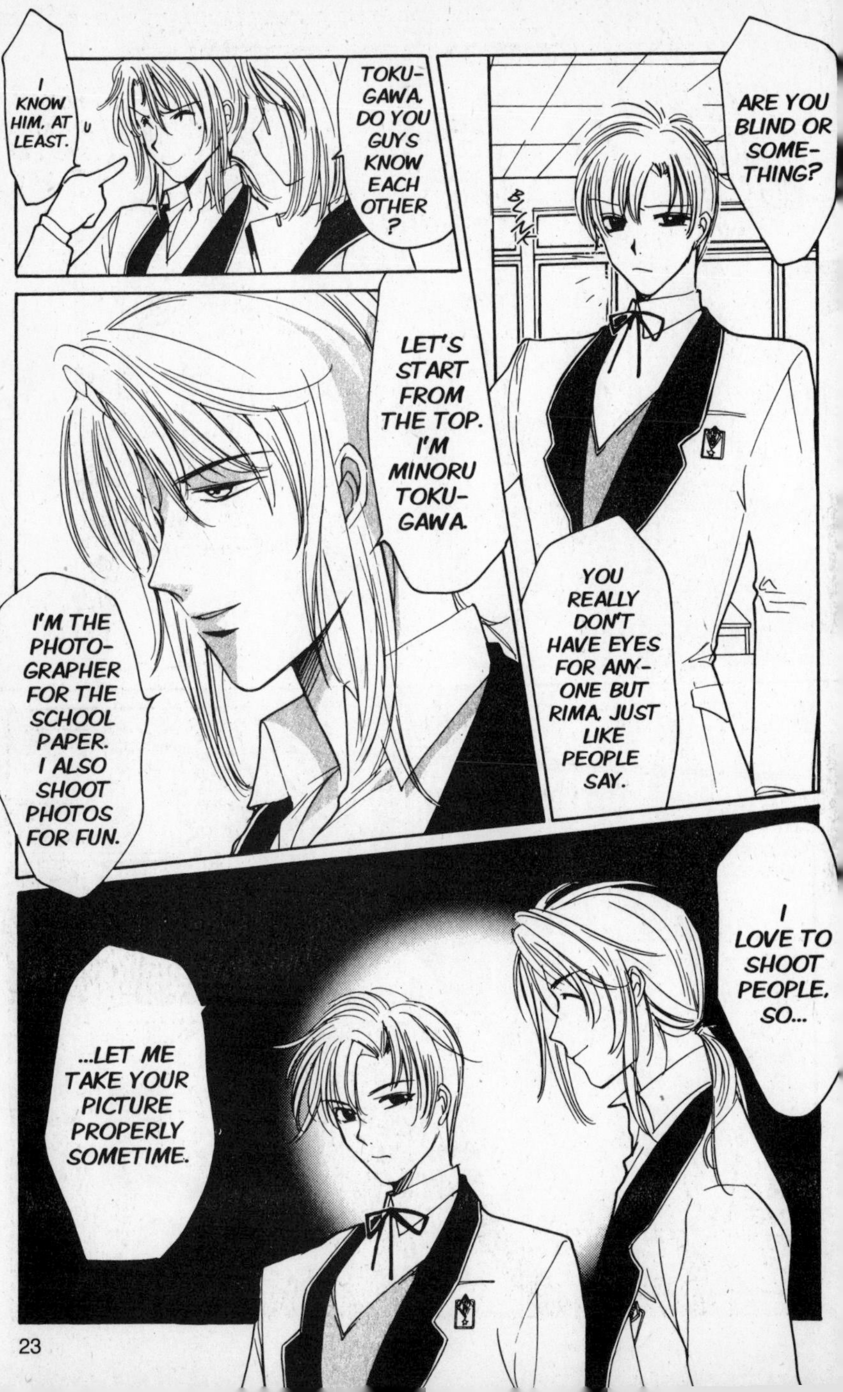

ARE YOU BLIND OR SOME-THING?
BLINK
YOU REALLY DON'T HAVE EYES FOR ANY-ONE BUT RIMA, JUST LIKE PEOPLE SAY.
TOKU-GAWA, DO YOU GUYS KNOW EACH OTHER?
I KNOW HIM, AT LEAST.
LET'S START FROM THE TOP. I'M MINORU TOKU-GAWA.
I'M THE PHOTO-GRAPHER FOR THE SCHOOL PAPER. I ALSO SHOOT PHOTOS FOR FUN.
I LOVE TO SHOOT PEOPLE, SO...
...LET ME TAKE YOUR PICTURE PROPERLY SOMETIME.

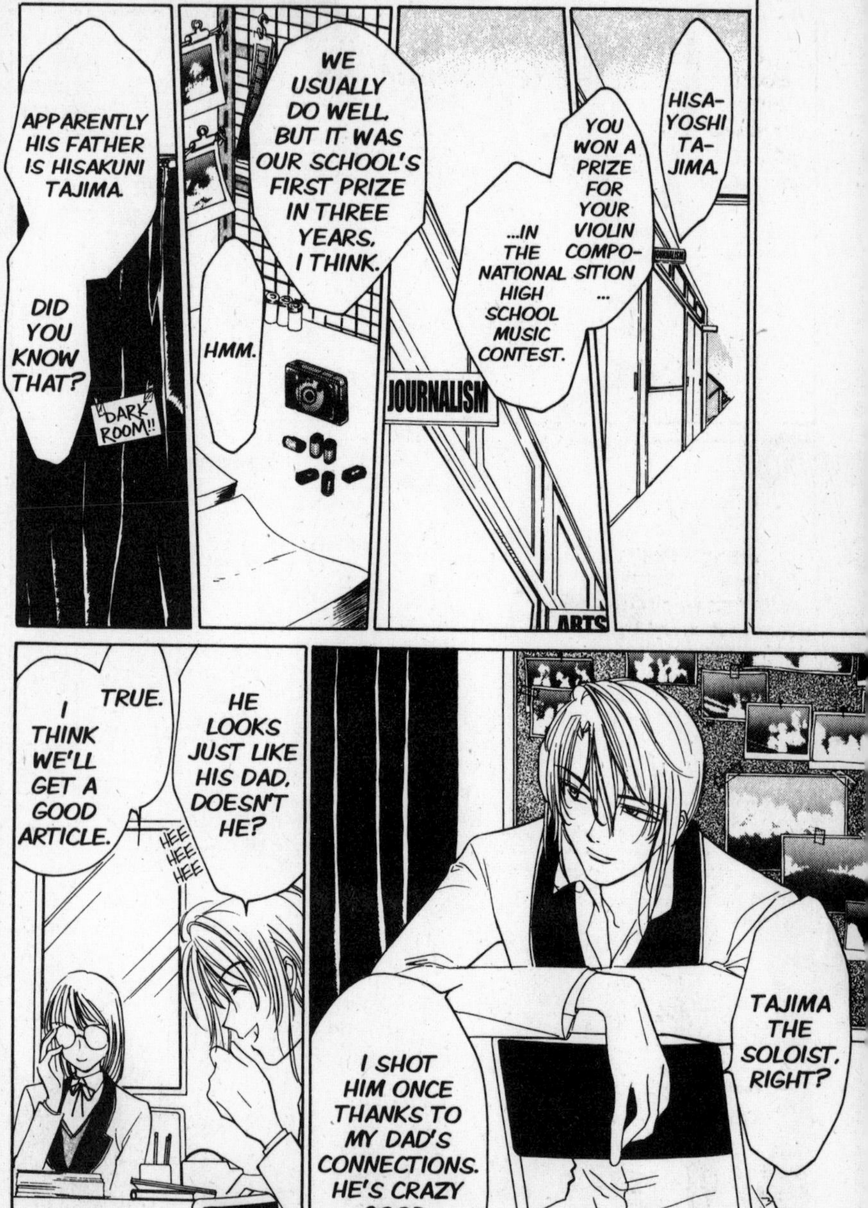
HISA-YOSHI TA-JIMA.
YOU WON A PRIZE FOR YOUR VIOLIN COMPOSITION...
...IN THE NATIONAL HIGH SCHOOL MUSIC CONTEST.
JOURNALISM
ARTS
WE USUALLY DO WELL, BUT IT WAS OUR SCHOOL'S FIRST PRIZE IN THREE YEARS, I THINK.
HMM.
JOURNALISM
APPARENTLY HIS FATHER IS HISAKUNI TAJIMA.
DID YOU KNOW THAT?
DARK ROOM!!
TAJIMA THE SOLOIST, RIGHT?
I SHOT HIM ONCE THANKS TO MY DAD'S CONNECTIONS. HE'S CRAZY GOOD LOOKING.
HE LOOKS JUST LIKE HIS DAD, DOESN'T HE?
HEE HEE HEE
TRUE.
I THINK WE'LL GET A GOOD ARTICLE.

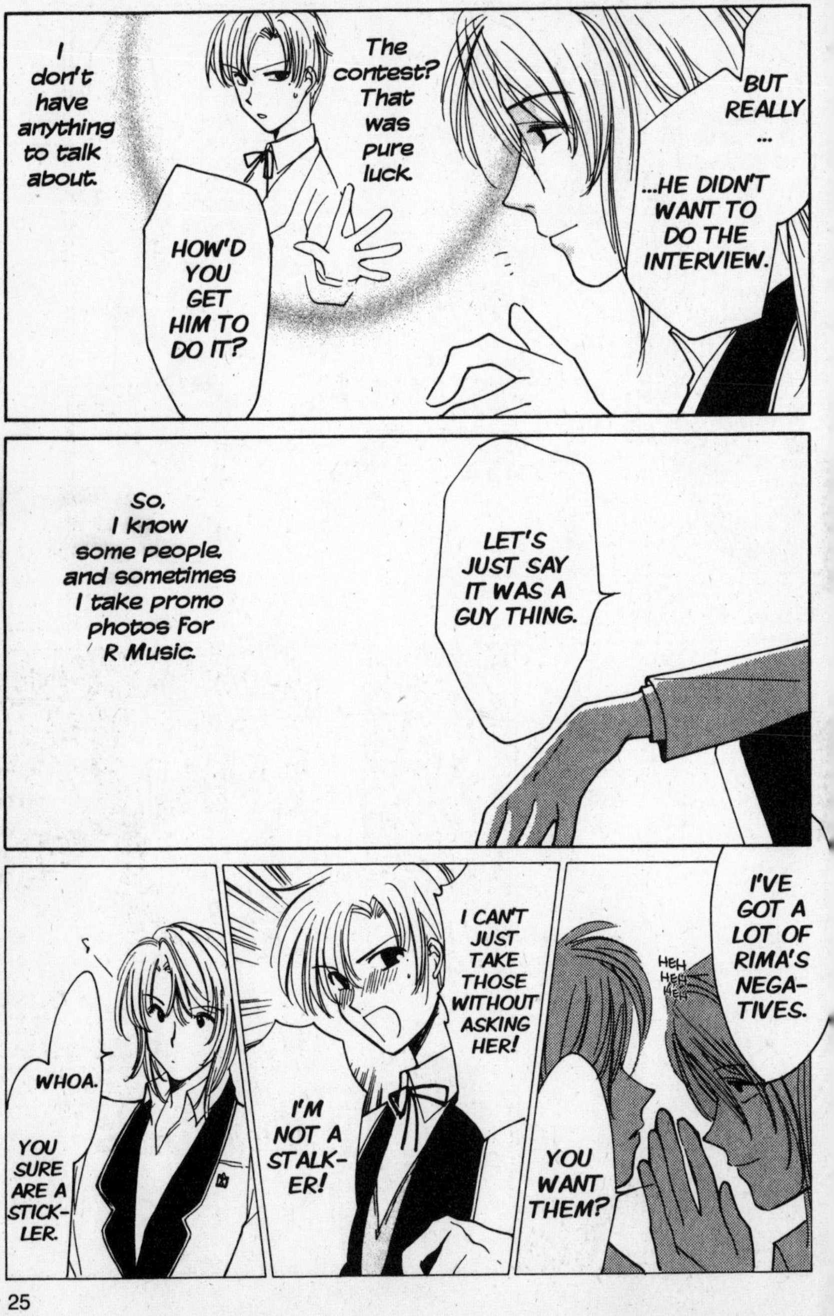
BUT REALLY ...
...HE DIDN'T WANT TO DO THE INTERVIEW.
The contest? That was pure luck.
I don't have anything to talk about.
HOW'D YOU GET HIM TO DO IT?
LET'S JUST SAY IT WAS A GUY THING.
So, I know some people, and sometimes I take promo photos for R Music.
I'VE GOT A LOT OF RIMA'S NEGA-TIVES.
HEH HEH HEH
YOU WANT THEM?
I CAN'T JUST TAKE THOSE WITHOUT ASKING HER!
I'M NOT A STALK-ER!
WHOA.
YOU SURE ARE A STICK-LER.

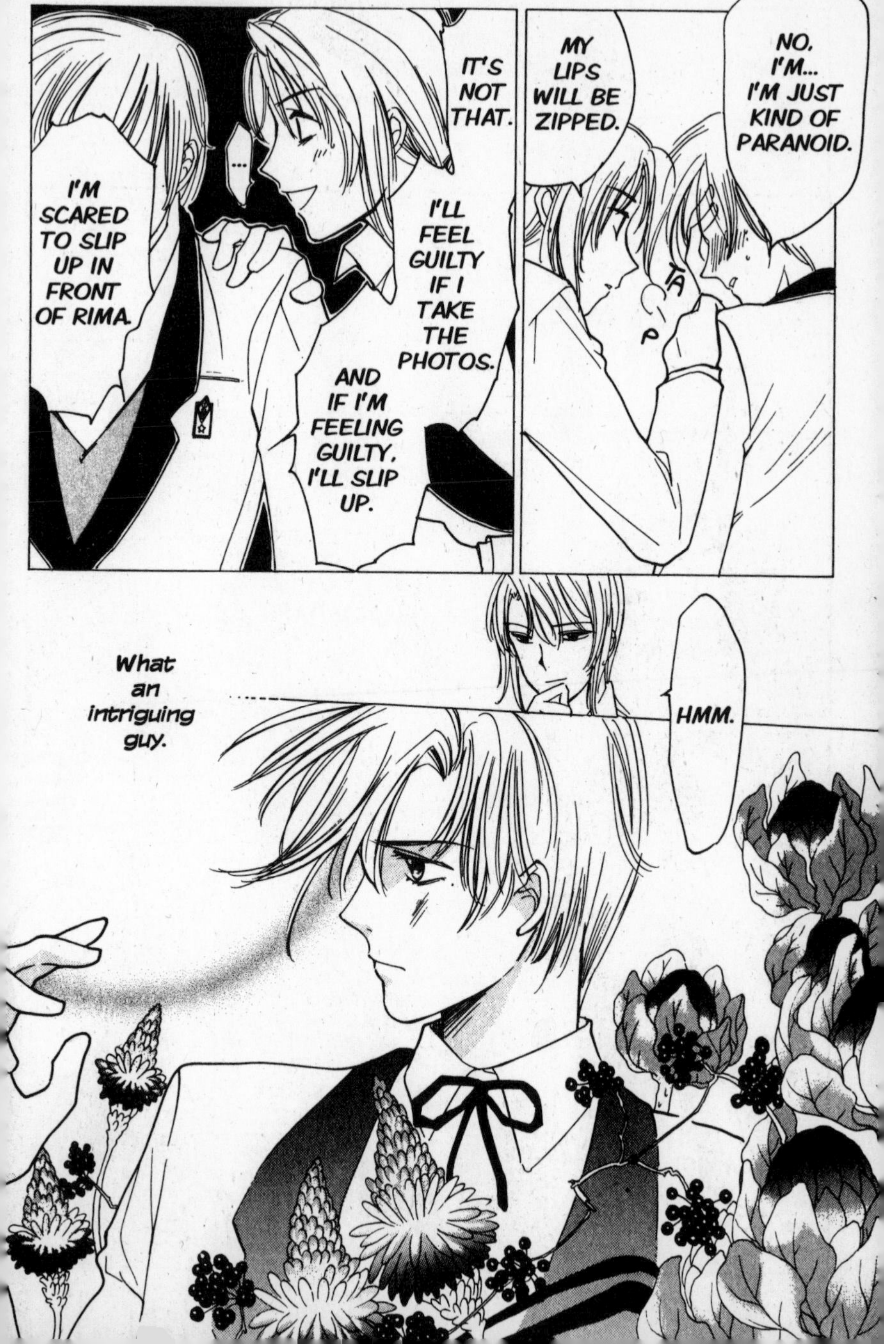
NO. I'M... I'M JUST KIND OF PARANOID.
MY LIPS WILL BE ZIPPED.
TAP
IT'S NOT THAT.
...
I'LL FEEL GUILTY IF I TAKE THE PHOTOS.
AND IF I'M FEELING GUILTY, I'LL SLIP UP.
I'M SCARED TO SLIP UP IN FRONT OF RIMA.
HMM.
What an intriguing guy.

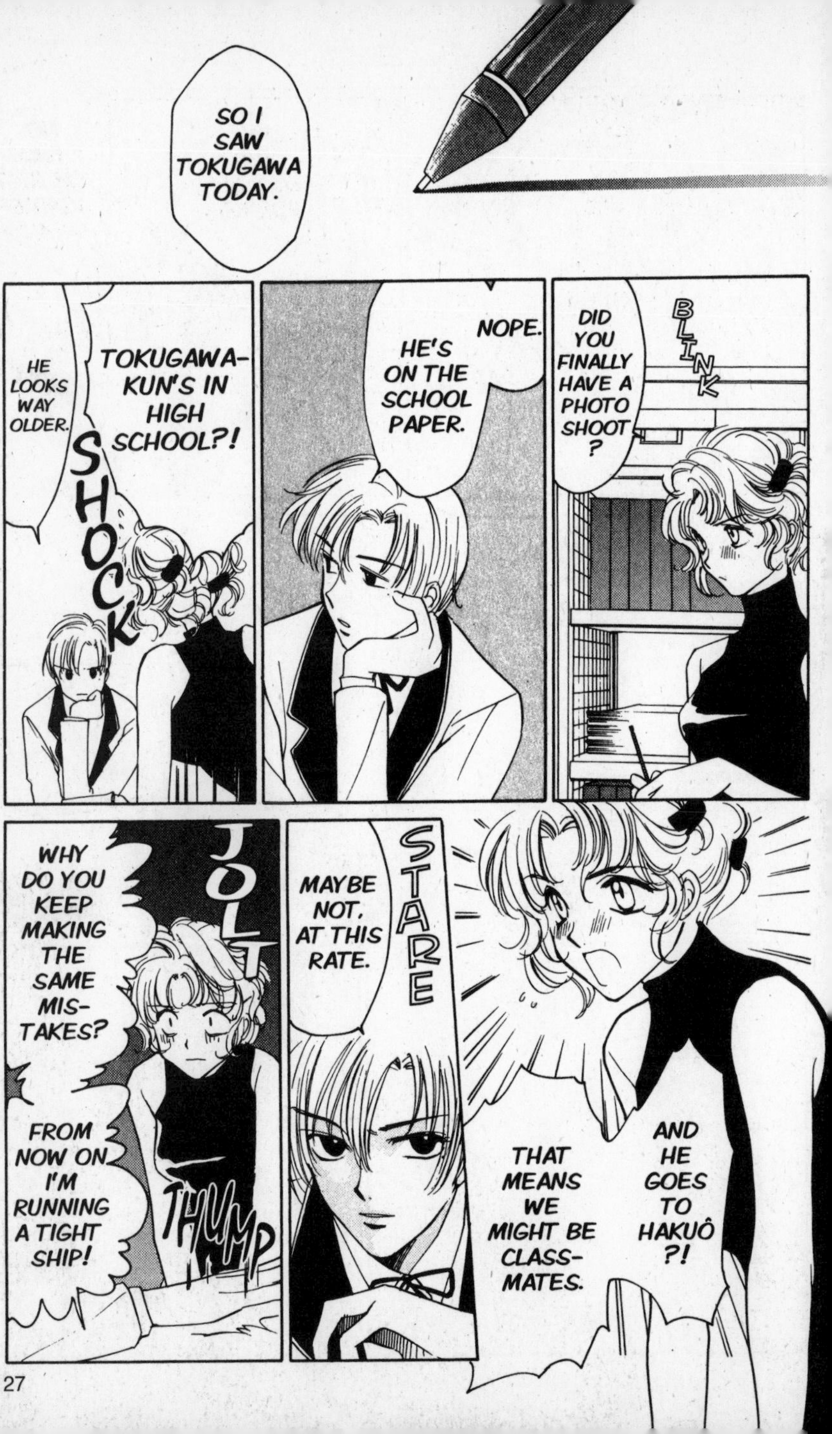
SO I SAW TOKUGAWA TODAY.
BLINK
DID YOU FINALLY HAVE A PHOTO SHOOT?
NOPE.
HE'S ON THE SCHOOL PAPER.
TOKUGAWA-KUN'S IN HIGH SCHOOL?!
SHOCK
HE LOOKS WAY OLDER.
AND HE GOES TO HAKUÔ?!
THAT MEANS WE MIGHT BE CLASS-MATES.
STARE
MAYBE NOT, AT THIS RATE.
JOLT
WHY DO YOU KEEP MAKING THE SAME MIS-TAKES?
FROM NOW ON I'M RUNNING A TIGHT SHIP!
THUMP

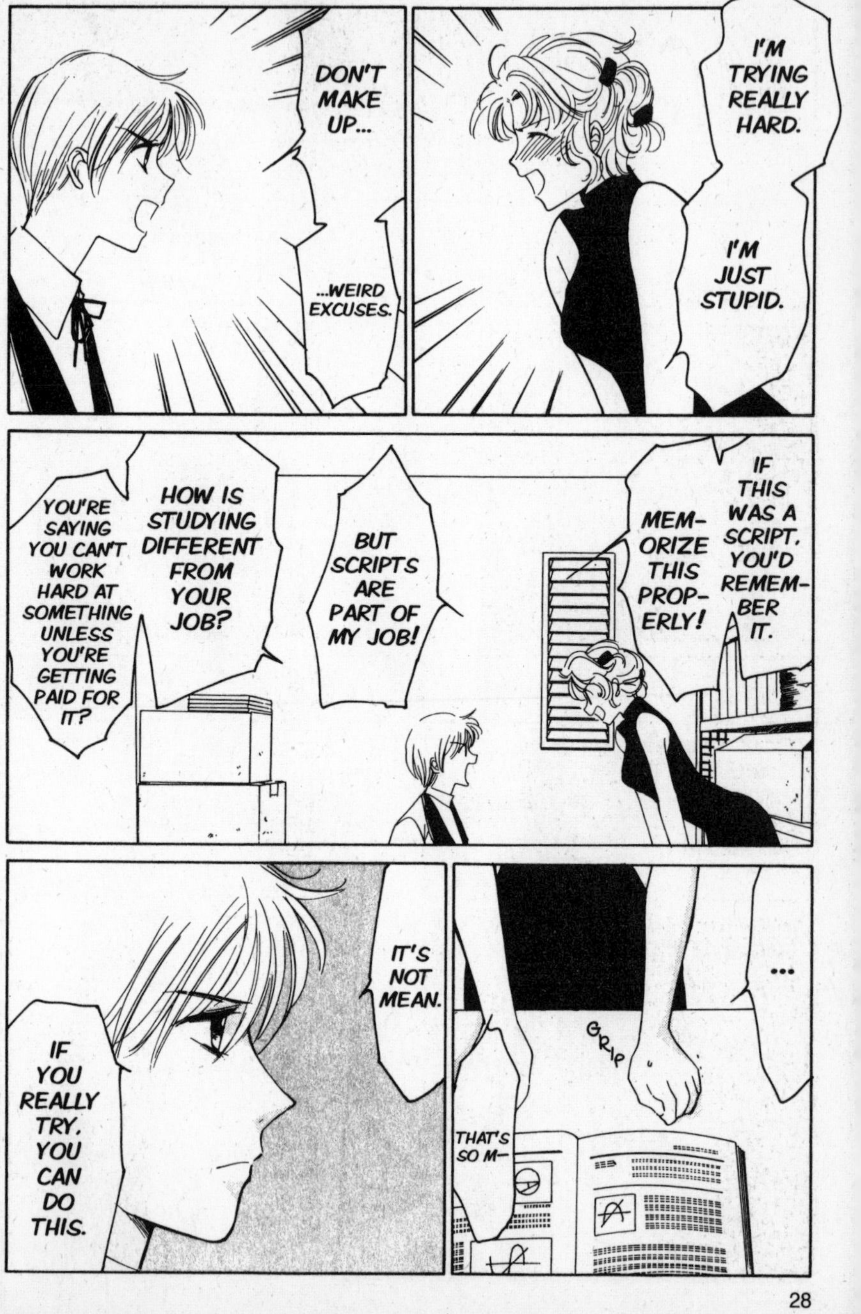
I'M TRYING REALLY HARD.
I'M JUST STUPID.
DON'T MAKE UP...
...WEIRD EXCUSES.
IF THIS WAS A SCRIPT, YOU'D REMEMBER IT.
MEMORIZE THIS PROPERLY!
BUT SCRIPTS ARE PART OF MY JOB!
HOW IS STUDYING DIFFERENT FROM YOUR JOB?
YOU'RE SAYING YOU CAN'T WORK HARD AT SOMETHING UNLESS YOU'RE GETTING PAID FOR IT?
...
GRIP
THAT'S SO M-
IT'S NOT MEAN.
IF YOU REALLY TRY, YOU CAN DO THIS.

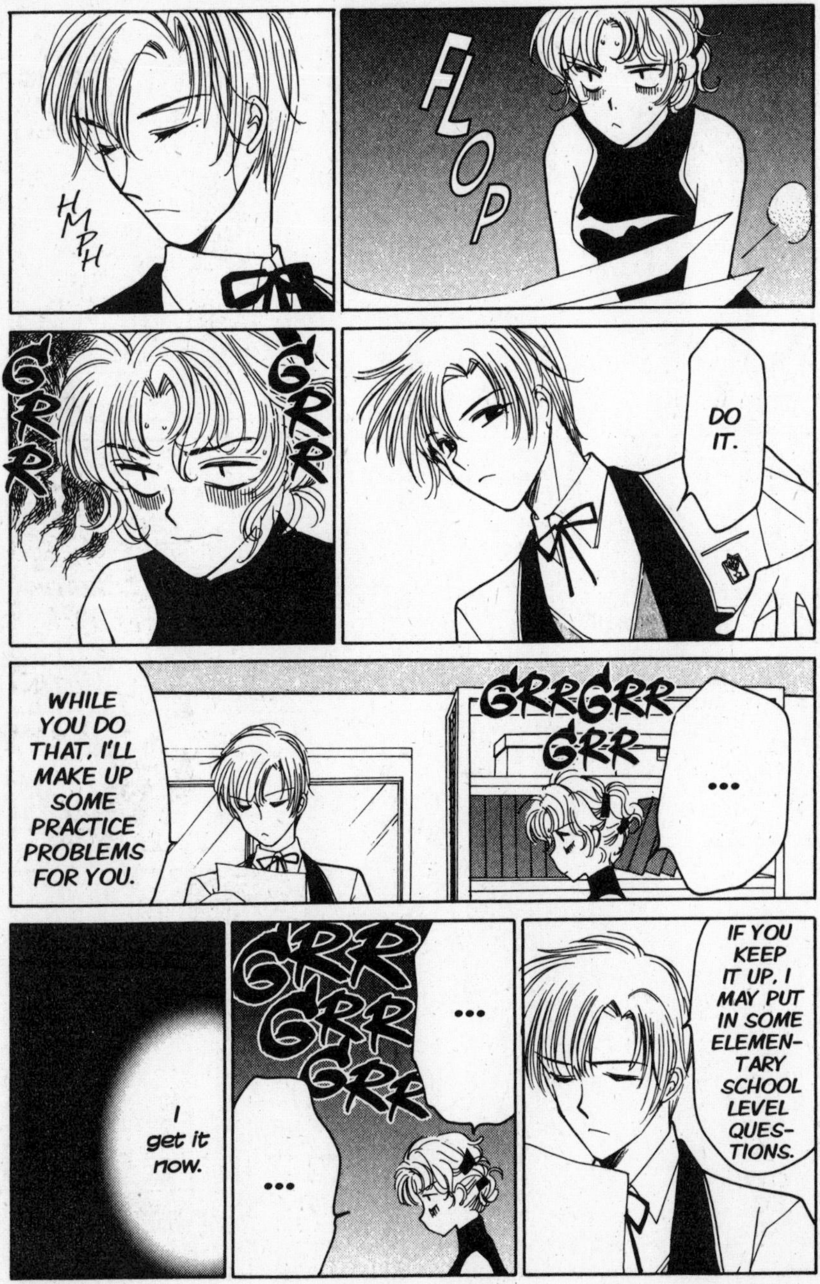
FLOP
HMPH
DO IT.
GRRR
GRRR
GRRGRR GRR
...
WHILE YOU DO THAT, I'LL MAKE UP SOME PRACTICE PROBLEMS FOR YOU.
IF YOU KEEP IT UP, I MAY PUT IN SOME ELEMENTARY SCHOOL LEVEL QUESTIONS.
GRR GRR GRR
...
...
I get it now.

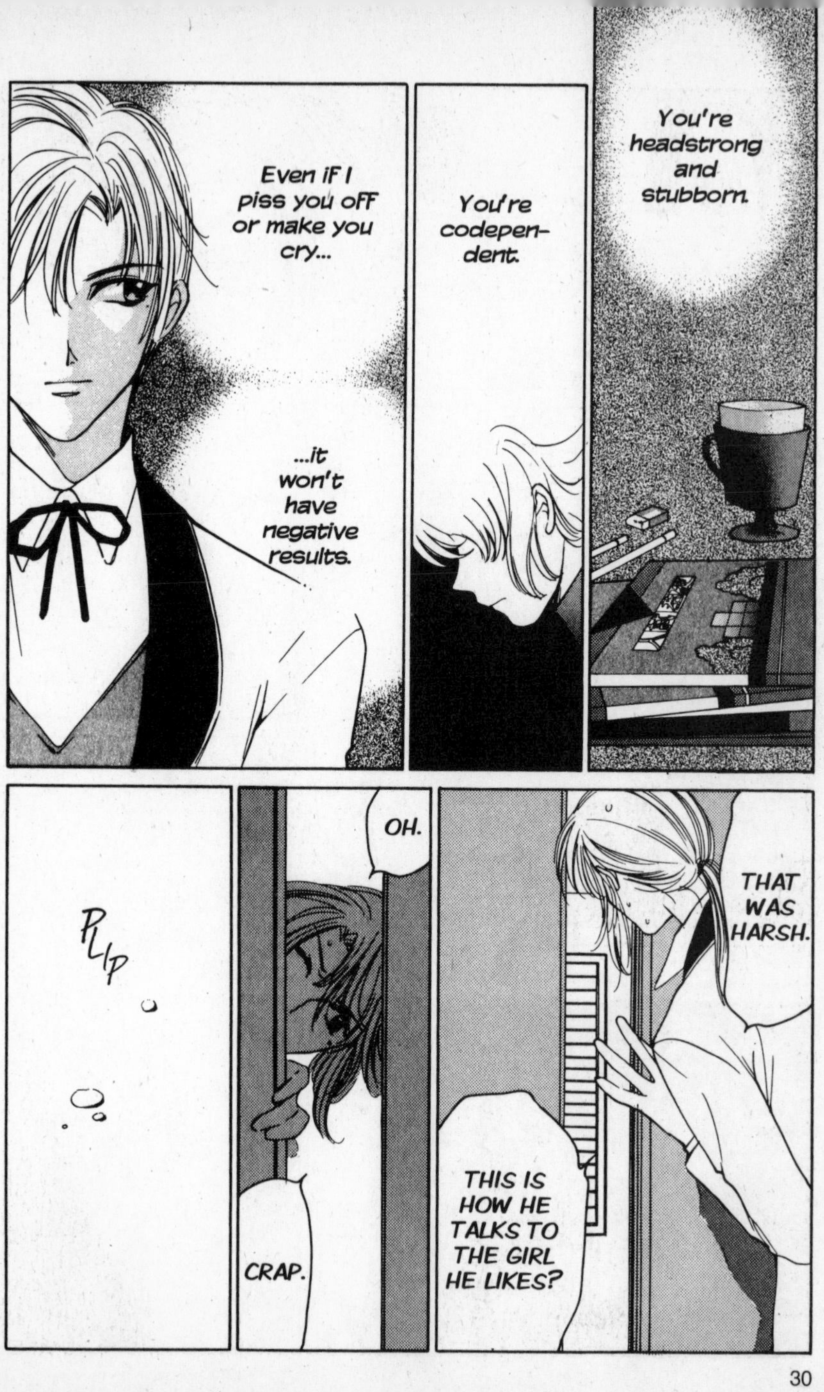
You're headstrong and stubborn.
You're codependent.
Even if I piss you off or make you cry...
...it won't have negative results.
THAT WAS HARSH.
THIS IS HOW HE TALKS TO THE GIRL HE LIKES?
OH.
CRAP.
PLIP

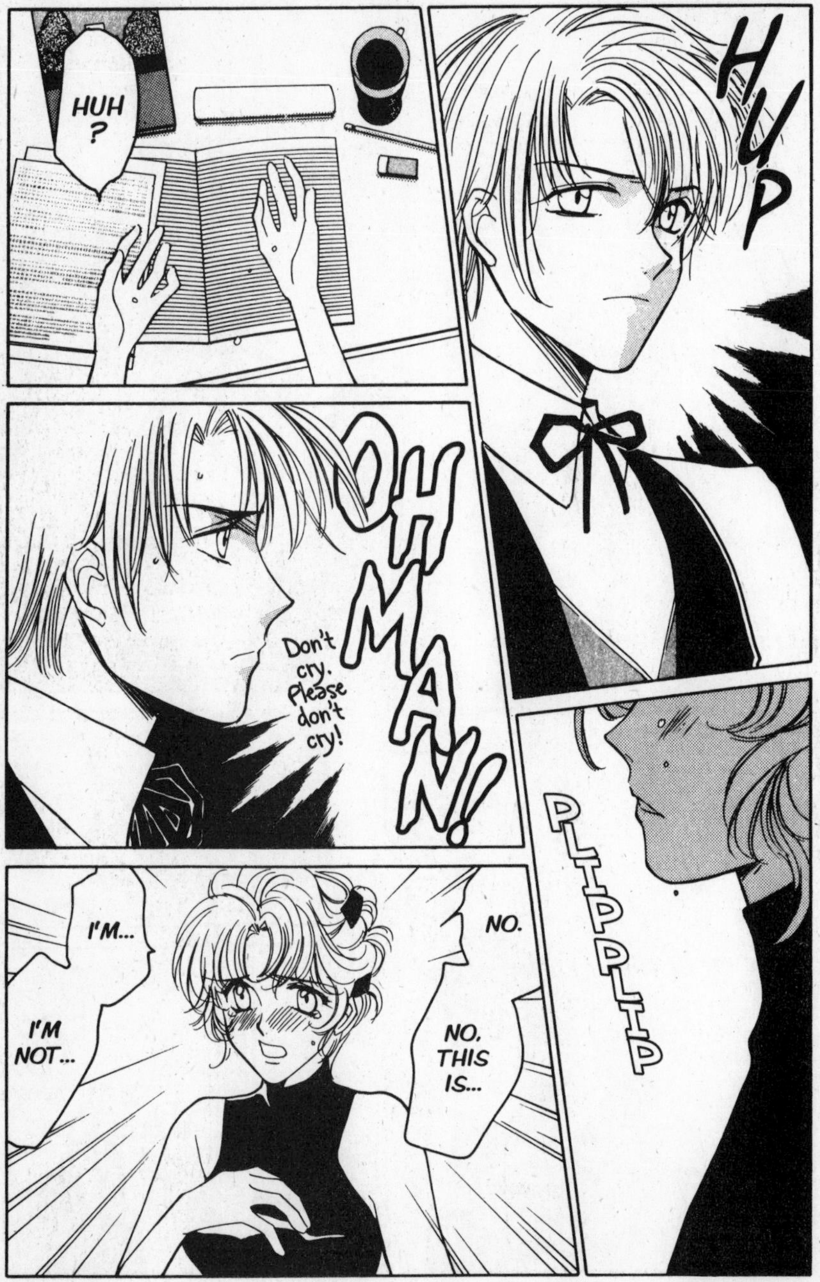
HUP
HUH ?
OH MAN!
Don't cry. Please don't cry!
PLIPPLIP
NO.
I'M...
NO, THIS IS...
I'M NOT...

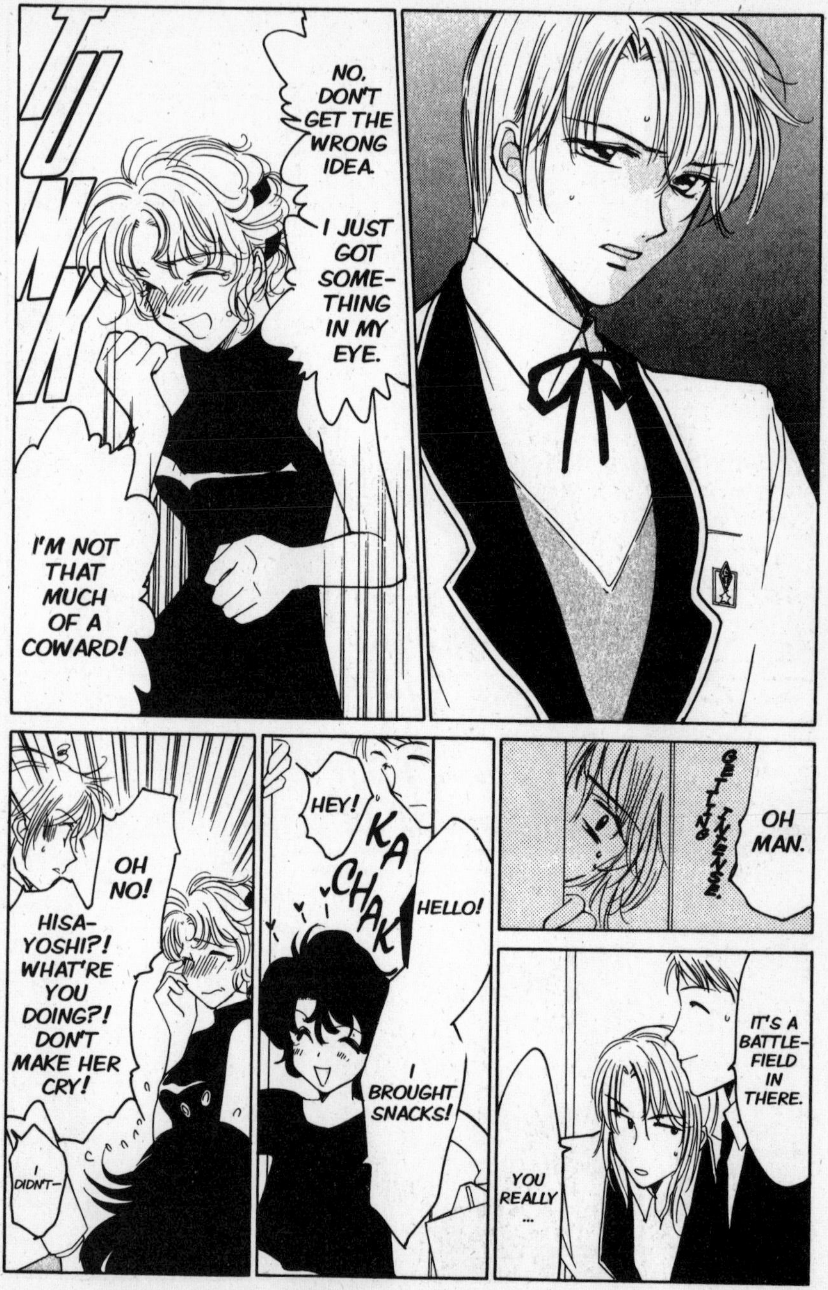
NO, DON'T GET THE WRONG IDEA.
I JUST GOT SOMETHING IN MY EYE.
TUNK
I'M NOT THAT MUCH OF A COWARD!
OH MAN.
GETTING INTENSE.
IT'S A BATTLE-FIELD IN THERE.
YOU REALLY...
HEY!
KA CHAK
HELLO!
I BROUGHT SNACKS!
OH NO!
HISA-YOSHI?! WHAT'RE YOU DOING?! DON'T MAKE HER CRY!
I DIDN'T-

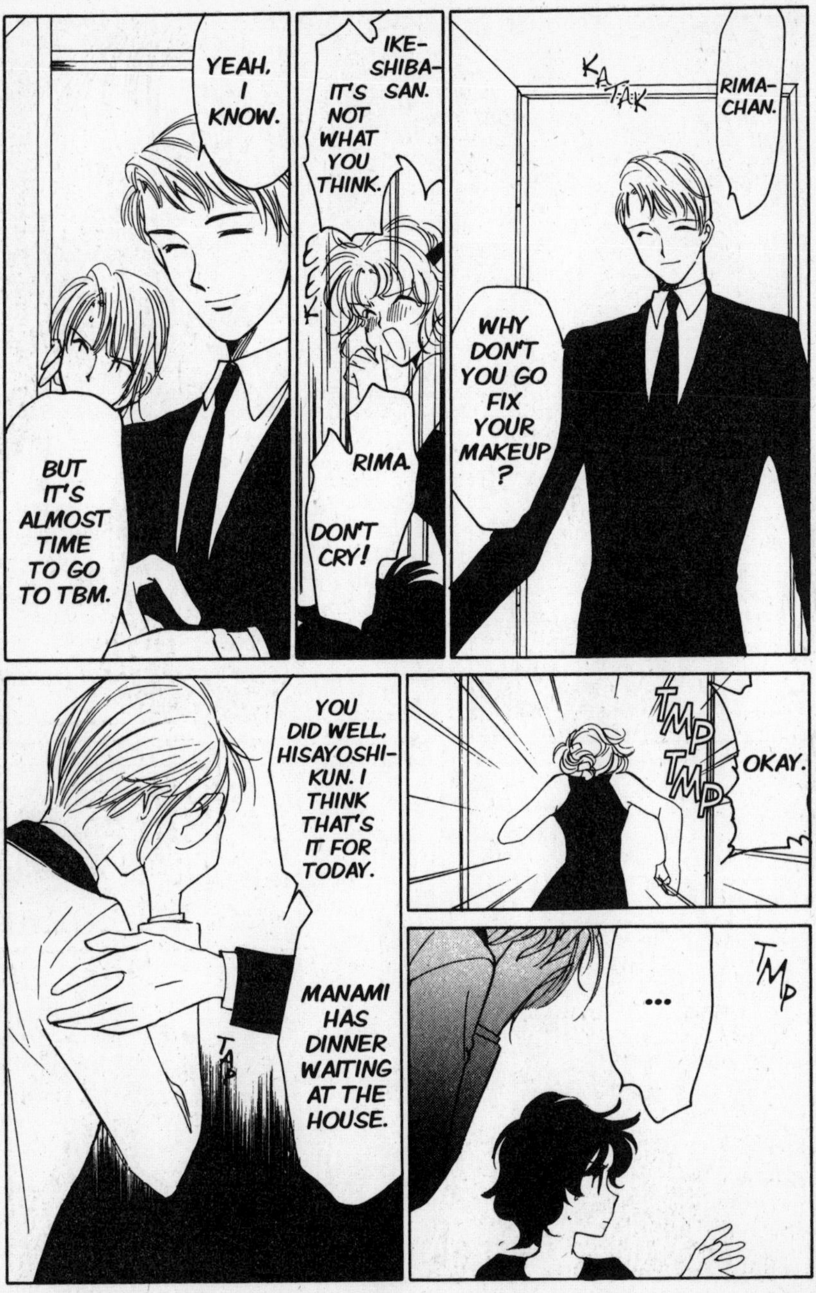
RIMA-CHAN.
KATAK
WHY DON'T YOU GO FIX YOUR MAKEUP?
IKE-SHIBA-SAN.
IT'S NOT WHAT YOU THINK.
RIMA.
DON'T CRY!
YEAH, I KNOW.
BUT IT'S ALMOST TIME TO GO TO TBM.
OKAY.
TMP TMP
TMP
...
YOU DID WELL, HISAYOSHI-KUN. I THINK THAT'S IT FOR TODAY.
MANAMI HAS DINNER WAITING AT THE HOUSE.
TAP

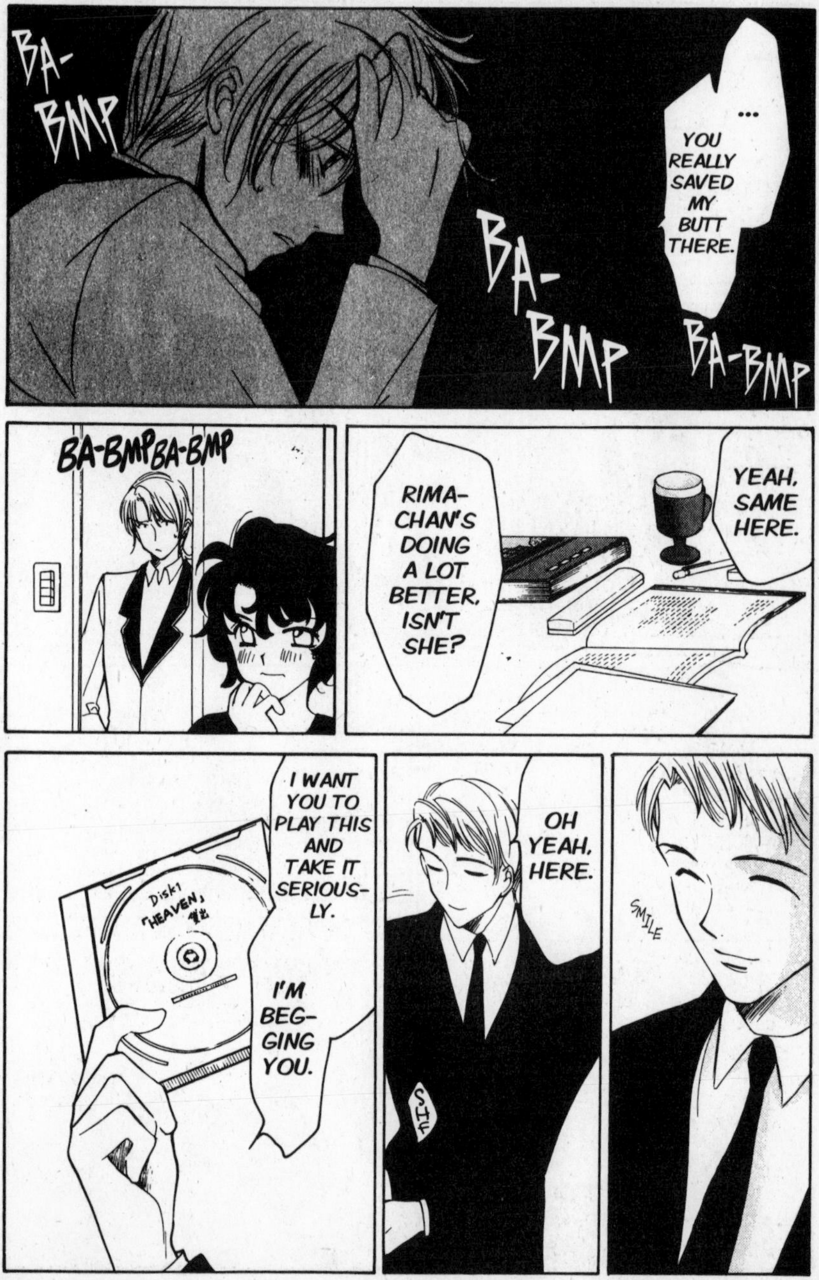
... YOU REALLY SAVED MY BUTT THERE.
BA-BMP
BA-BMP
BA-BMP
YEAH, SAME HERE.
RIMA-CHAN'S DOING A LOT BETTER, ISN'T SHE?
BA-BMP BA-BMP
SMILE
OH YEAH, HERE.
SHF
I WANT YOU TO PLAY THIS AND TAKE IT SERIOUSLY.
Disk1
「HEAVEN」
I'M BEGGING YOU.

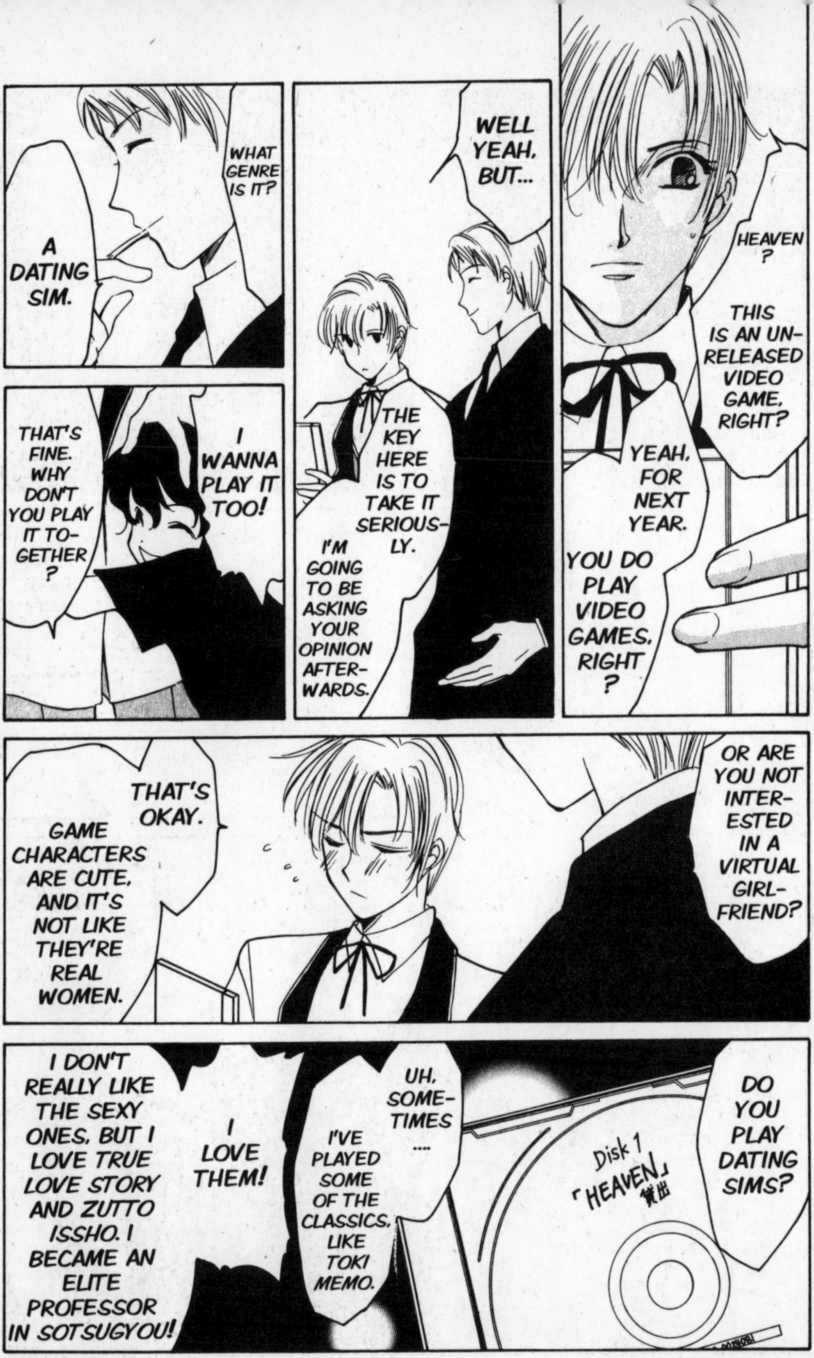

HEAVEN?
THIS IS AN UNRELEASED VIDEO GAME, RIGHT?
YEAH, FOR NEXT YEAR.
YOU DO PLAY VIDEO GAMES, RIGHT?
WELL YEAH, BUT...
THE KEY HERE IS TO TAKE IT SERIOUSLY.
I'M GOING TO BE ASKING YOUR OPINION AFTERWARDS.
WHAT GENRE IS IT?
A DATING SIM.
I WANNA PLAY IT TOO!
THAT'S FINE. WHY DON'T YOU PLAY IT TOGETHER?
OR ARE YOU NOT INTERESTED IN A VIRTUAL GIRLFRIEND?
THAT'S OKAY.
GAME CHARACTERS ARE CUTE, AND IT'S NOT LIKE THEY'RE REAL WOMEN.
DO YOU PLAY DATING SIMS?
Disk 1 「HEAVEN」 貸出
UH, SOMETIMES....
I'VE PLAYED SOME OF THE CLASSICS, LIKE TOKI MEMO.
I LOVE THEM!
I DON'T REALLY LIKE THE SEXY ONES, BUT I LOVE TRUE LOVE STORY AND ZUTTO ISSHO. I BECAME AN ELITE PROFESSOR IN SOTSUGYOU!

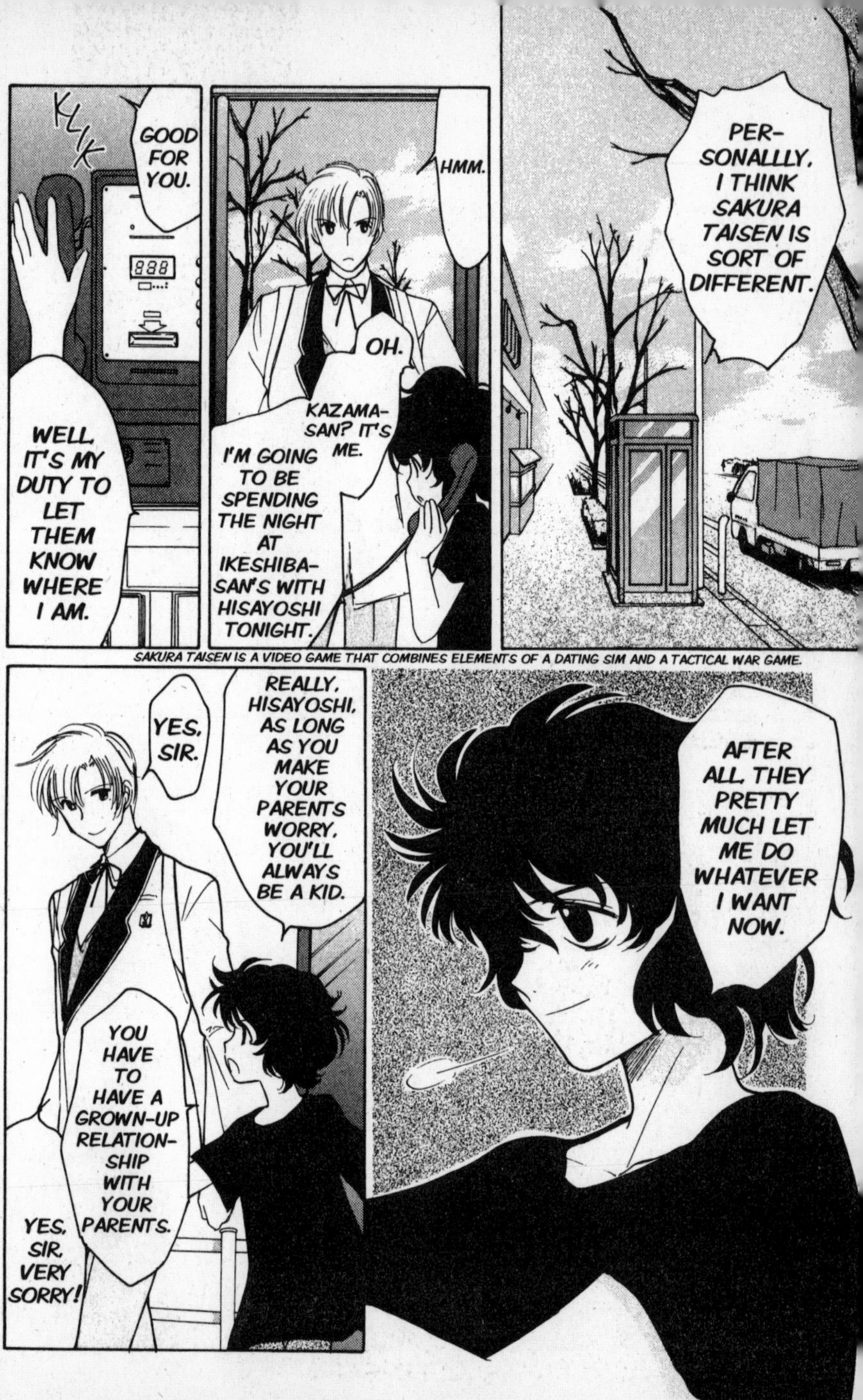
PER-SONALLLY, I THINK SAKURA TAISEN IS SORT OF DIFFERENT.
HMM.
OH.
KAZAMA-SAN? IT'S ME.
I'M GOING TO BE SPENDING THE NIGHT AT IKESHIBA-SAN'S WITH HISAYOSHI TONIGHT.
GOOD FOR YOU.
KLIK
WELL, IT'S MY DUTY TO LET THEM KNOW WHERE I AM.
AFTER ALL, THEY PRETTY MUCH LET ME DO WHATEVER I WANT NOW.
REALLY, HISAYOSHI, AS LONG AS YOU MAKE YOUR PARENTS WORRY, YOU'LL ALWAYS BE A KID.
YES, SIR.
YOU HAVE TO HAVE A GROWN-UP RELATION-SHIP WITH YOUR PARENTS.
YES, SIR, VERY SORRY!

SAKURA TAISEN IS A VIDEO GAME THAT COMBINES ELEMENTS OF A DATING SIM AND A TACTICAL WAR GAME.

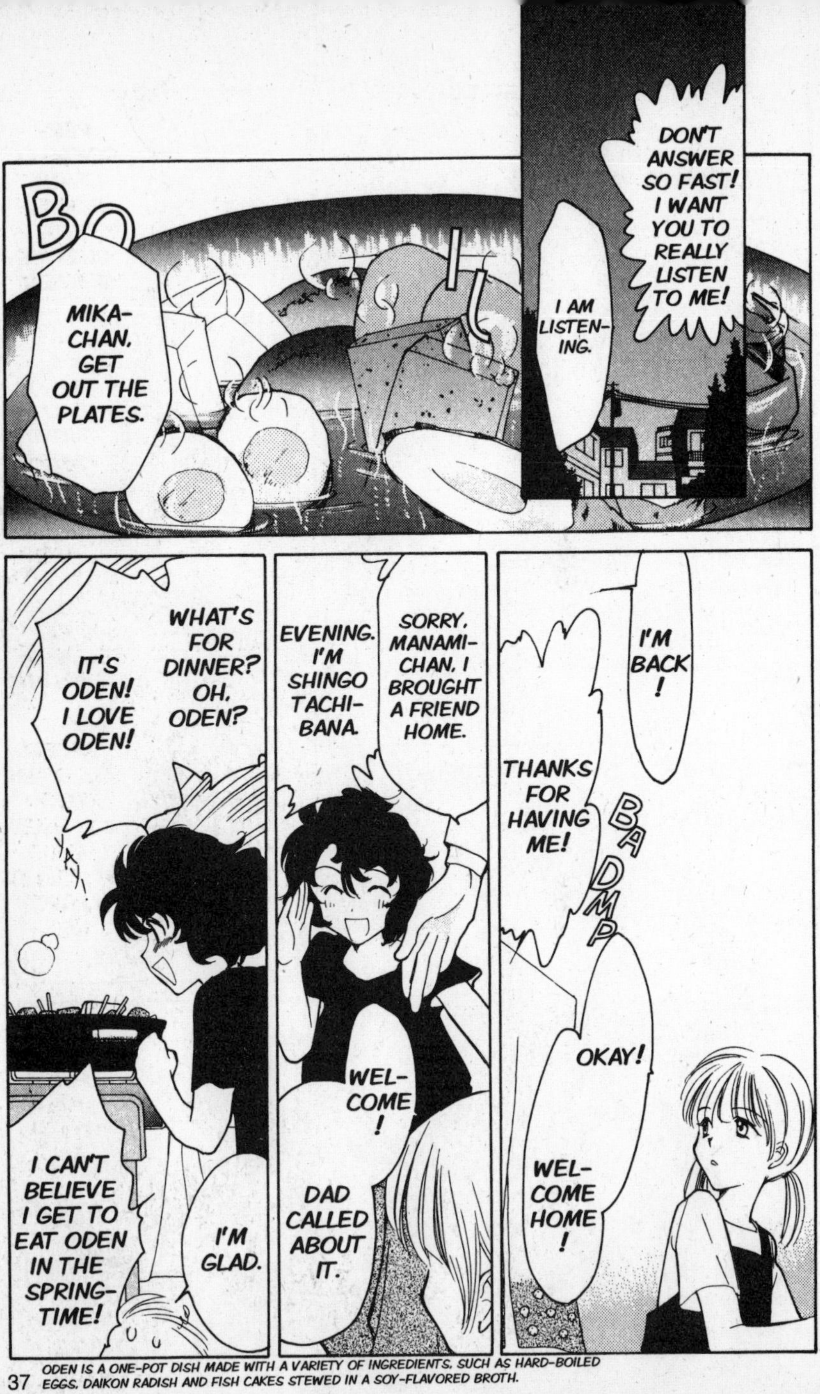
DON'T ANSWER SO FAST! I WANT YOU TO REALLY LISTEN TO ME!
I AM LISTENING.
BO
MIKA-CHAN, GET OUT THE PLATES.
I'M BACK!
THANKS FOR HAVING ME!
BADMP
OKAY!
WELCOME HOME!
SORRY, MANAMI-CHAN, I BROUGHT A FRIEND HOME.
EVENING. I'M SHINGO TACHIBANA.
WELCOME!
DAD CALLED ABOUT IT.
WHAT'S FOR DINNER? OH, ODEN?
IT'S ODEN! I LOVE ODEN!
I'M GLAD.
I CAN'T BELIEVE I GET TO EAT ODEN IN THE SPRINGTIME!

ODEN IS A ONE-POT DISH MADE WITH A VARIETY OF INGREDIENTS, SUCH AS HARD-BOILED EGGS, DAIKON RADISH AND FISH CAKES STEWED IN A SOY-FLAVORED BROTH.

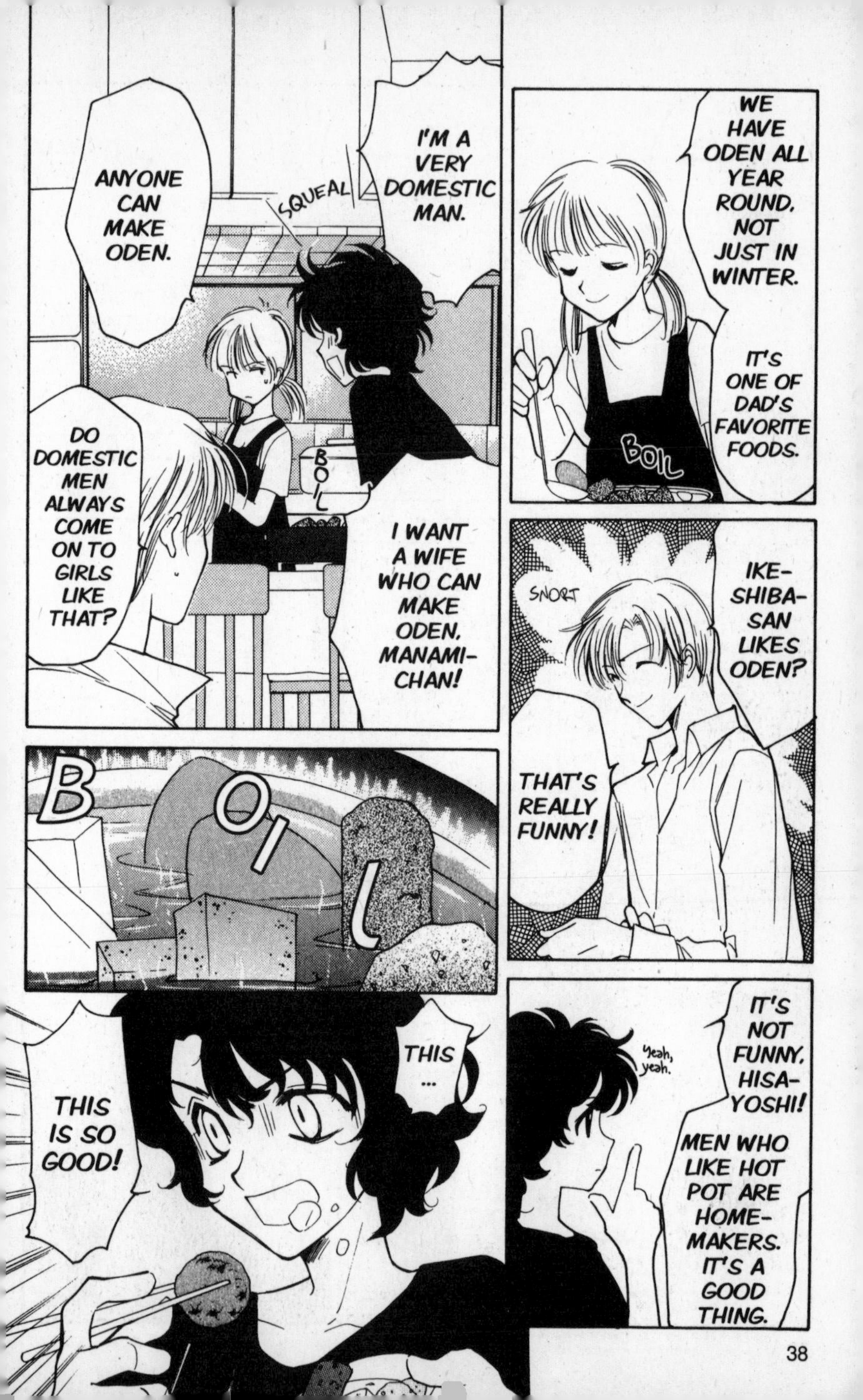
WE HAVE ODEN ALL YEAR ROUND, NOT JUST IN WINTER.
BOIL
IT'S ONE OF DAD'S FAVORITE FOODS.
I'M A VERY DOMESTIC MAN.
SQUEAL
ANYONE CAN MAKE ODEN.
I WANT A WIFE WHO CAN MAKE ODEN, MANAMI-CHAN!
BOIL
DO DOMESTIC MEN ALWAYS COME ON TO GIRLS LIKE THAT?
IKE-SHIBA-SAN LIKES ODEN?
SNORT
THAT'S REALLY FUNNY!
BOIL
IT'S NOT FUNNY, HISA-YOSHI!
yeah, yeah.
MEN WHO LIKE HOT POT ARE HOME-MAKERS. IT'S A GOOD THING.
THIS ...
THIS IS SO GOOD!

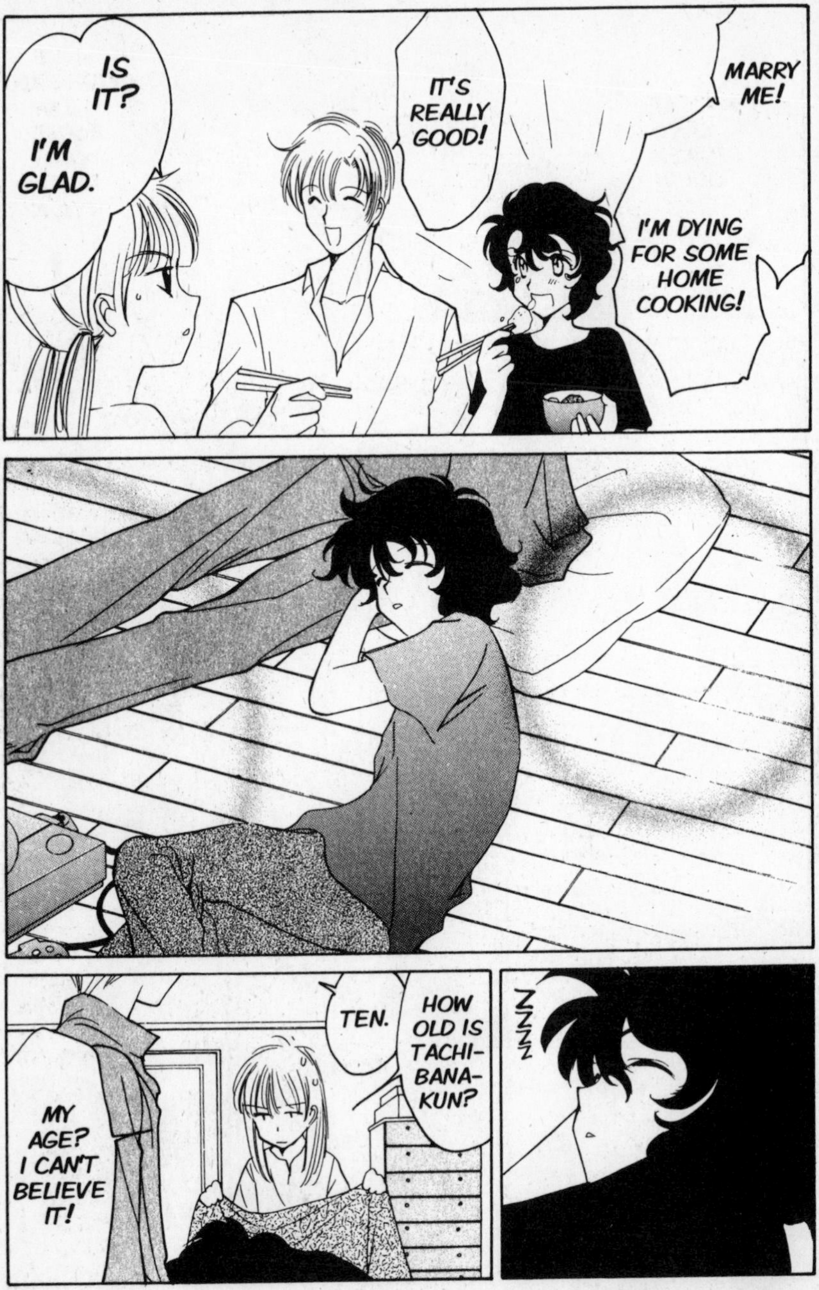
MARRY ME!
I'M DYING FOR SOME HOME COOKING!
IT'S REALLY GOOD!
IS IT?
I'M GLAD.
ZZZZ
HOW OLD IS TACHIBANA-KUN?
TEN.
MY AGE? I CAN'T BELIEVE IT!

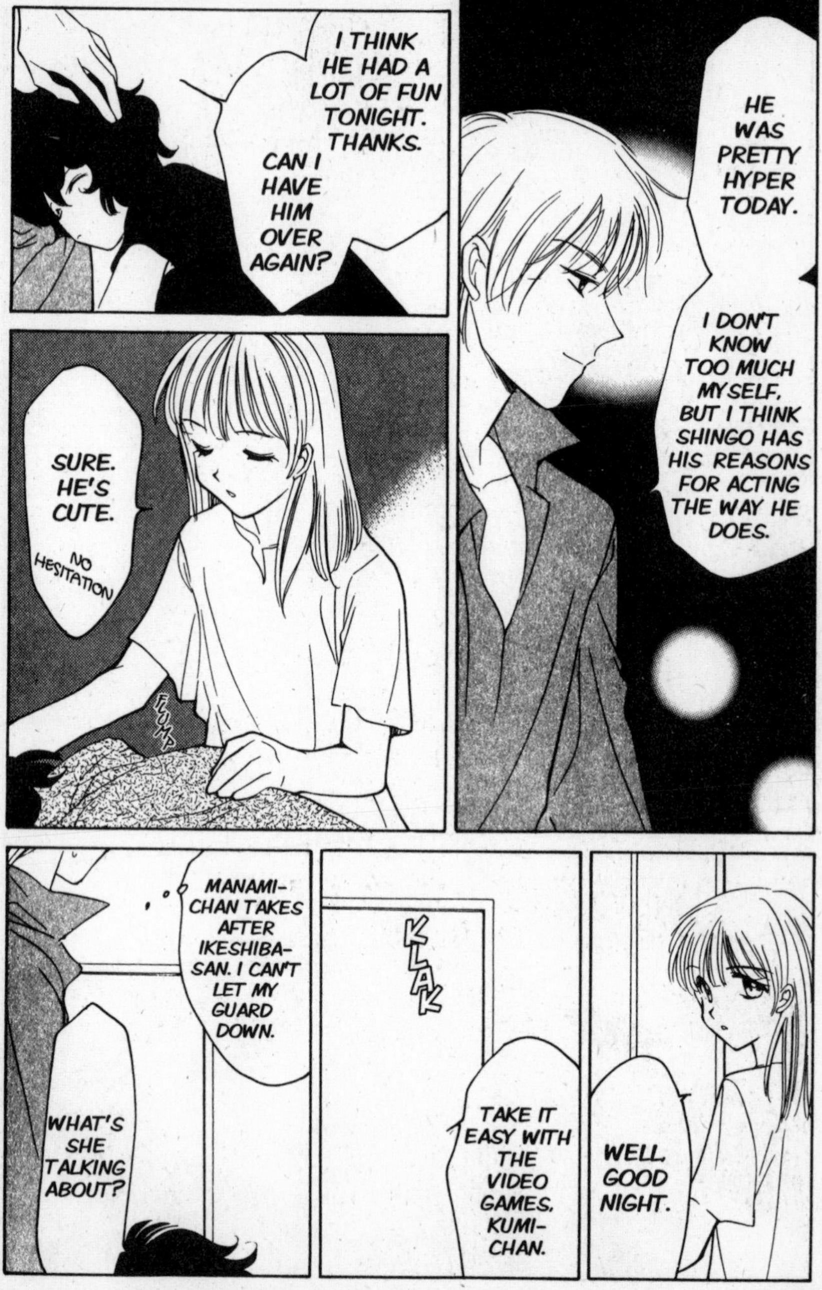
HE WAS PRETTY HYPER TODAY.
I DON'T KNOW TOO MUCH MYSELF, BUT I THINK SHINGO HAS HIS REASONS FOR ACTING THE WAY HE DOES.
I THINK HE HAD A LOT OF FUN TONIGHT. THANKS.
CAN I HAVE HIM OVER AGAIN?
SURE. HE'S CUTE.
NO HESITATION
FLUMP
WELL, GOOD NIGHT.
TAKE IT EASY WITH THE VIDEO GAMES, KUMI-CHAN.
KLAK
MANAMI-CHAN TAKES AFTER IKESHIBA-SAN. I CAN'T LET MY GUARD DOWN.
WHAT'S SHE TALKING ABOUT?

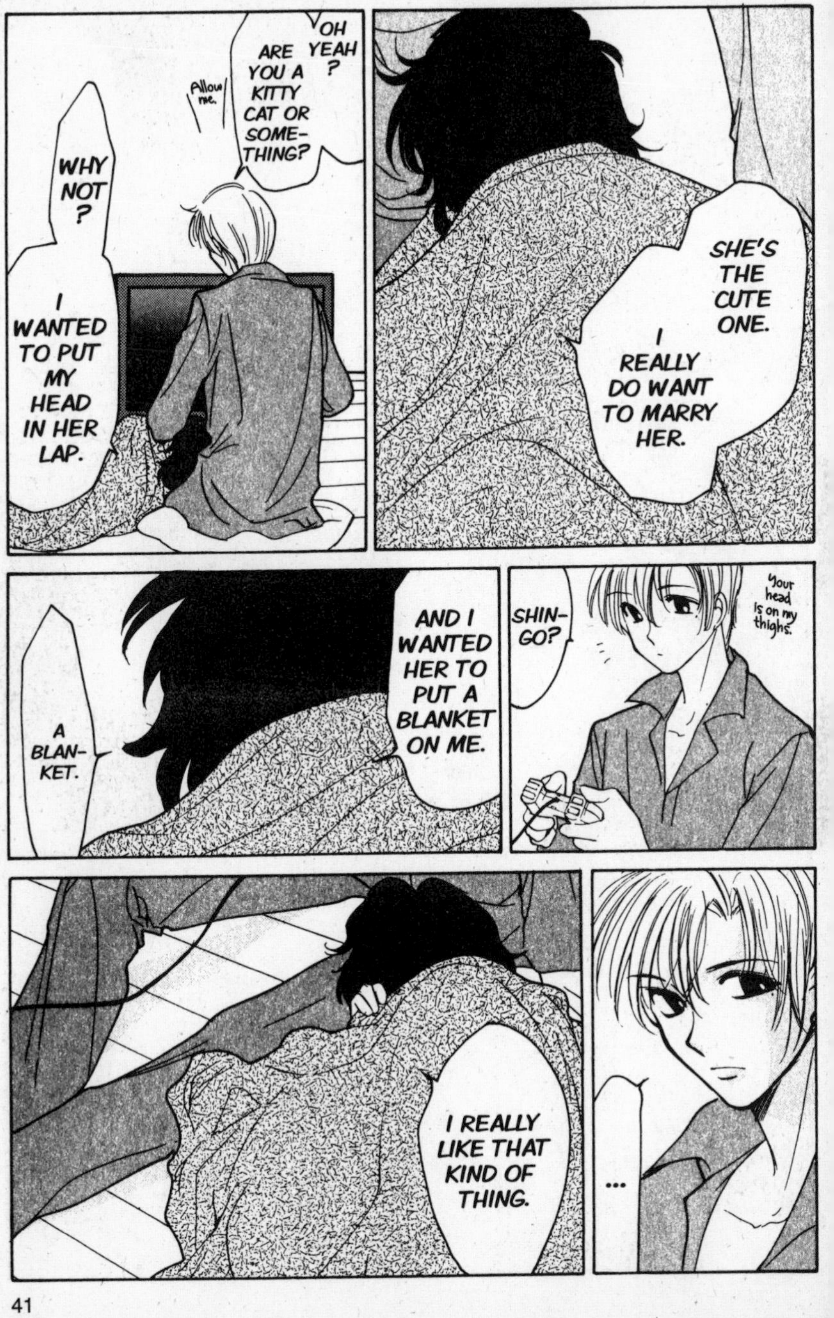
SHE'S THE CUTE ONE.
I REALLY DO WANT TO MARRY HER.
OH YEAH?
ARE YOU A KITTY CAT OR SOME-THING?
Allow me.
WHY NOT?
I WANTED TO PUT MY HEAD IN HER LAP.
Your head is on my thighs.
SHIN-GO?
AND I WANTED HER TO PUT A BLANKET ON ME.
A BLAN-KET.
...
I REALLY LIKE THAT KIND OF THING.

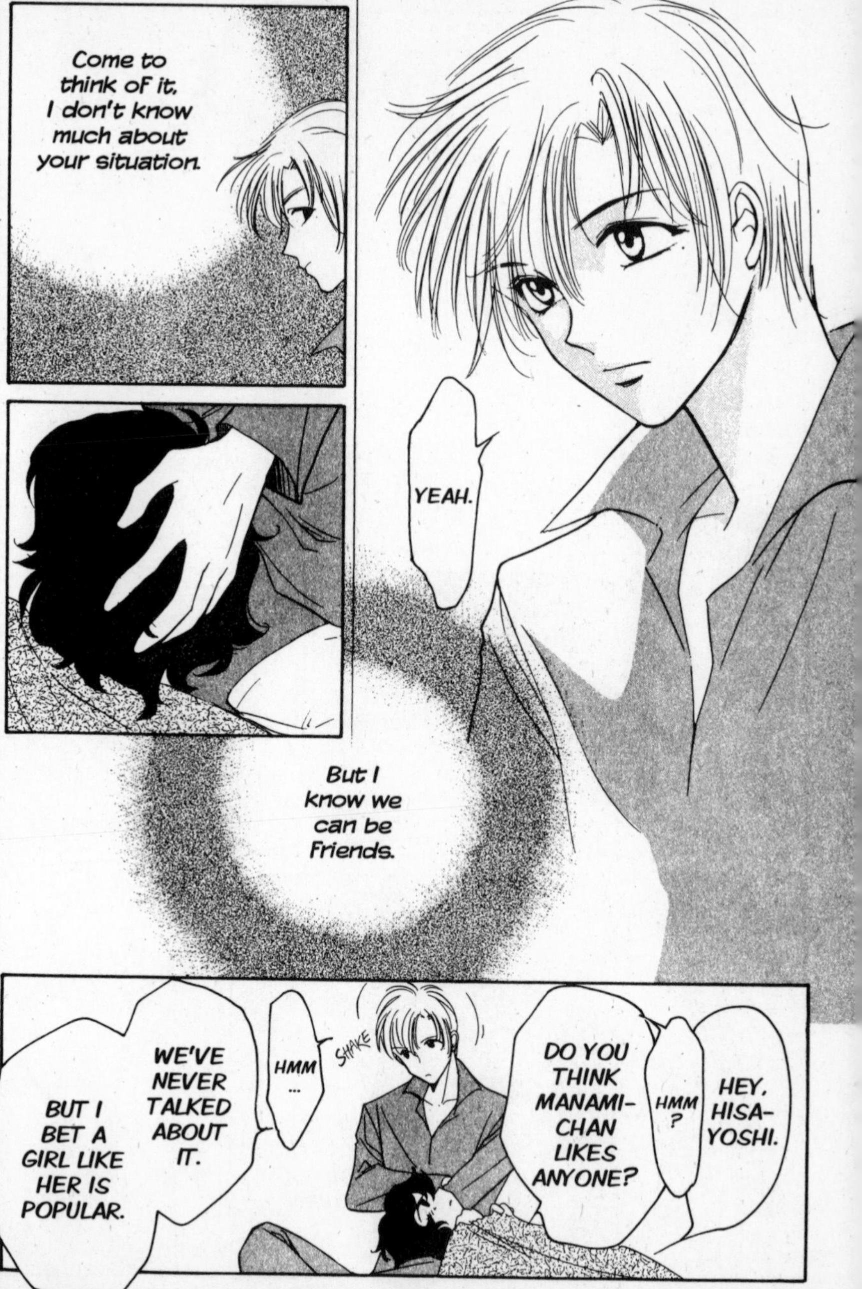
YEAH.
But I know we can be friends.
Come to think of it, I don't know much about your situation.
HEY, HISA-YOSHI.
HMM?
DO YOU THINK MANAMI-CHAN LIKES ANYONE?
SHAKE
HMM...
WE'VE NEVER TALKED ABOUT IT.
BUT I BET A GIRL LIKE HER IS POPULAR.

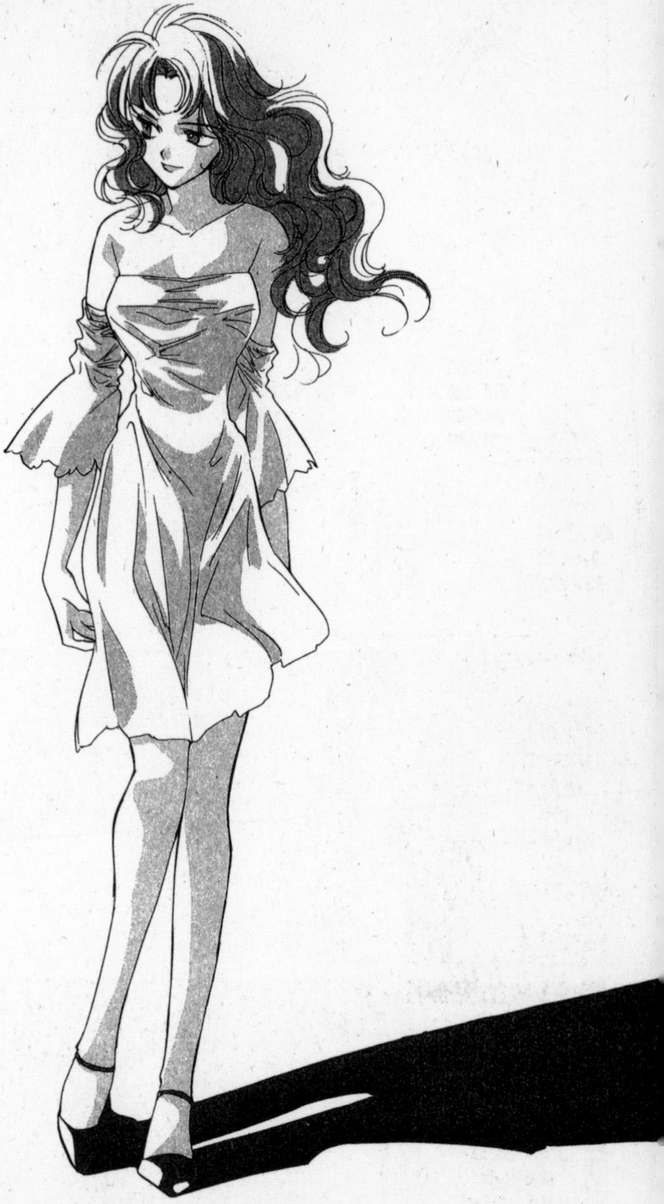

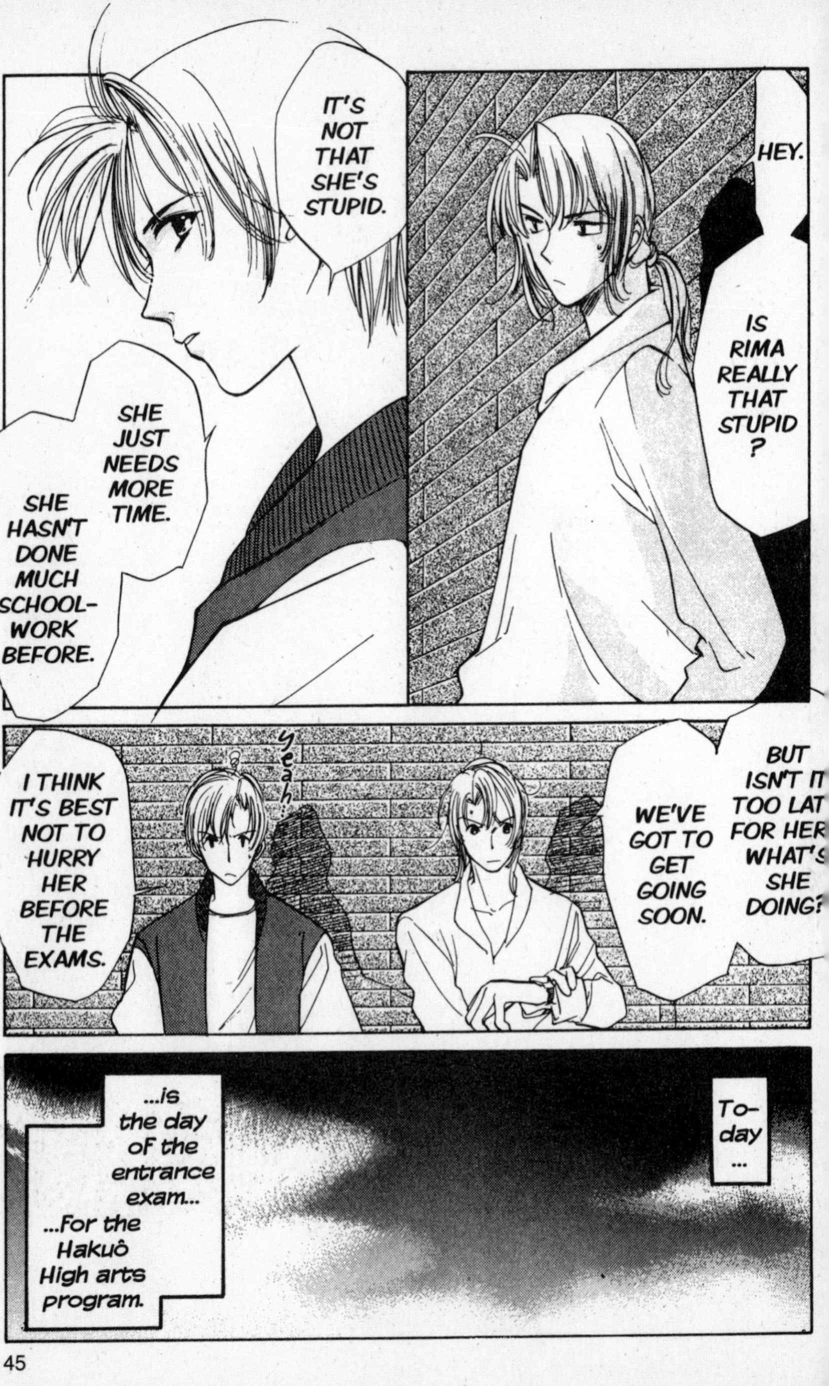
HEY.
IS RIMA REALLY THAT STUPID?
IT'S NOT THAT SHE'S STUPID.
SHE JUST NEEDS MORE TIME.
SHE HASN'T DONE MUCH SCHOOL-WORK BEFORE.
BUT ISN'T IT TOO LAT FOR HER WHAT'S SHE DOING?
WE'VE GOT TO GET GOING SOON.
yeah...
I THINK IT'S BEST NOT TO HURRY HER BEFORE THE EXAMS.
To-day...
...is the day oF the entrance exam...
...For the Hakuô High arts program.

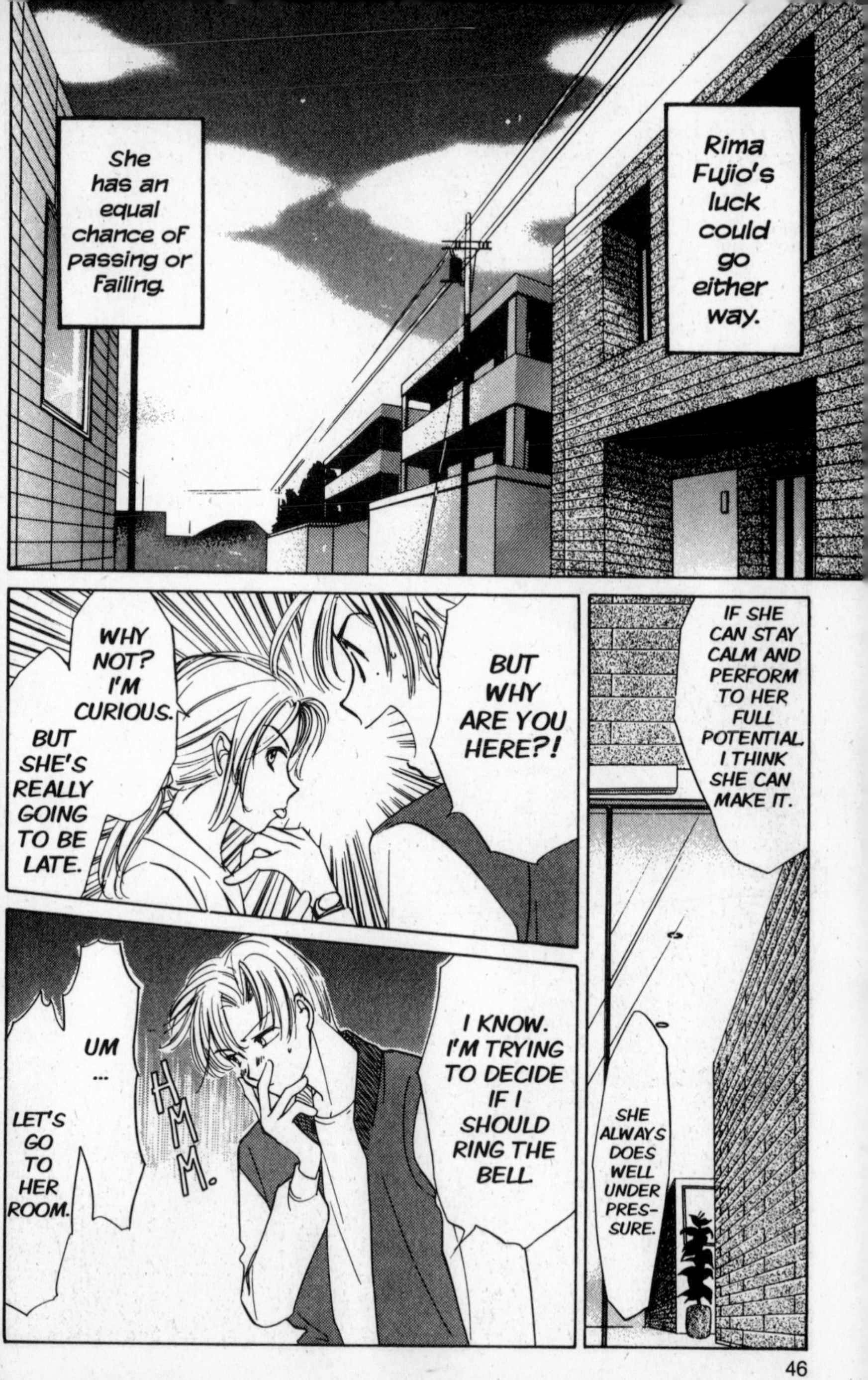
Rima Fujio's luck could go either way.
She has an equal chance of passing or failing.
IF SHE CAN STAY CALM AND PERFORM TO HER FULL POTENTIAL, I THINK SHE CAN MAKE IT.
SHE ALWAYS DOES WELL UNDER PRES-SURE.
BUT WHY ARE YOU HERE?!
WHY NOT? I'M CURIOUS.
BUT SHE'S REALLY GOING TO BE LATE.
I KNOW. I'M TRYING TO DECIDE IF I SHOULD RING THE BELL.
HMMM.
UM ...
LET'S GO TO HER ROOM.

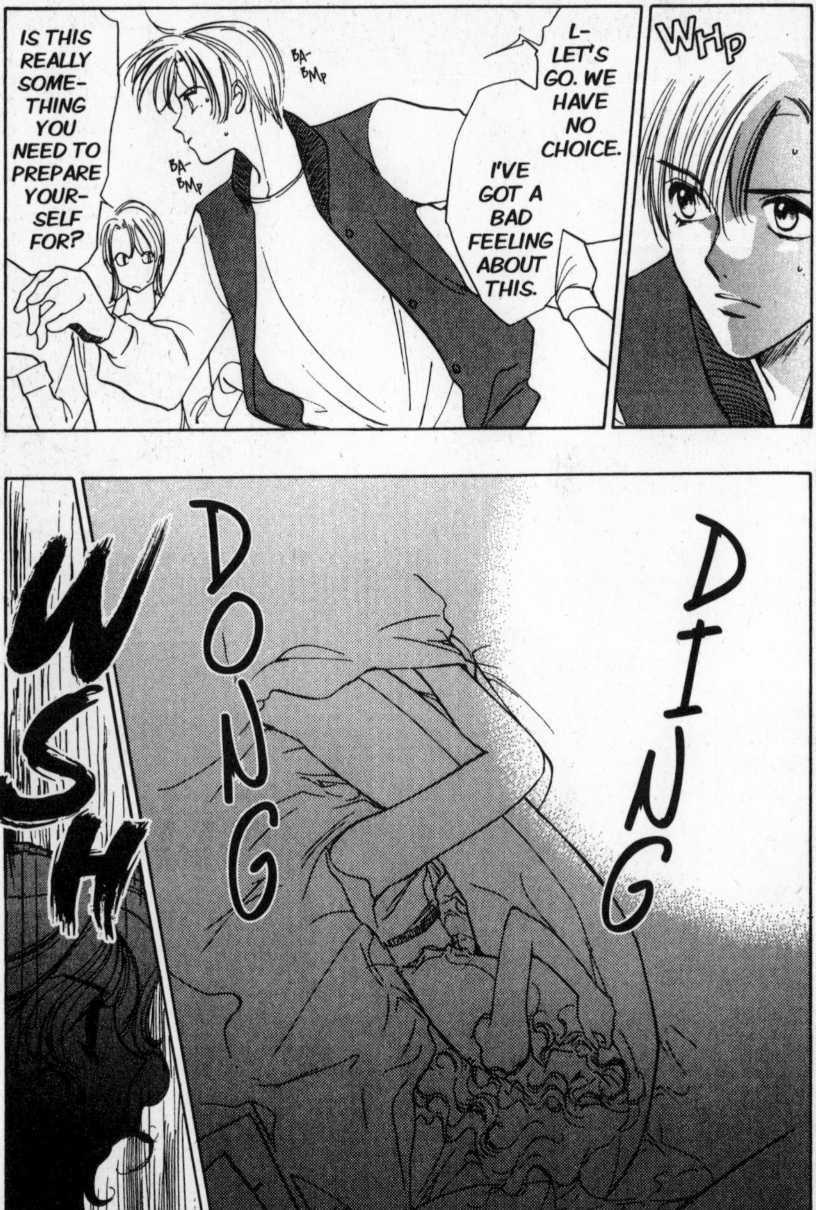
WHIP
L- LET'S GO. WE HAVE NO CHOICE.
I'VE GOT A BAD FEELING ABOUT THIS.
BA-BMP
BA-BMP
IS THIS REALLY SOMETHING YOU NEED TO PREPARE YOURSELF FOR?
DING
DONG
WSH

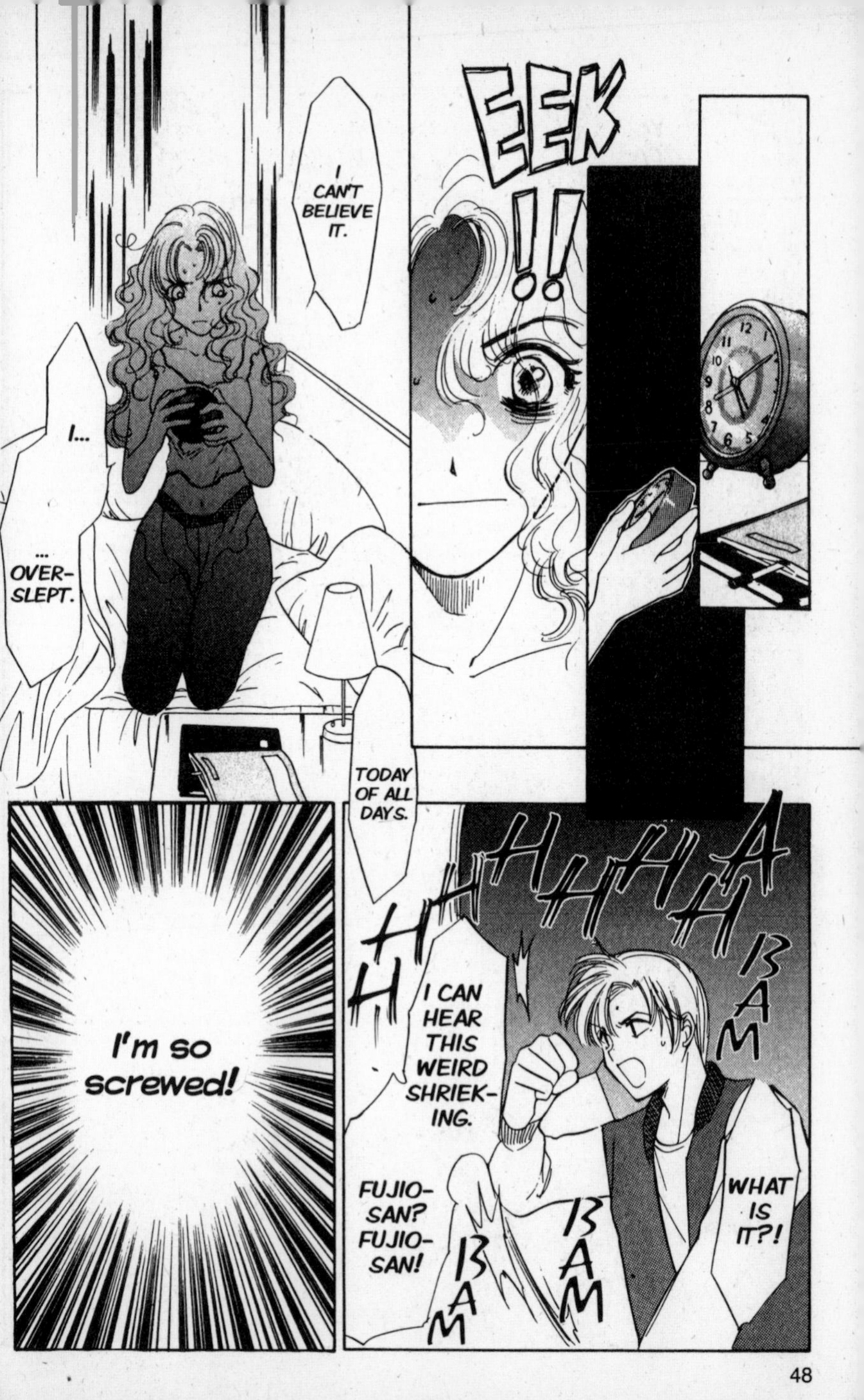
EEK!!
I CAN'T BELIEVE IT.
I...
... OVER-SLEPT.
TODAY OF ALL DAYS.
HHHHHHHHA
BAM
I CAN HEAR THIS WEIRD SHRIEK-ING.
WHAT IS IT?!
FUJIO-SAN? FUJIO-SAN!
BAM
BAM
I'm so screwed!

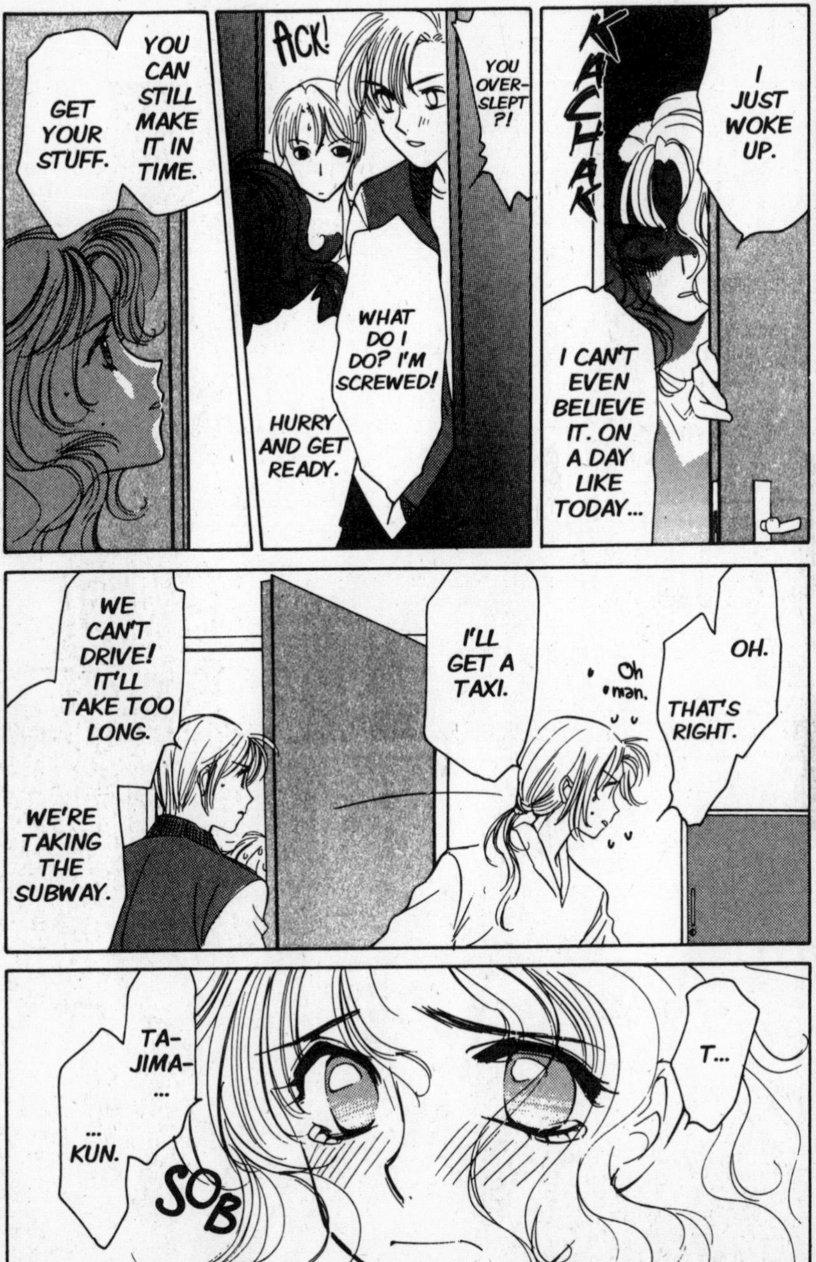
KACHAK
I JUST WOKE UP.
I CAN'T EVEN BELIEVE IT. ON A DAY LIKE TODAY...
YOU OVER-SLEPT?!
ACK!
WHAT DO I DO? I'M SCREWED!
HURRY AND GET READY.
YOU CAN STILL MAKE IT IN TIME.
GET YOUR STUFF.
OH.
THAT'S RIGHT.
Oh man.
I'LL GET A TAXI.
WE CAN'T DRIVE! IT'LL TAKE TOO LONG.
WE'RE TAKING THE SUBWAY.
T...
TA-JIMA-...
...KUN.
SOB

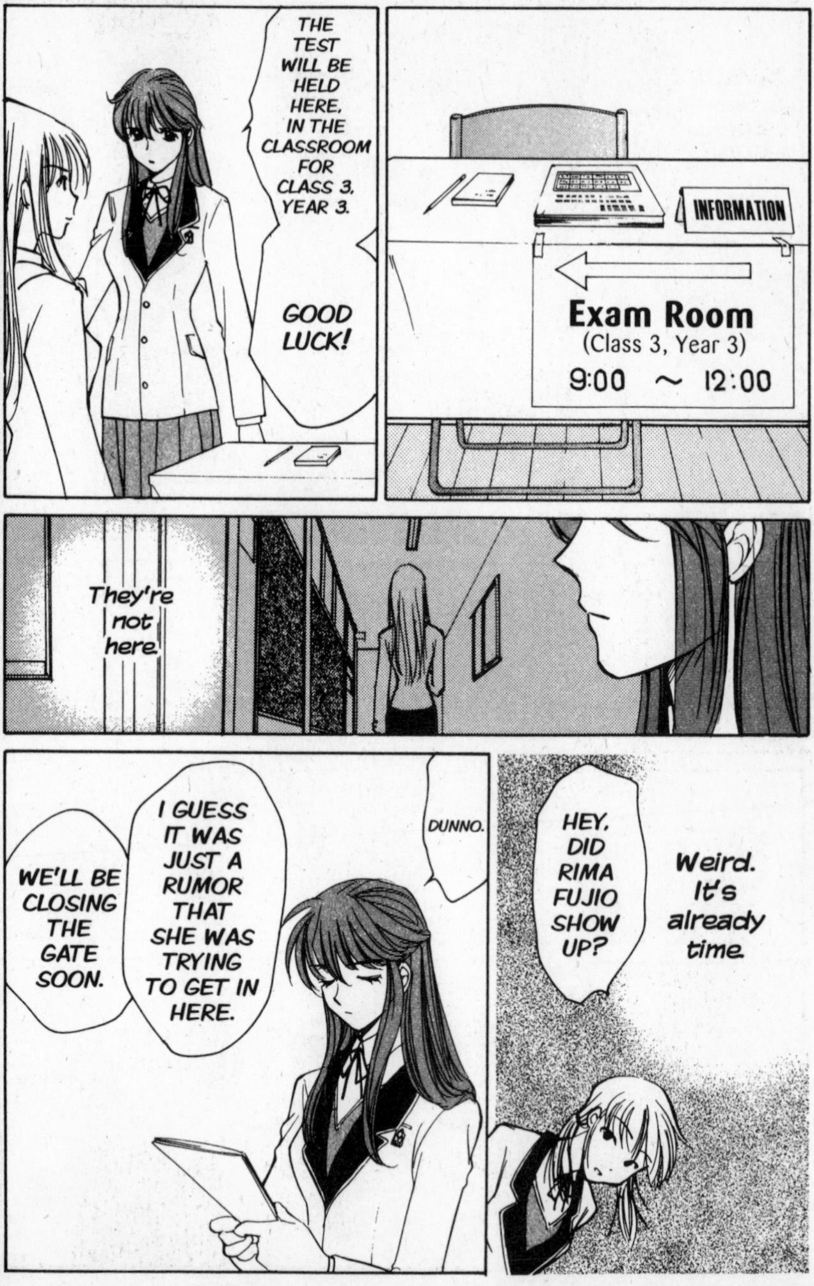
INFORMATION
Exam Room
(Class 3, Year 3)
9:00 ~ 12:00
THE TEST WILL BE HELD HERE, IN THE CLASSROOM FOR CLASS 3, YEAR 3.
GOOD LUCK!
They're not here.
HEY, DID RIMA FUJIO SHOW UP?
Weird. It's already time.
DUNNO.
I GUESS IT WAS JUST A RUMOR THAT SHE WAS TRYING TO GET IN HERE.
WE'LL BE CLOSING THE GATE SOON.

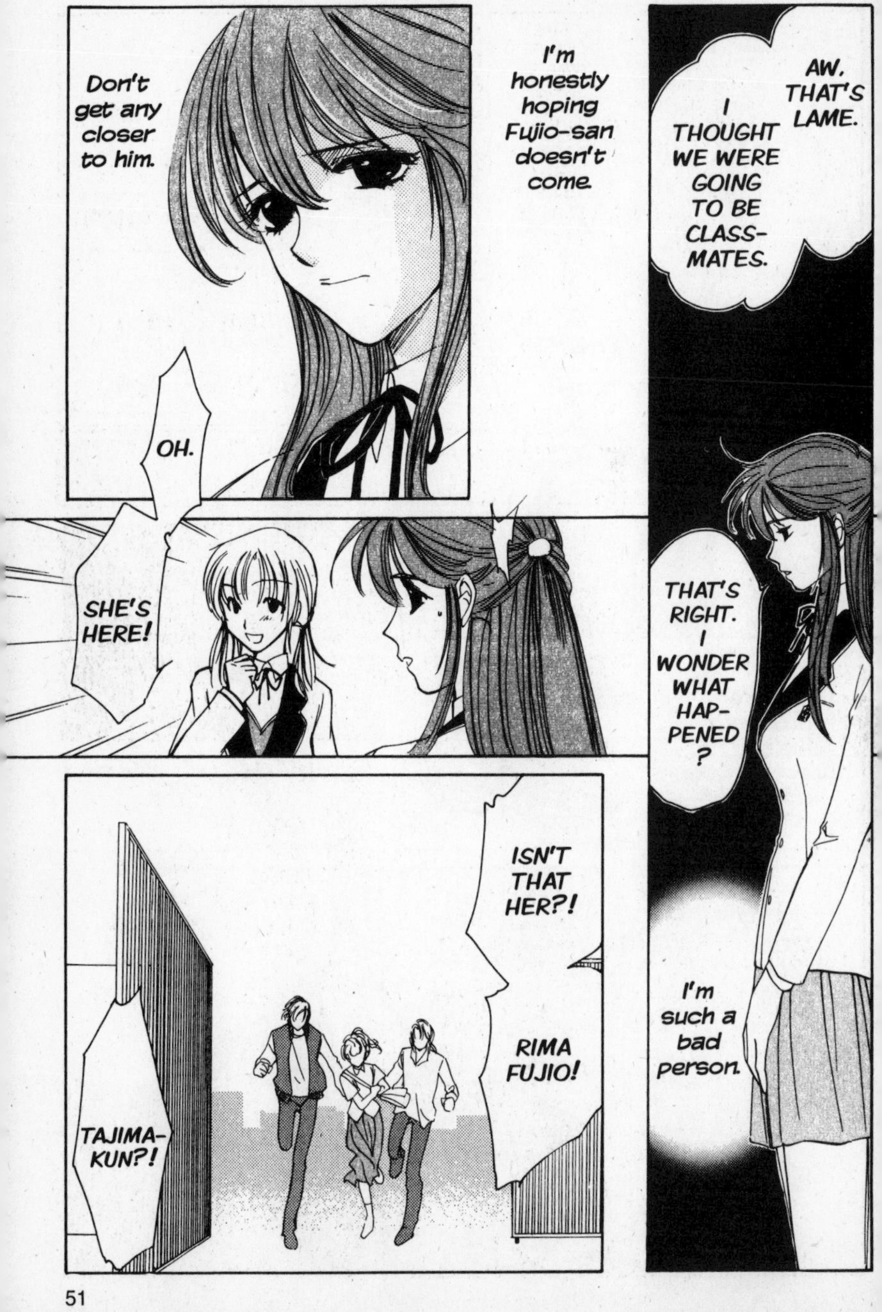

AW. THAT'S LAME.
I THOUGHT WE WERE GOING TO BE CLASS-MATES.
THAT'S RIGHT. I WONDER WHAT HAP-PENED?
I'm such a bad person.
I'm honestly hoping Fujio-san doesn't come.
Don't get any closer to him.
OH.
SHE'S HERE!
ISN'T THAT HER?!
RIMA FUJIO!
TAJIMA-KUN?!

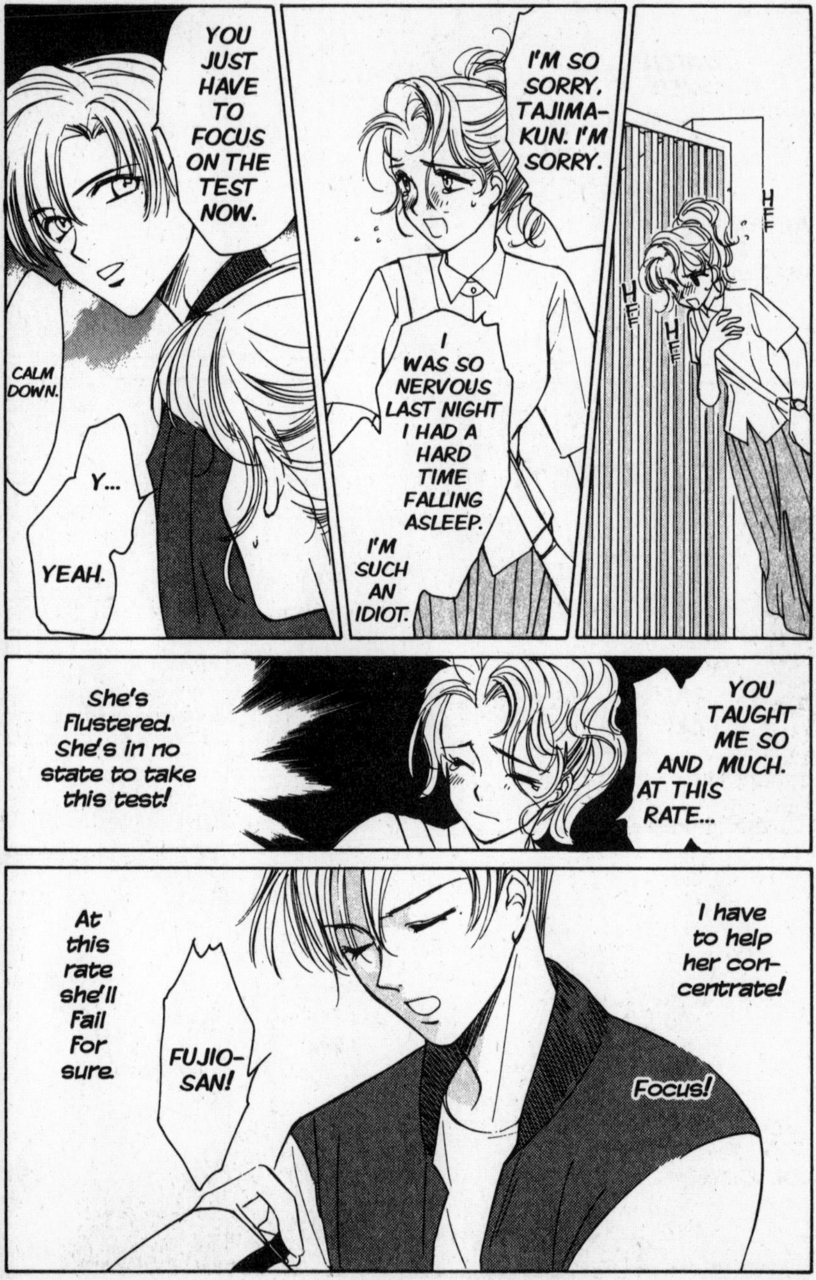
HEF
HEF
HEF
I'M SO SORRY, TAJIMA-KUN. I'M SORRY.
I WAS SO NERVOUS LAST NIGHT I HAD A HARD TIME FALLING ASLEEP.
I'M SUCH AN IDIOT.
YOU JUST HAVE TO FOCUS ON THE TEST NOW.
CALM DOWN.
Y...
YEAH.
YOU TAUGHT ME SO MUCH. AND AT THIS RATE...
She's flustered. She's in no state to take this test!
I have to help her con-centrate!
Focus!
FUJIO-SAN!
At this rate she'll fail for sure.

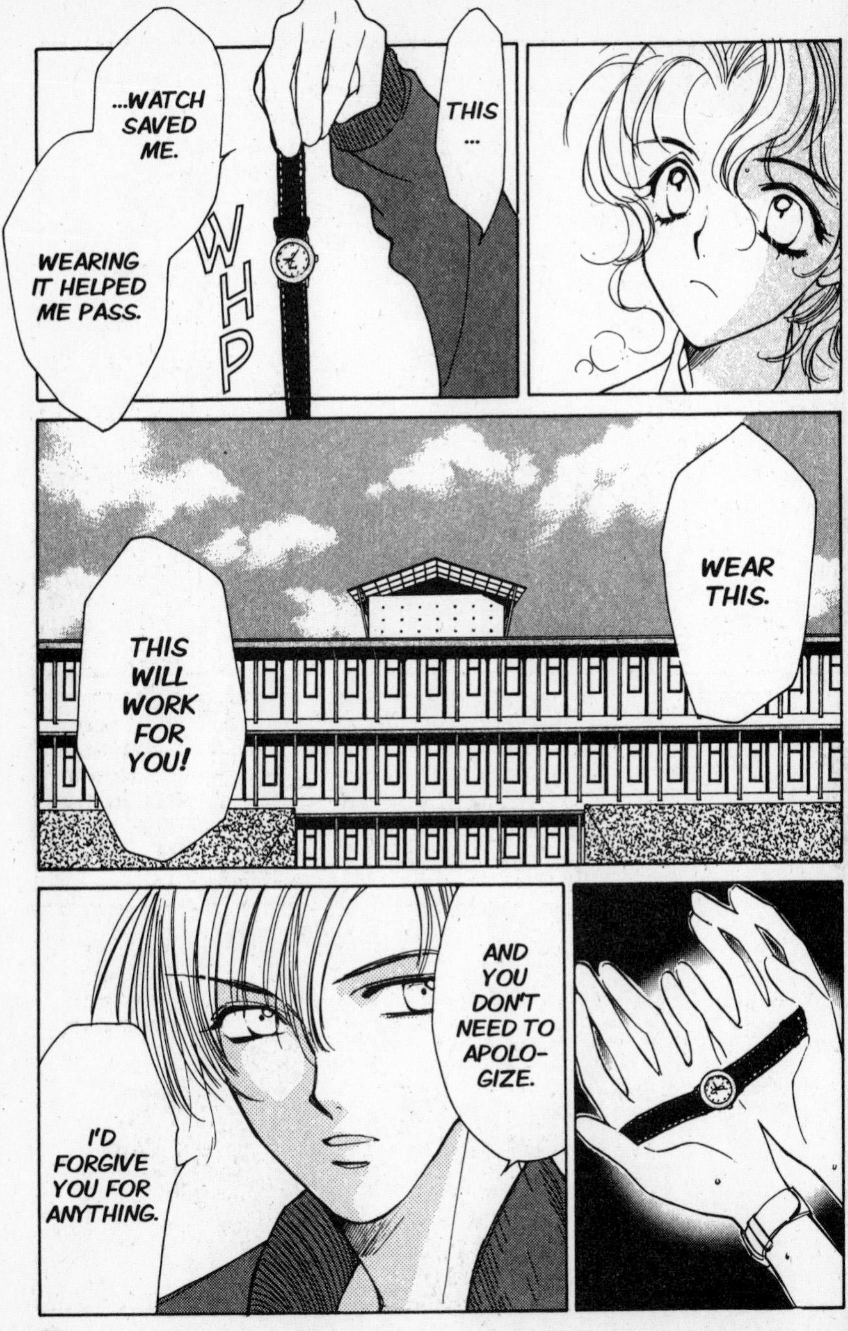
THIS ...
...WATCH SAVED ME.
WHP
WEARING IT HELPED ME PASS.
WEAR THIS.
THIS WILL WORK FOR YOU!
AND YOU DON'T NEED TO APOLOGIZE.
I'D FORGIVE YOU FOR ANYTHING.

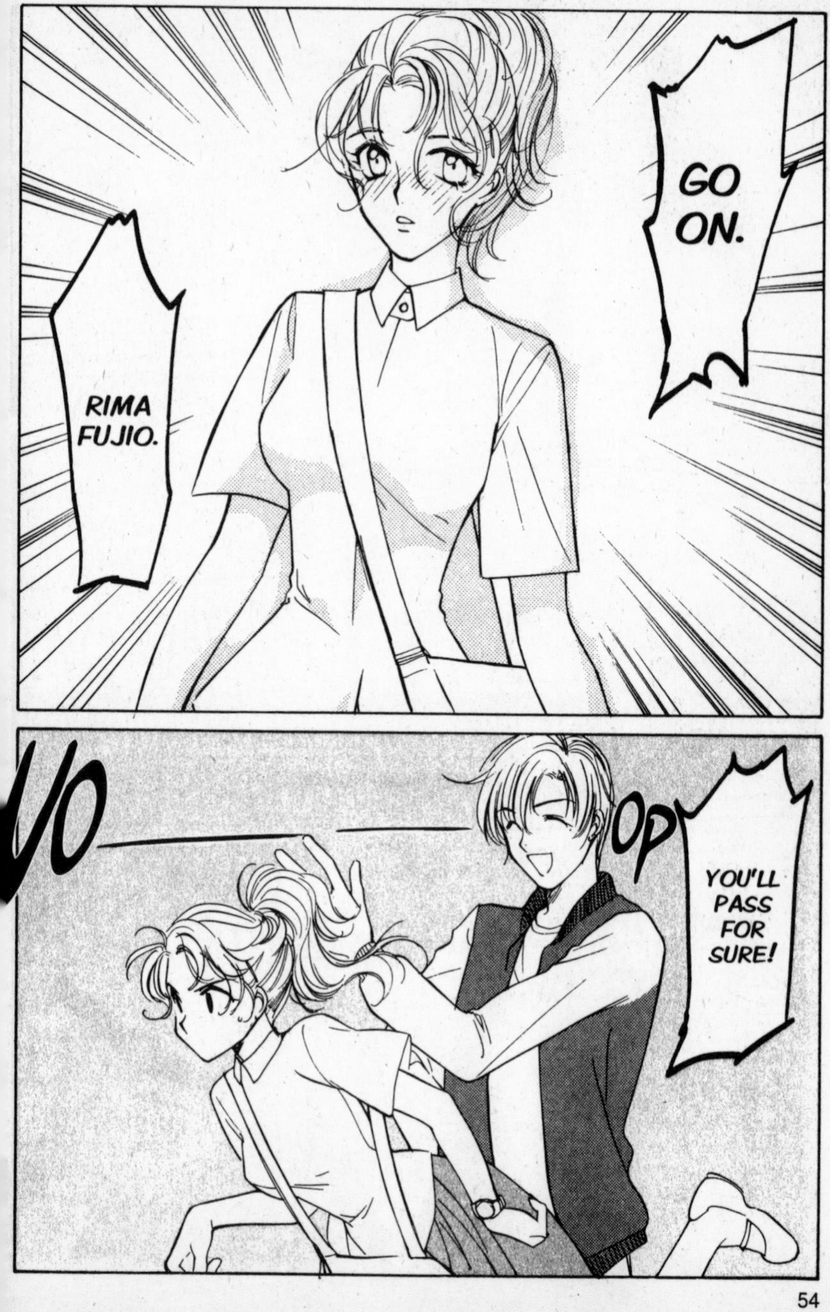
GO ON.
RIMA FUJIO.
YOU'LL PASS FOR SURE!
OP

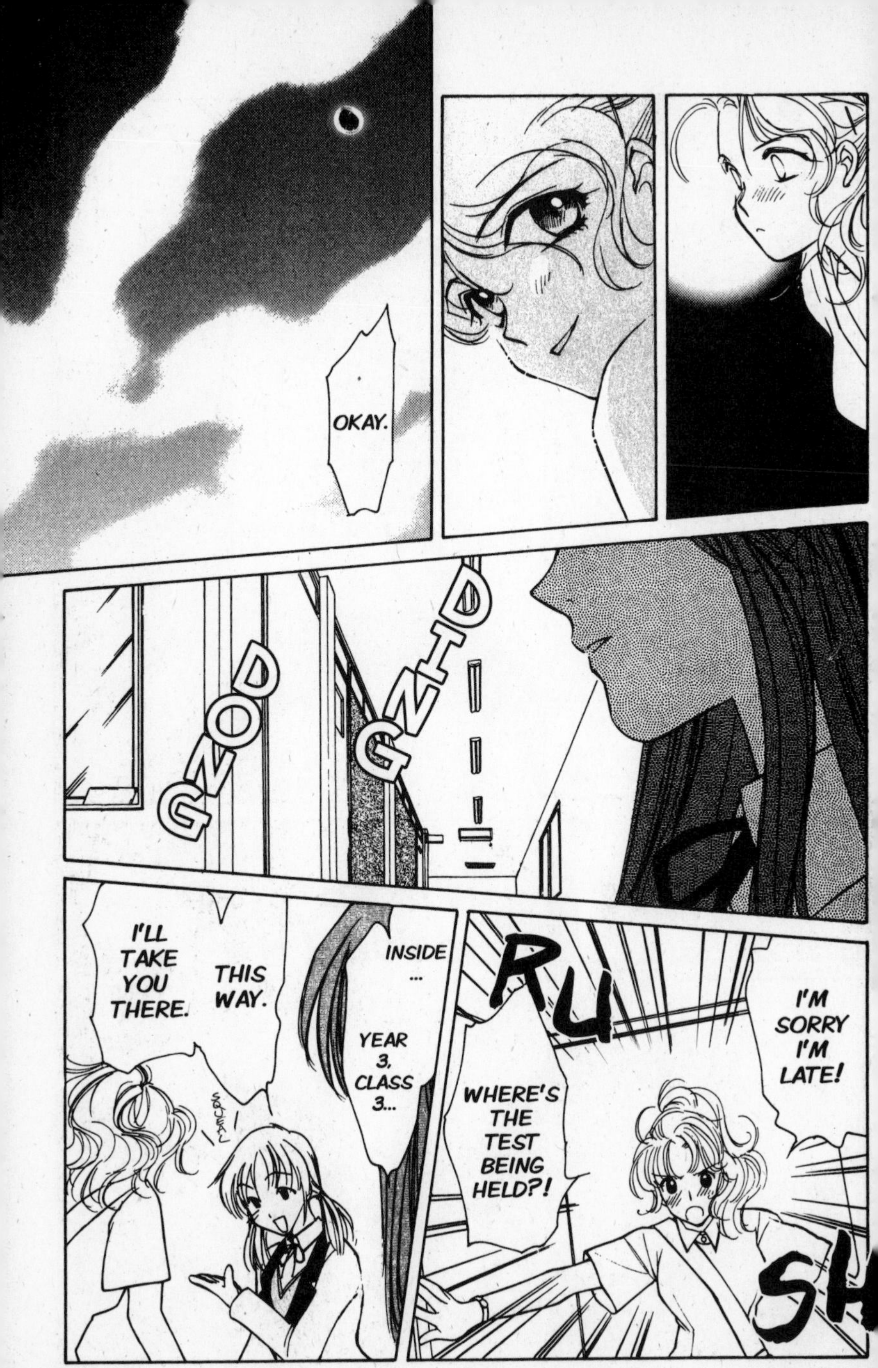
OKAY.
DING
DONG
RUSH
I'M SORRY I'M LATE!
WHERE'S THE TEST BEING HELD?!
INSIDE ...
YEAR 3, CLASS 3...
THIS WAY.
I'LL TAKE YOU THERE.

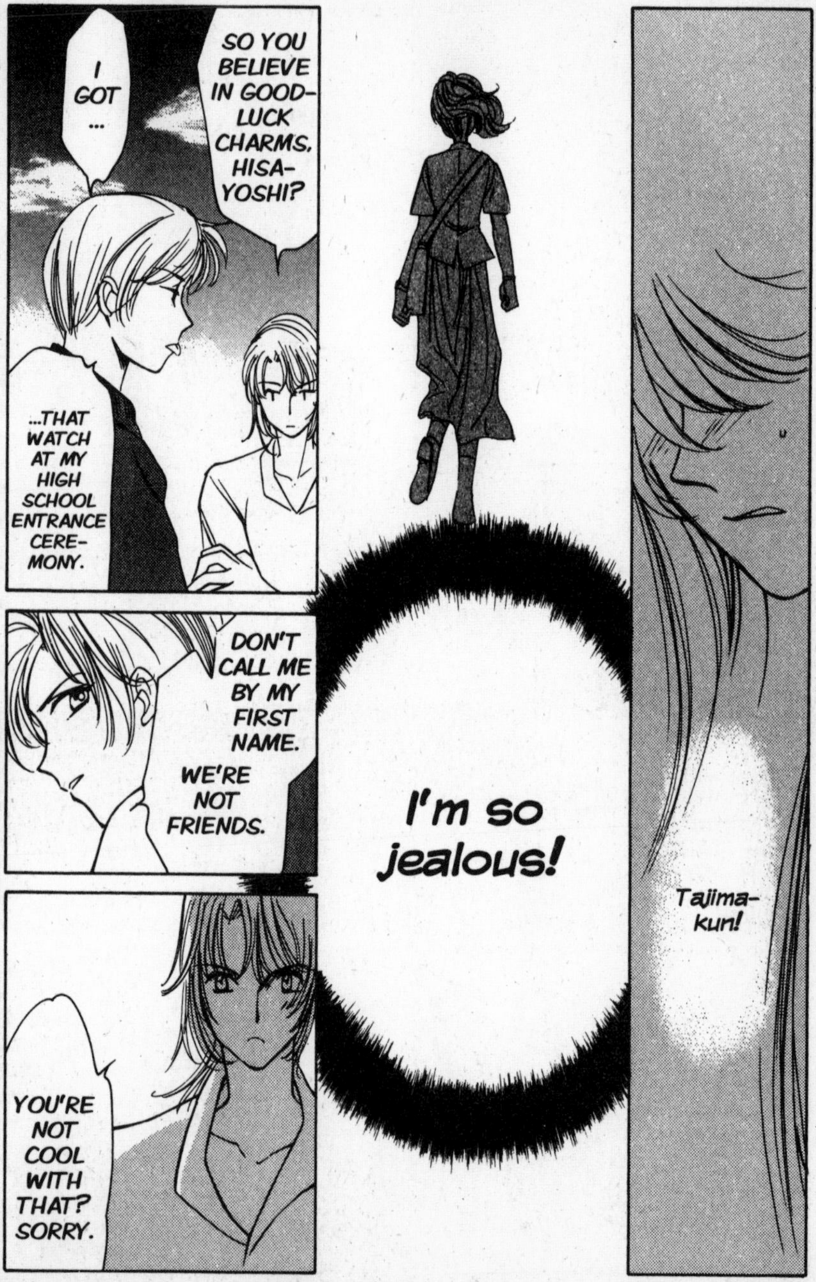
Tajima-kun!
I'm so jealous!
SO YOU BELIEVE IN GOOD-LUCK CHARMS, HISA-YOSHI?
I GOT ...
...THAT WATCH AT MY HIGH SCHOOL ENTRANCE CERE-MONY.
DON'T CALL ME BY MY FIRST NAME.
WE'RE NOT FRIENDS.
YOU'RE NOT COOL WITH THAT? SORRY.

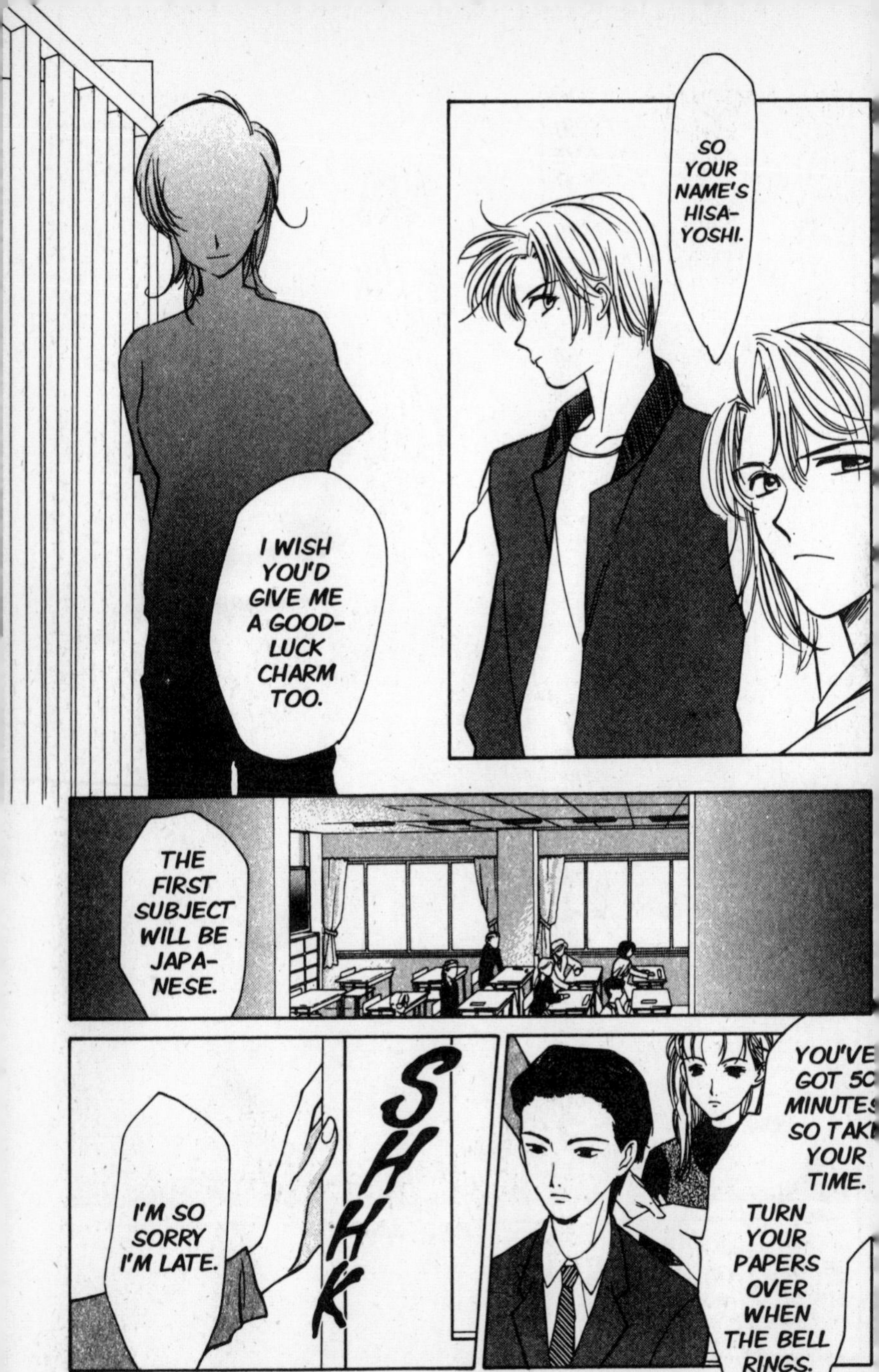
SO YOUR NAME'S HISA-YOSHI.
I WISH YOU'D GIVE ME A GOOD-LUCK CHARM TOO.
THE FIRST SUBJECT WILL BE JAPA-NESE.
YOU'VE GOT 50 MINUTES SO TAKE YOUR TIME.
TURN YOUR PAPERS OVER WHEN THE BELL RINGS.
SHHK
I'M SO SORRY I'M LATE.

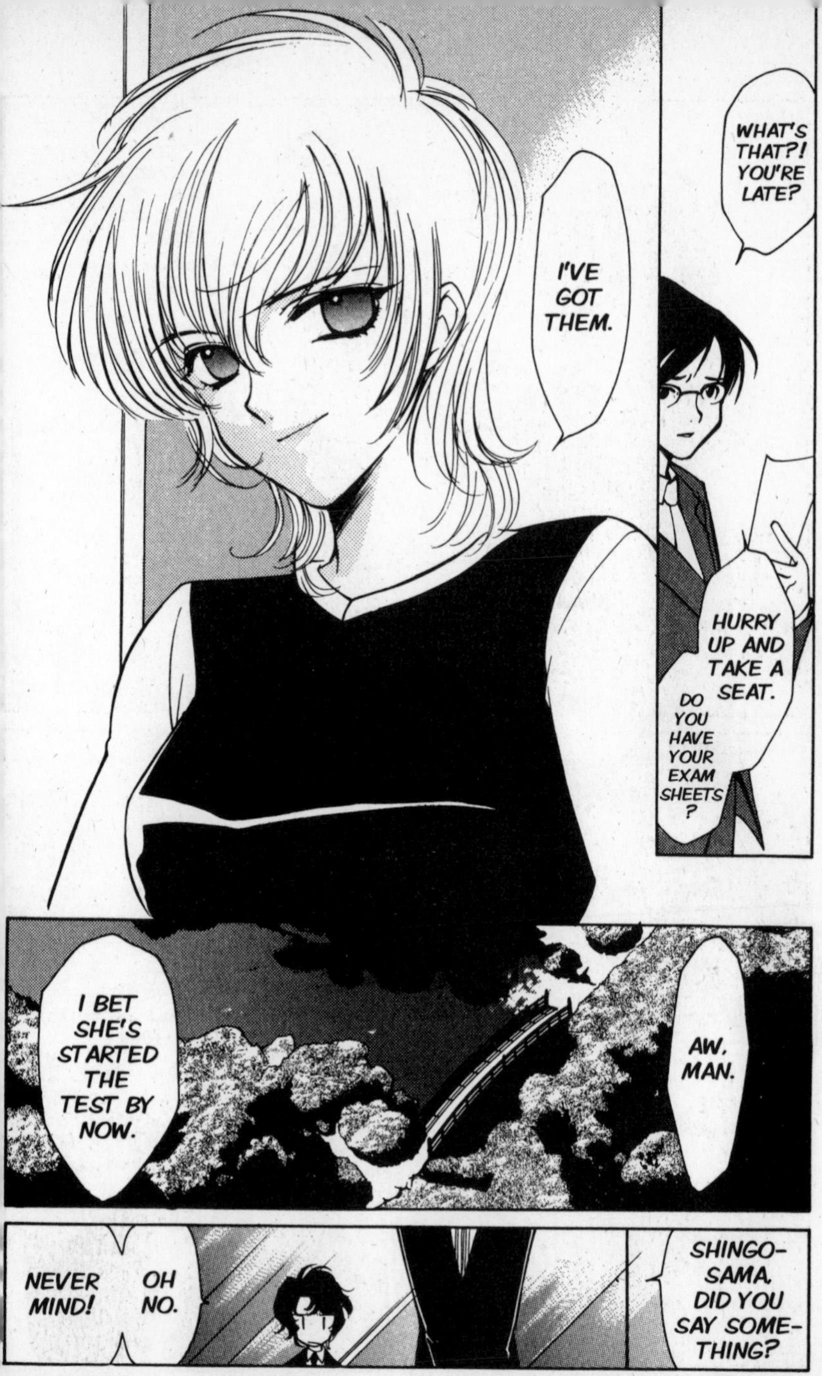
WHAT'S THAT?! YOU'RE LATE?
HURRY UP AND TAKE A SEAT.
DO YOU HAVE YOUR EXAM SHEETS?
I'VE GOT THEM.
AW, MAN.
I BET SHE'S STARTED THE TEST BY NOW.
SHINGO-SAMA, DID YOU SAY SOME-THING?
OH NO.
NEVER MIND!

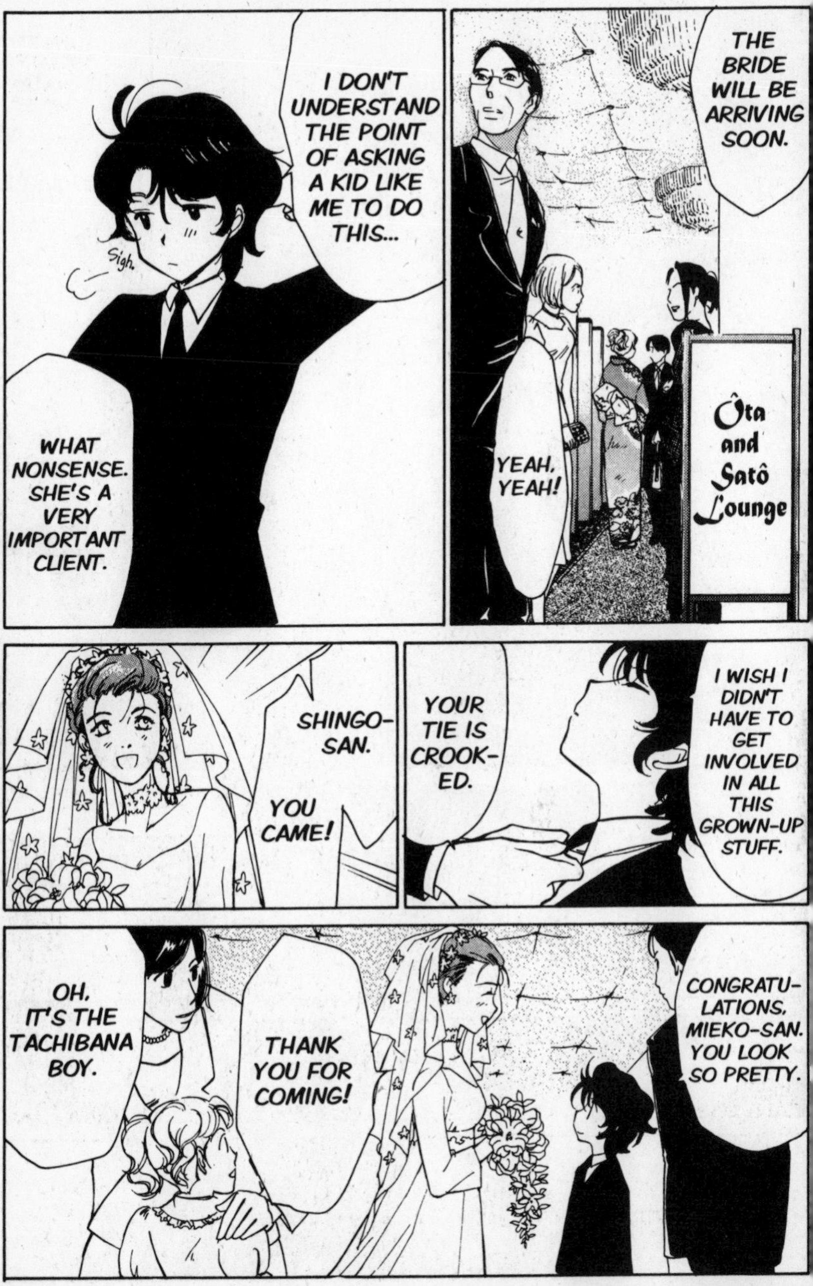
THE BRIDE WILL BE ARRIVING SOON.
Ôta and Satô Lounge
YEAH, YEAH!
I DON'T UNDERSTAND THE POINT OF ASKING A KID LIKE ME TO DO THIS...
Sigh.
WHAT NONSENSE. SHE'S A VERY IMPORTANT CLIENT.
I WISH I DIDN'T HAVE TO GET INVOLVED IN ALL THIS GROWN-UP STUFF.
YOUR TIE IS CROOK-ED.
SHINGO-SAN.
YOU CAME!
CONGRATU-LATIONS, MIEKO-SAN. YOU LOOK SO PRETTY.
THANK YOU FOR COMING!
OH, IT'S THE TACHIBANA BOY.

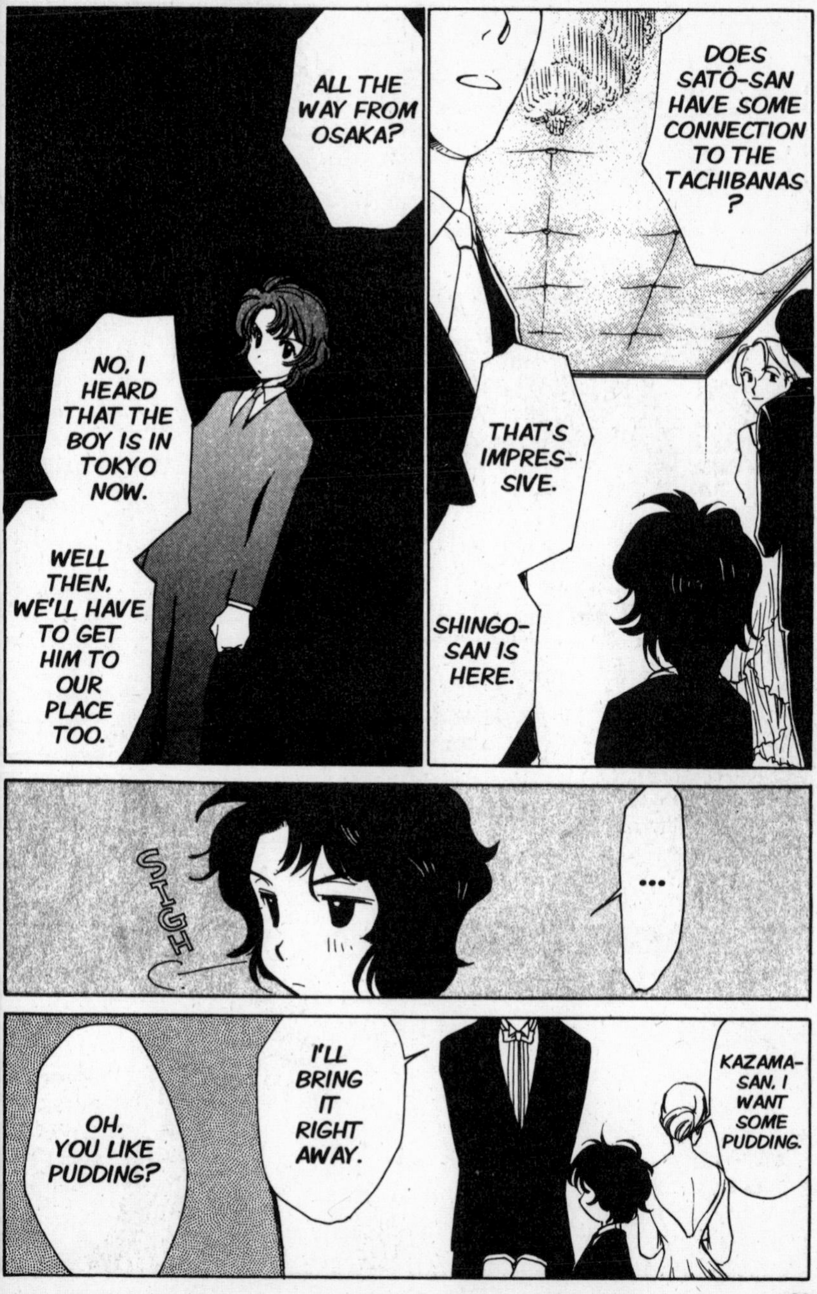
DOES SATÔ-SAN HAVE SOME CONNECTION TO THE TACHIBANAS?
THAT'S IMPRES-SIVE.
SHINGO-SAN IS HERE.
ALL THE WAY FROM OSAKA?
NO, I HEARD THAT THE BOY IS IN TOKYO NOW.
WELL THEN, WE'LL HAVE TO GET HIM TO OUR PLACE TOO.
...
SIGH
KAZAMA-SAN, I WANT SOME PUDDING.
I'LL BRING IT RIGHT AWAY.
OH, YOU LIKE PUDDING?

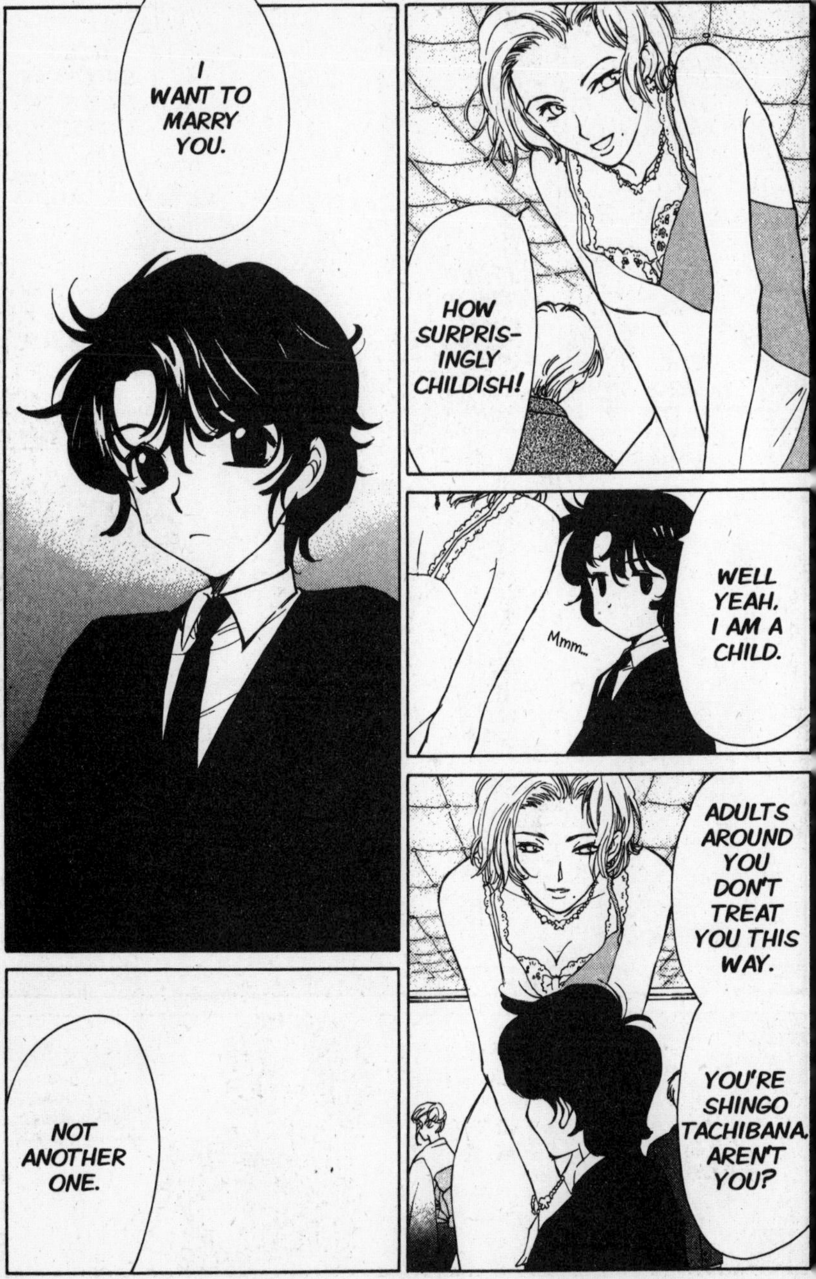
HOW SURPRIS-INGLY CHILDISH!
WELL YEAH, I AM A CHILD.
Mmm...
ADULTS AROUND YOU DON'T TREAT YOU THIS WAY.
YOU'RE SHINGO TACHIBANA, AREN'T YOU?
I WANT TO MARRY YOU.
NOT ANOTHER ONE.

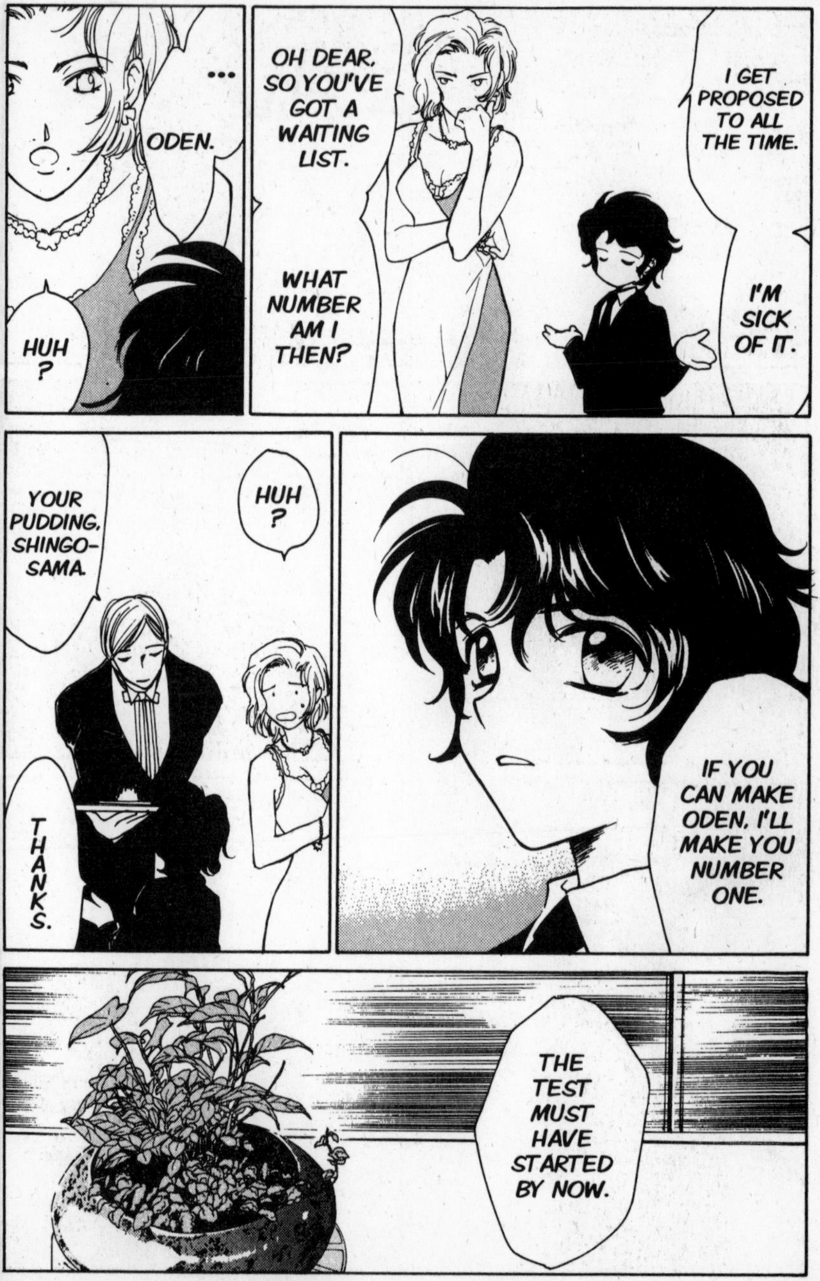
I GET PROPOSED TO ALL THE TIME.
I'M SICK OF IT.
OH DEAR. SO YOU'VE GOT A WAITING LIST.
WHAT NUMBER AM I THEN?
... ODEN.
HUH?
IF YOU CAN MAKE ODEN, I'LL MAKE YOU NUMBER ONE.
HUH?
YOUR PUDDING, SHINGO-SAMA.
THANKS.
THE TEST MUST HAVE STARTED BY NOW.

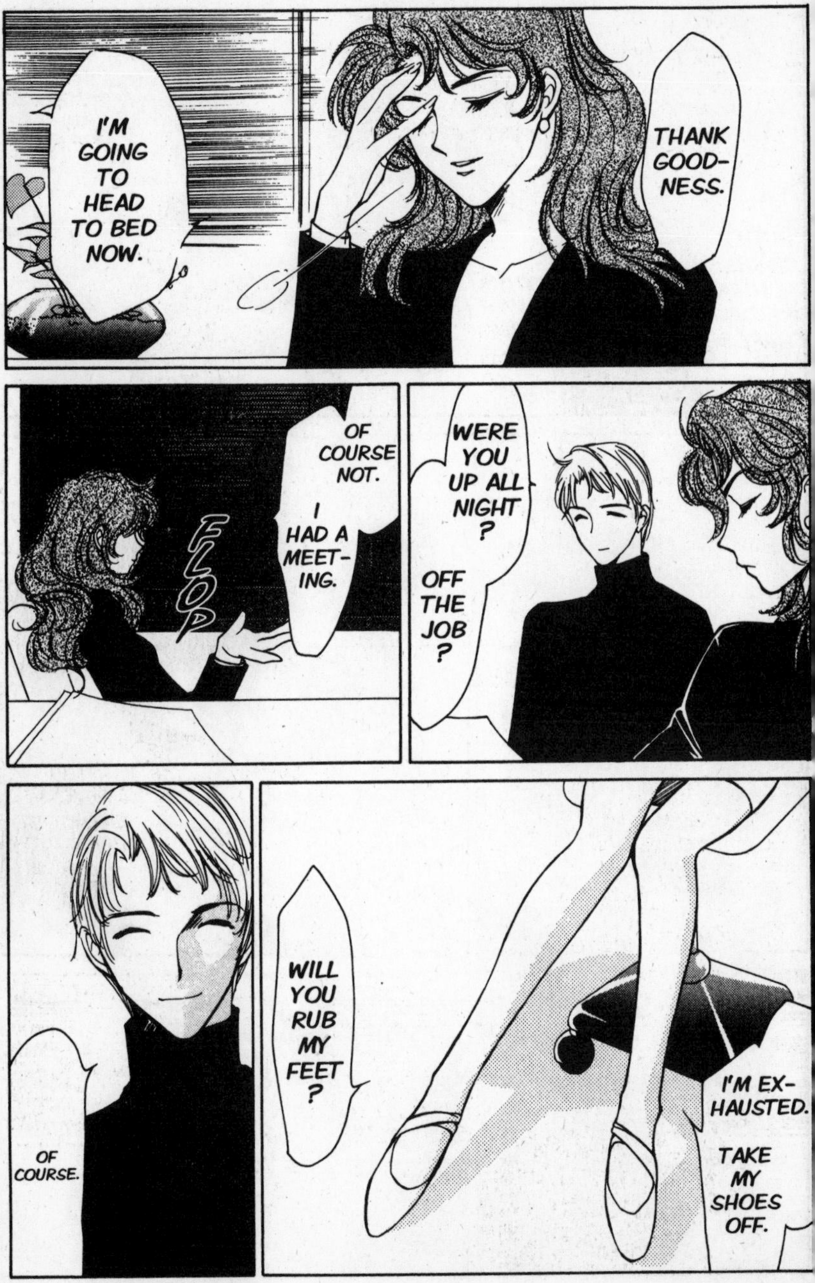
THANK GOOD-NESS.
I'M GOING TO HEAD TO BED NOW.
WERE YOU UP ALL NIGHT?
OFF THE JOB?
OF COURSE NOT.
I HAD A MEET-ING.
FLOP
I'M EX-HAUSTED.
TAKE MY SHOES OFF.
WILL YOU RUB MY FEET?
OF COURSE.

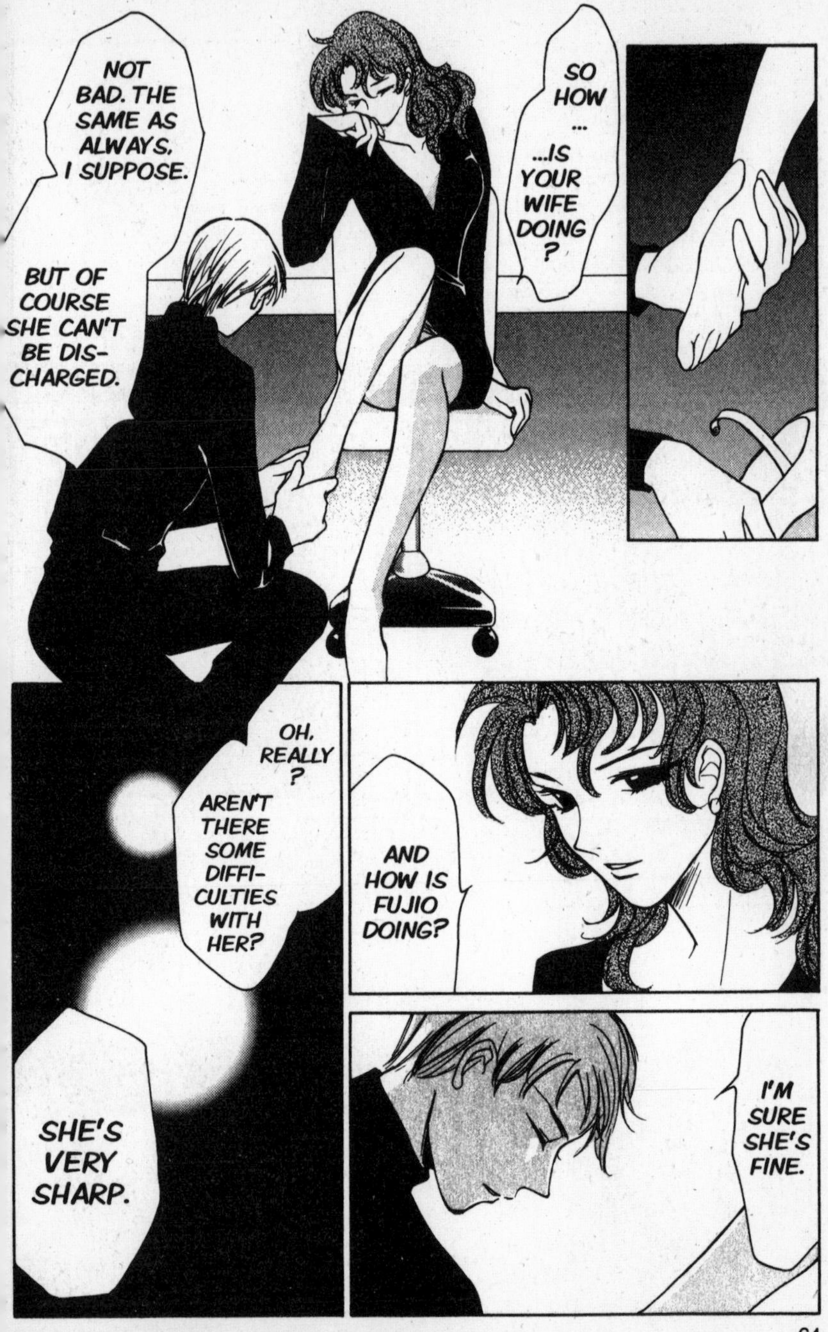
SO HOW ... ...IS YOUR WIFE DOING?
NOT BAD. THE SAME AS ALWAYS. I SUPPOSE.
BUT OF COURSE SHE CAN'T BE DIS-CHARGED.
AND HOW IS FUJIO DOING?
I'M SURE SHE'S FINE.
OH, REALLY?
AREN'T THERE SOME DIFFI-CULTIES WITH HER?
SHE'S VERY SHARP.

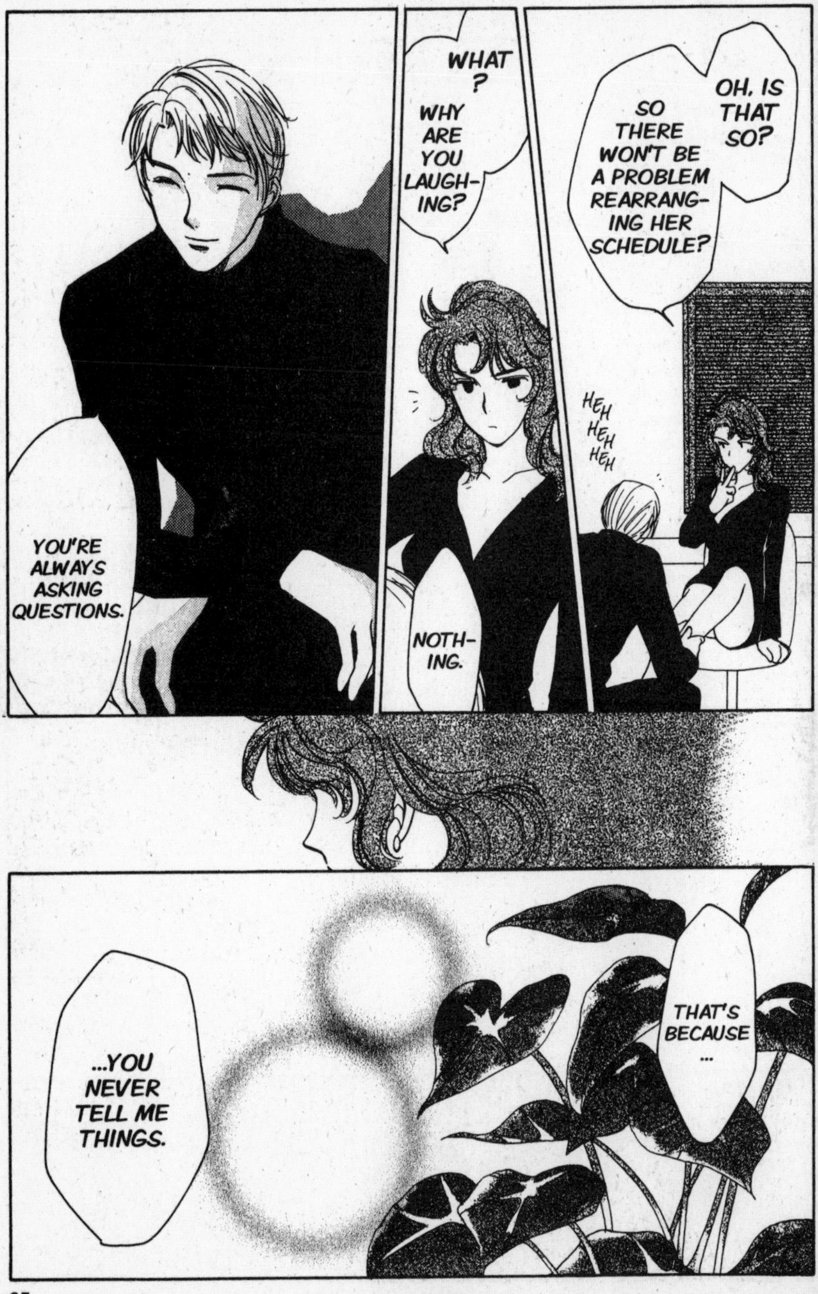
OH, IS THAT SO?
SO THERE WON'T BE A PROBLEM REARRANGING HER SCHEDULE?
HEH HEH HEH
WHAT? WHY ARE YOU LAUGHING?
NOTHING.
YOU'RE ALWAYS ASKING QUESTIONS.
THAT'S BECAUSE ...
...YOU NEVER TELL ME THINGS.

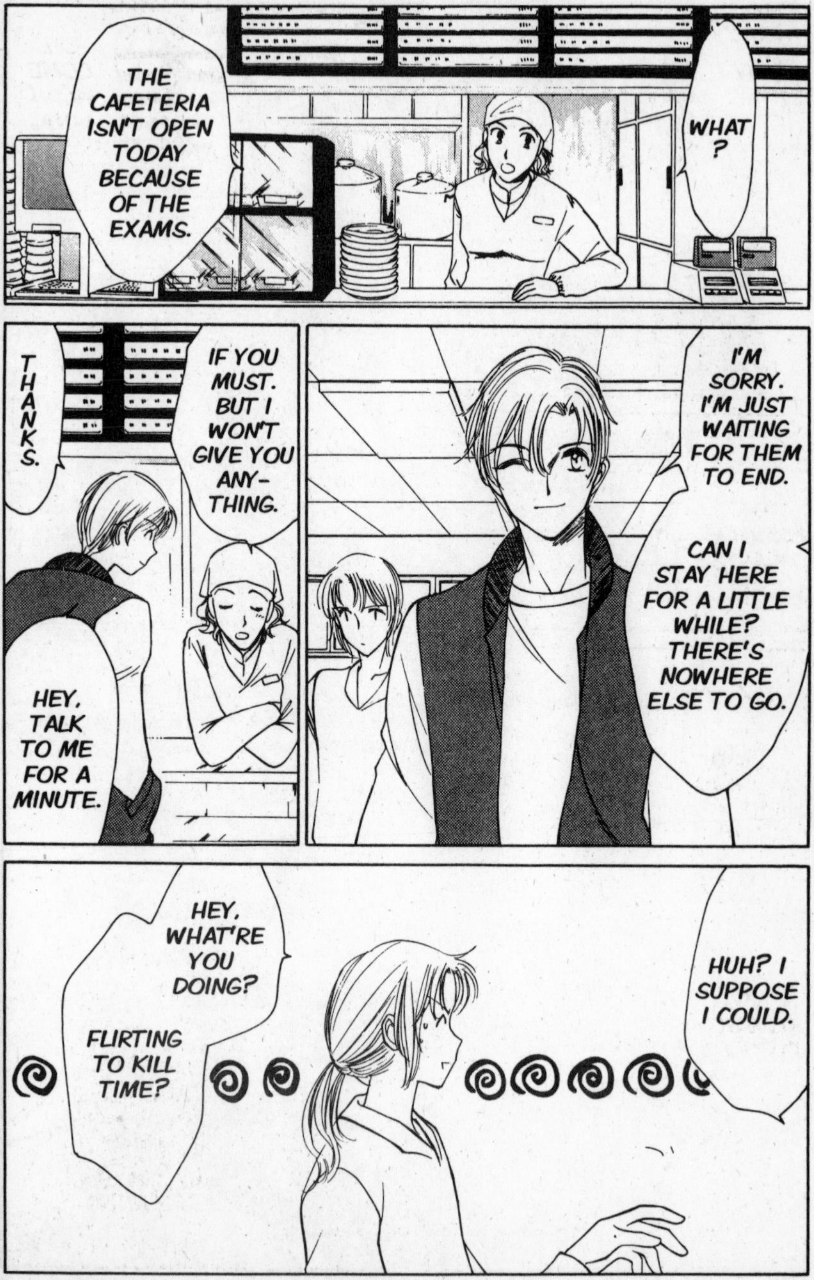
WHAT?
THE CAFETERIA ISN'T OPEN TODAY BECAUSE OF THE EXAMS.
I'M SORRY. I'M JUST WAITING FOR THEM TO END.
CAN I STAY HERE FOR A LITTLE WHILE? THERE'S NOWHERE ELSE TO GO.
IF YOU MUST. BUT I WON'T GIVE YOU ANY-THING.
THANKS.
HEY. TALK TO ME FOR A MINUTE.
HUH? I SUPPOSE I COULD.
HEY, WHAT'RE YOU DOING?
FLIRTING TO KILL TIME?

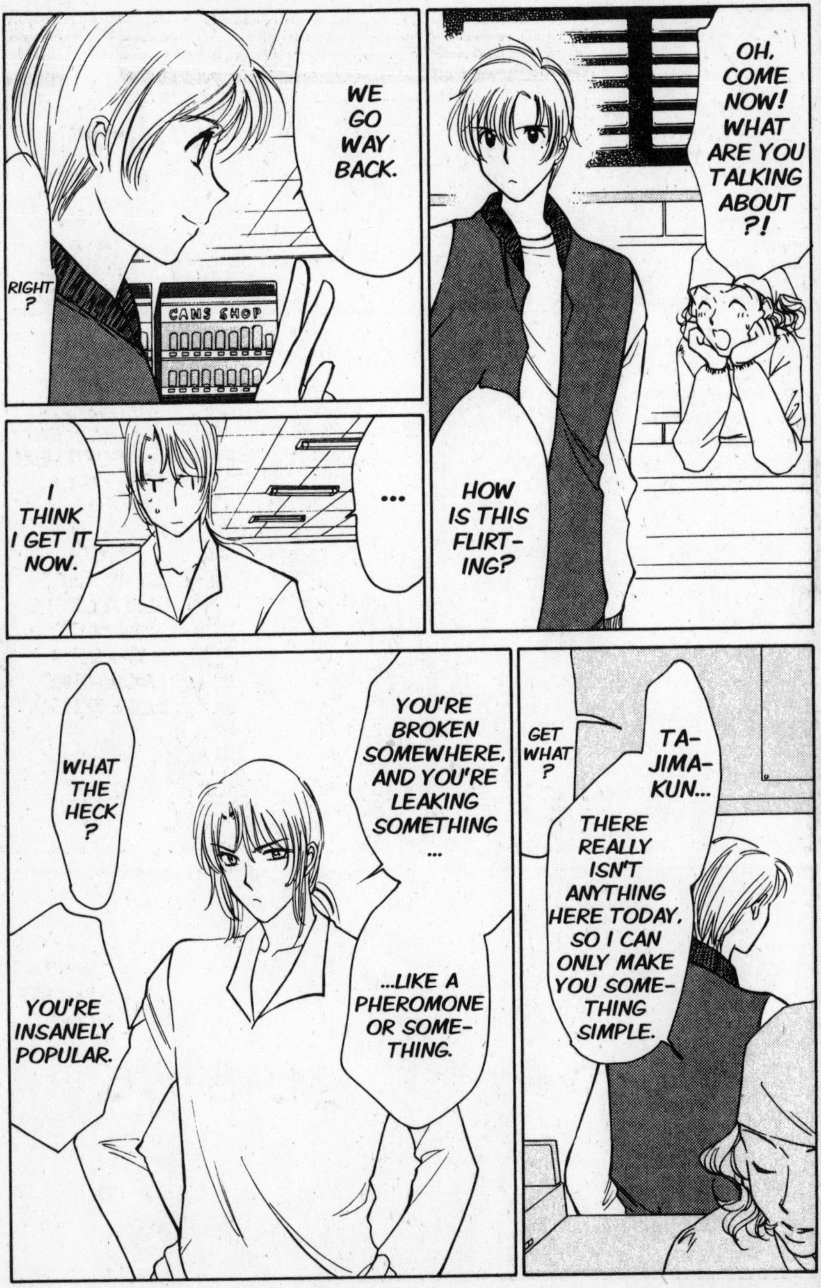
OH, COME NOW! WHAT ARE YOU TALKING ABOUT?!
HOW IS THIS FLIRTING?
WE GO WAY BACK.
RIGHT?
CANS SHOP
...
I THINK I GET IT NOW.
TA-JIMA-KUN...
THERE REALLY ISN'T ANYTHING HERE TODAY, SO I CAN ONLY MAKE YOU SOMETHING SIMPLE.
GET WHAT?
YOU'RE BROKEN SOMEWHERE, AND YOU'RE LEAKING SOMETHING...
WHAT THE HECK?
...LIKE A PHEROMONE OR SOMETHING.
YOU'RE INSANELY POPULAR.

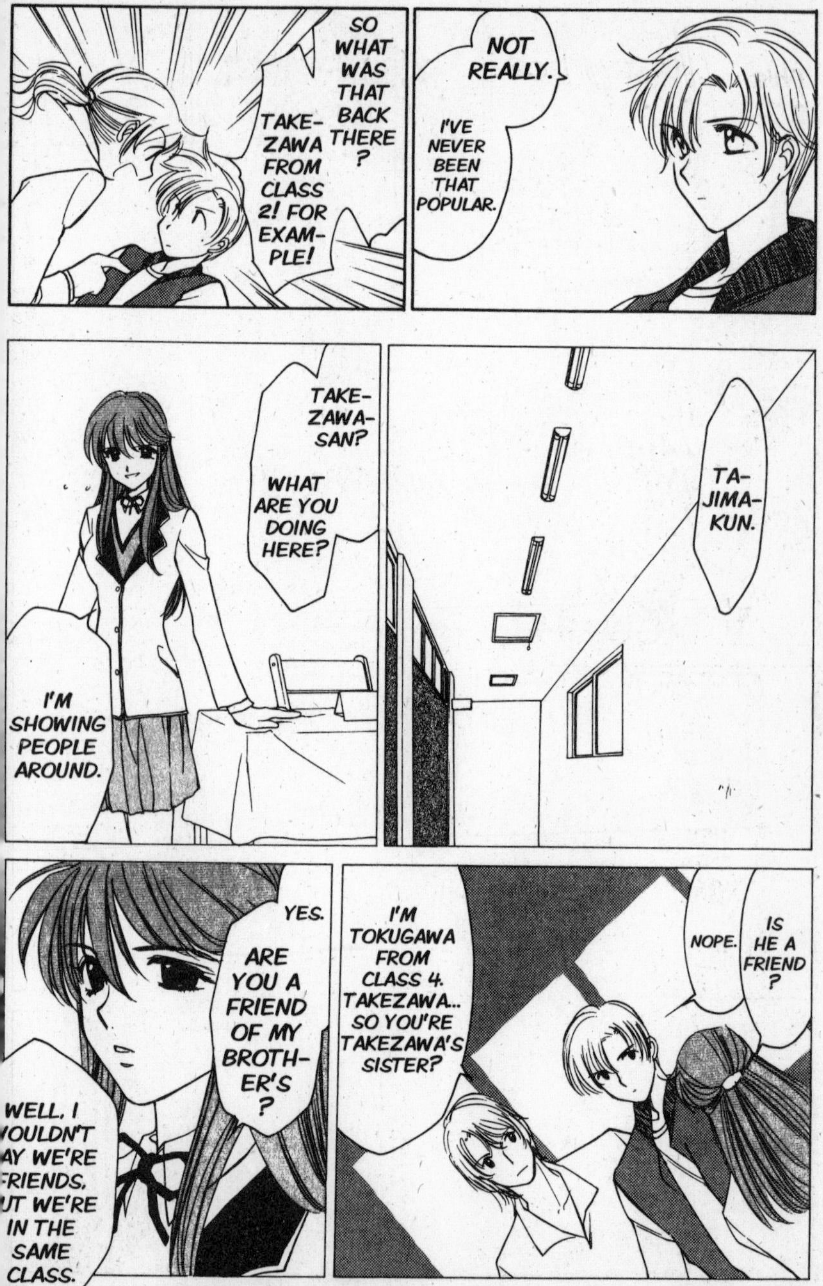
NOT REALLY.
I'VE NEVER BEEN THAT POPULAR.
SO WHAT WAS THAT BACK THERE?
TAKE-ZAWA FROM CLASS 2! FOR EXAM-PLE!
TA-JIMA-KUN.
TAKE-ZAWA-SAN?
WHAT ARE YOU DOING HERE?
I'M SHOWING PEOPLE AROUND.
IS HE A FRIEND?
NOPE.
I'M TOKUGAWA FROM CLASS 4. TAKEZAWA... SO YOU'RE TAKEZAWA'S SISTER?
YES.
ARE YOU A FRIEND OF MY BROTH-ER'S?
WELL, I OULDN'T AY WE'RE RIENDS, UT WE'RE IN THE SAME CLASS.

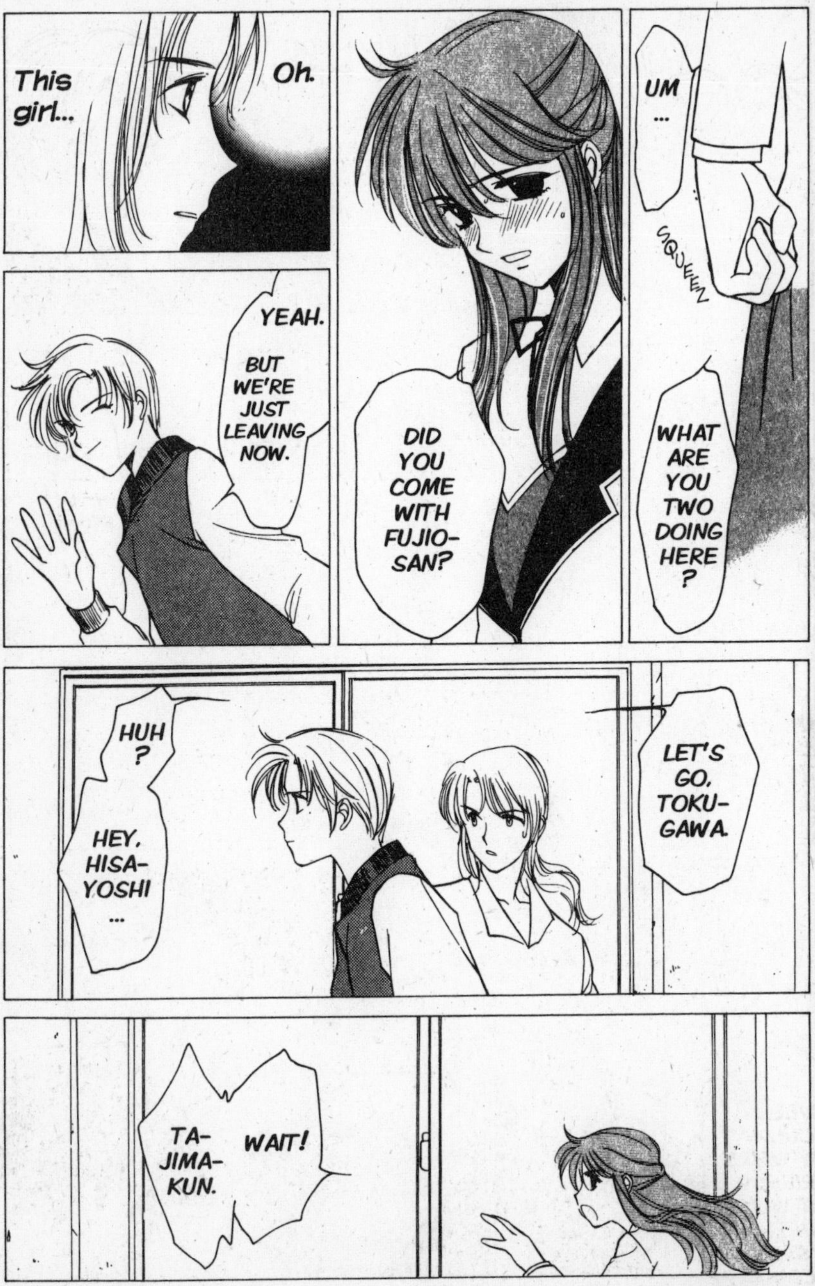
UM ...
SQUEEN
WHAT ARE YOU TWO DOING HERE?
DID YOU COME WITH FUJIO-SAN?
Oh.
This girl...
YEAH.
BUT WE'RE JUST LEAVING NOW.
LET'S GO, TOKUGAWA.
HUH?
HEY, HISAYOSHI ...
WAIT!
TA-JIMA-KUN.

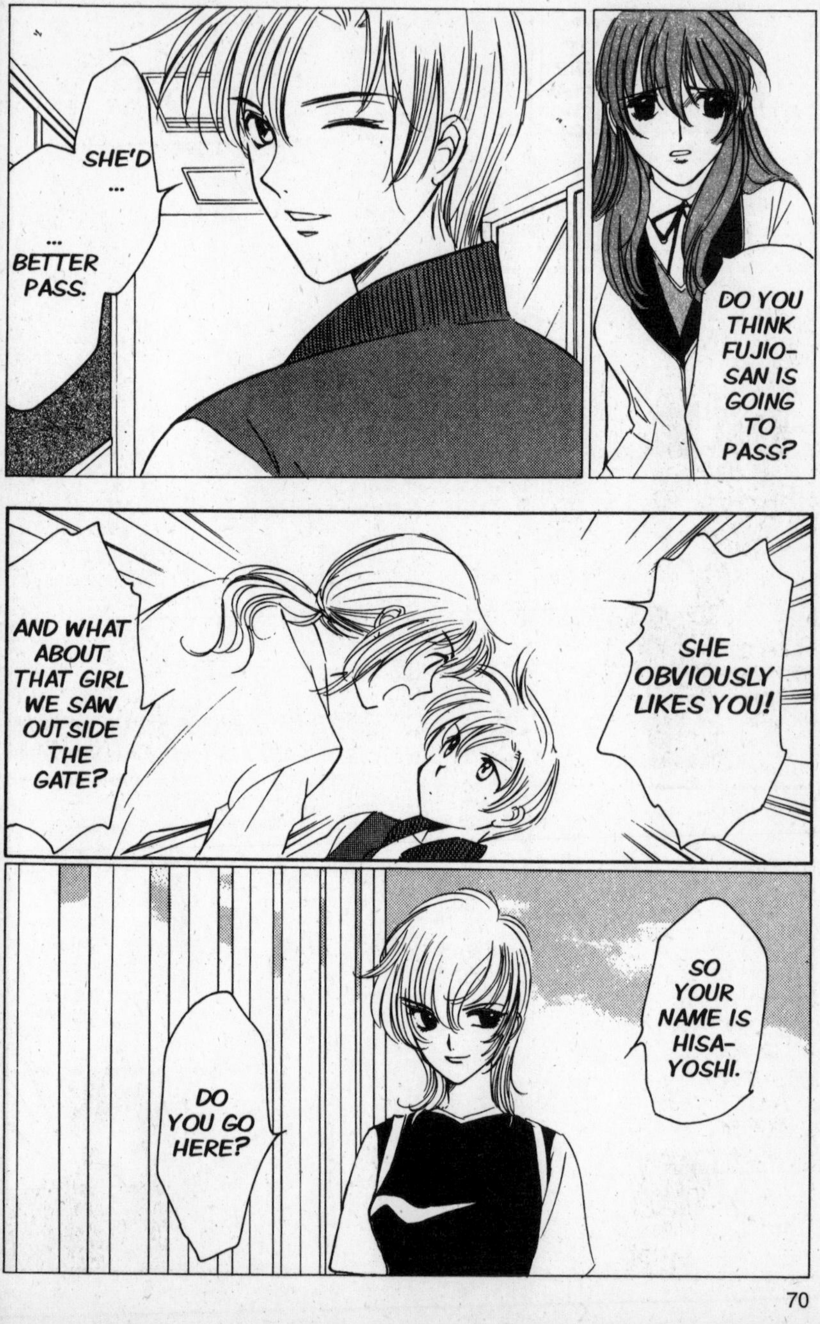
DO YOU THINK FUJIO-SAN IS GOING TO PASS?
SHE'D ...
... BETTER PASS.
SHE OBVIOUSLY LIKES YOU!
AND WHAT ABOUT THAT GIRL WE SAW OUTSIDE THE GATE?
SO YOUR NAME IS HISA-YOSHI.
DO YOU GO HERE?

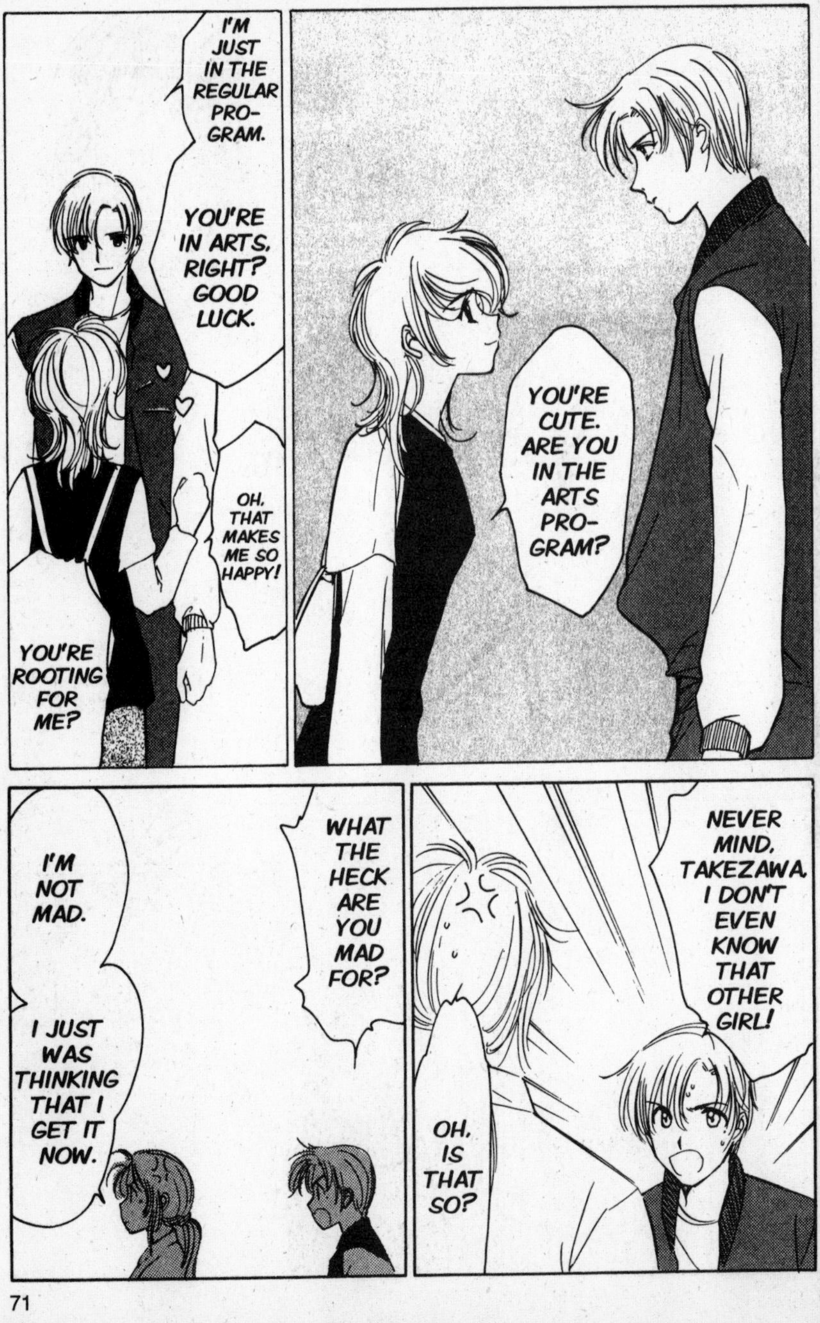
YOU'RE CUTE. ARE YOU IN THE ARTS PROGRAM?
I'M JUST IN THE REGULAR PROGRAM.
YOU'RE IN ARTS, RIGHT? GOOD LUCK.
OH. THAT MAKES ME SO HAPPY!
YOU'RE ROOTING FOR ME?
NEVER MIND, TAKEZAWA. I DON'T EVEN KNOW THAT OTHER GIRL!
OH. IS THAT SO?
WHAT THE HECK ARE YOU MAD FOR?
I'M NOT MAD.
I JUST WAS THINKING THAT I GET IT NOW.

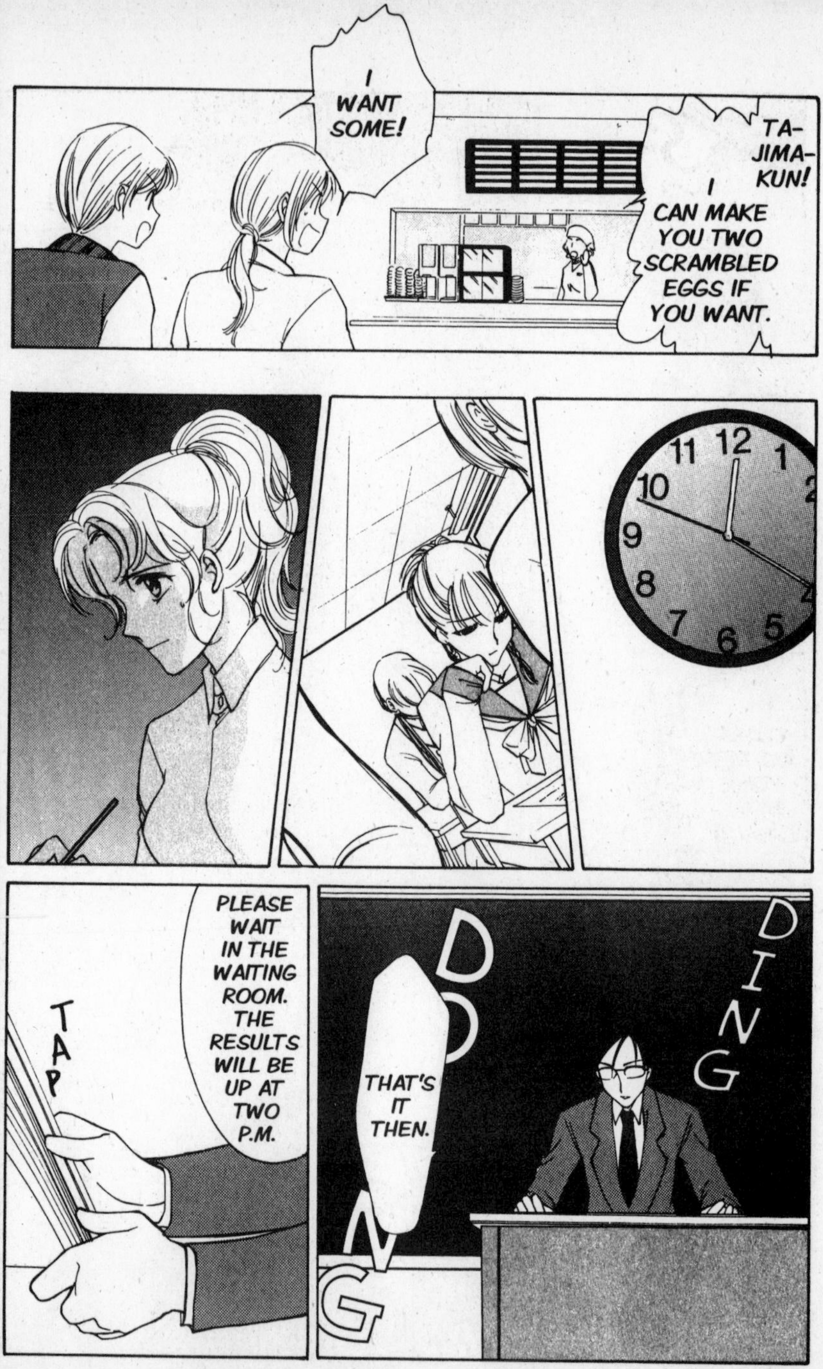
TA-JIMA-KUN! I CAN MAKE YOU TWO SCRAMBLED EGGS IF YOU WANT.
I WANT SOME!
DING
DONG
THAT'S IT THEN.
PLEASE WAIT IN THE WAITING ROOM. THE RESULTS WILL BE UP AT TWO P.M.
TAP

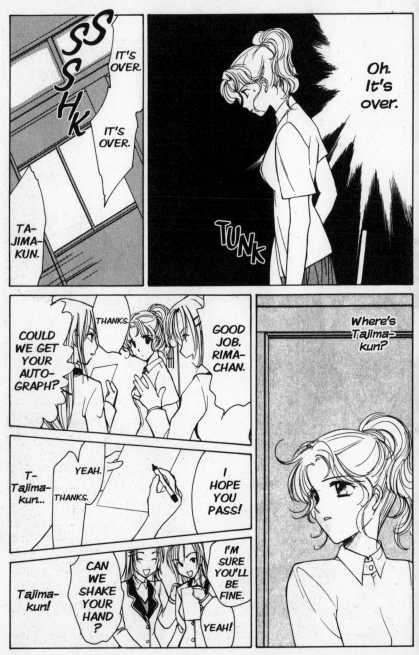

Oh. It's over.
TUNK
IT'S OVER.
SSSHK
IT'S OVER.
TA-JIMA-KUN.
Where's Tajima-kun?
GOOD JOB, RIMA-CHAN.
THANKS.
COULD WE GET YOUR AUTO-GRAPH?
I HOPE YOU PASS!
YEAH.
THANKS.
T-Tajima-kun...
I'M SURE YOU'LL BE FINE.
YEAH!
CAN WE SHAKE YOUR HAND?
Tajima-kun!

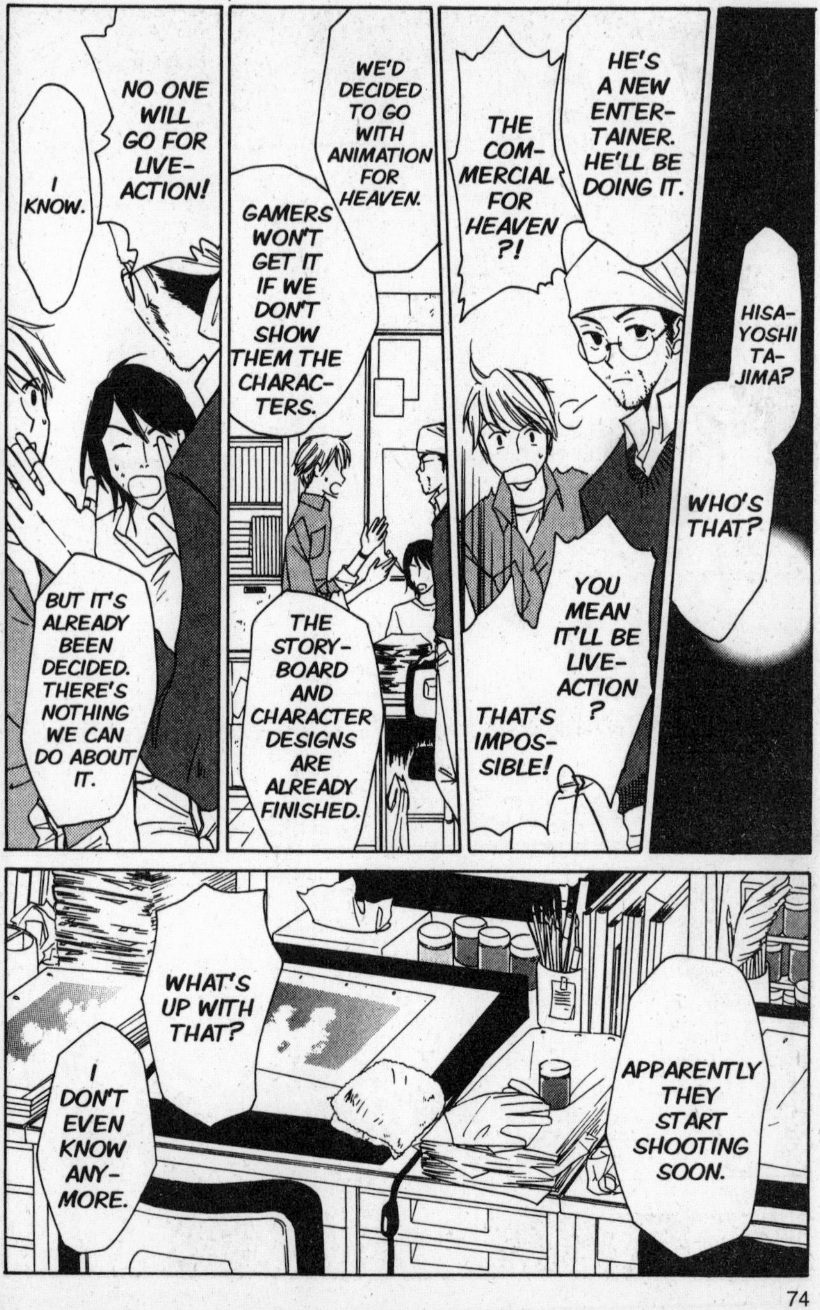
HISAYOSHI TAJIMA?
WHO'S THAT?
HE'S A NEW ENTERTAINER. HE'LL BE DOING IT.
THE COMMERCIAL FOR HEAVEN?!
YOU MEAN IT'LL BE LIVE-ACTION?
THAT'S IMPOSSIBLE!
WE'D DECIDED TO GO WITH ANIMATION FOR HEAVEN.
GAMERS WON'T GET IT IF WE DON'T SHOW THEM THE CHARACTERS.
THE STORYBOARD AND CHARACTER DESIGNS ARE ALREADY FINISHED.
NO ONE WILL GO FOR LIVE-ACTION!
I KNOW.
BUT IT'S ALREADY BEEN DECIDED. THERE'S NOTHING WE CAN DO ABOUT IT.
APPARENTLY THEY START SHOOTING SOON.
WHAT'S UP WITH THAT?
I DON'T EVEN KNOW ANYMORE.

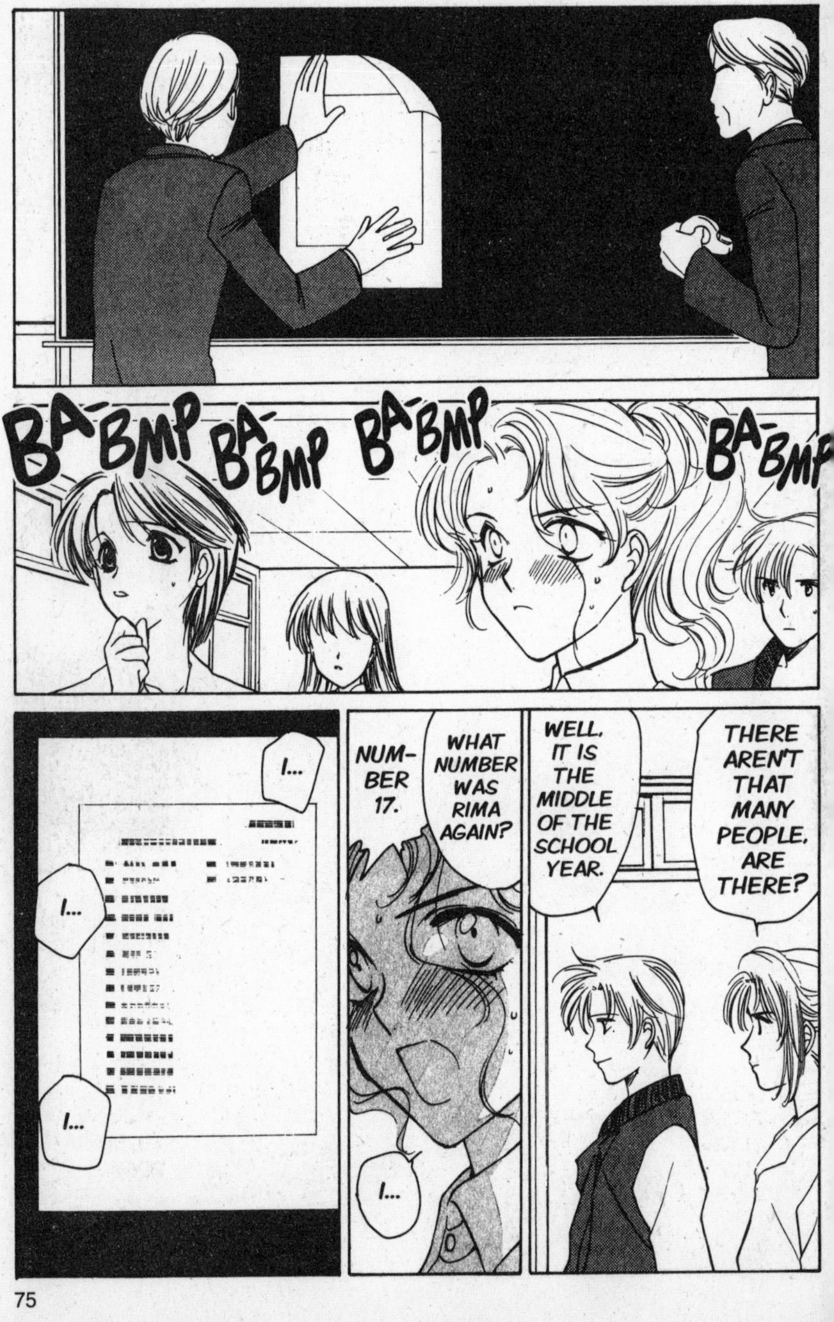
BA-BMP
BA-BMP
BA-BMP
BA-BMP
THERE AREN'T THAT MANY PEOPLE. ARE THERE?
WELL. IT IS THE MIDDLE OF THE SCHOOL YEAR.
WHAT NUMBER WAS RIMA AGAIN?
NUMBER 17.
I...
I...
I...
I...

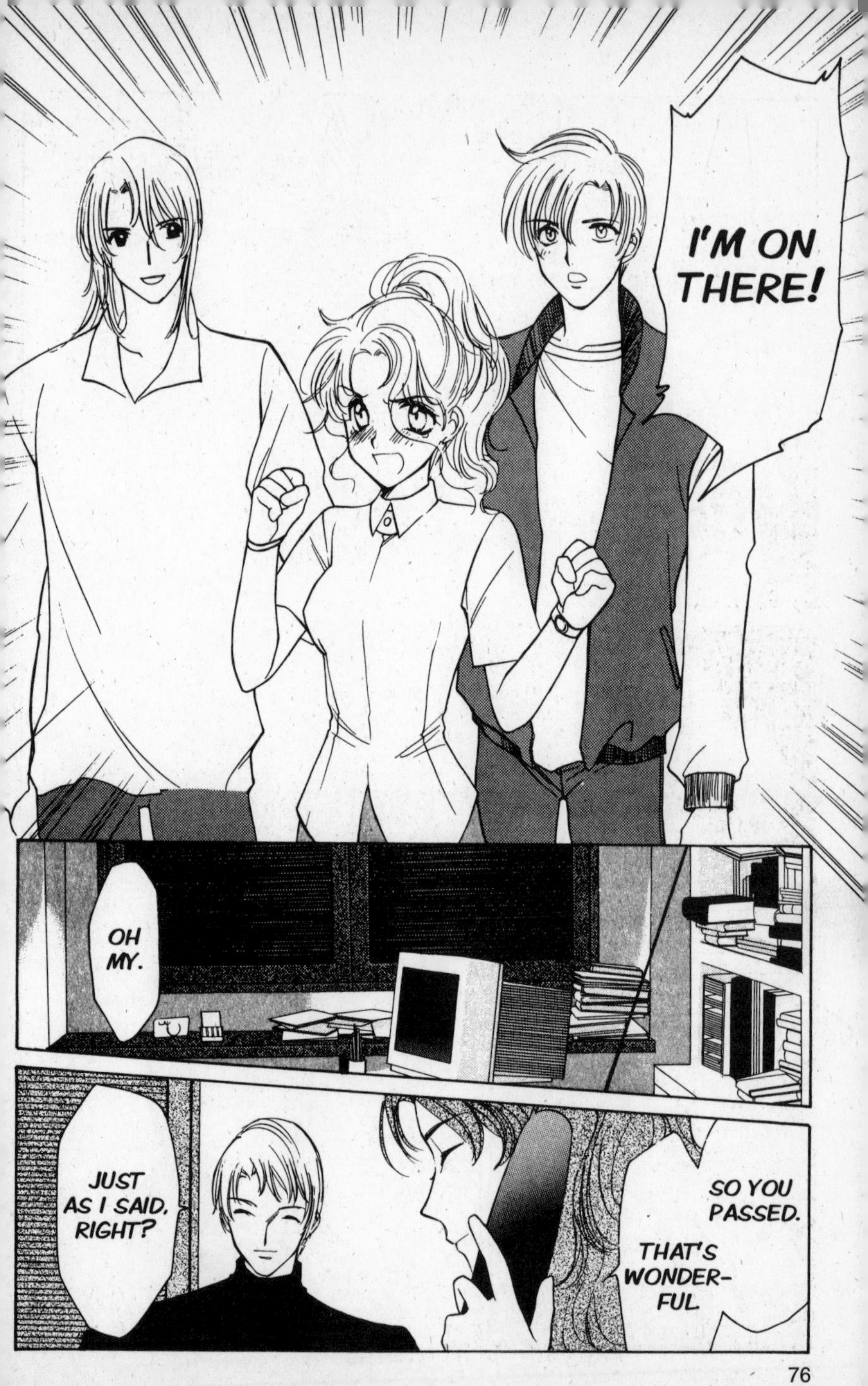
I'M ON THERE!
OH MY.
SO YOU PASSED.
THAT'S WONDER-FUL.
JUST AS I SAID. RIGHT?

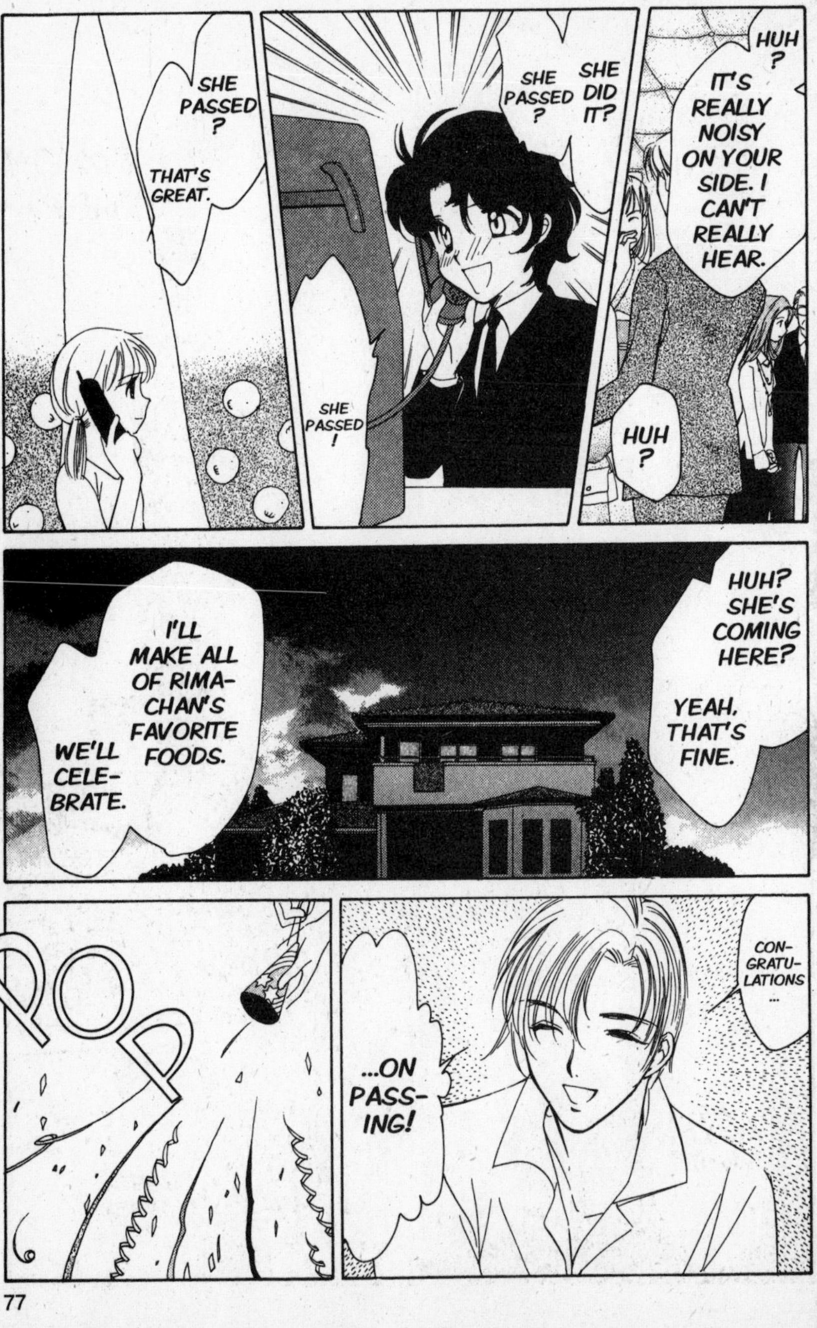
HUH?
IT'S REALLY NOISY ON YOUR SIDE. I CAN'T REALLY HEAR.
HUH?
SHE DID IT?
SHE PASSED?
SHE PASSED!
SHE PASSED?
THAT'S GREAT.
HUH? SHE'S COMING HERE?
YEAH, THAT'S FINE.
I'LL MAKE ALL OF RIMA-CHAN'S FAVORITE FOODS.
WE'LL CELE-BRATE.
CON-GRATU-LATIONS...
...ON PASS-ING!
POP

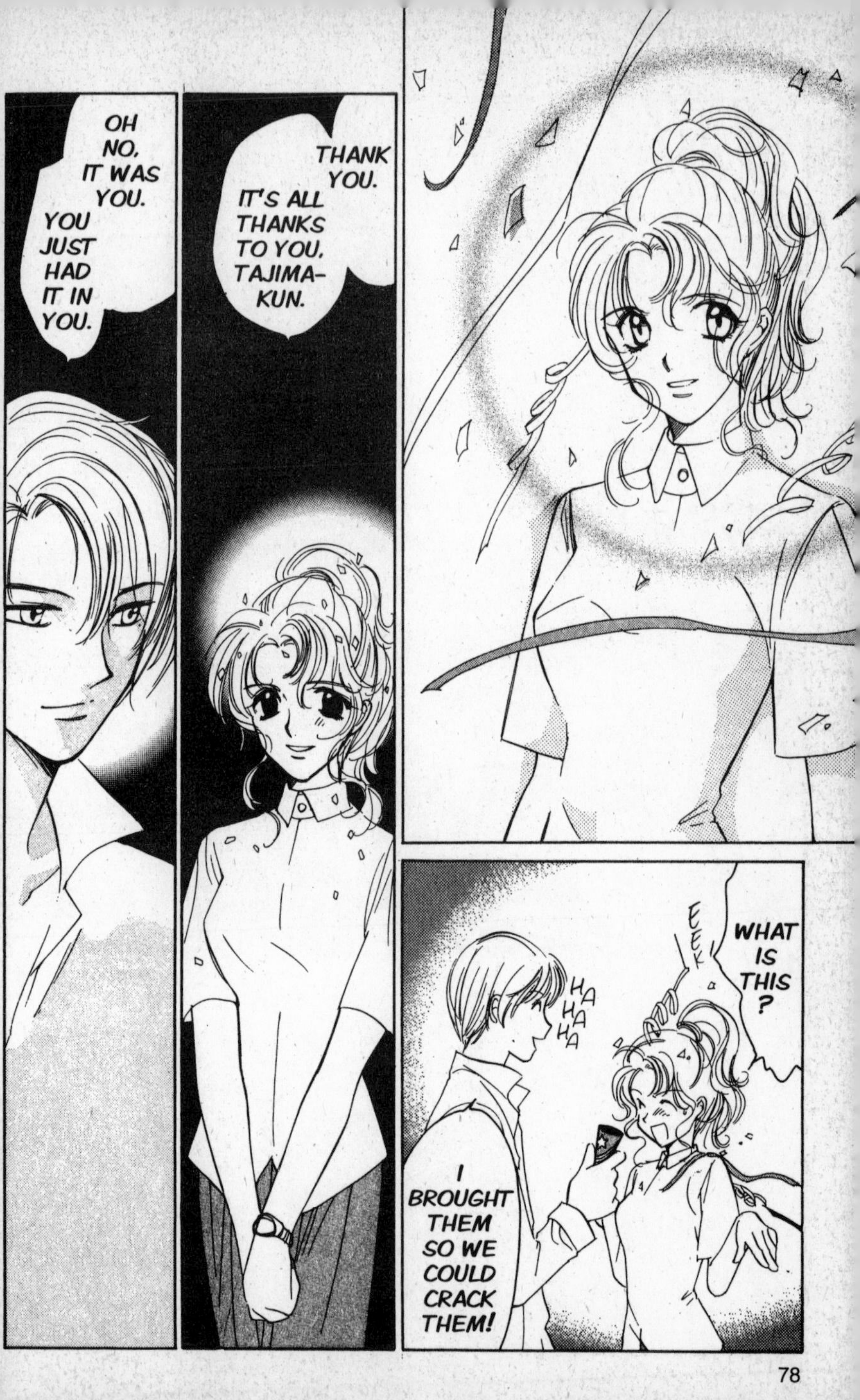
WHAT IS THIS?
EEK
HA HA HA HA
I BROUGHT THEM SO WE COULD CRACK THEM!
THANK YOU. IT'S ALL THANKS TO YOU, TAJIMA-KUN.
OH NO, IT WAS YOU. YOU JUST HAD IT IN YOU.

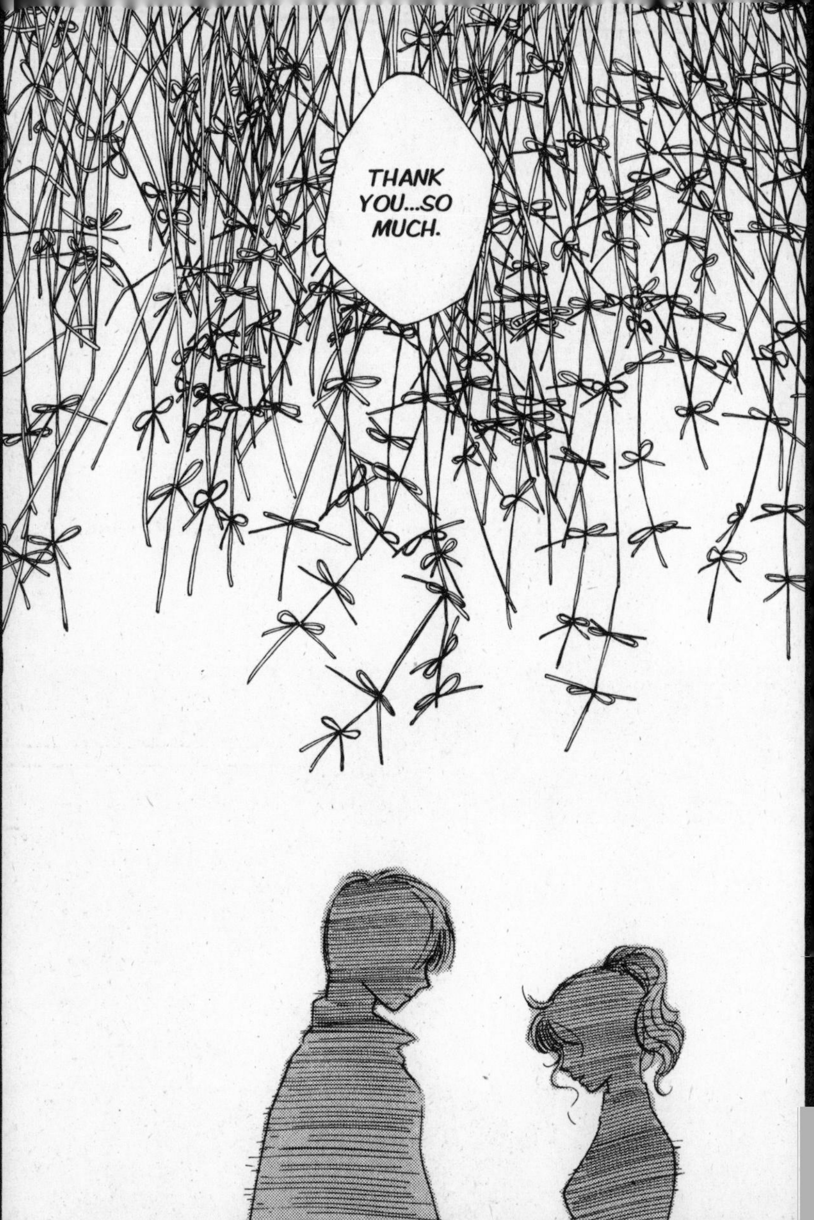
THANK YOU...SO MUCH.

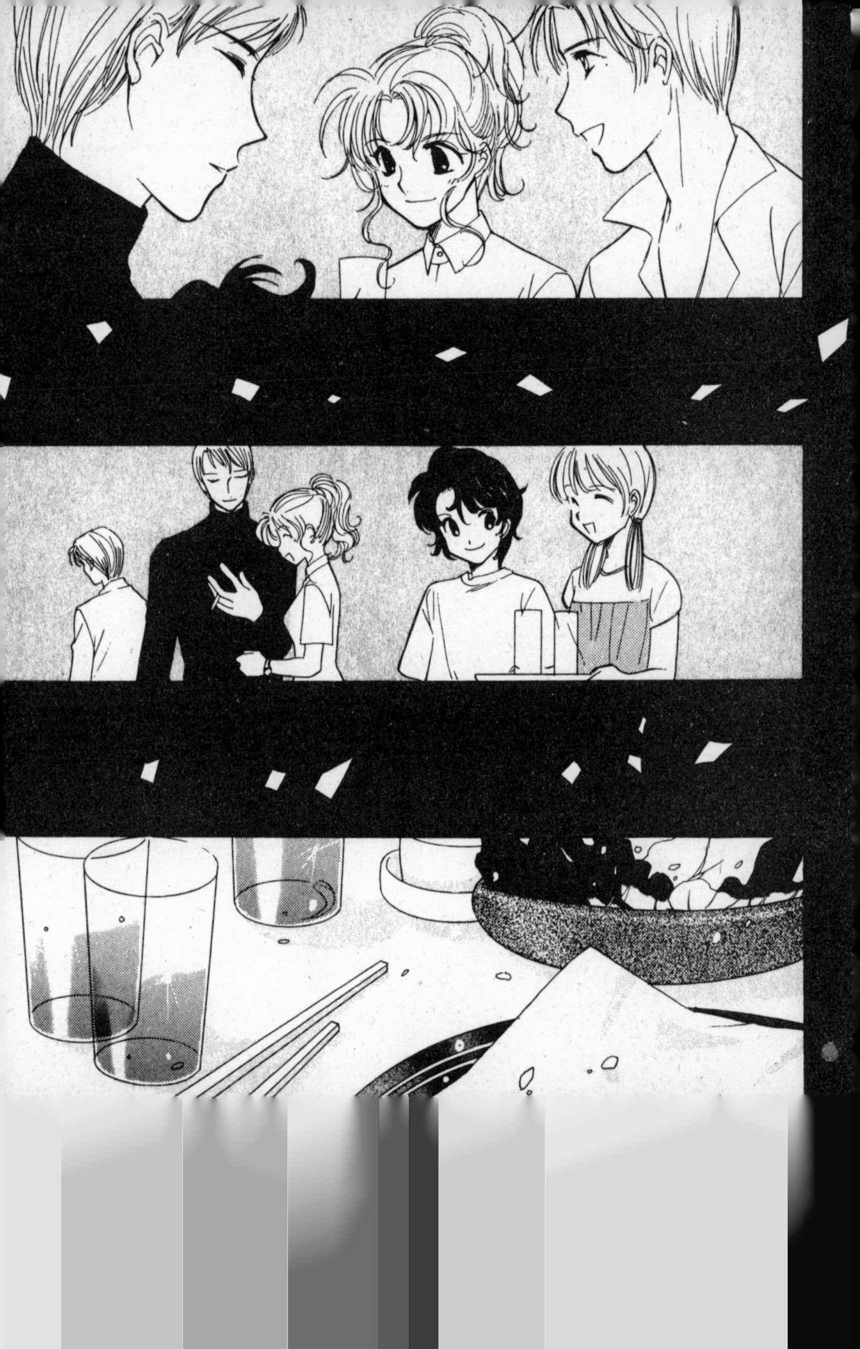

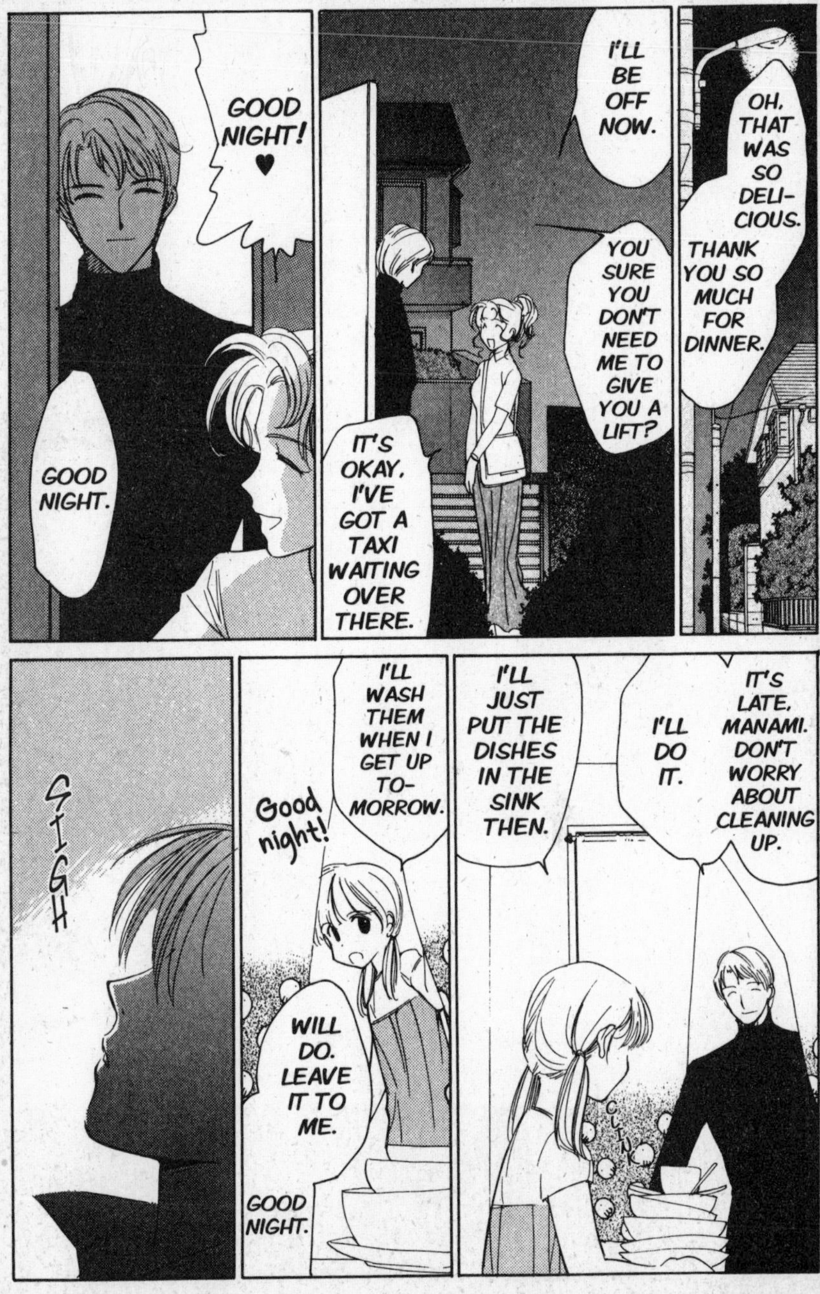
OH, THAT WAS SO DELICIOUS.
THANK YOU SO MUCH FOR DINNER.
I'LL BE OFF NOW.
YOU SURE YOU DON'T NEED ME TO GIVE YOU A LIFT?
IT'S OKAY, I'VE GOT A TAXI WAITING OVER THERE.
GOOD NIGHT! ♥
GOOD NIGHT.
IT'S LATE, MANAMI. DON'T WORRY ABOUT CLEANING UP.
I'LL DO IT.
I'LL JUST PUT THE DISHES IN THE SINK THEN.
CLINK
I'LL WASH THEM WHEN I GET UP TO-MORROW.
Good night!
WILL DO. LEAVE IT TO ME.
GOOD NIGHT.
SIGH

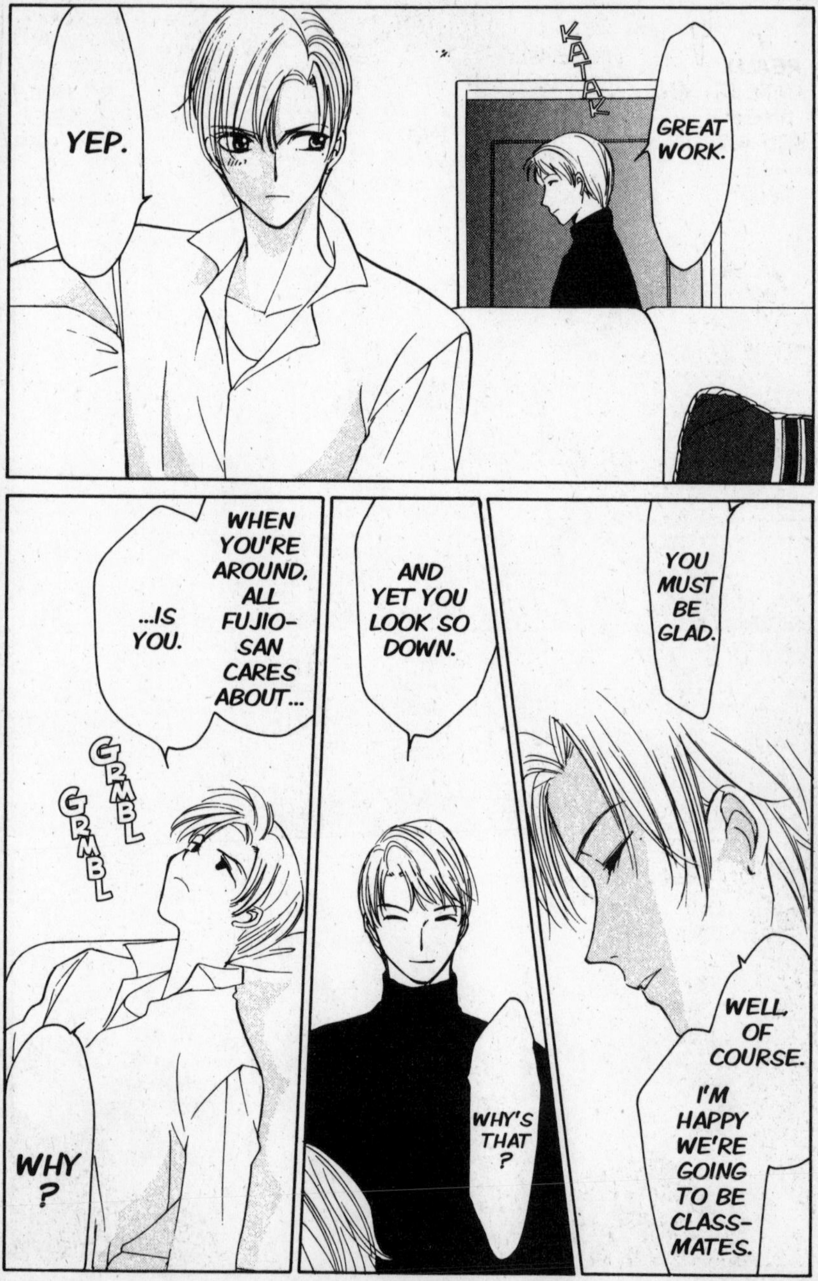
GREAT WORK.
KATAN
YEP.
YOU MUST BE GLAD.
WELL, OF COURSE.
I'M HAPPY WE'RE GOING TO BE CLASSMATES.
AND YET YOU LOOK SO DOWN.
WHY'S THAT?
WHEN YOU'RE AROUND, ALL FUJIO-SAN CARES ABOUT...
...IS YOU.
GRMBL
GRMBL
WHY?

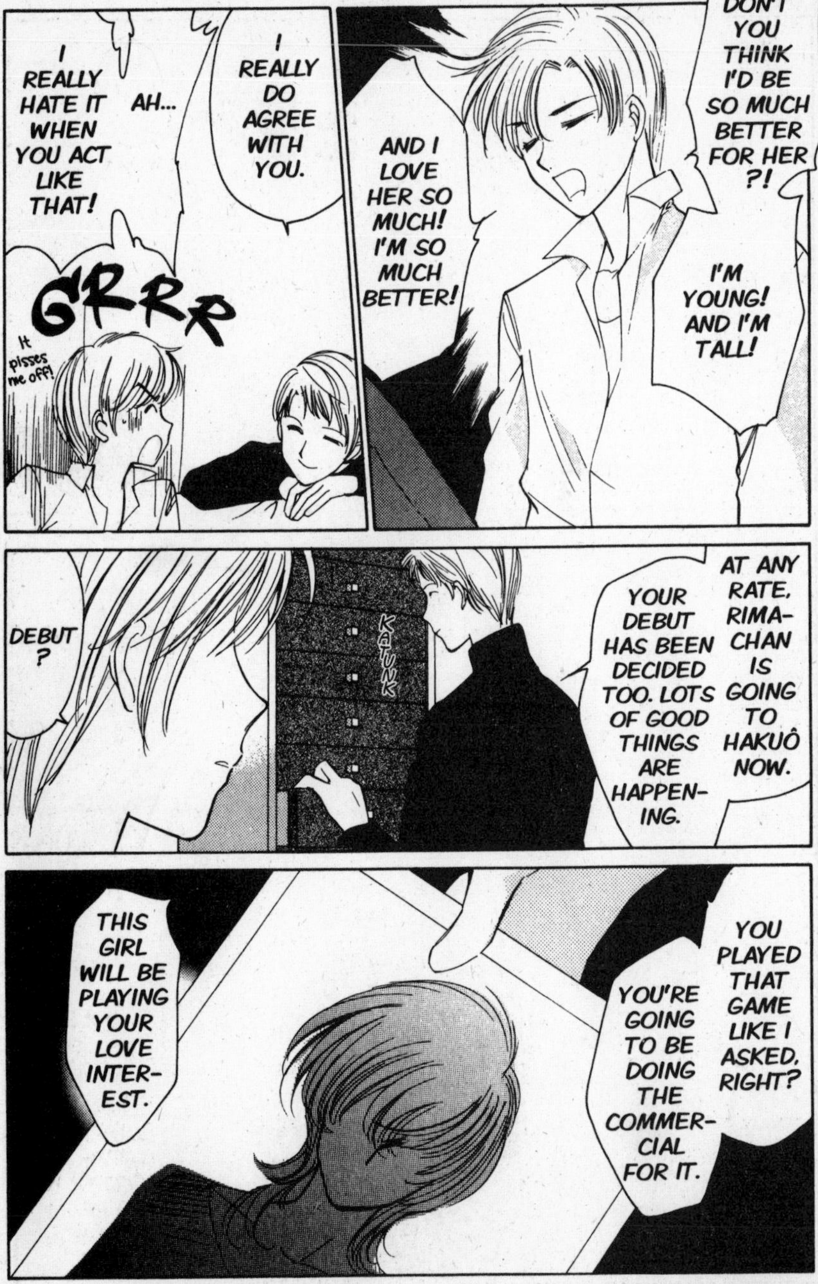
DON'T YOU THINK I'D BE SO MUCH BETTER FOR HER?!
I'M YOUNG! AND I'M TALL!
AND I LOVE HER SO MUCH! I'M SO MUCH BETTER!
I REALLY DO AGREE WITH YOU.
AH...
I REALLY HATE IT WHEN YOU ACT LIKE THAT!
GRRR
It pisses me off!
AT ANY RATE, RIMA-CHAN IS GOING TO HAKUÔ NOW.
YOUR DEBUT HAS BEEN DECIDED TOO. LOTS OF GOOD THINGS ARE HAPPENING.
KATUNK
DEBUT?
YOU PLAYED THAT GAME LIKE I ASKED, RIGHT?
YOU'RE GOING TO BE DOING THE COMMERCIAL FOR IT.
THIS GIRL WILL BE PLAYING YOUR LOVE INTEREST.

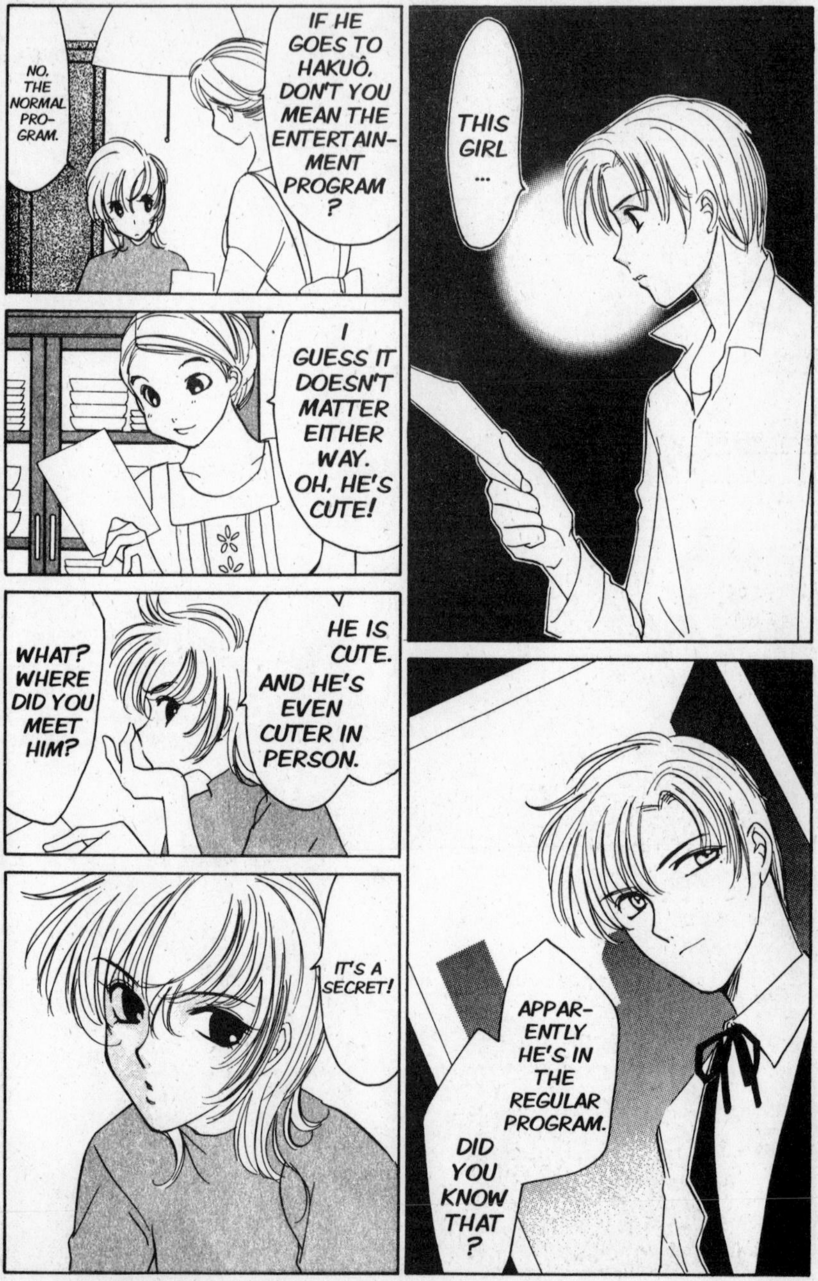
THIS GIRL ...
APPARENTLY HE'S IN THE REGULAR PROGRAM.
DID YOU KNOW THAT?
IF HE GOES TO HAKUÔ, DON'T YOU MEAN THE ENTERTAINMENT PROGRAM?
NO. THE NORMAL PROGRAM.
I GUESS IT DOESN'T MATTER EITHER WAY. OH, HE'S CUTE!
HE IS CUTE. AND HE'S EVEN CUTER IN PERSON.
WHAT? WHERE DID YOU MEET HIM?
IT'S A SECRET!

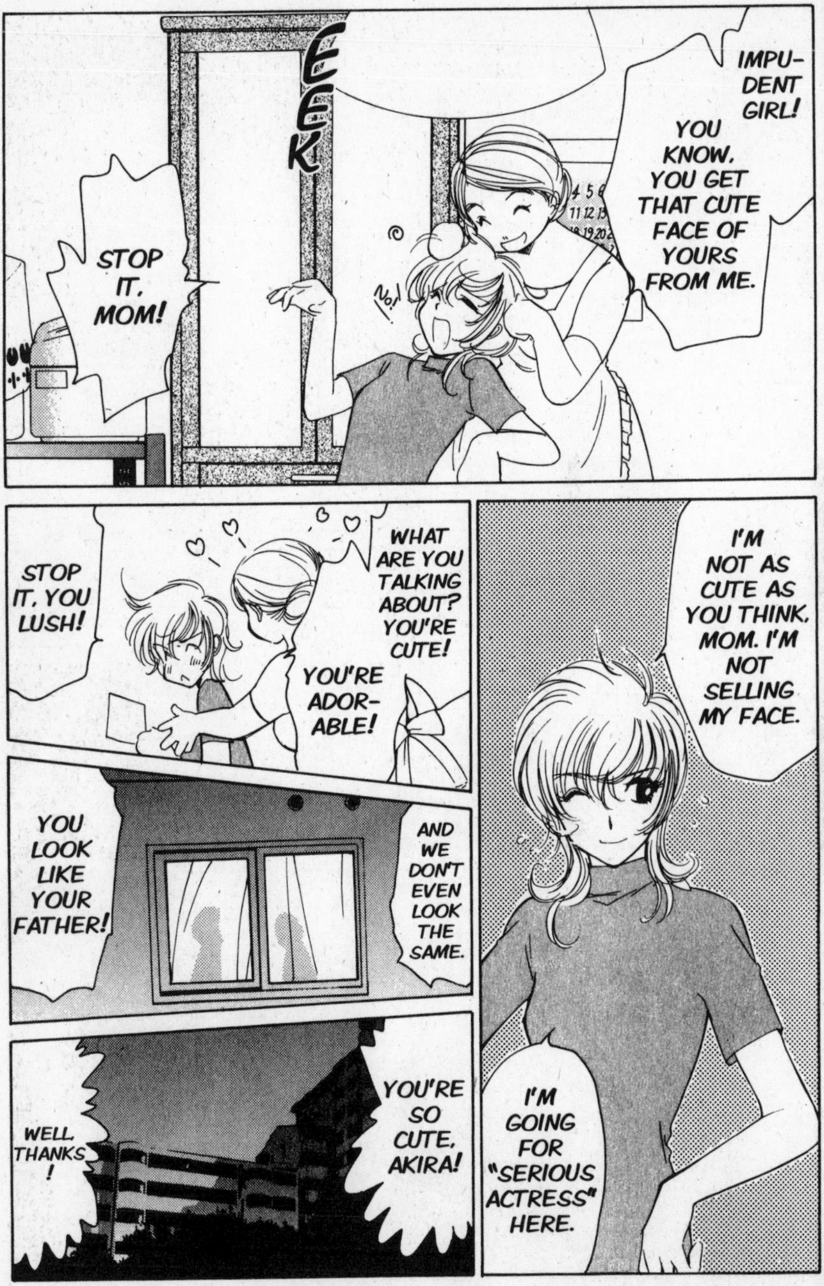
IMPUDENT GIRL!
YOU KNOW, YOU GET THAT CUTE FACE OF YOURS FROM ME.
EEEK
No!
STOP IT, MOM!
I'M NOT AS CUTE AS YOU THINK, MOM. I'M NOT SELLING MY FACE.
I'M GOING FOR "SERIOUS ACTRESS" HERE.
WHAT ARE YOU TALKING ABOUT? YOU'RE CUTE!
YOU'RE ADORABLE!
STOP IT, YOU LUSH!
AND WE DON'T EVEN LOOK THE SAME.
YOU LOOK LIKE YOUR FATHER!
YOU'RE SO CUTE, AKIRA!
WELL, THANKS!

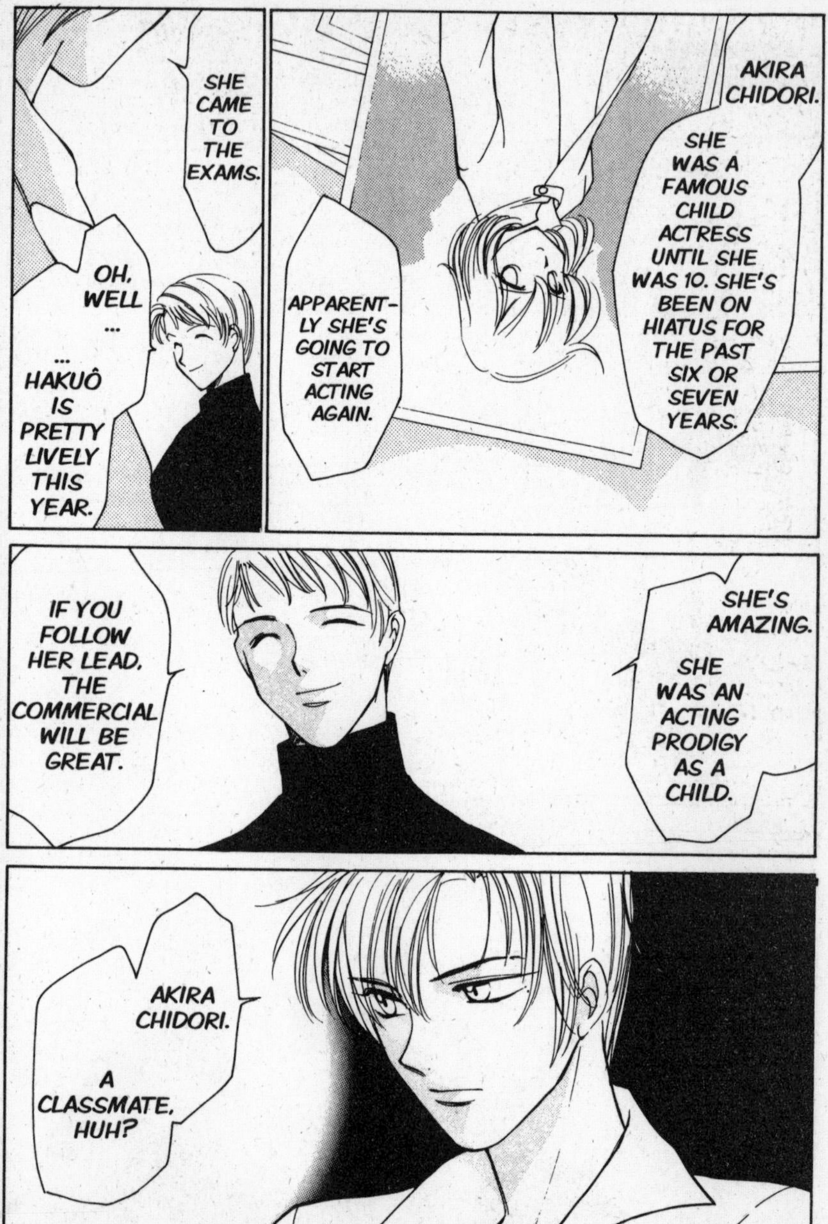
AKIRA CHIDORI.
SHE WAS A FAMOUS CHILD ACTRESS UNTIL SHE WAS 10. SHE'S BEEN ON HIATUS FOR THE PAST SIX OR SEVEN YEARS.
APPARENT-LY SHE'S GOING TO START ACTING AGAIN.
SHE CAME TO THE EXAMS.
OH, WELL ...
... HAKUÔ IS PRETTY LIVELY THIS YEAR.
SHE'S AMAZING.
SHE WAS AN ACTING PRODIGY AS A CHILD.
IF YOU FOLLOW HER LEAD, THE COMMERCIAL WILL BE GREAT.
AKIRA CHIDORI.
A CLASSMATE, HUH?

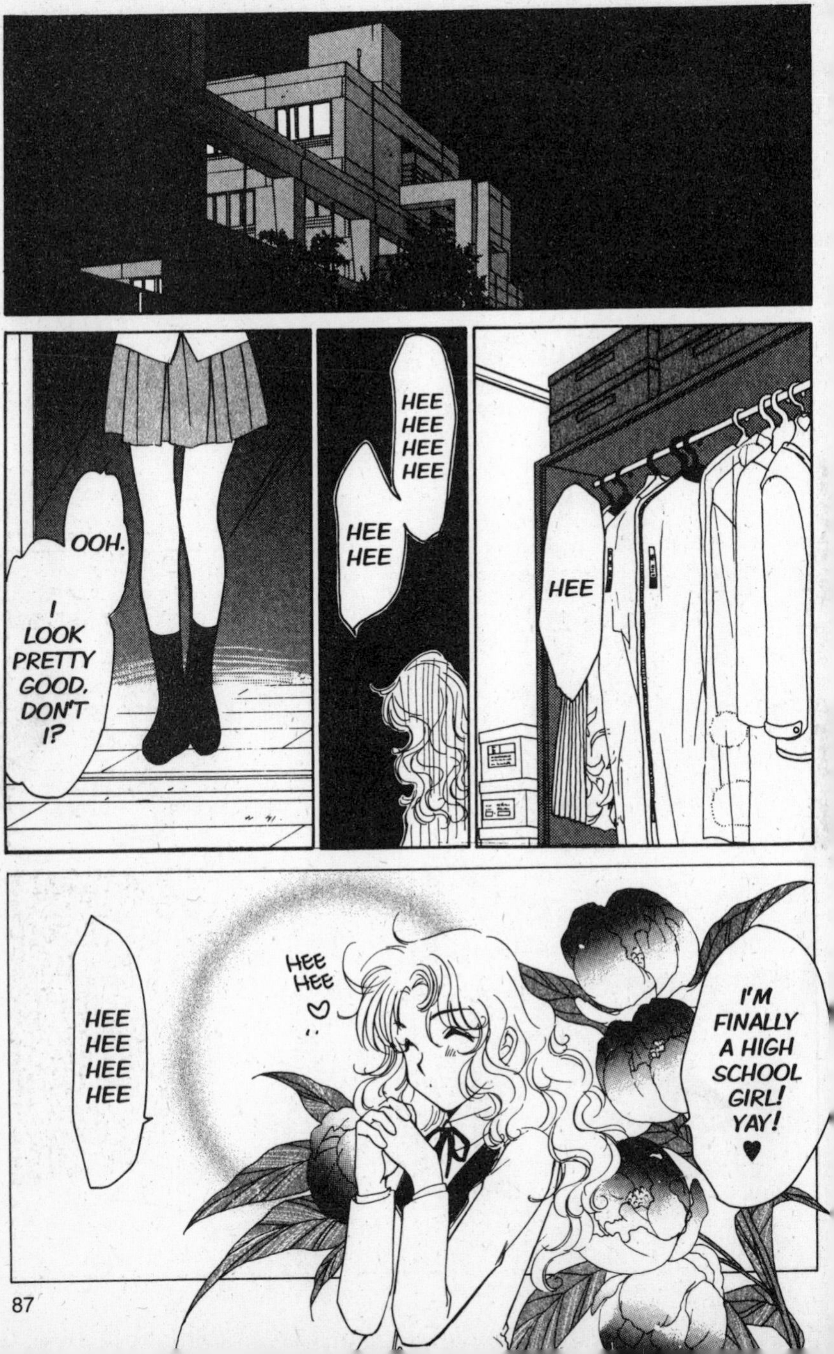
HEE
HEE HEE HEE HEE
HEE HEE
OOH.
I LOOK PRETTY GOOD. DON'T I?
I'M FINALLY A HIGH SCHOOL GIRL! YAY! ♥
HEE HEE ♡
HEE HEE HEE HEE

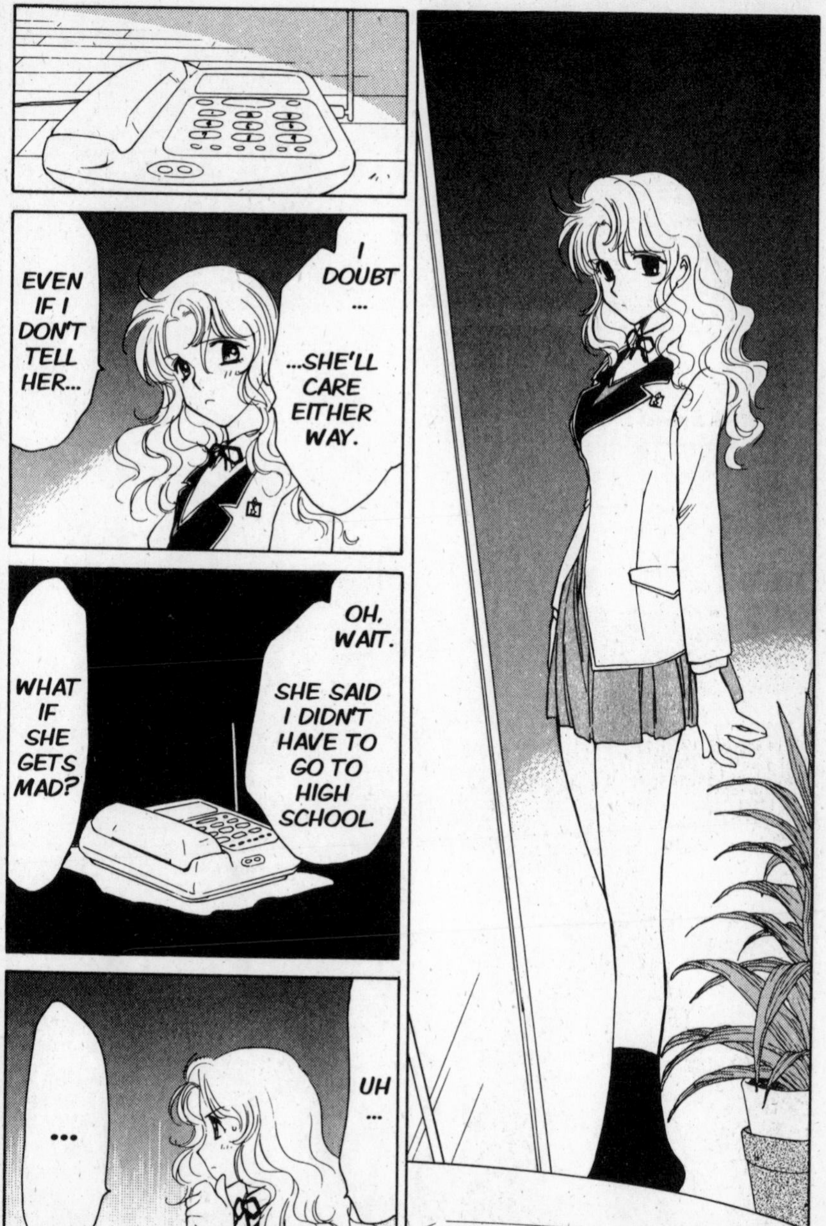
I DOUBT ...
...SHE'LL CARE EITHER WAY.
EVEN IF I DON'T TELL HER...
OH, WAIT.
SHE SAID I DIDN'T HAVE TO GO TO HIGH SCHOOL.
WHAT IF SHE GETS MAD?
UH ...
...

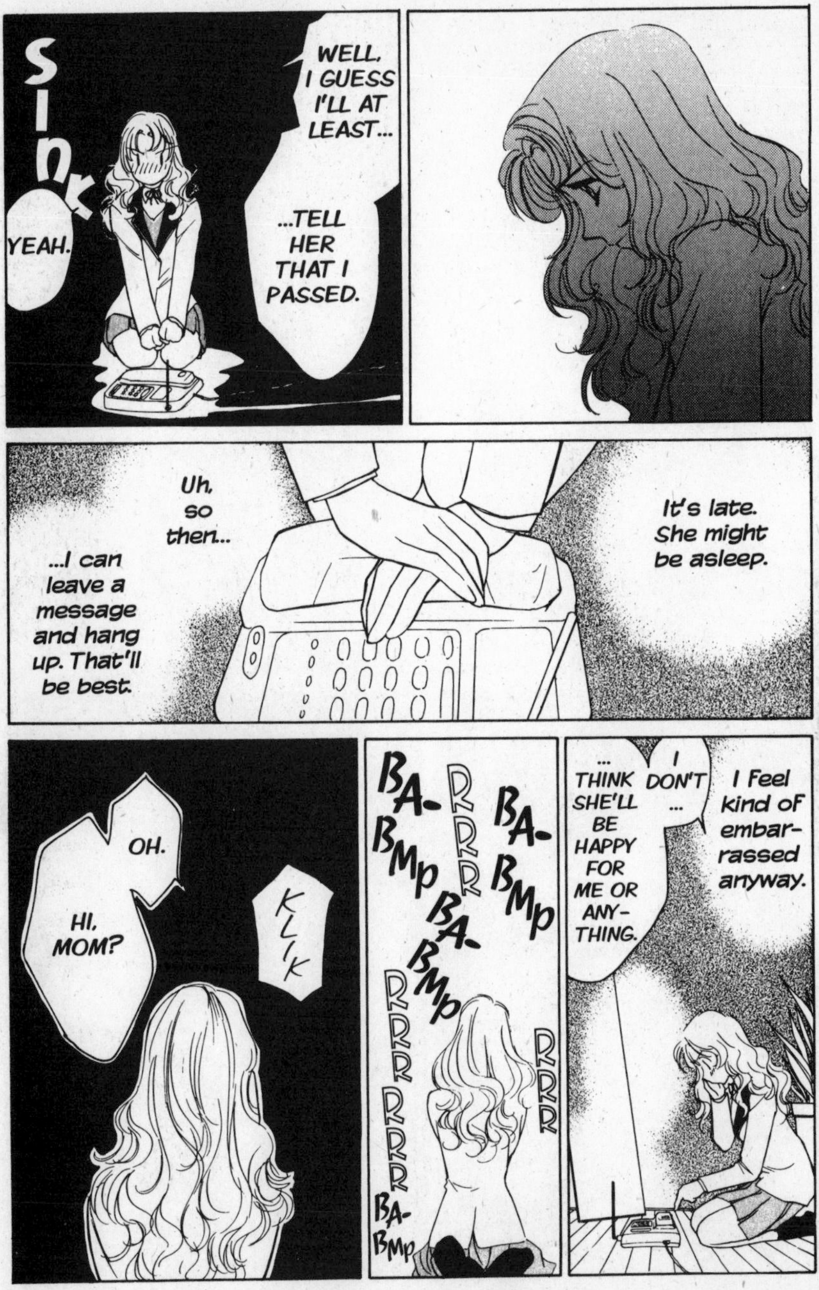
WELL, I GUESS I'LL AT LEAST...
...TELL HER THAT I PASSED.
SINK
YEAH.
It's late. She might be asleep.
Uh, so then...
...I can leave a message and hang up. That'll be best.
I Feel kind of embarrassed anyway.
I DON'T...
...THINK SHE'LL BE HAPPY FOR ME OR ANYTHING.
BA-BMP
RRR
BA-BMP
BA-BMP
RRR
RRR
BA-BMP
KLIK
OH.
HI, MOM?

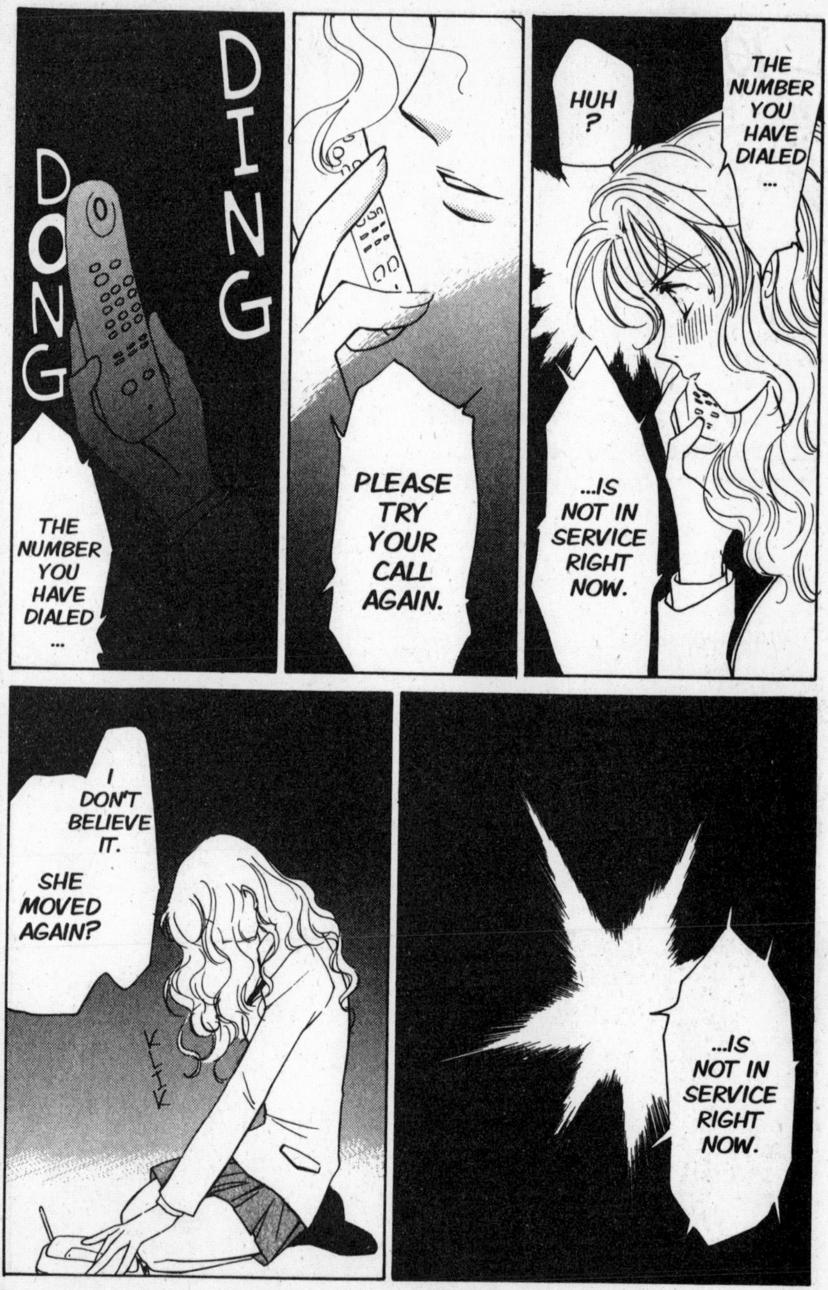
THE NUMBER YOU HAVE DIALED...
HUH?
...IS NOT IN SERVICE RIGHT NOW.
PLEASE TRY YOUR CALL AGAIN.
DING
DONG
THE NUMBER YOU HAVE DIALED...
...IS NOT IN SERVICE RIGHT NOW.
I DON'T BELIEVE IT.
SHE MOVED AGAIN?
KLIK

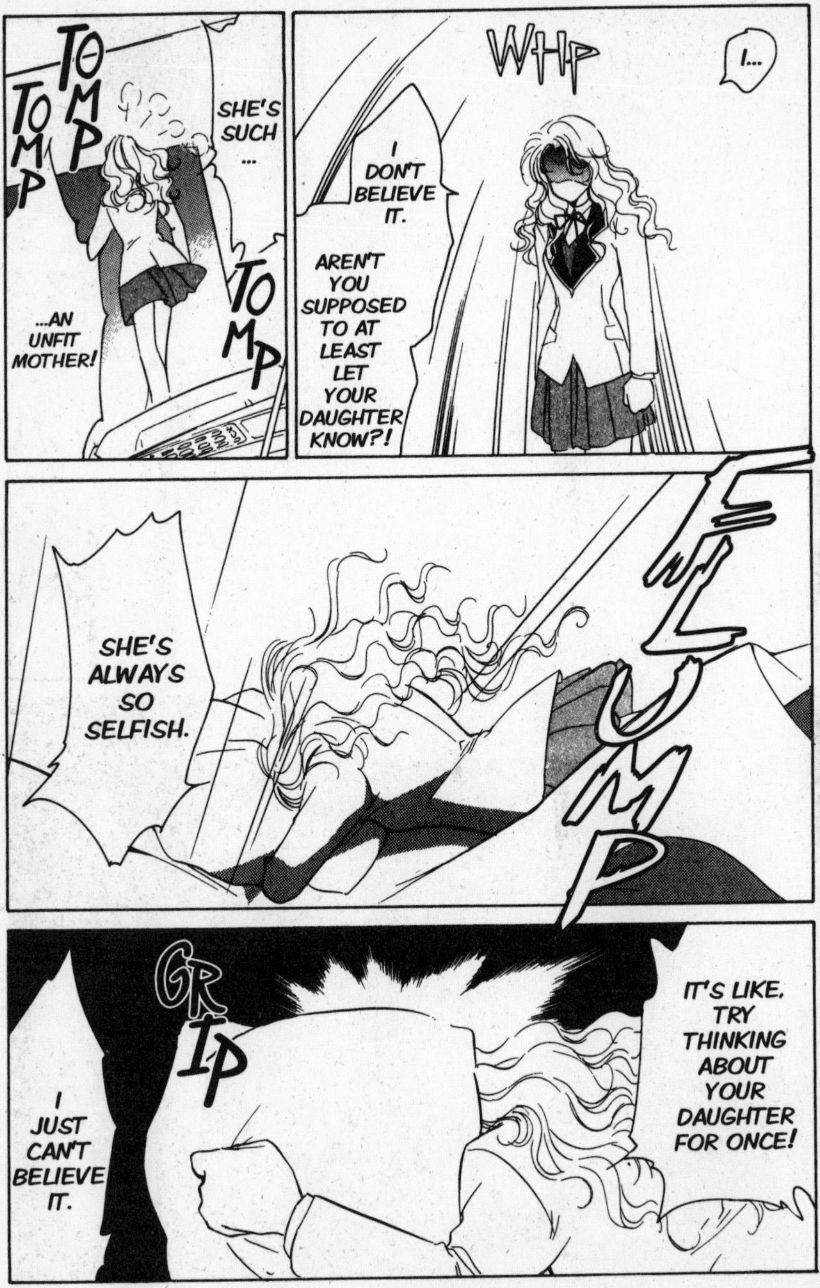
I...
WHIP
I DON'T BELIEVE IT.
AREN'T YOU SUPPOSED TO AT LEAST LET YOUR DAUGHTER KNOW?!
SHE'S SUCH ...
TOMP
TOMP
TOMP
...AN UNFIT MOTHER!
TOMP
FLUMP
SHE'S ALWAYS SO SELFISH.
IT'S LIKE, TRY THINKING ABOUT YOUR DAUGHTER FOR ONCE!
GRIP
I JUST CAN'T BELIEVE IT.

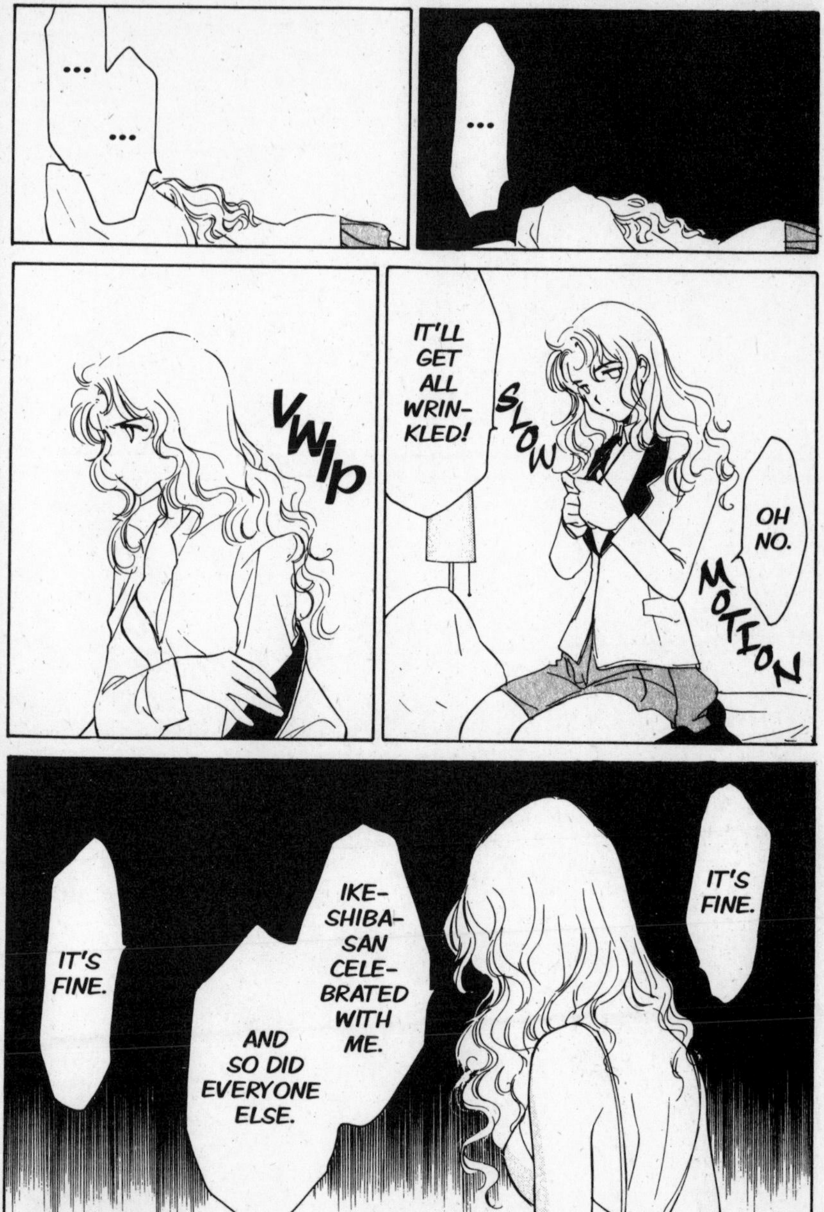
...
...
...
OH NO.
MOTION
IT'LL GET ALL WRINKLED!
SLOW
VWIP
IT'S FINE.
IKE-SHIBA-SAN CELEBRATED WITH ME.
AND SO DID EVERYONE ELSE.
IT'S FINE.

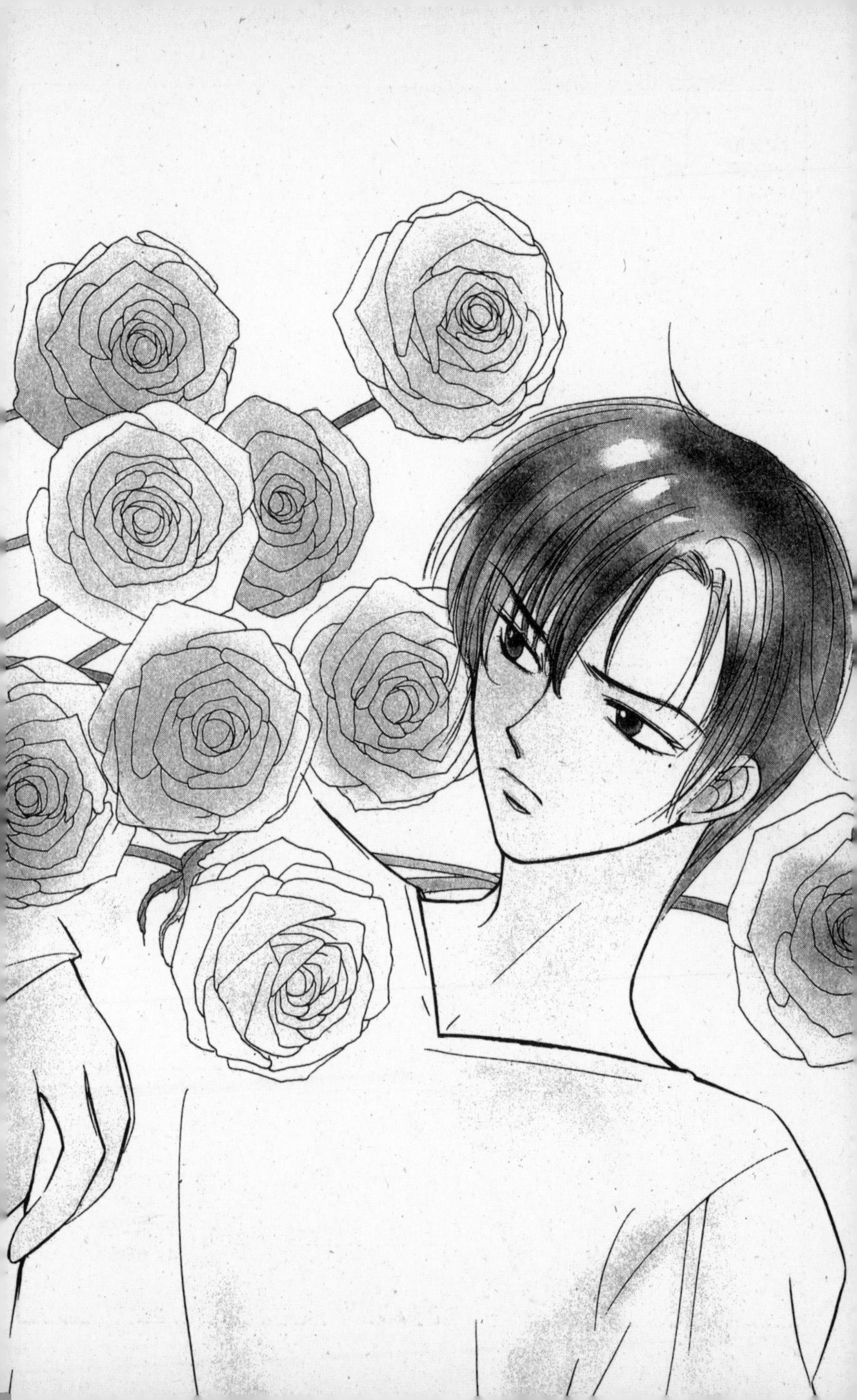

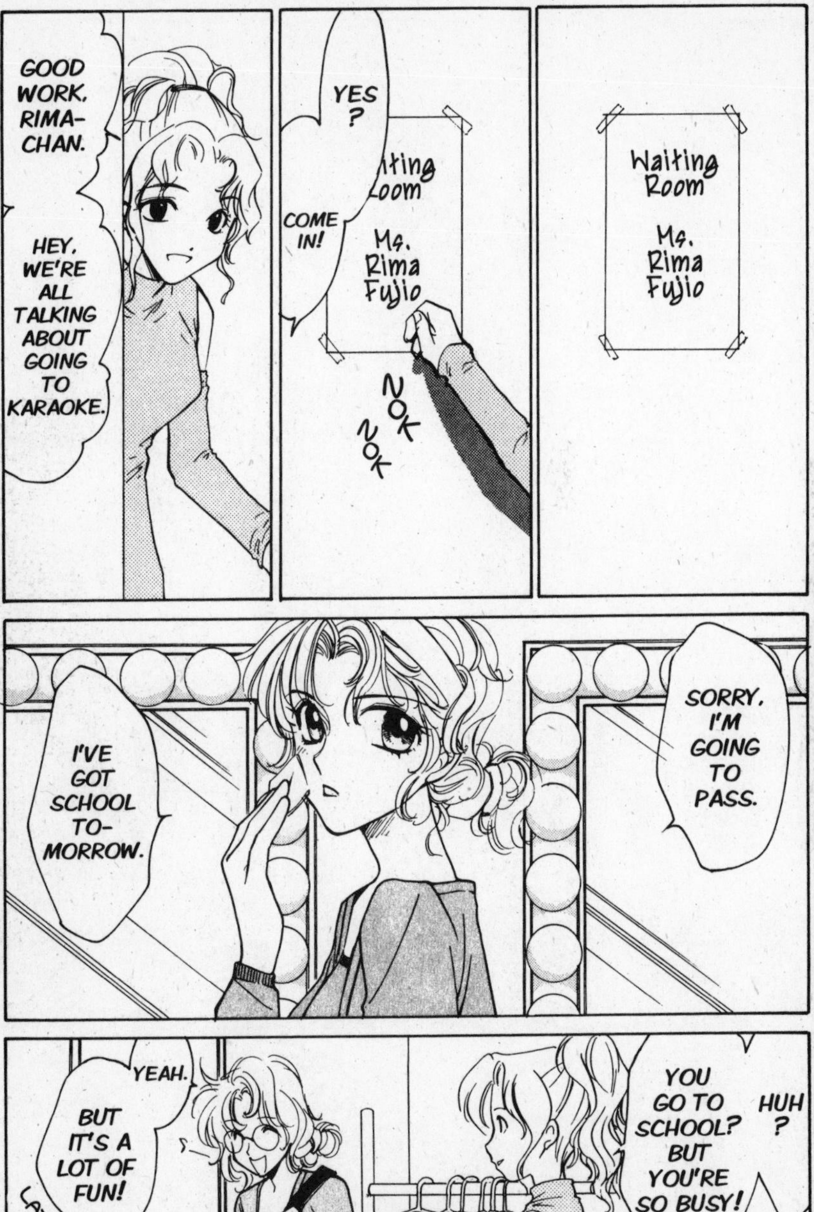
Waiting Room
Ms. Rima Fujio
Ms. Rima Fujio
NOK NOK
YES? COME IN!
GOOD WORK, RIMA-CHAN.
HEY, WE'RE ALL TALKING ABOUT GOING TO KARAOKE.
SORRY, I'M GOING TO PASS.
I'VE GOT SCHOOL TO-MORROW.
HUH?
YOU GO TO SCHOOL? BUT YOU'RE SO BUSY!
YEAH.
BUT IT'S A LOT OF FUN!
LATER!

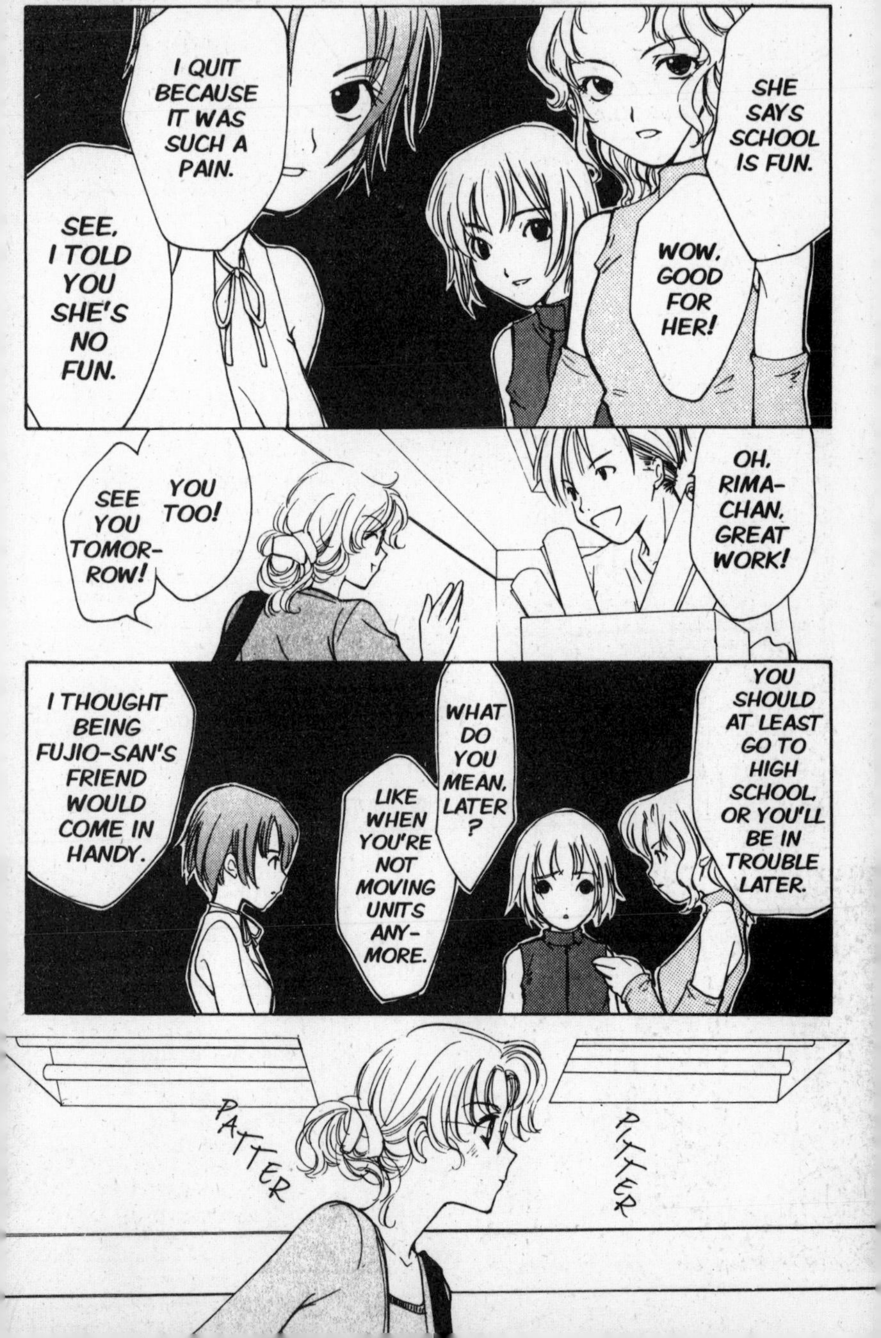
SHE SAYS SCHOOL IS FUN.
WOW, GOOD FOR HER!
I QUIT BECAUSE IT WAS SUCH A PAIN.
SEE, I TOLD YOU SHE'S NO FUN.
OH, RIMA-CHAN, GREAT WORK!
YOU TOO!
SEE YOU TOMOR-ROW!
YOU SHOULD AT LEAST GO TO HIGH SCHOOL, OR YOU'LL BE IN TROUBLE LATER.
WHAT DO YOU MEAN, LATER?
LIKE WHEN YOU'RE NOT MOVING UNITS ANY-MORE.
I THOUGHT BEING FUJIO-SAN'S FRIEND WOULD COME IN HANDY.
PITTER
PATTER

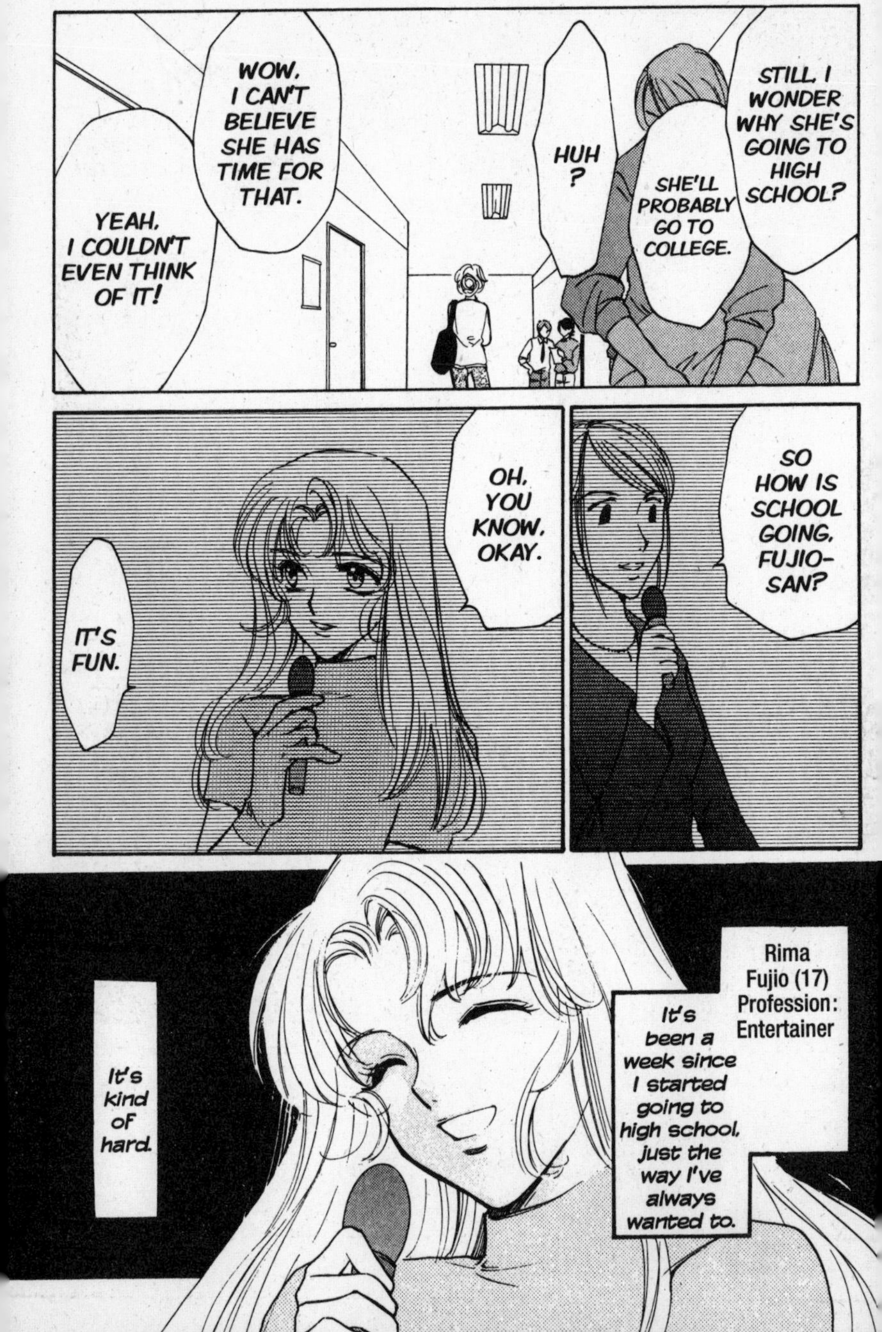
STILL, I WONDER WHY SHE'S GOING TO HIGH SCHOOL?
SHE'LL PROBABLY GO TO COLLEGE.
HUH?
WOW, I CAN'T BELIEVE SHE HAS TIME FOR THAT.
YEAH, I COULDN'T EVEN THINK OF IT!
SO HOW IS SCHOOL GOING, FUJIO-SAN?
OH, YOU KNOW, OKAY.
IT'S FUN.
Rima Fujio (17) Profession: Entertainer
It's been a week since I started going to high school, just the way I've always wanted to.
It's kind of hard.

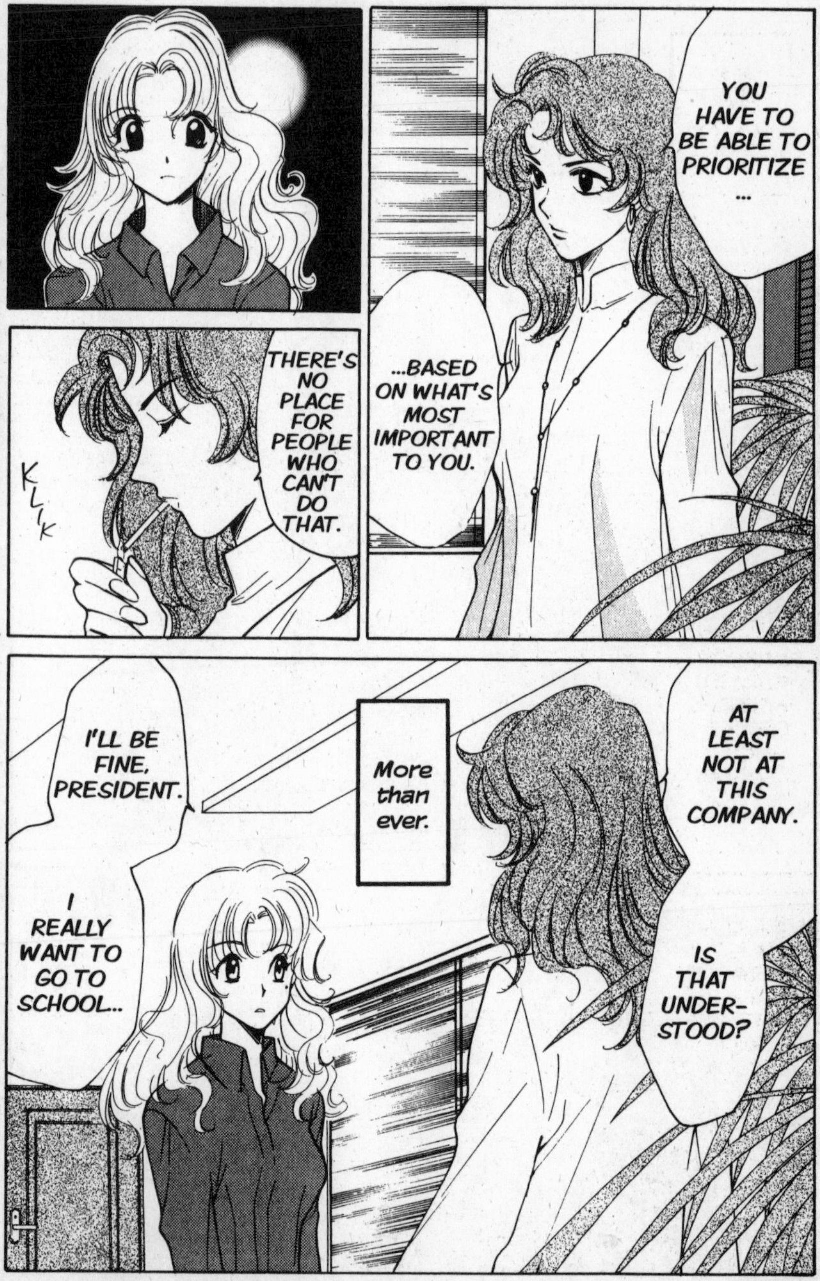
YOU HAVE TO BE ABLE TO PRIORITIZE ...
...BASED ON WHAT'S MOST IMPORTANT TO YOU.
THERE'S NO PLACE FOR PEOPLE WHO CAN'T DO THAT.
KLIK
AT LEAST NOT AT THIS COMPANY.
IS THAT UNDERSTOOD?
I'LL BE FINE, PRESIDENT.
I REALLY WANT TO GO TO SCHOOL...
More than ever.

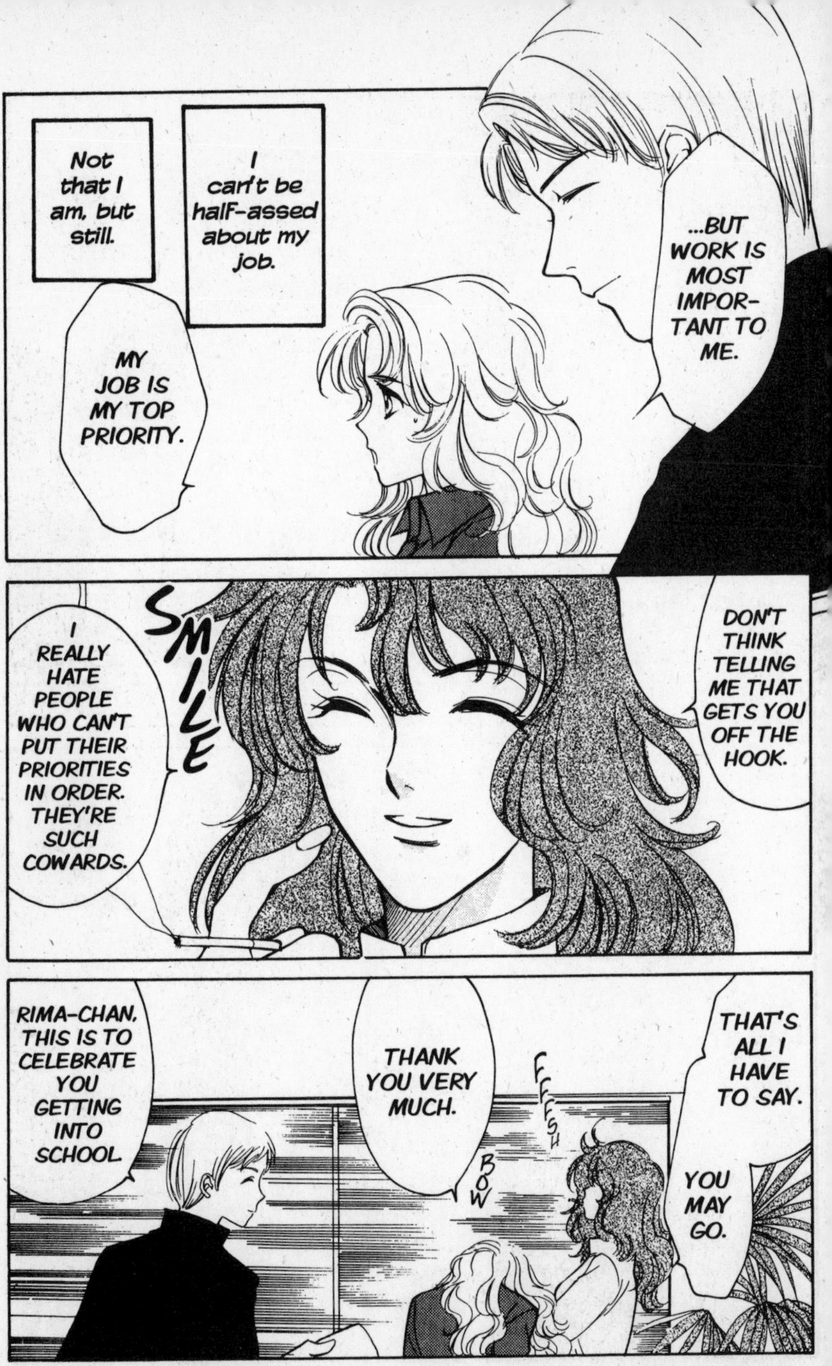
...BUT WORK IS MOST IMPOR-TANT TO ME.
I can't be half-assed about my job.
Not that I am, but still.
MY JOB IS MY TOP PRIORITY.
DON'T THINK TELLING ME THAT GETS YOU OFF THE HOOK.
SMILE
I REALLY HATE PEOPLE WHO CAN'T PUT THEIR PRIORITIES IN ORDER. THEY'RE SUCH COWARDS.
THAT'S ALL I HAVE TO SAY.
YOU MAY GO.
FFFSH
THANK YOU VERY MUCH.
BOW
RIMA-CHAN, THIS IS TO CELEBRATE YOU GETTING INTO SCHOOL.

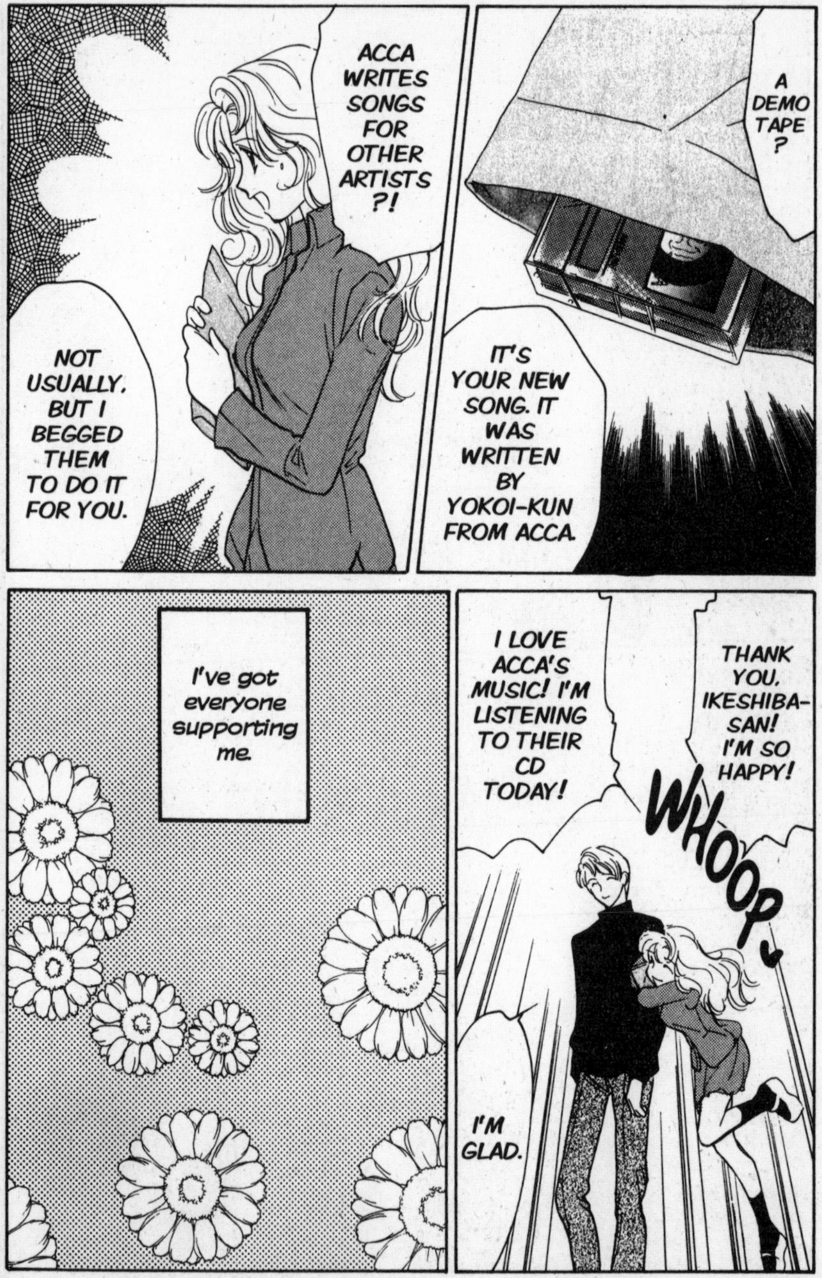
A DEMO TAPE?
IT'S YOUR NEW SONG. IT WAS WRITTEN BY YOKOI-KUN FROM ACCA.
ACCA WRITES SONGS FOR OTHER ARTISTS?!
NOT USUALLY. BUT I BEGGED THEM TO DO IT FOR YOU.
THANK YOU, IKESHIBA-SAN! I'M SO HAPPY!
I LOVE ACCA'S MUSIC! I'M LISTENING TO THEIR CD TODAY!
WHOOP
I'M GLAD.
I've got everyone supporting me.

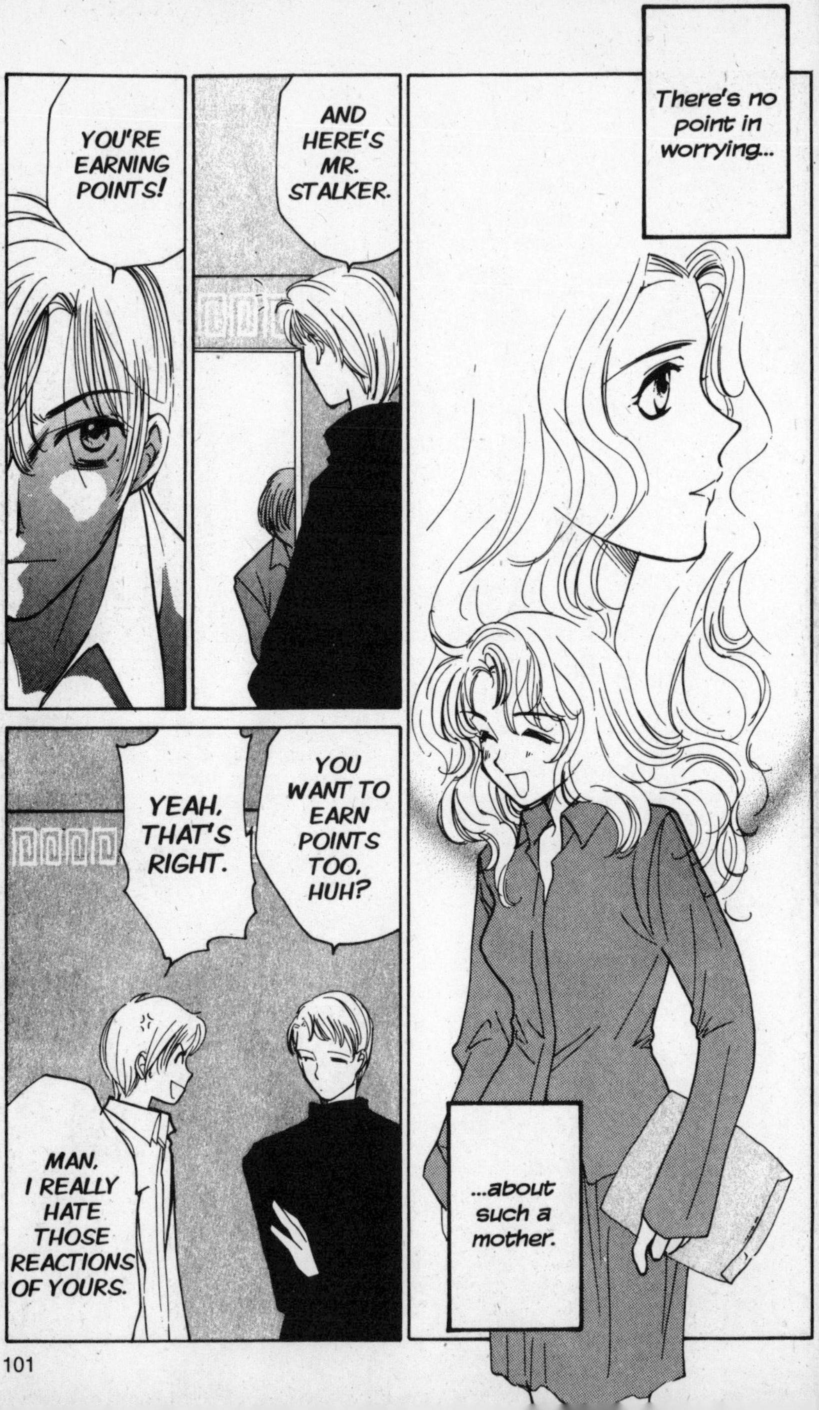
There's no point in worrying...
...about such a mother.
AND HERE'S MR. STALKER.
YOU'RE EARNING POINTS!
YOU WANT TO EARN POINTS TOO, HUH?
YEAH, THAT'S RIGHT.
MAN, I REALLY HATE THOSE REACTIONS OF YOURS.

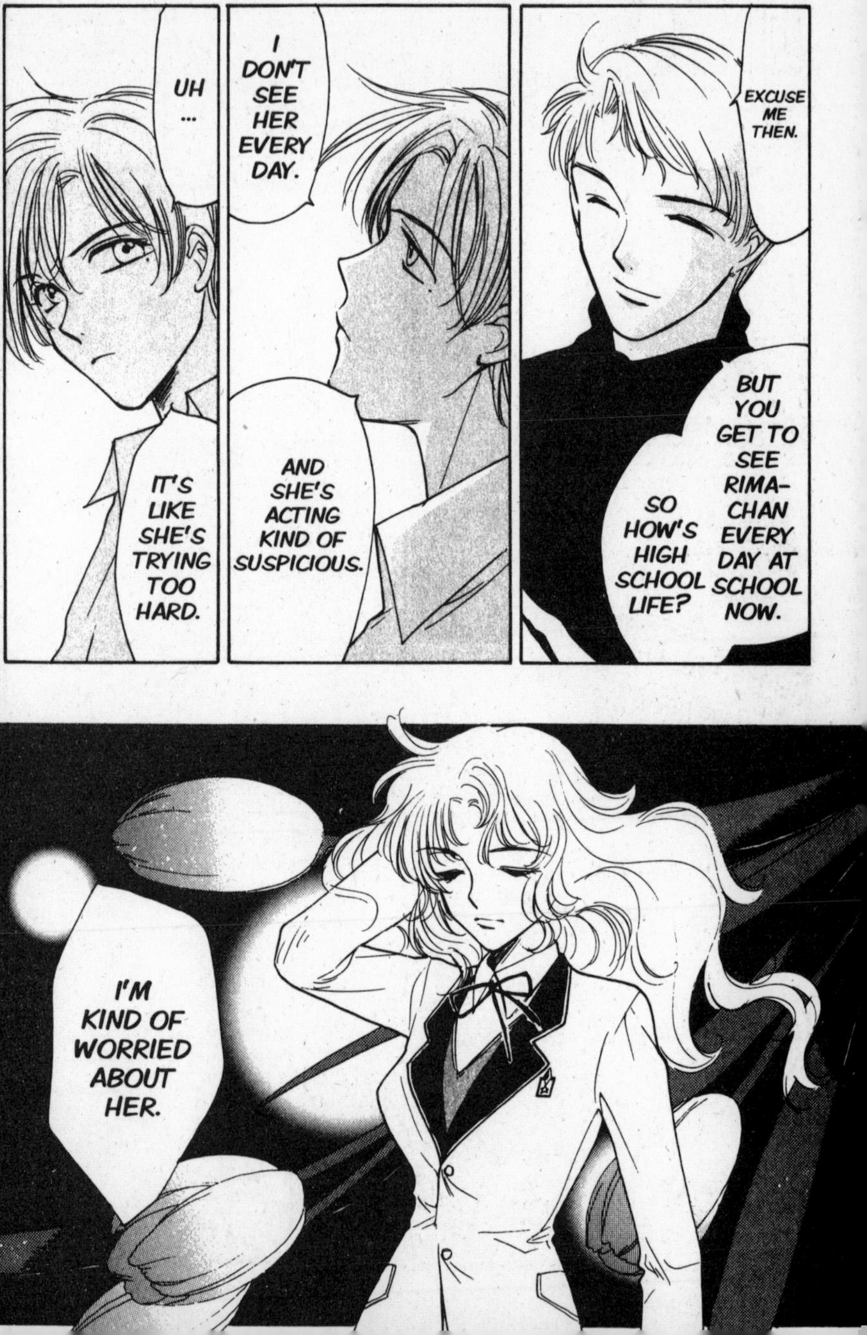
EXCUSE ME THEN.
BUT YOU GET TO SEE RIMA-CHAN EVERY DAY AT SCHOOL NOW.
SO HOW'S HIGH SCHOOL LIFE?
I DON'T SEE HER EVERY DAY.
AND SHE'S ACTING KIND OF SUSPICIOUS.
UH ...
IT'S LIKE SHE'S TRYING TOO HARD.
I'M KIND OF WORRIED ABOUT HER.

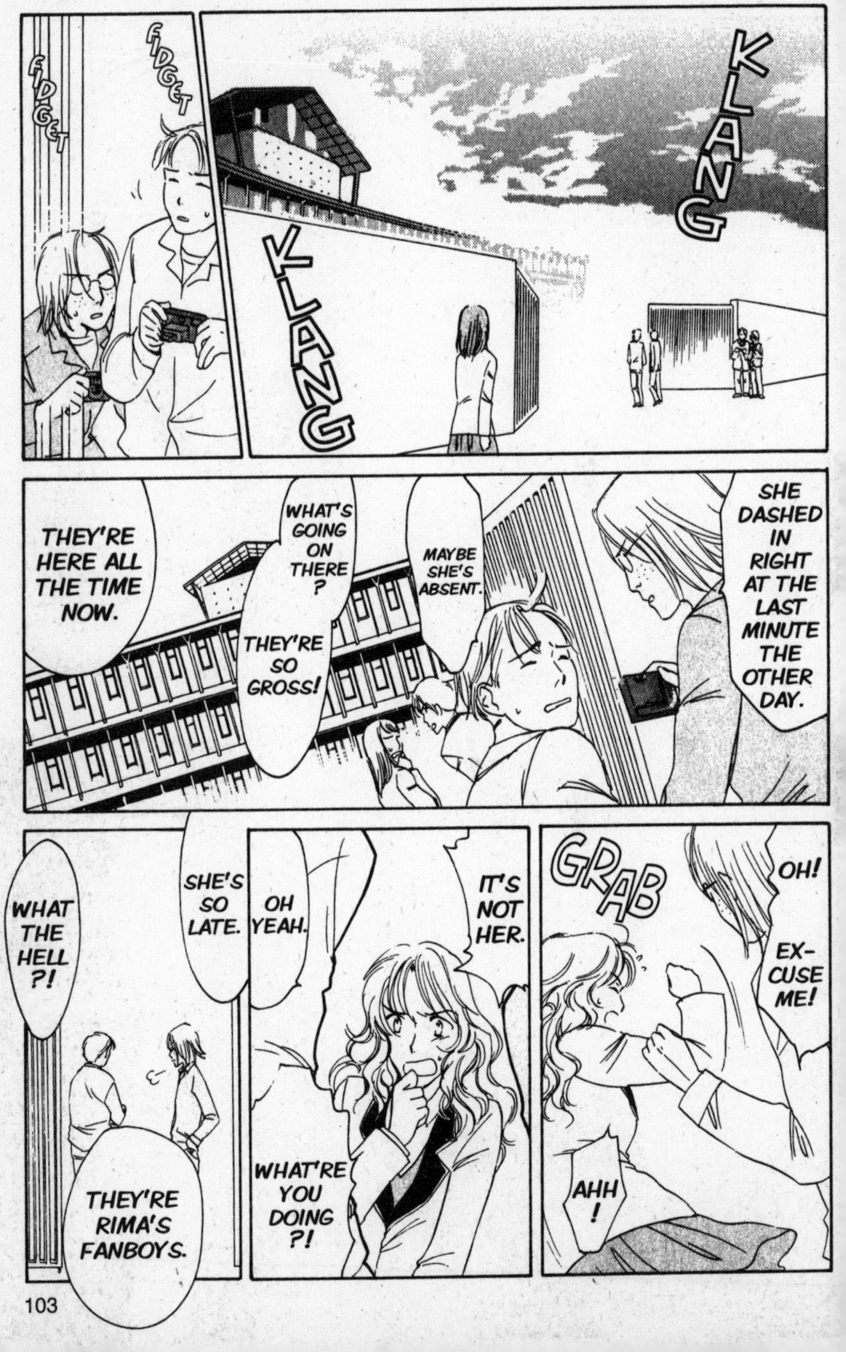
KLANG
KLANG
FIDGET
FIDGET
SHE DASHED IN RIGHT AT THE LAST MINUTE THE OTHER DAY.
MAYBE SHE'S ABSENT.
WHAT'S GOING ON THERE?
THEY'RE SO GROSS!
THEY'RE HERE ALL THE TIME NOW.
OH!
EX-CUSE ME!
GRAB
AHH!
IT'S NOT HER.
OH YEAH.
WHAT'RE YOU DOING?!
SHE'S SO LATE.
WHAT THE HELL?!
THEY'RE RIMA'S FANBOYS.

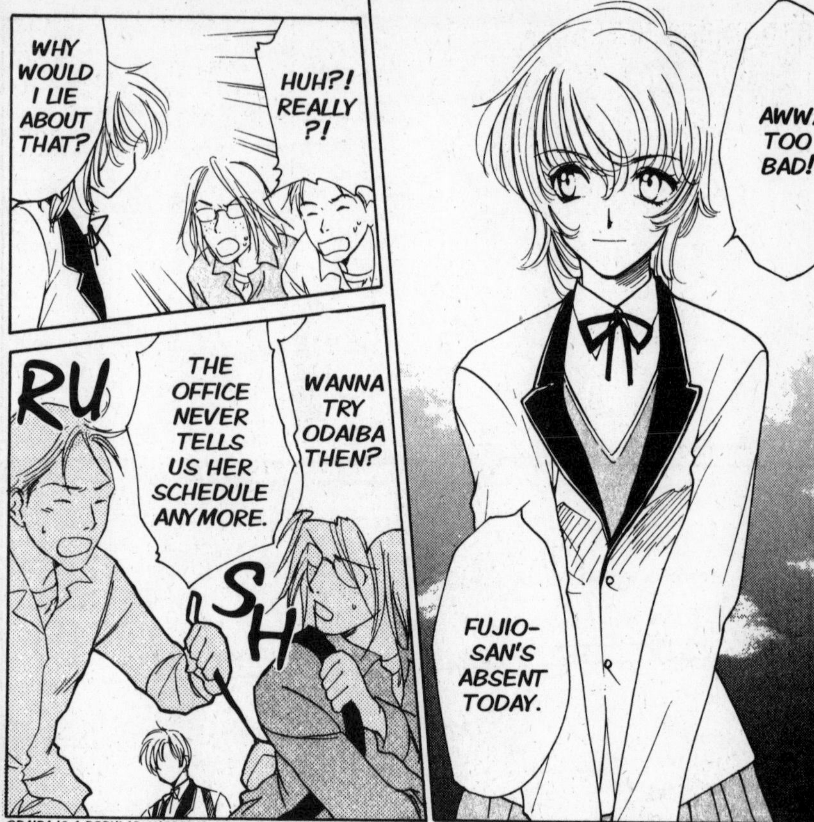
AWW. TOO BAD!
FUJIO-SAN'S ABSENT TODAY.
HUH?! REALLY?!
WHY WOULD I LIE ABOUT THAT?
WANNA TRY ODAIBA THEN?
THE OFFICE NEVER TELLS US HER SCHEDULE ANYMORE.
RU
SH

ODAIBA IS A POPULAR SHOPPING AND ENTERTAINMENT SPOT IN TOKYO BAY.

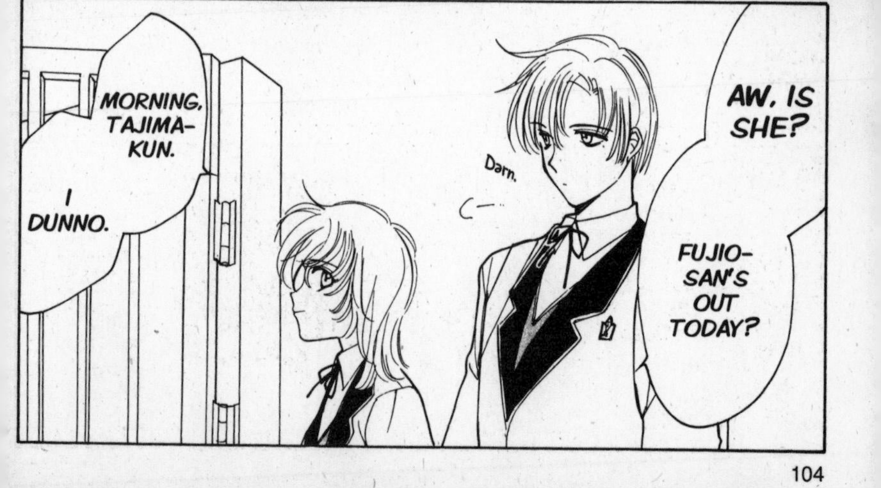
AW, IS SHE?
FUJIO-SAN'S OUT TODAY?
Darn.
MORNING, TAJIMA-KUN.
I DUNNO.

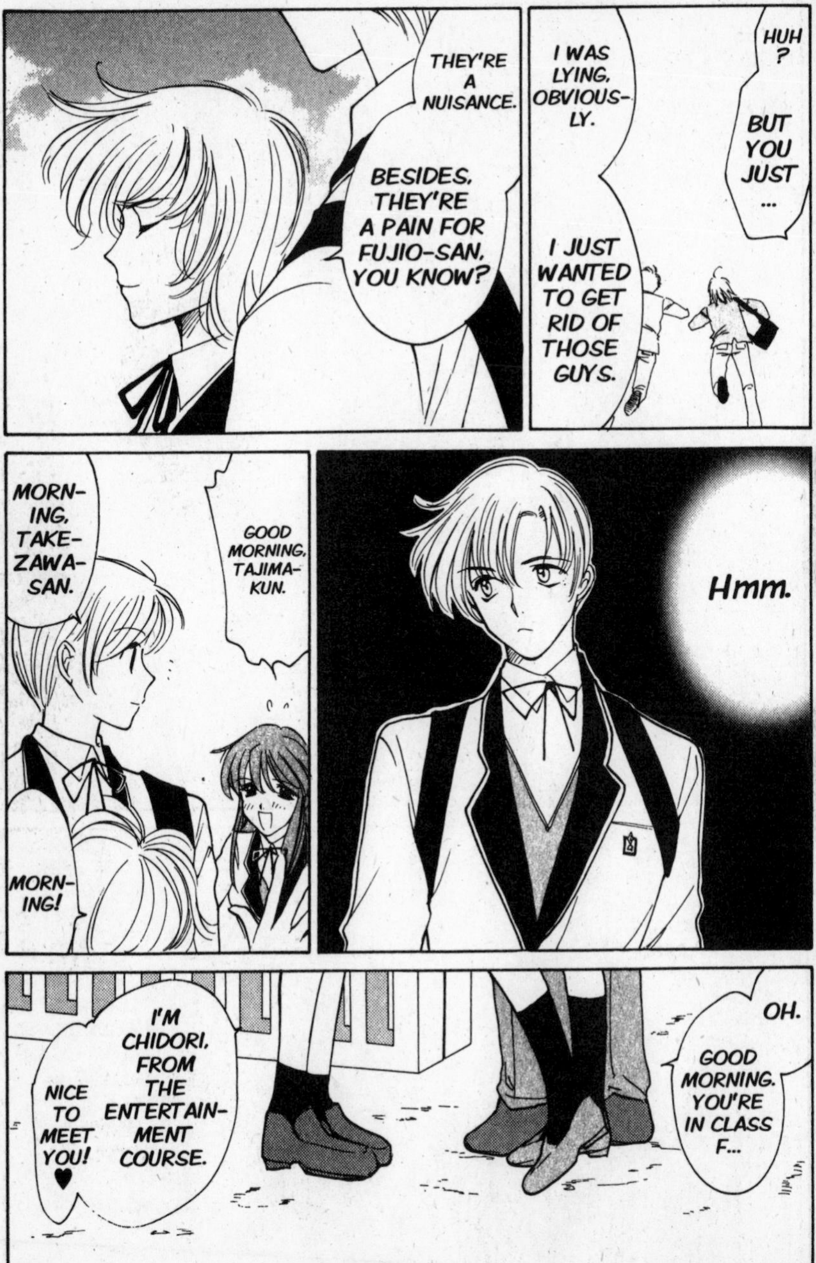
HUH? BUT YOU JUST...
I WAS LYING, OBVIOUSLY.
I JUST WANTED TO GET RID OF THOSE GUYS.
THEY'RE A NUISANCE.
BESIDES, THEY'RE A PAIN FOR FUJIO-SAN, YOU KNOW?
Hmm.
GOOD MORNING, TAJIMA-KUN.
MORNING, TAKEZAWA-SAN.
MORNING!
OH.
GOOD MORNING. YOU'RE IN CLASS F...
I'M CHIDORI, FROM THE ENTERTAINMENT COURSE.
NICE TO MEET YOU! ♥

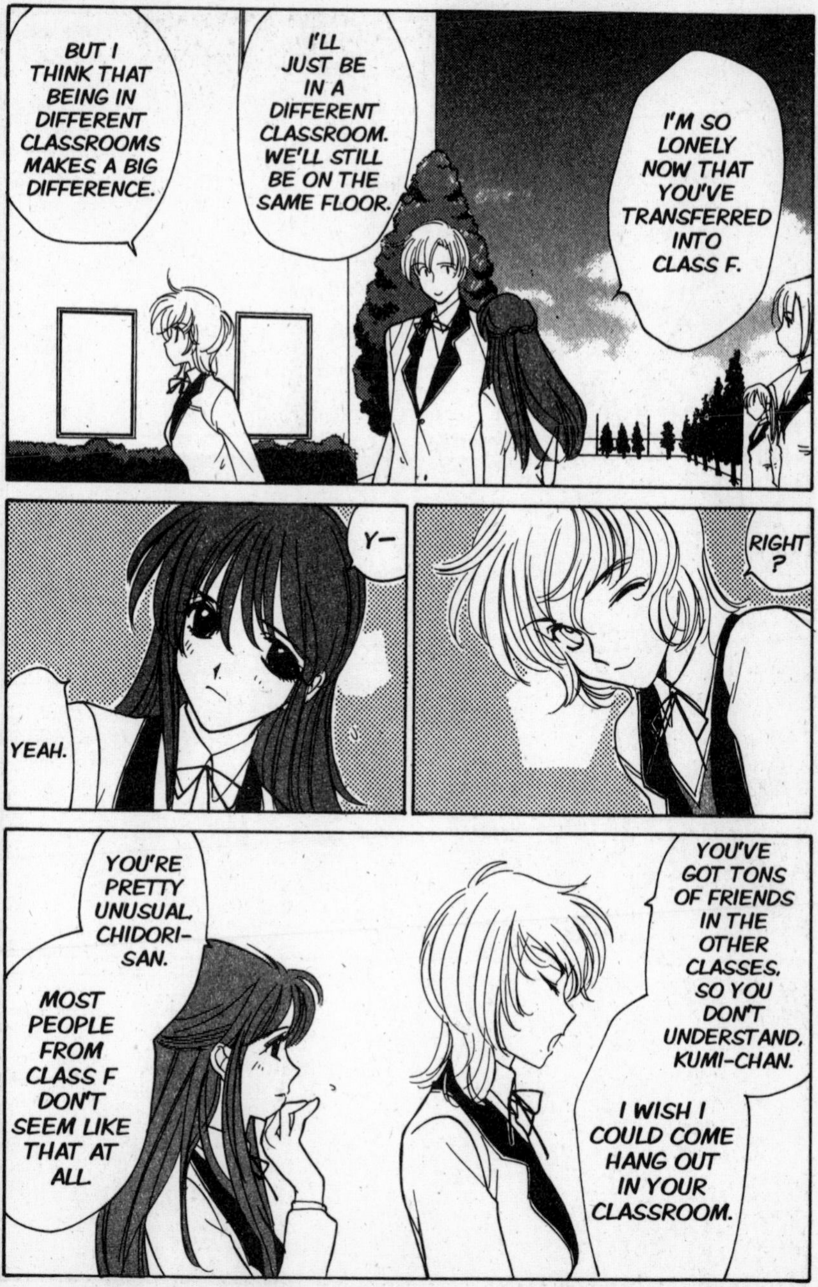
I'M SO LONELY NOW THAT YOU'VE TRANSFERRED INTO CLASS F.
I'LL JUST BE IN A DIFFERENT CLASSROOM. WE'LL STILL BE ON THE SAME FLOOR.
BUT I THINK THAT BEING IN DIFFERENT CLASSROOMS MAKES A BIG DIFFERENCE.
RIGHT?
Y—
YEAH.
YOU'VE GOT TONS OF FRIENDS IN THE OTHER CLASSES, SO YOU DON'T UNDERSTAND, KUMI-CHAN.
I WISH I COULD COME HANG OUT IN YOUR CLASSROOM.
YOU'RE PRETTY UNUSUAL, CHIDORI-SAN.
MOST PEOPLE FROM CLASS F DON'T SEEM LIKE THAT AT ALL.

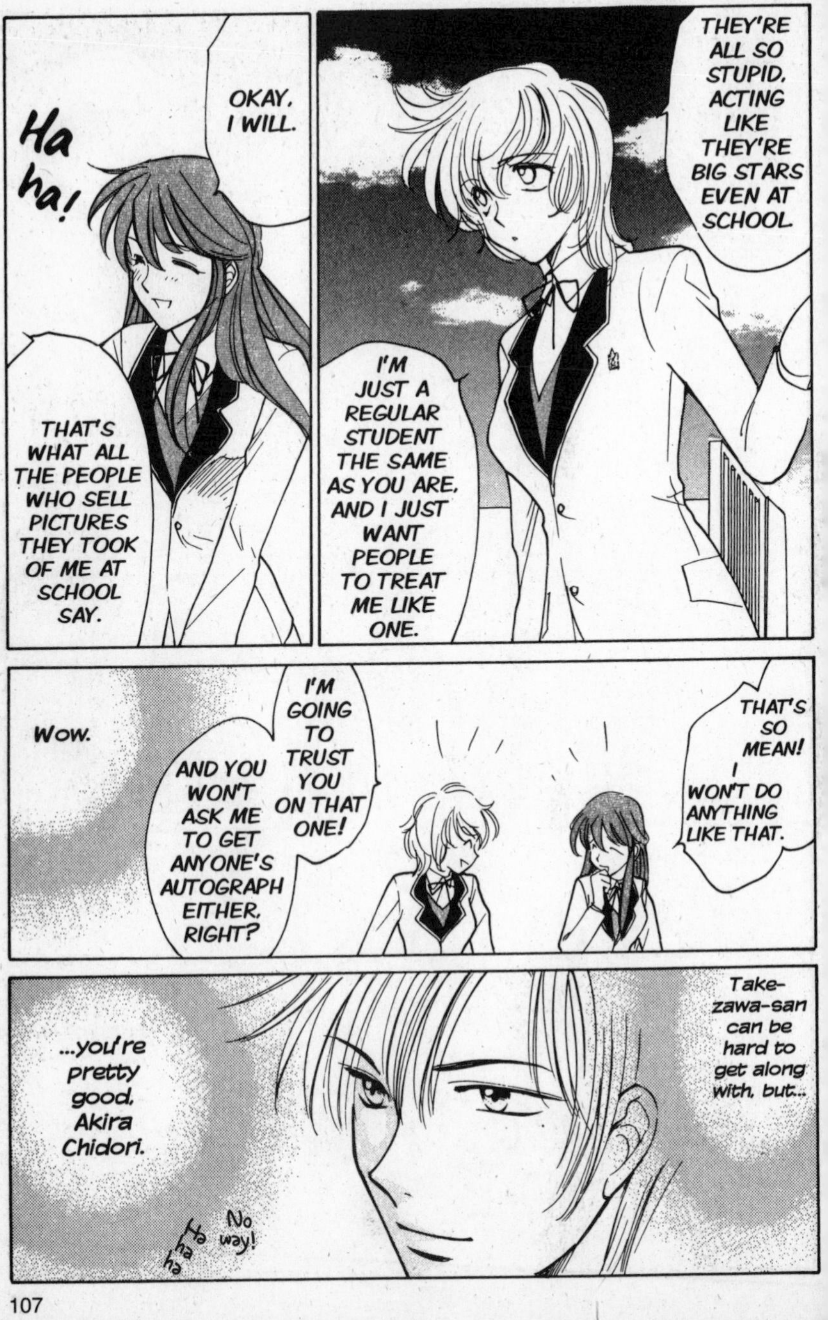
THEY'RE ALL SO STUPID, ACTING LIKE THEY'RE BIG STARS EVEN AT SCHOOL.
I'M JUST A REGULAR STUDENT THE SAME AS YOU ARE, AND I JUST WANT PEOPLE TO TREAT ME LIKE ONE.
OKAY, I WILL.
Ha ha!
THAT'S WHAT ALL THE PEOPLE WHO SELL PICTURES THEY TOOK OF ME AT SCHOOL SAY.
THAT'S SO MEAN! I WON'T DO ANYTHING LIKE THAT.
I'M GOING TO TRUST YOU ON THAT ONE!
AND YOU WON'T ASK ME TO GET ANYONE'S AUTOGRAPH EITHER, RIGHT?
Wow.
Take-zawa-san can be hard to get along with, but...
...you're pretty good, Akira Chidori.
No way!
Ha ha ha

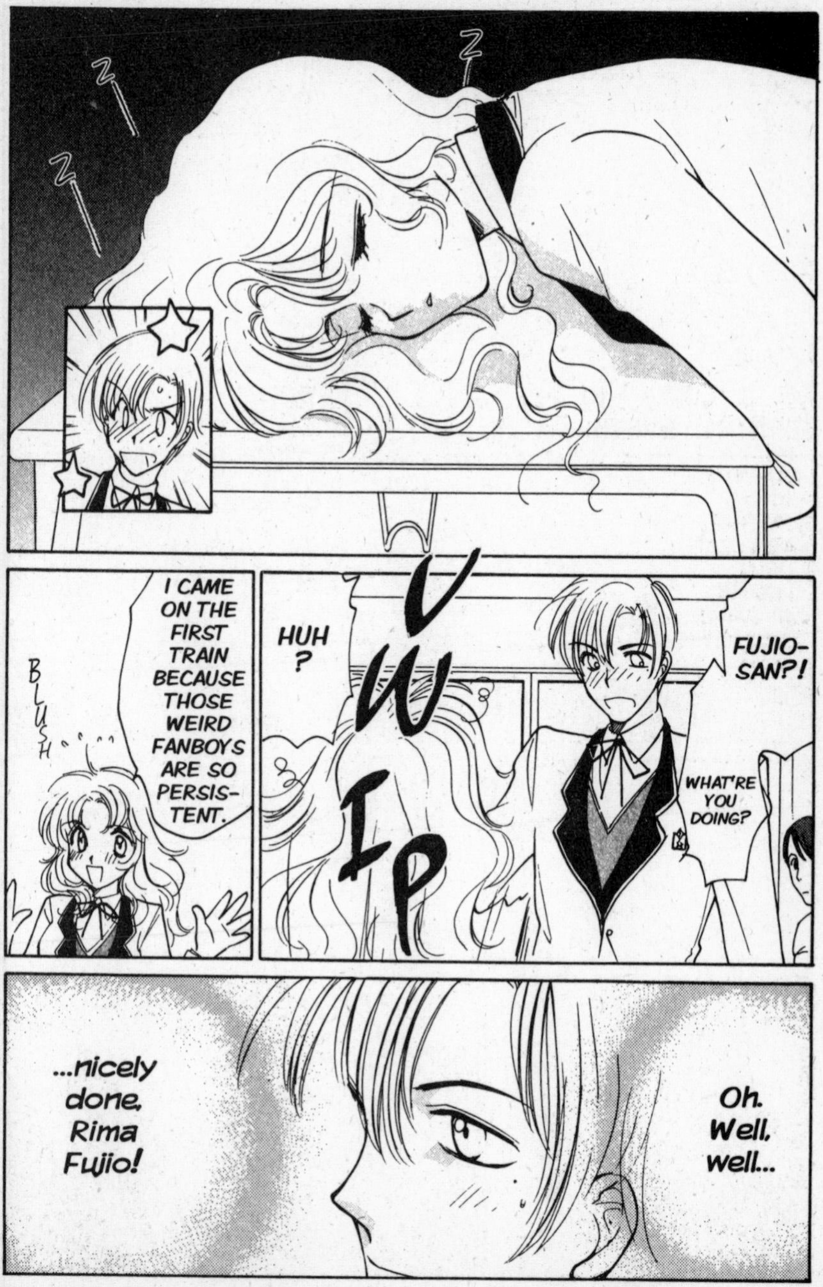
Z
Z
Z
FUJIO-SAN?!
WHAT'RE YOU DOING?
HUH?
I CAME ON THE FIRST TRAIN BECAUSE THOSE WEIRD FANBOYS ARE SO PERSISTENT.
BLUSH
Oh. Well, well...
...nicely done, Rima Fujio!

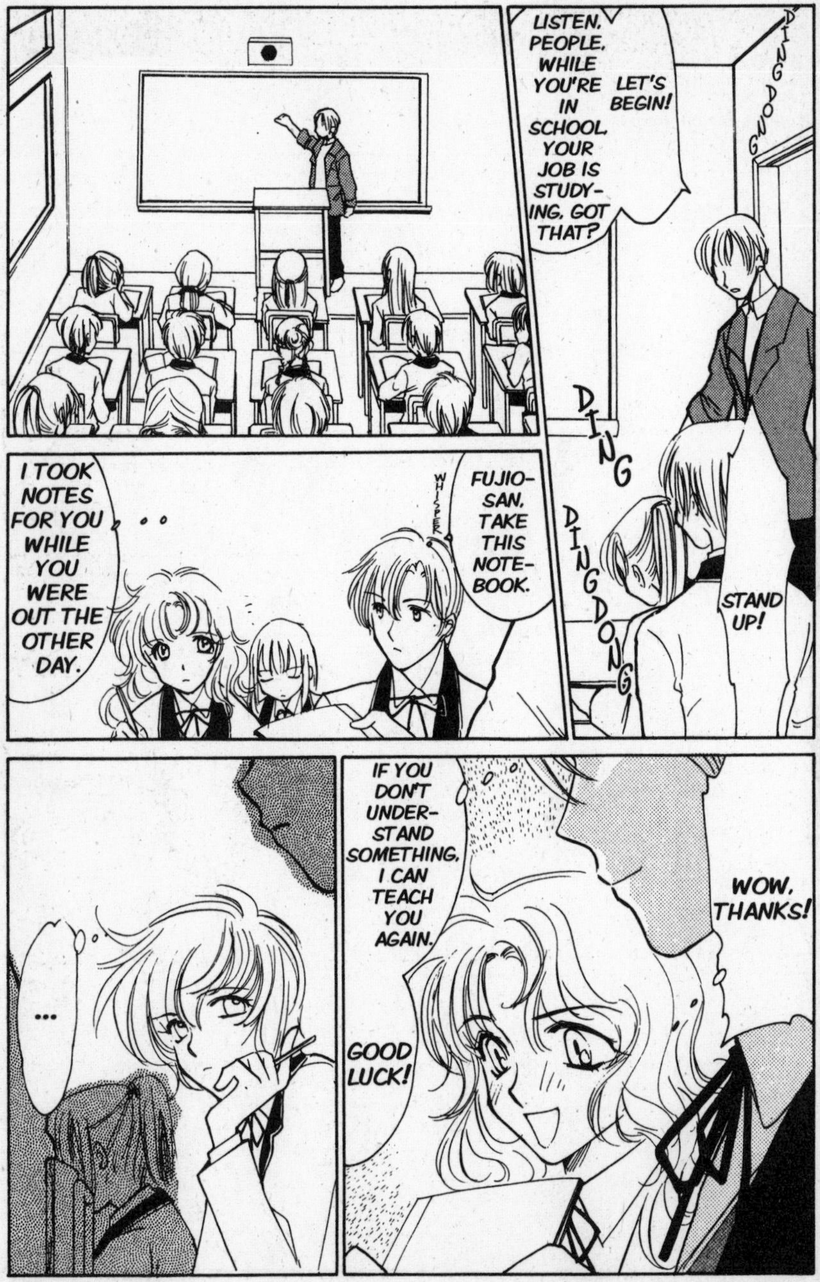
DING DONG
LET'S BEGIN!
LISTEN, PEOPLE, WHILE YOU'RE IN SCHOOL, YOUR JOB IS STUDYING. GOT THAT?
DING DONG DING DONG
STAND UP!
WHISPER
FUJIO-SAN, TAKE THIS NOTEBOOK.
I TOOK NOTES FOR YOU WHILE YOU WERE OUT THE OTHER DAY.
WOW, THANKS!
IF YOU DON'T UNDERSTAND SOMETHING, I CAN TEACH YOU AGAIN.
GOOD LUCK!
...

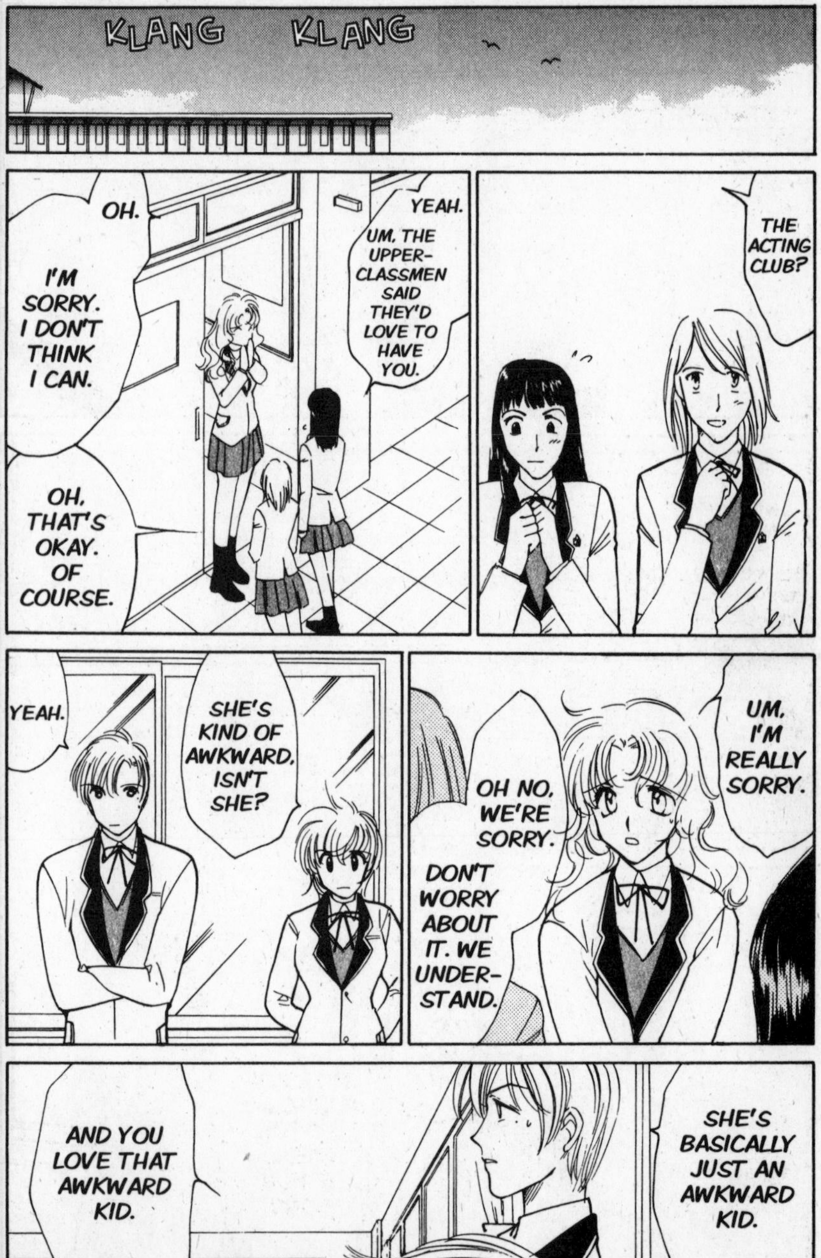
KLANG KLANG
THE ACTING CLUB?
YEAH.
UM, THE UPPER-CLASSMEN SAID THEY'D LOVE TO HAVE YOU.
OH.
I'M SORRY. I DON'T THINK I CAN.
OH, THAT'S OKAY. OF COURSE.
UM, I'M REALLY SORRY.
OH NO, WE'RE SORRY.
DON'T WORRY ABOUT IT. WE UNDER-STAND.
SHE'S KIND OF AWKWARD, ISN'T SHE?
YEAH.
SHE'S BASICALLY JUST AN AWKWARD KID.
AND YOU LOVE THAT AWKWARD KID.

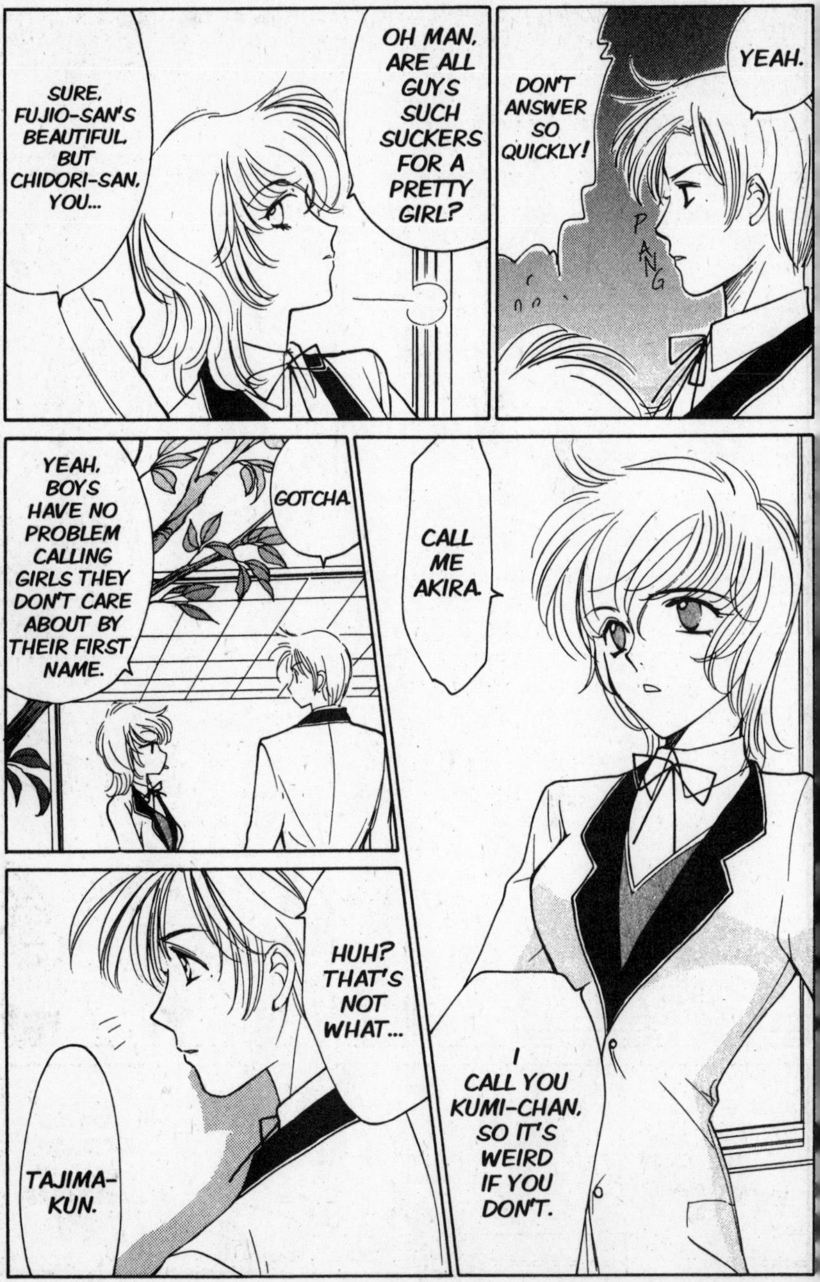
YEAH.
DON'T ANSWER SO QUICKLY!
PANG
OH MAN, ARE ALL GUYS SUCH SUCKERS FOR A PRETTY GIRL?
SURE, FUJIO-SAN'S BEAUTIFUL, BUT CHIDORI-SAN, YOU...
CALL ME AKIRA.
I CALL YOU KUMI-CHAN, SO IT'S WEIRD IF YOU DON'T.
GOTCHA
YEAH, BOYS HAVE NO PROBLEM CALLING GIRLS THEY DON'T CARE ABOUT BY THEIR FIRST NAME.
HUH? THAT'S NOT WHAT...
TAJIMA-KUN.

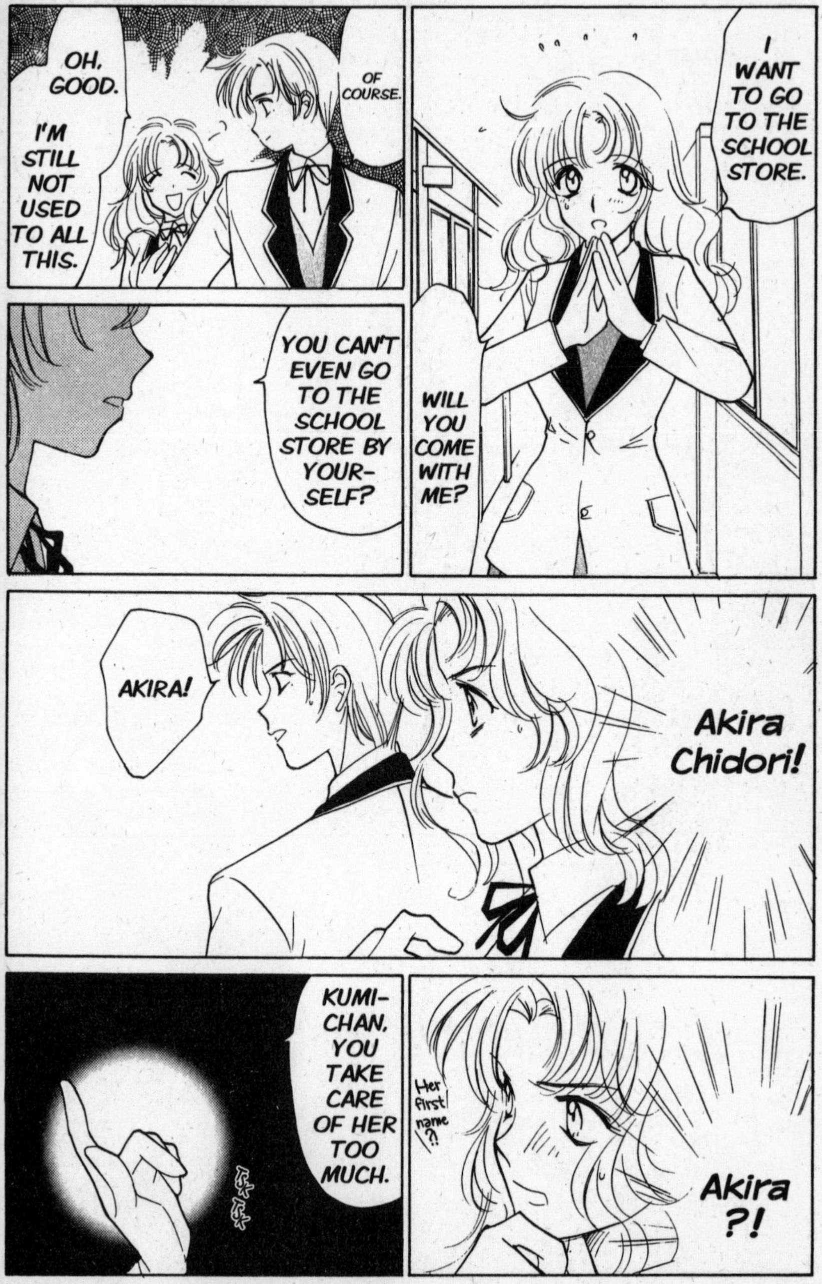

I WANT TO GO TO THE SCHOOL STORE.
WILL YOU COME WITH ME?
OF COURSE.
OH, GOOD.
I'M STILL NOT USED TO ALL THIS.
YOU CAN'T EVEN GO TO THE SCHOOL STORE BY YOURSELF?
Akira Chidori!
AKIRA!
Akira?!
Her first name?!
KUMI-CHAN, YOU TAKE CARE OF HER TOO MUCH.

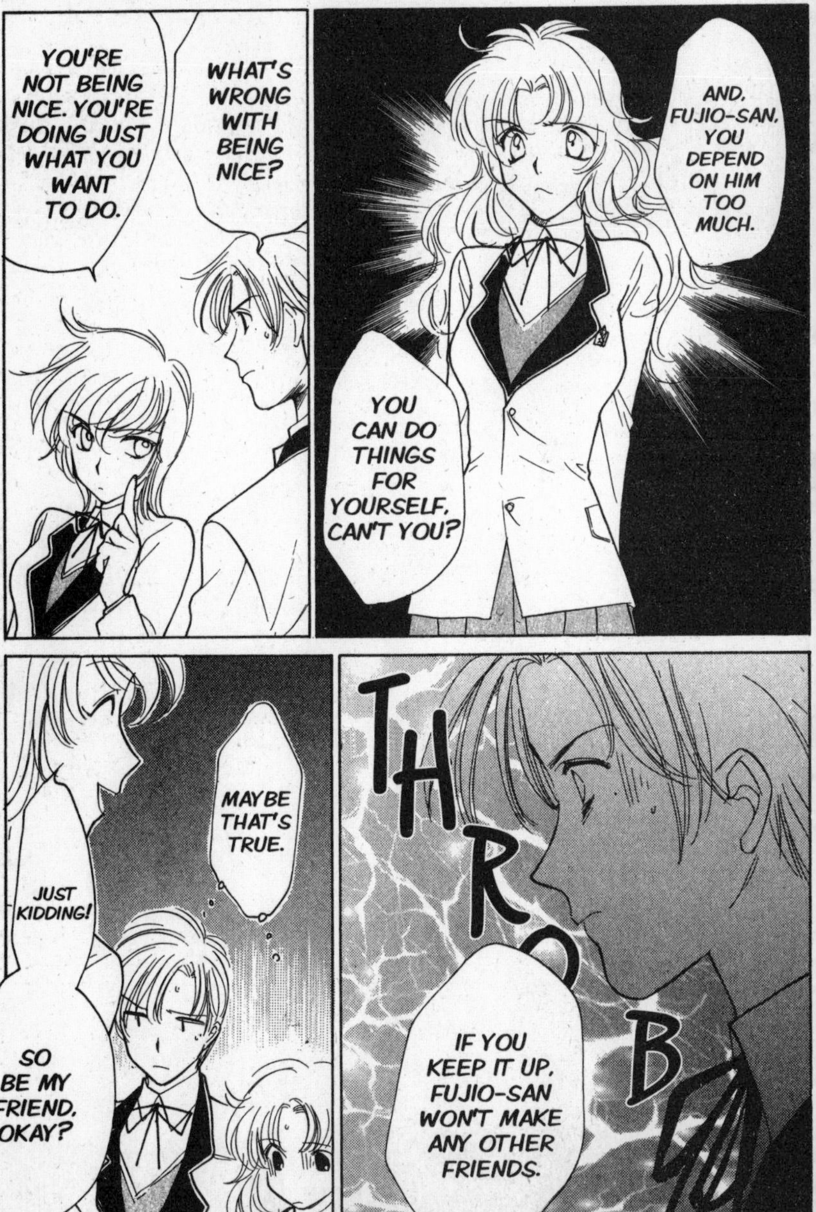
AND, FUJIO-SAN, YOU DEPEND ON HIM TOO MUCH.
YOU CAN DO THINGS FOR YOURSELF, CAN'T YOU?
WHAT'S WRONG WITH BEING NICE?
YOU'RE NOT BEING NICE. YOU'RE DOING JUST WHAT YOU WANT TO DO.
THROB
IF YOU KEEP IT UP, FUJIO-SAN WON'T MAKE ANY OTHER FRIENDS.
MAYBE THAT'S TRUE.
JUST KIDDING!
SO BE MY FRIEND, OKAY?

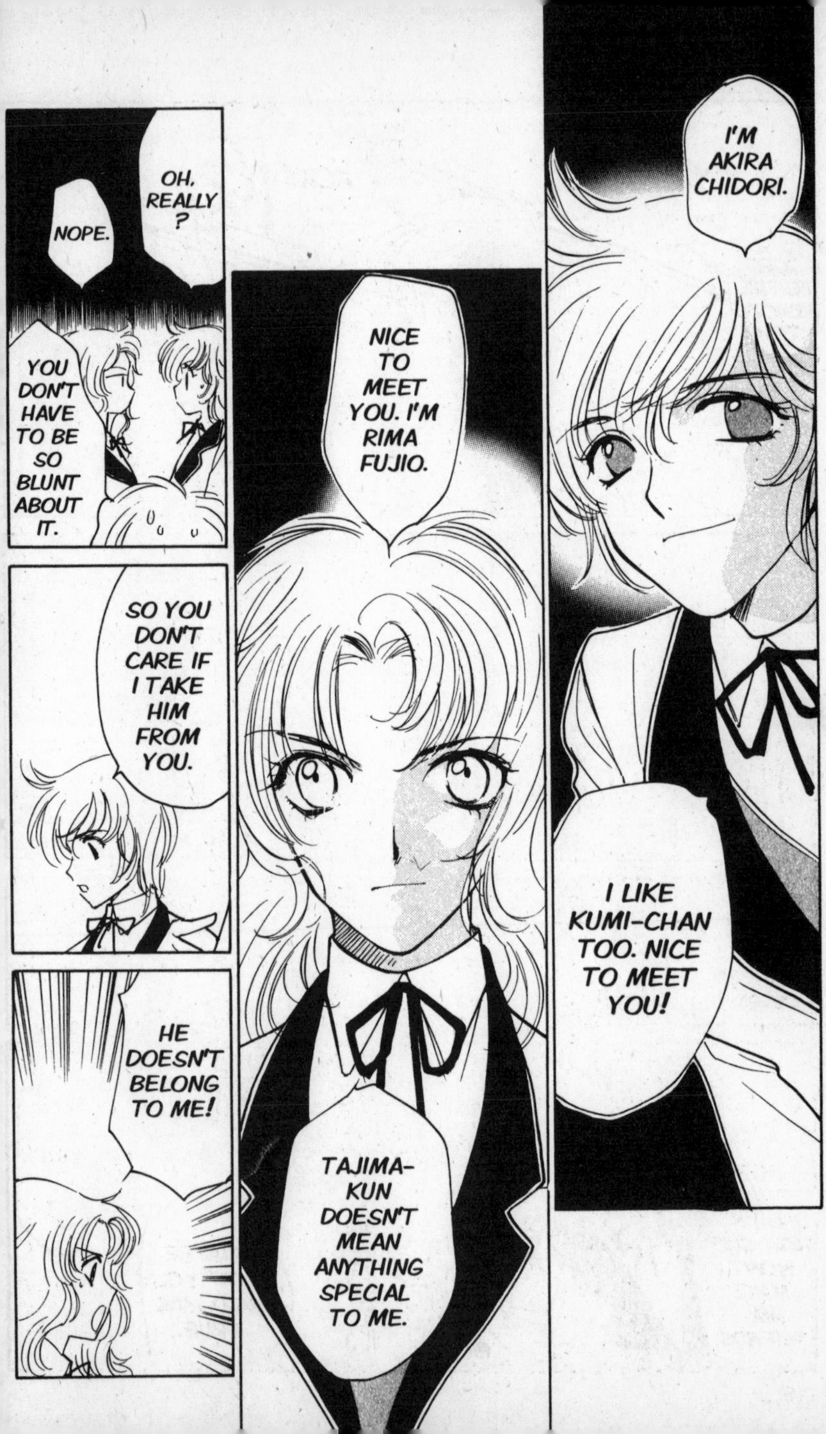
I'M AKIRA CHIDORI.
I LIKE KUMI-CHAN TOO. NICE TO MEET YOU!
NICE TO MEET YOU. I'M RIMA FUJIO.
TAJIMA-KUN DOESN'T MEAN ANYTHING SPECIAL TO ME.
OH, REALLY?
NOPE.
YOU DON'T HAVE TO BE SO BLUNT ABOUT IT.
SO YOU DON'T CARE IF I TAKE HIM FROM YOU.
HE DOESN'T BELONG TO ME!

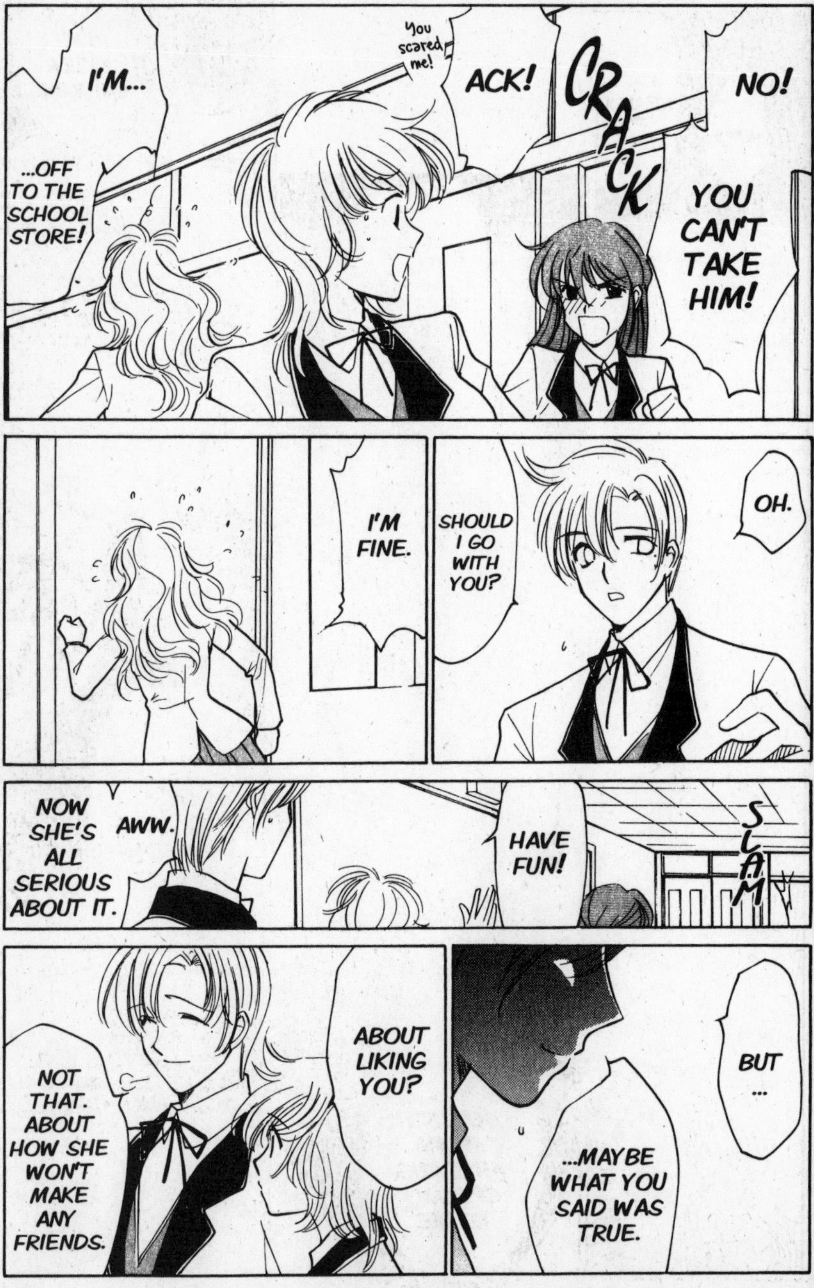
NO!
YOU CAN'T TAKE HIM!
CRACK
ACK!
You scared me!
I'M...
...OFF TO THE SCHOOL STORE!
OH.
SHOULD I GO WITH YOU?
I'M FINE.
SLAM
HAVE FUN!
AWW.
NOW SHE'S ALL SERIOUS ABOUT IT.
BUT ...
...MAYBE WHAT YOU SAID WAS TRUE.
ABOUT LIKING YOU?
NOT THAT. ABOUT HOW SHE WON'T MAKE ANY FRIENDS.

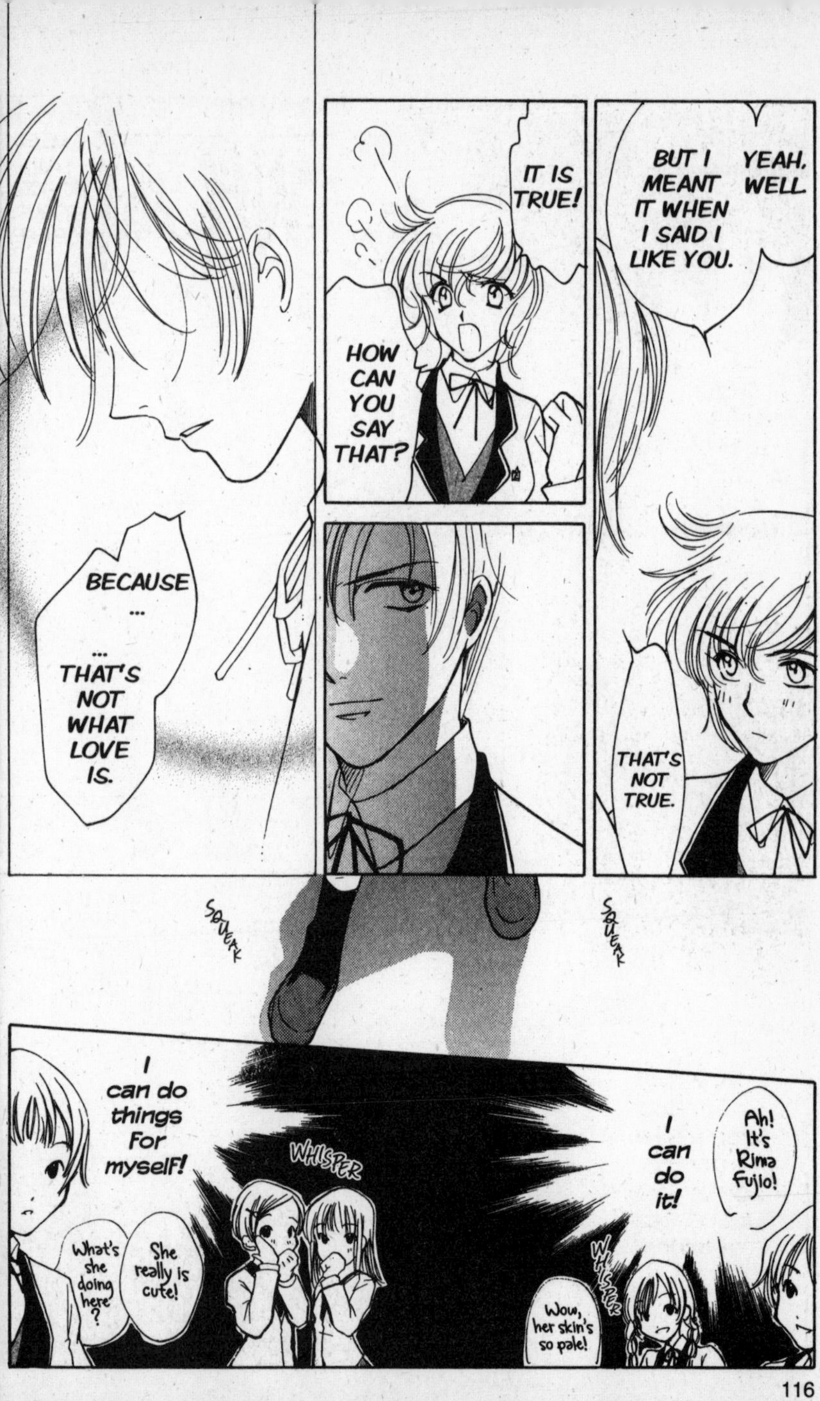
YEAH. WELL.
BUT I MEANT IT WHEN I SAID I LIKE YOU.
IT IS TRUE!
HOW CAN YOU SAY THAT?
THAT'S NOT TRUE.
BECAUSE ...
... THAT'S NOT WHAT LOVE IS.
SQUEAK
SQUEAK
Ah! It's Rima Fujio!
I can do it!
WHISPER
Wow, her skin's so pale!
WHISPER
She really is cute!
What's she doing here?
I can do things For myself!

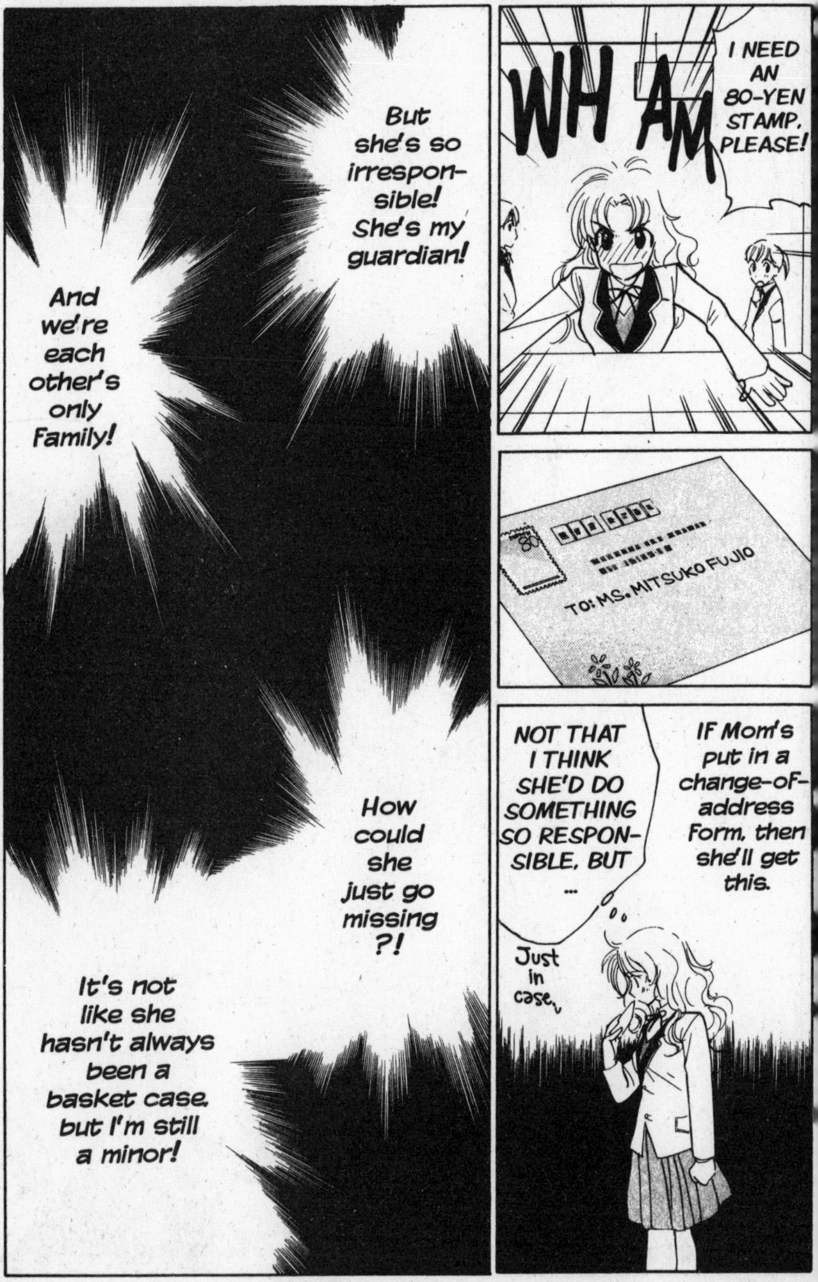
WHAM
I NEED AN 80-YEN STAMP, PLEASE!
80
TO: MS. MITSUKO FUJIO
IF Mom's put in a change-of-address form, then she'll get this.
NOT THAT I THINK SHE'D DO SOMETHING SO RESPONSIBLE, BUT ...
Just in case.
But she's so irresponsible! She's my guardian!
And we're each other's only family!
How could she just go missing?!
It's not like she hasn't always been a basket case, but I'm still a minor!

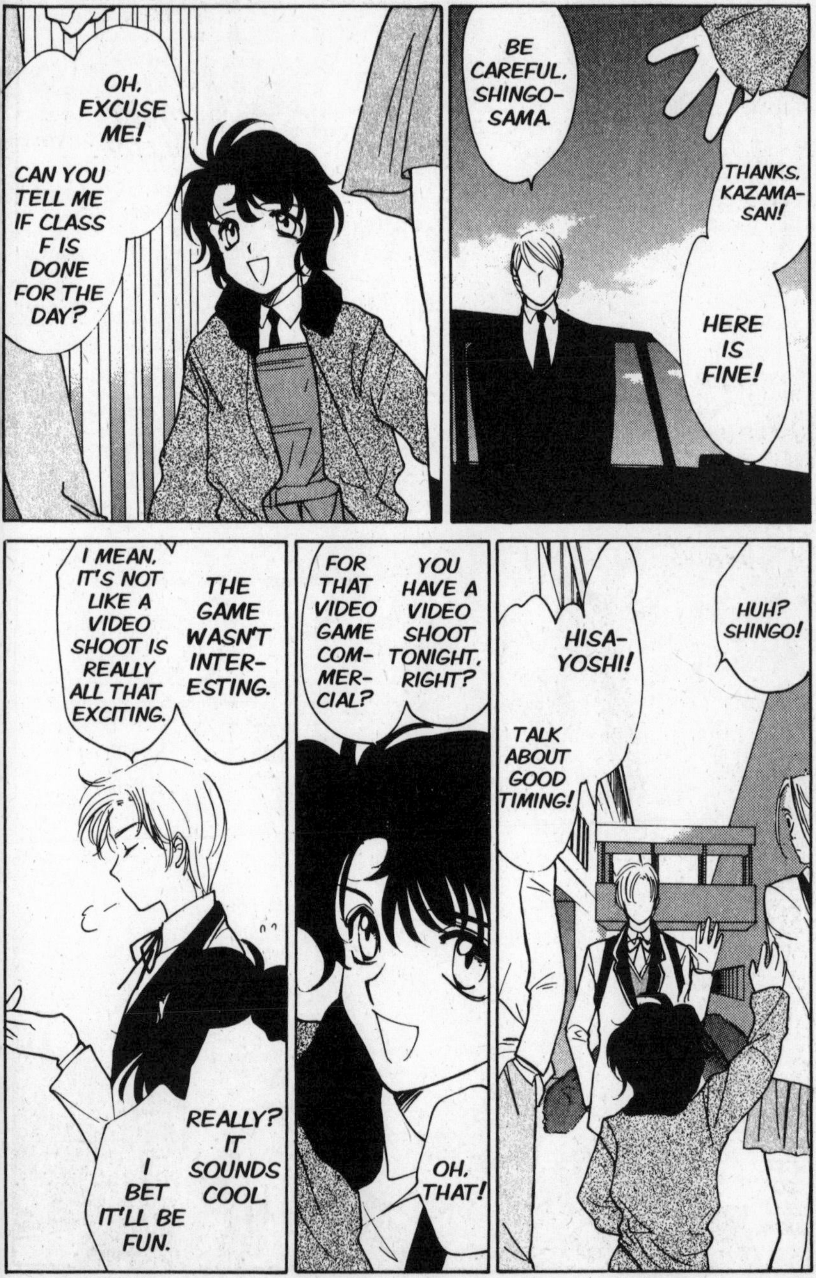
THANKS, KAZAMA-SAN!
HERE IS FINE!
BE CAREFUL, SHINGO-SAMA.
OH, EXCUSE ME!
CAN YOU TELL ME IF CLASS F IS DONE FOR THE DAY?
HUH? SHINGO!
HISA-YOSHI!
TALK ABOUT GOOD TIMING!
YOU HAVE A VIDEO SHOOT TONIGHT, RIGHT?
FOR THAT VIDEO GAME COM-MER-CIAL?
OH, THAT!
THE GAME WASN'T INTER-ESTING.
I MEAN, IT'S NOT LIKE A VIDEO SHOOT IS REALLY ALL THAT EXCITING.
REALLY? IT SOUNDS COOL.
I BET IT'LL BE FUN.

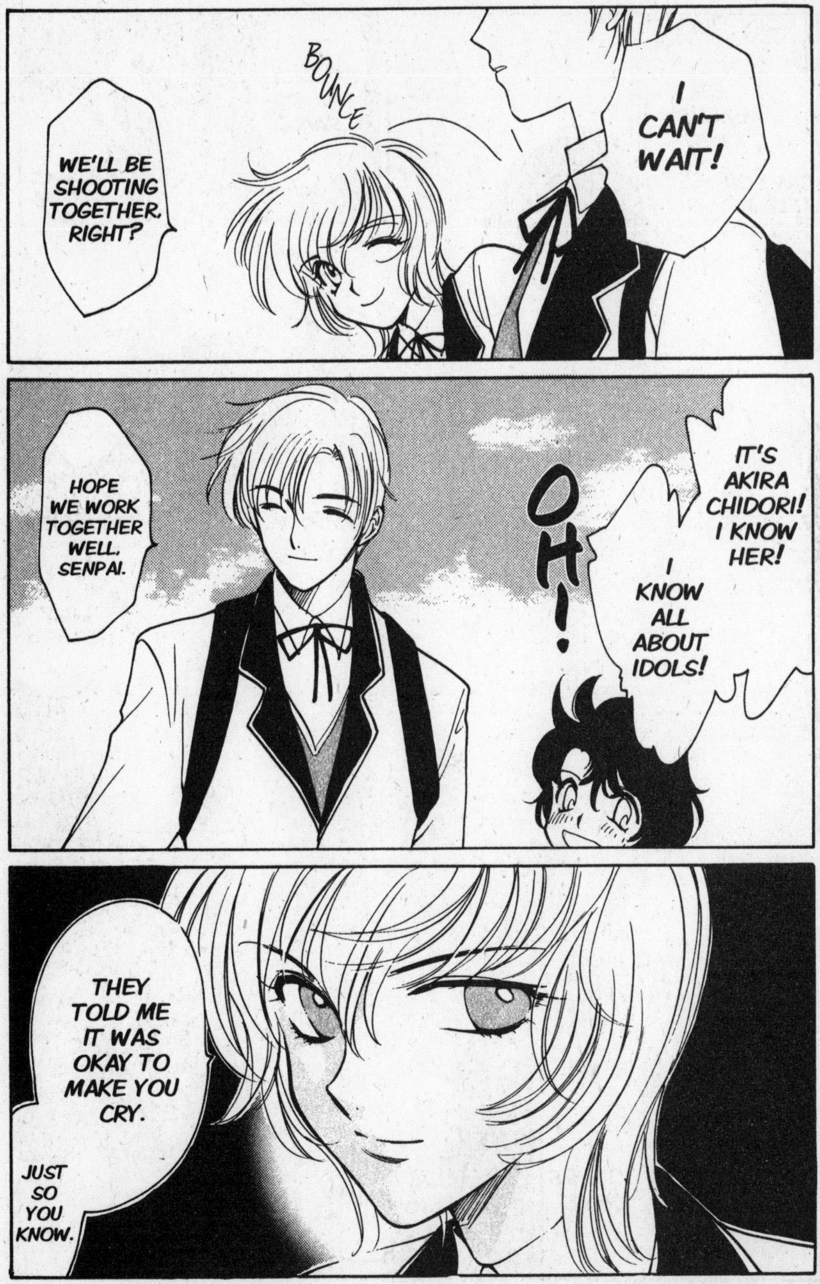
I CAN'T WAIT!
BOUNCE
WE'LL BE SHOOTING TOGETHER, RIGHT?
IT'S AKIRA CHIDORI! I KNOW HER!
I KNOW ALL ABOUT IDOLS!
OH!
HOPE WE WORK TOGETHER WELL, SENPAI.
THEY TOLD ME IT WAS OKAY TO MAKE YOU CRY.
JUST SO YOU KNOW.

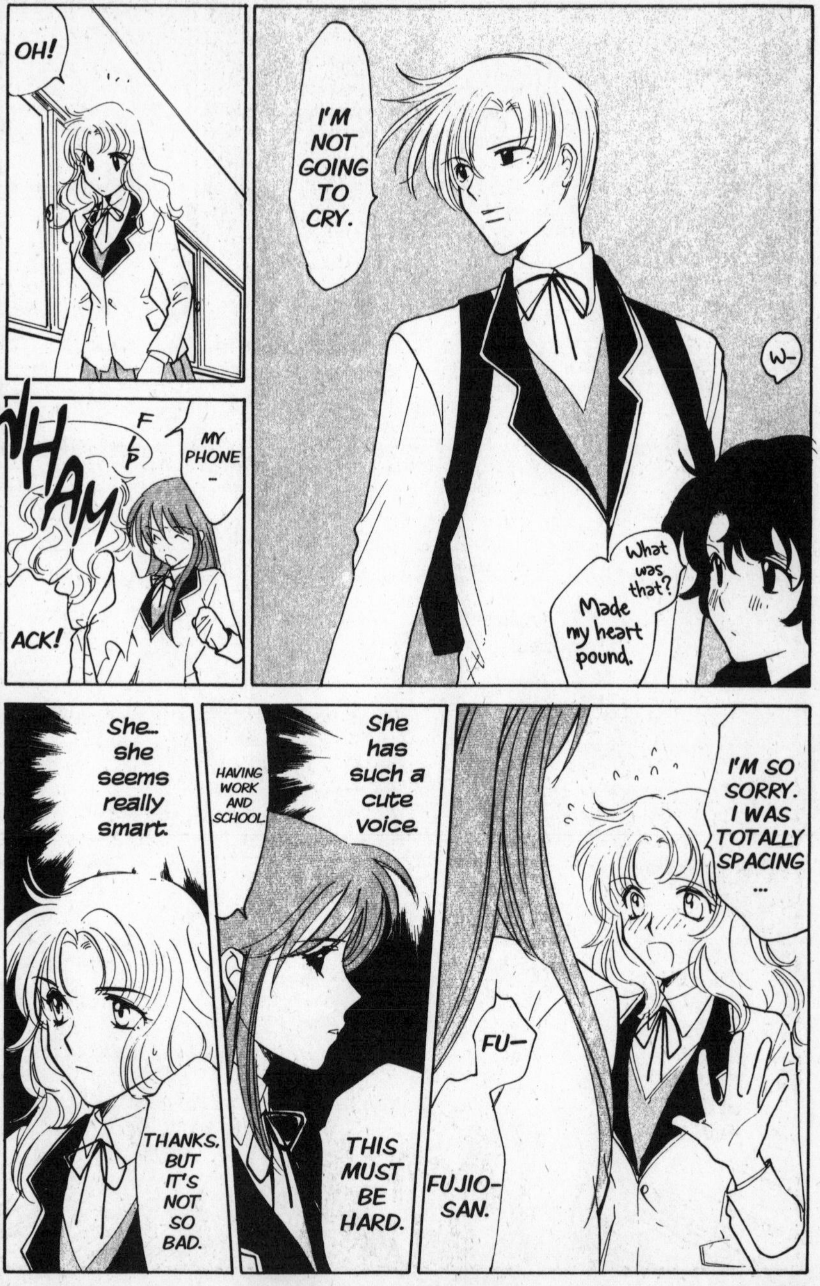
I'M NOT GOING TO CRY.
W–
What was that? Made my heart pound.
OH!
MY PHONE ...
FLP
WHAM
ACK!
I'M SO SORRY. I WAS TOTALLY SPACING ...
FU–
FUJIO-SAN.
She has such a cute voice.
HAVING WORK AND SCHOOL
THIS MUST BE HARD.
She... she seems really smart.
THANKS, BUT IT'S NOT SO BAD.

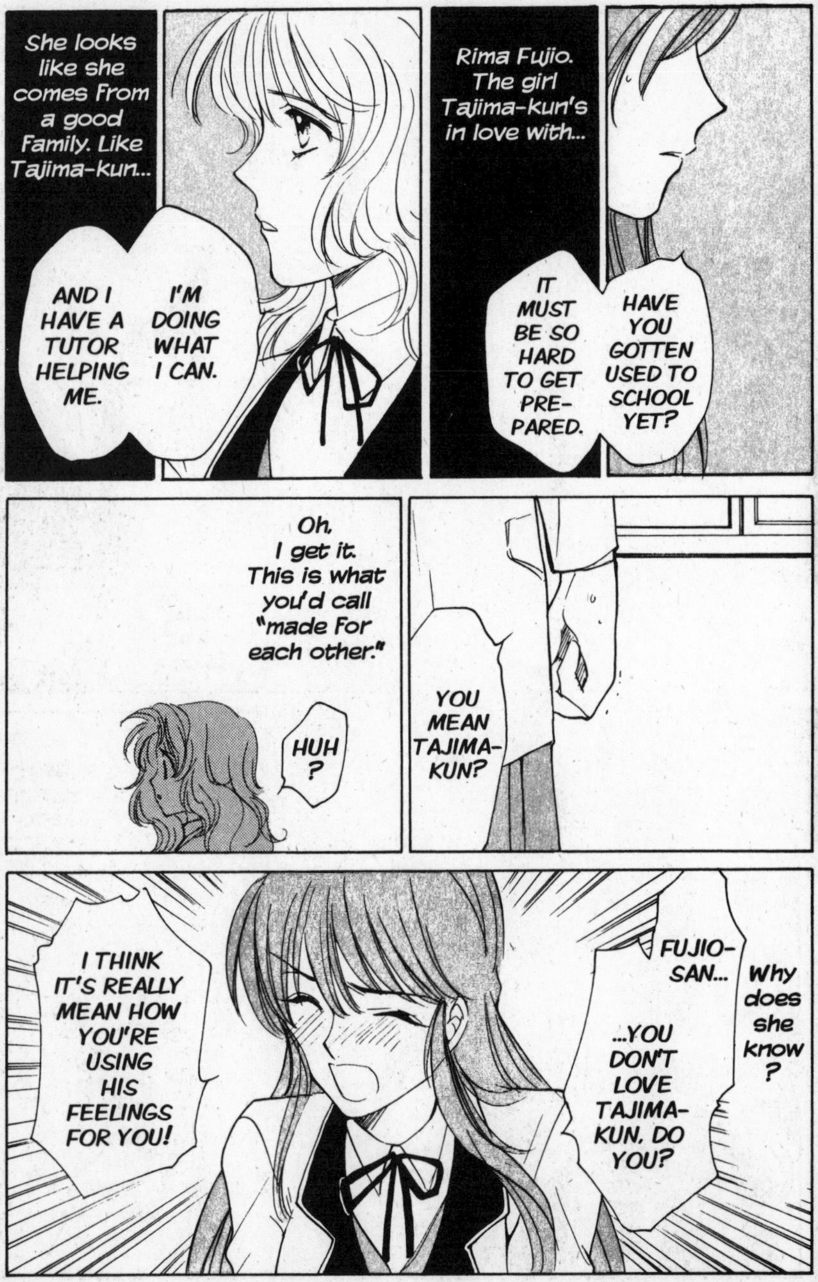
Rima Fujio. The girl Tajima-kun's in love with...
HAVE YOU GOTTEN USED TO SCHOOL YET?
IT MUST BE SO HARD TO GET PRE-PARED.
She looks like she comes from a good family. Like Tajima-kun...
I'M DOING WHAT I CAN.
AND I HAVE A TUTOR HELPING ME.
YOU MEAN TAJIMA-KUN?
Oh, I get it. This is what you'd call "made for each other."
HUH?
FUJIO-SAN...
...YOU DON'T LOVE TAJIMA-KUN, DO YOU?
Why does she know?
I THINK IT'S REALLY MEAN HOW YOU'RE USING HIS FEELINGS FOR YOU!

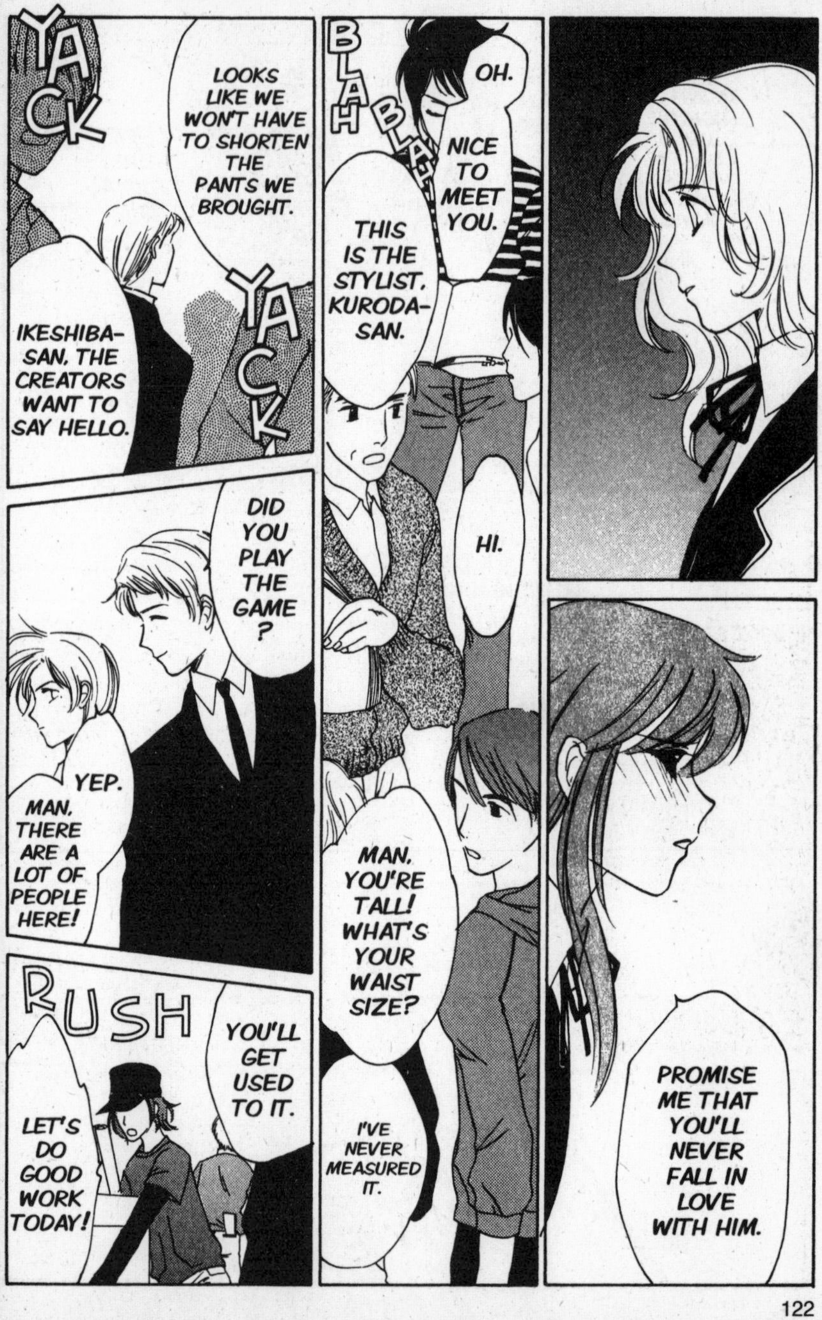
PROMISE ME THAT YOU'LL NEVER FALL IN LOVE WITH HIM.
BLAH
BLAH
OH.
NICE TO MEET YOU.
THIS IS THE STYLIST, KURODA-SAN.
HI.
MAN, YOU'RE TALL! WHAT'S YOUR WAIST SIZE?
I'VE NEVER MEASURED IT.
YACK
LOOKS LIKE WE WON'T HAVE TO SHORTEN THE PANTS WE BROUGHT.
YACK
IKESHIBA-SAN, THE CREATORS WANT TO SAY HELLO.
DID YOU PLAY THE GAME?
YEP. MAN, THERE ARE A LOT OF PEOPLE HERE!
RUSH
YOU'LL GET USED TO IT.
LET'S DO GOOD WORK TODAY!

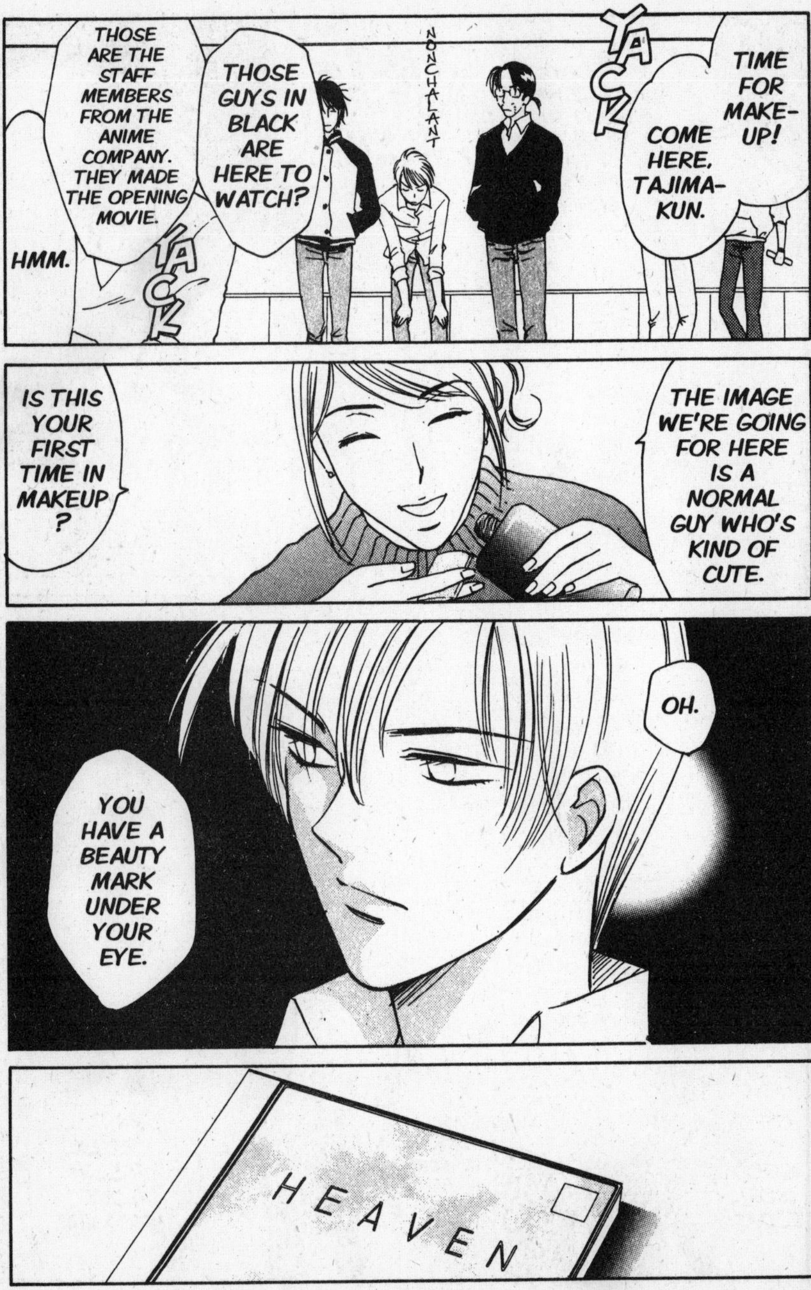
TIME FOR MAKE-UP!
COME HERE, TAJIMA-KUN.
YACK
NONCHALANT
THOSE GUYS IN BLACK ARE HERE TO WATCH?
THOSE ARE THE STAFF MEMBERS FROM THE ANIME COMPANY. THEY MADE THE OPENING MOVIE.
HMM.
YACK
THE IMAGE WE'RE GOING FOR HERE IS A NORMAL GUY WHO'S KIND OF CUTE.
IS THIS YOUR FIRST TIME IN MAKEUP?
OH.
YOU HAVE A BEAUTY MARK UNDER YOUR EYE.
HEAVEN

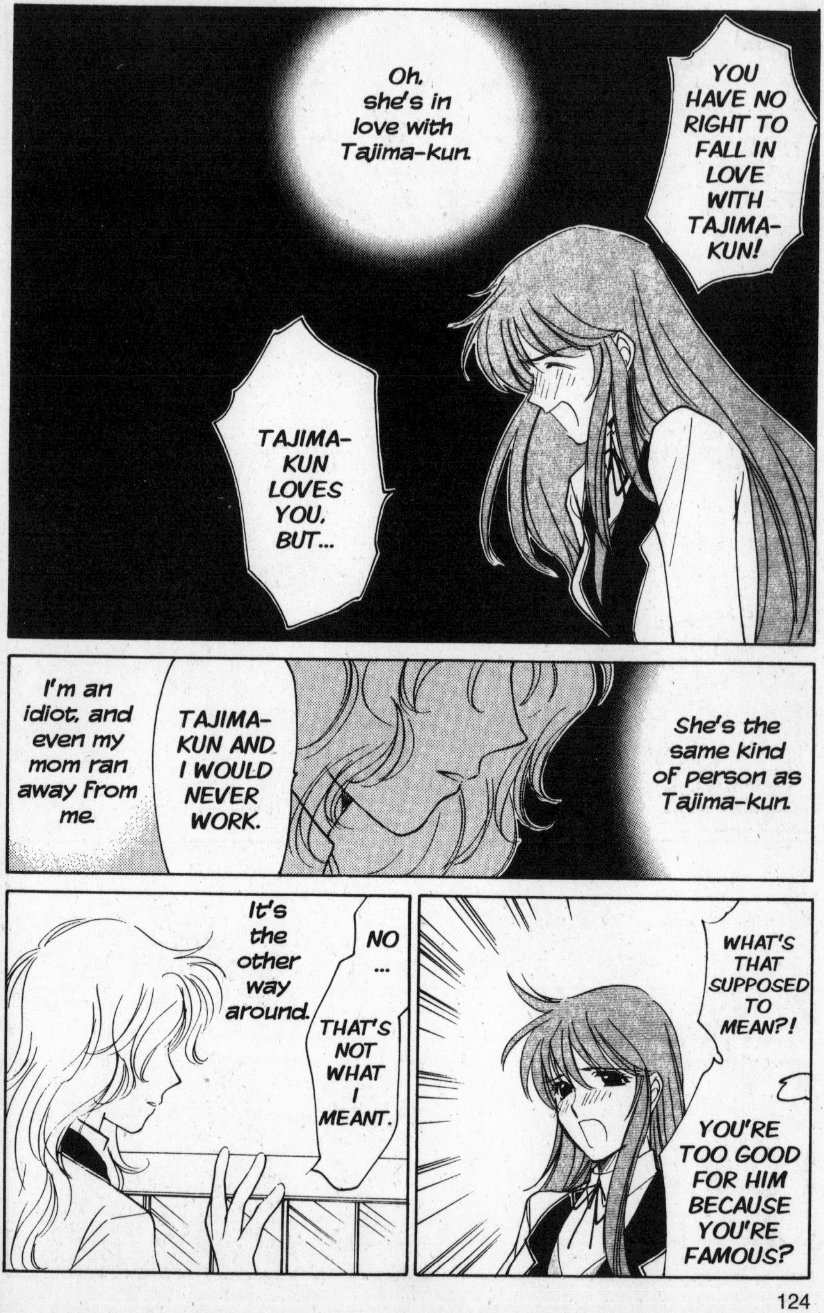
YOU HAVE NO RIGHT TO FALL IN LOVE WITH TAJIMA-KUN!
Oh, she's in love with Tajima-kun.
TAJIMA-KUN LOVES YOU, BUT...
She's the same kind of person as Tajima-kun.
TAJIMA-KUN AND I WOULD NEVER WORK.
I'm an idiot, and even my mom ran away from me.
WHAT'S THAT SUPPOSED TO MEAN?!
YOU'RE TOO GOOD FOR HIM BECAUSE YOU'RE FAMOUS?
NO ...
THAT'S NOT WHAT I MEANT.
It's the other way around.

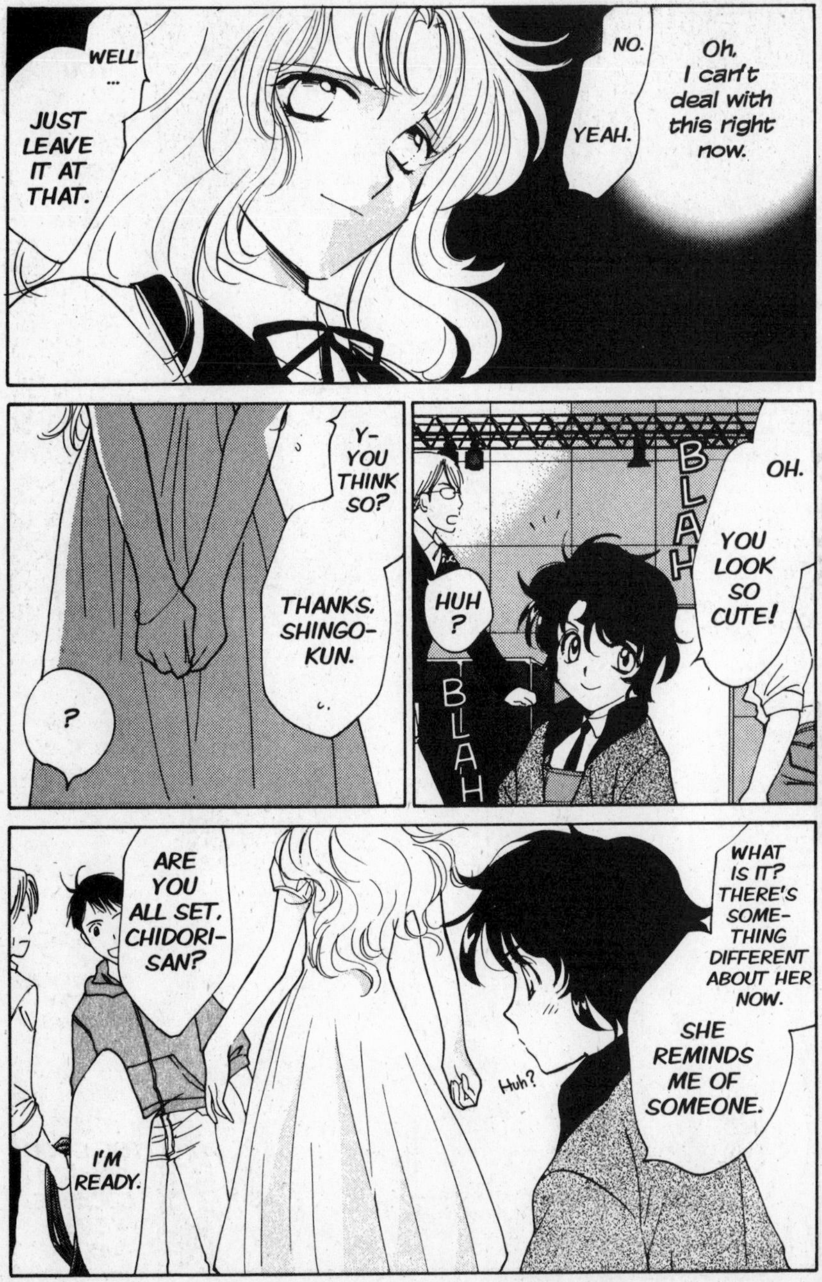
Oh, I can't deal with this right now.
NO.
YEAH.
WELL ... JUST LEAVE IT AT THAT.
OH.
YOU LOOK SO CUTE!
BLAH
HUH?
BLAH
Y-YOU THINK SO?
THANKS, SHINGO-KUN.
?
WHAT IS IT? THERE'S SOME-THING DIFFERENT ABOUT HER NOW.
SHE REMINDS ME OF SOMEONE.
Huh?
ARE YOU ALL SET, CHIDORI-SAN?
I'M READY.

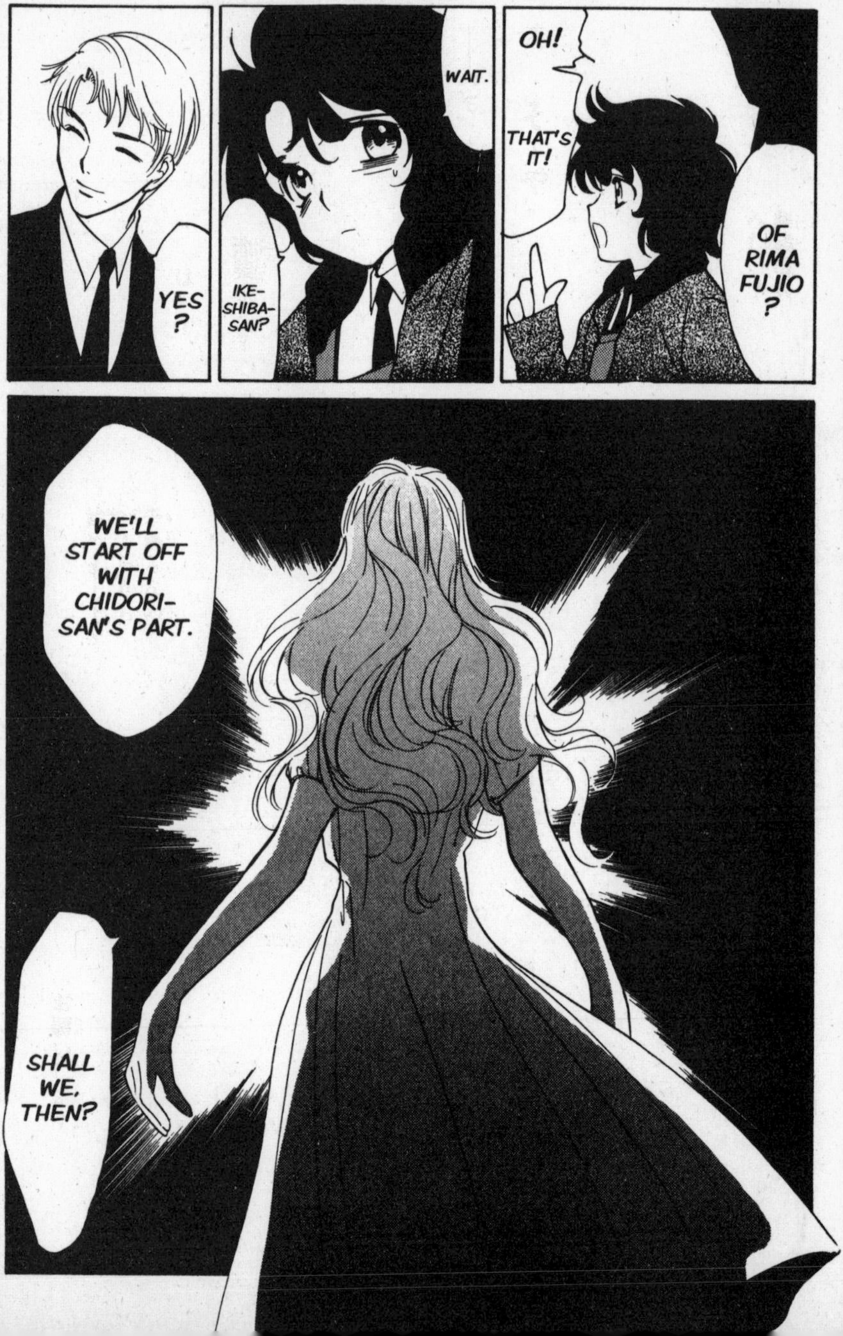
OF RIMA FUJIO?
OH!
THAT'S IT!
WAIT.
IKE-SHIBA-SAN?
YES?
WE'LL START OFF WITH CHIDORI-SAN'S PART.
SHALL WE, THEN?

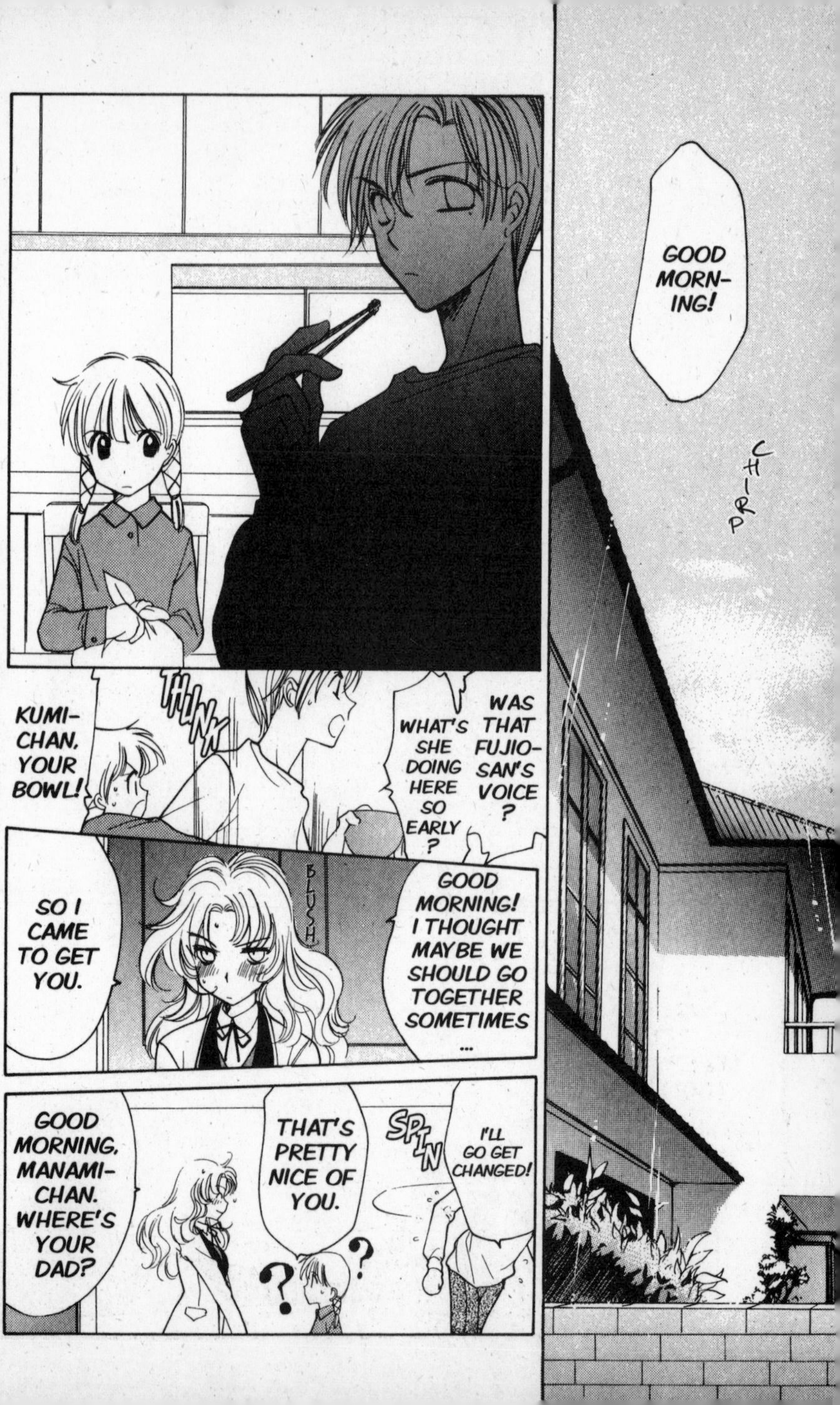
GOOD MORNING!
CHIRP
WAS THAT FUJIO-SAN'S VOICE?
WHAT'S SHE DOING HERE SO EARLY?
THINK
KUMI-CHAN, YOUR BOWL!
GOOD MORNING! I THOUGHT MAYBE WE SHOULD GO TOGETHER SOMETIMES...
BLUSH
SO I CAME TO GET YOU.
I'LL GO GET CHANGED!
SPIN
THAT'S PRETTY NICE OF YOU.
GOOD MORNING, MANAMI-CHAN. WHERE'S YOUR DAD?

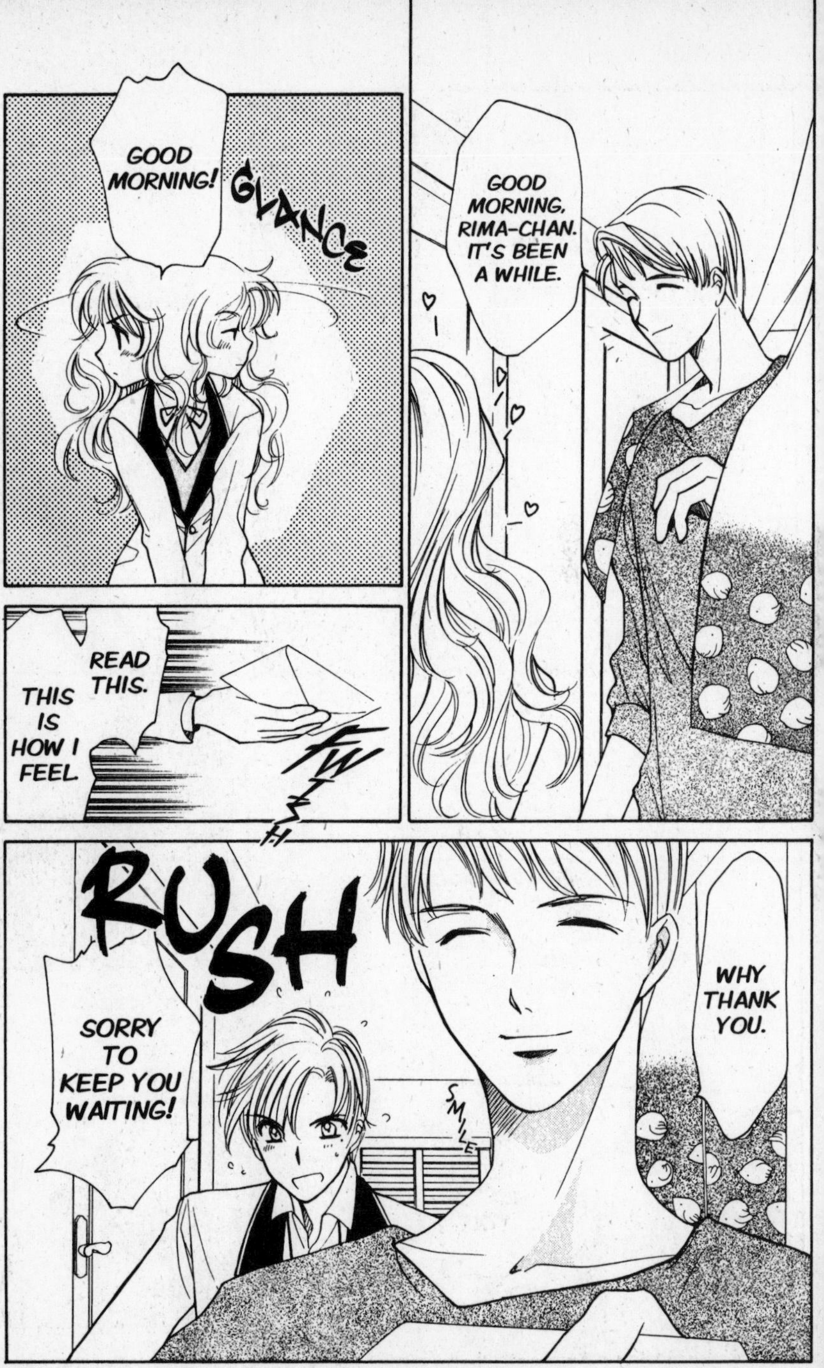
GOOD MORNING, RIMA-CHAN. IT'S BEEN A WHILE.
GOOD MORNING!
GLANCE
READ THIS.
THIS IS HOW I FEEL.
FWISH
WHY THANK YOU.
RUSH
SMILE
SORRY TO KEEP YOU WAITING!

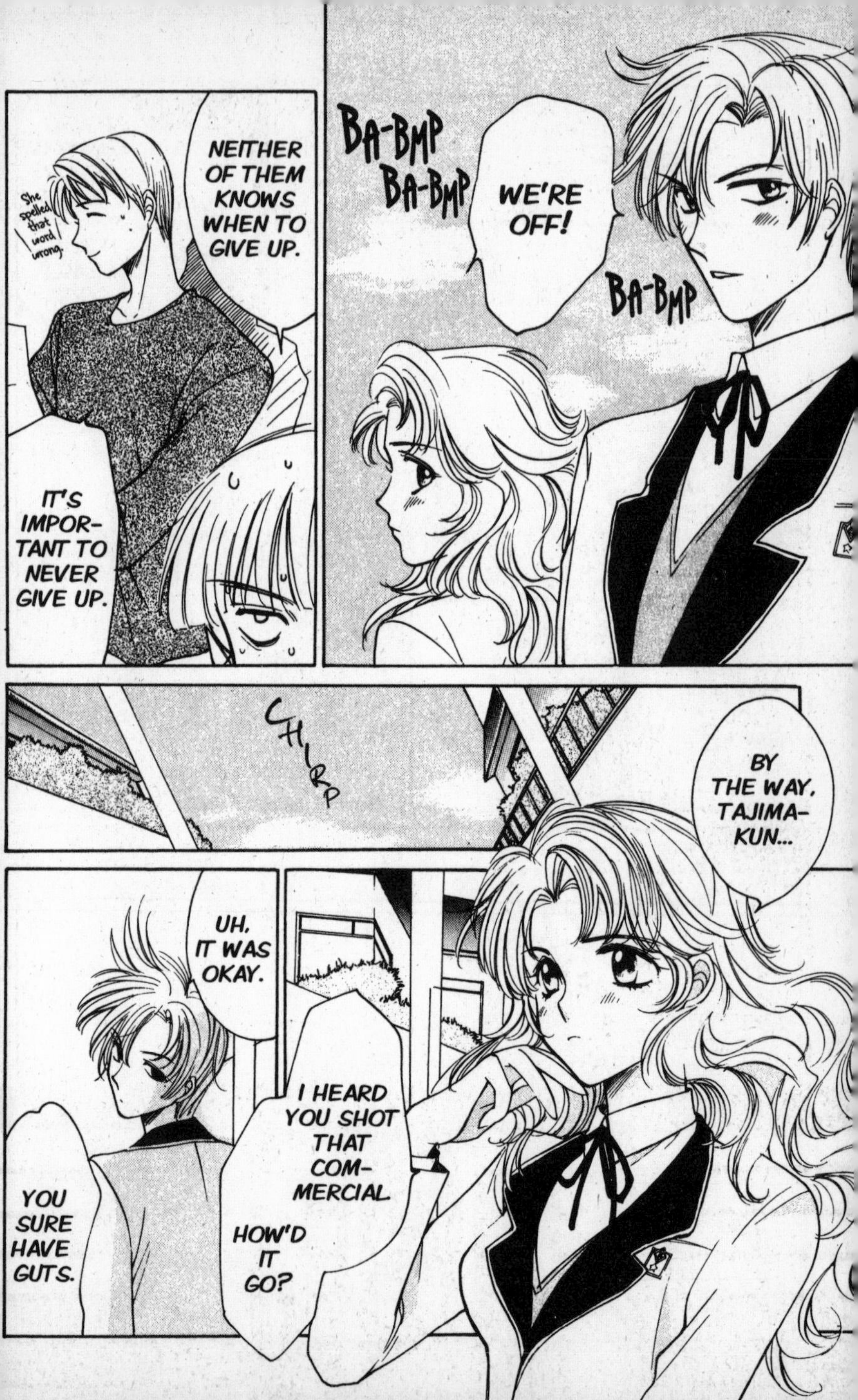
BA-BMP
BA-BMP
WE'RE OFF!
BA-BMP
NEITHER OF THEM KNOWS WHEN TO GIVE UP.
She spelled that word wrong.
IT'S IMPOR-TANT TO NEVER GIVE UP.
BY THE WAY, TAJIMA-KUN...
I HEARD YOU SHOT THAT COM-MERCIAL
HOW'D IT GO?
CHIRP
UH. IT WAS OKAY.
YOU SURE HAVE GUTS.

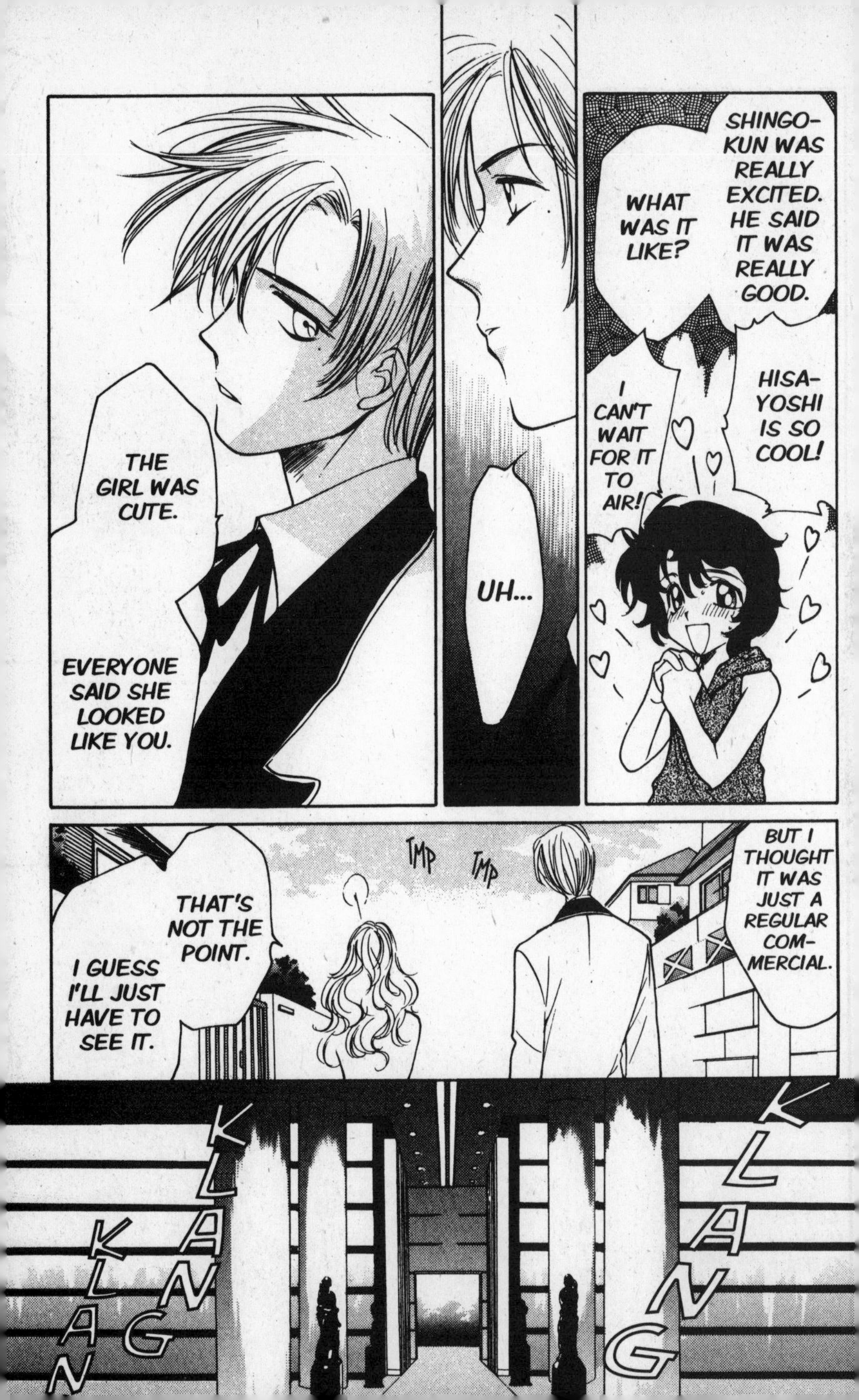
SHINGO-KUN WAS REALLY EXCITED. HE SAID IT WAS REALLY GOOD.
WHAT WAS IT LIKE?
HISA-YOSHI IS SO COOL!
I CAN'T WAIT FOR IT TO AIR!
UH...
THE GIRL WAS CUTE.
EVERYONE SAID SHE LOOKED LIKE YOU.
BUT I THOUGHT IT WAS JUST A REGULAR COM-MERCIAL.
TMP
TMP
THAT'S NOT THE POINT.
I GUESS I'LL JUST HAVE TO SEE IT.
KLANG
KLANG
KLANG

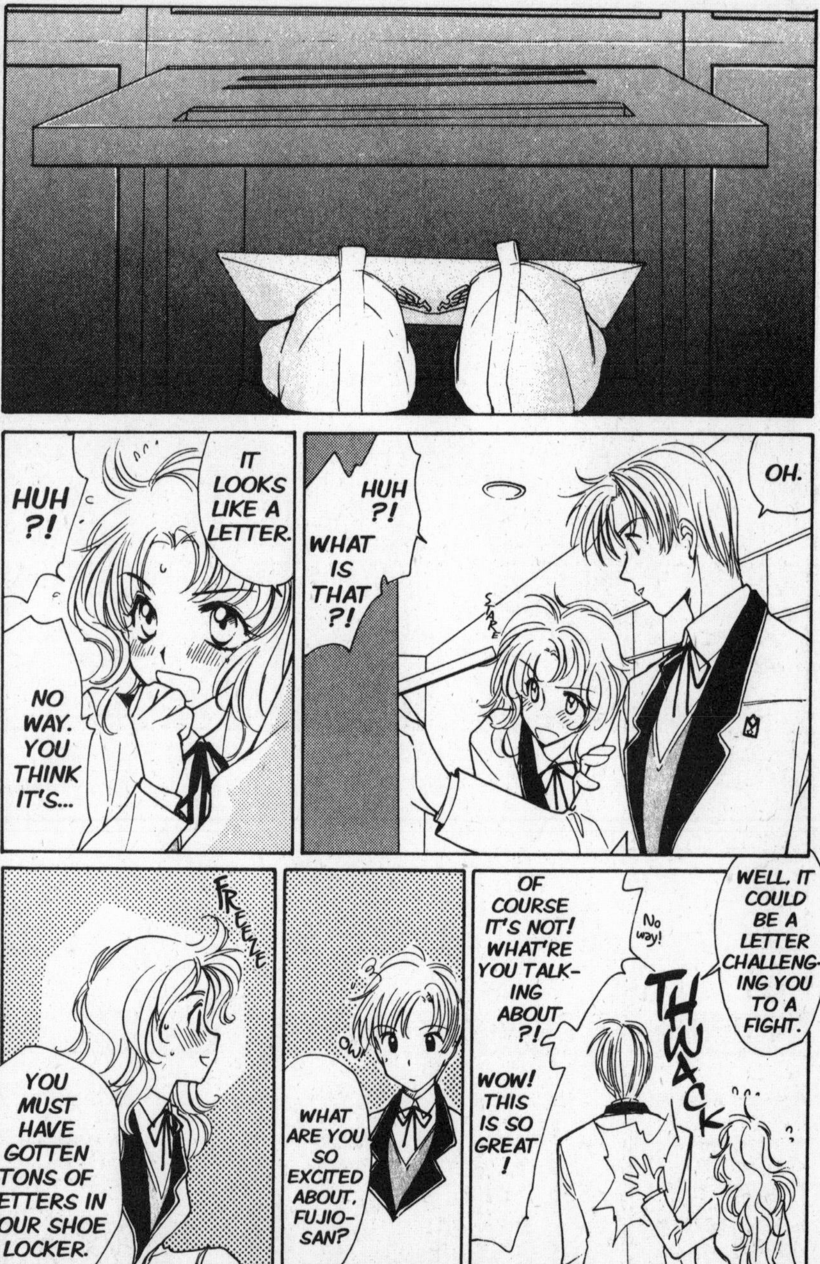
OH.
STARE
HUH ?! WHAT IS THAT ?!
IT LOOKS LIKE A LETTER.
HUH ?!
NO WAY. YOU THINK IT'S...
WELL. IT COULD BE A LETTER CHALLENG-ING YOU TO A FIGHT.
No way!
OF COURSE IT'S NOT! WHAT'RE YOU TALK-ING ABOUT ?!
THWACK
WOW! THIS IS SO GREAT !
OW!
WHAT ARE YOU SO EXCITED ABOUT, FUJIO-SAN?
FREEZE
YOU MUST HAVE GOTTEN TONS OF LETTERS IN YOUR SHOE LOCKER.

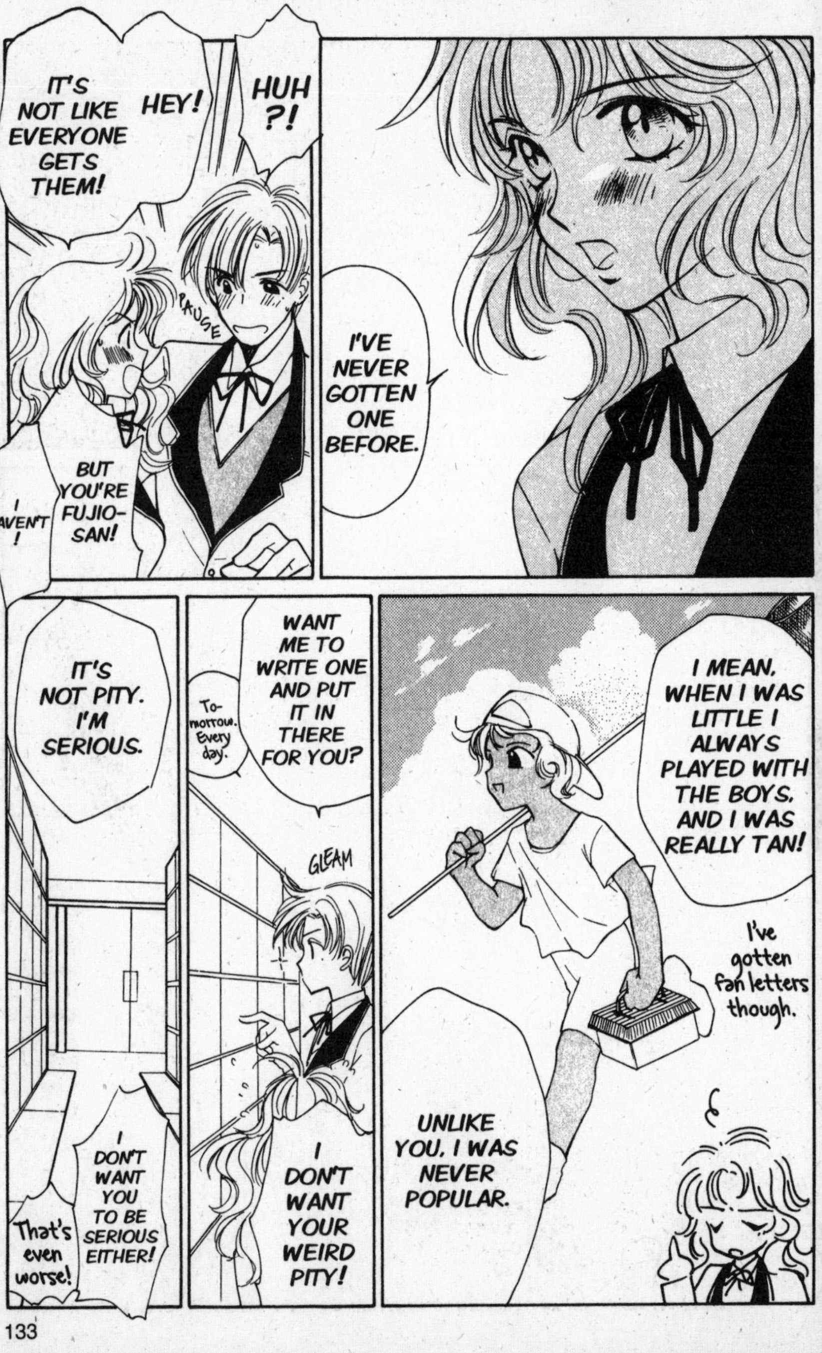
I'VE NEVER GOTTEN ONE BEFORE.
HUH?!
HEY!
IT'S NOT LIKE EVERYONE GETS THEM!
PAUSE
BUT YOU'RE FUJIO-SAN!
I HAVEN'T!
I MEAN, WHEN I WAS LITTLE I ALWAYS PLAYED WITH THE BOYS, AND I WAS REALLY TAN!
I've gotten fan letters though.
UNLIKE YOU, I WAS NEVER POPULAR.
WANT ME TO WRITE ONE AND PUT IT IN THERE FOR YOU?
To-morrow. Every day.
GLEAM
I DON'T WANT YOUR WEIRD PITY!
IT'S NOT PITY. I'M SERIOUS.
I DON'T WANT YOU TO BE SERIOUS EITHER!
That's even worse!

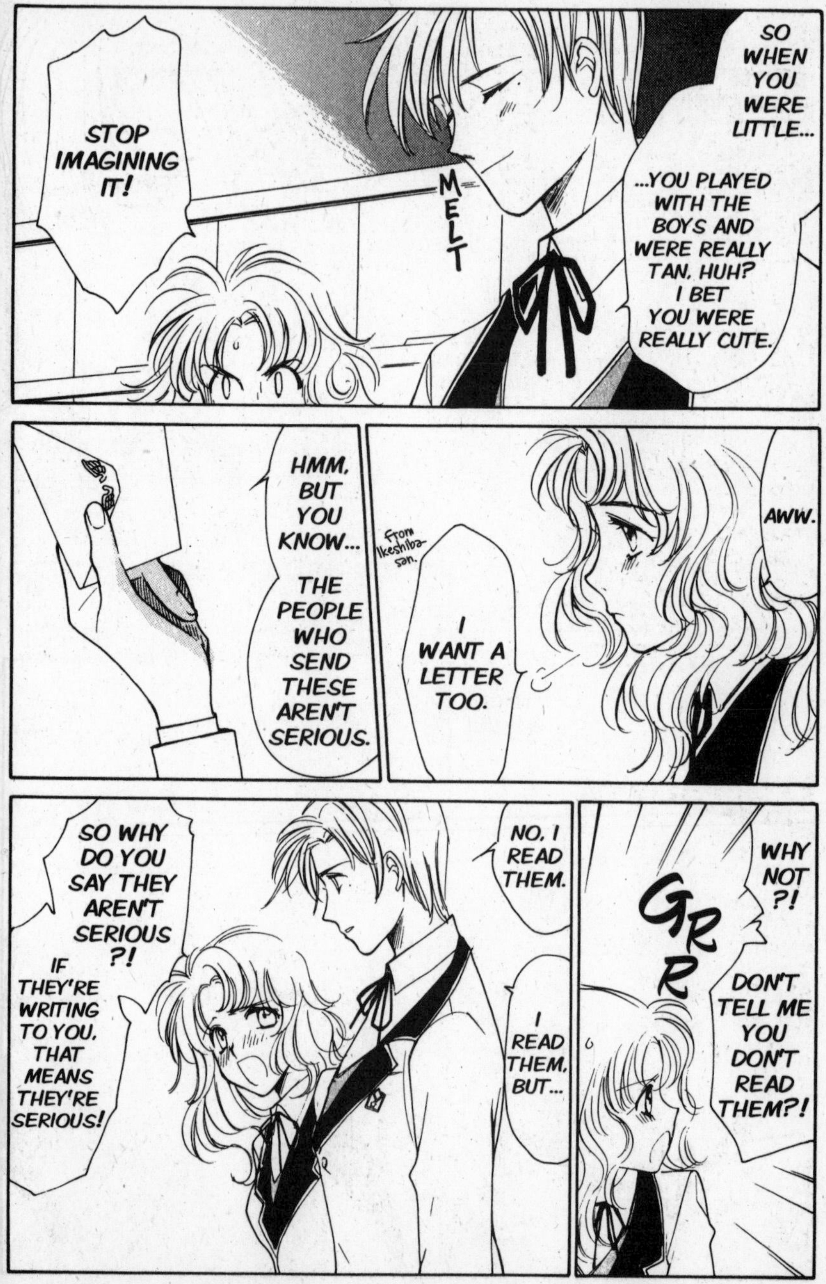
SO WHEN YOU WERE LITTLE...
...YOU PLAYED WITH THE BOYS AND WERE REALLY TAN, HUH? I BET YOU WERE REALLY CUTE.
MELT
STOP IMAGINING IT!
AWW.
I WANT A LETTER TOO.
from Ikeshiba-san.
HMM, BUT YOU KNOW...
THE PEOPLE WHO SEND THESE AREN'T SERIOUS.
WHY NOT?!
GRR
DON'T TELL ME YOU DON'T READ THEM?!
NO, I READ THEM.
I READ THEM, BUT...
SO WHY DO YOU SAY THEY AREN'T SERIOUS?!
IF THEY'RE WRITING TO YOU, THAT MEANS THEY'RE SERIOUS!

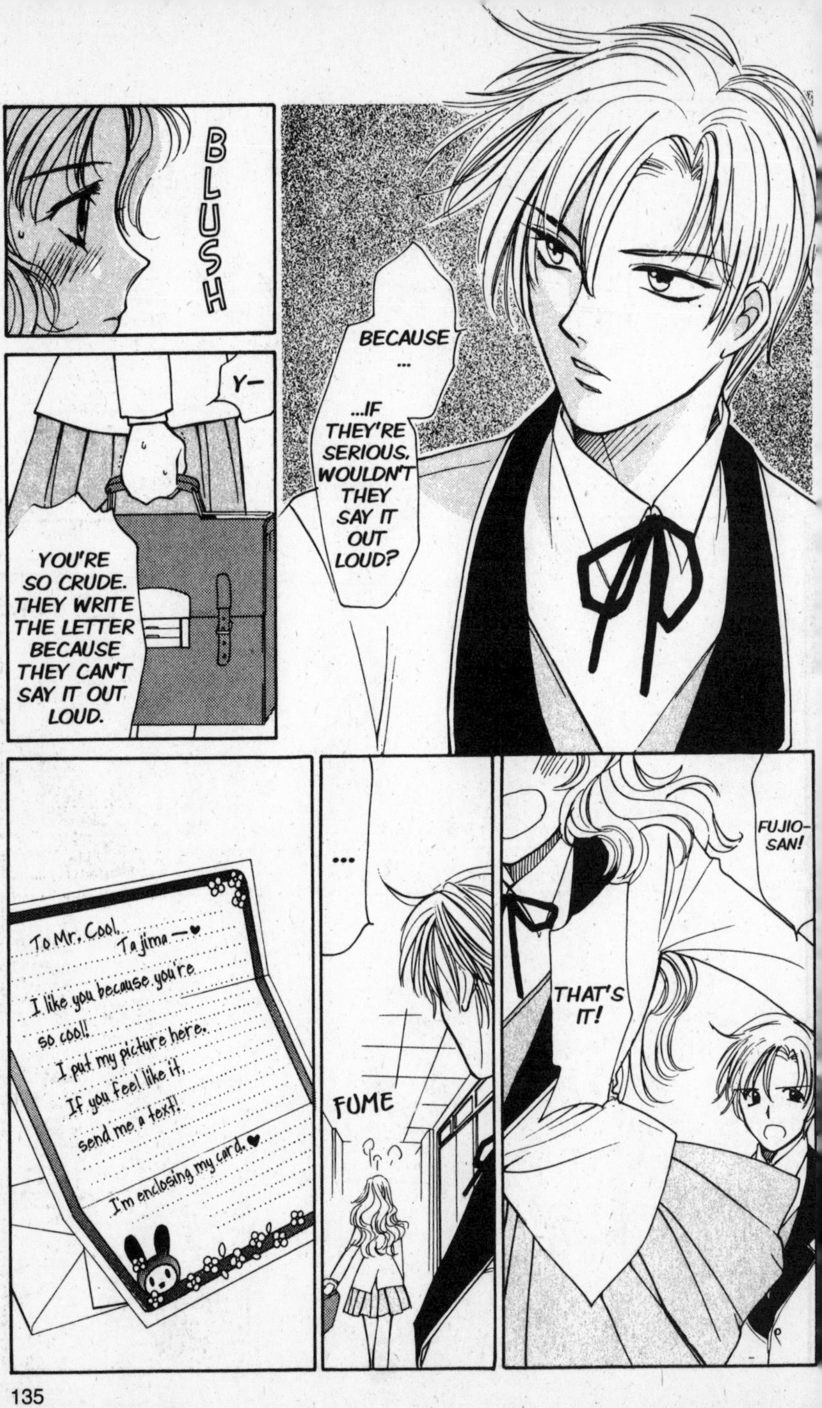
BECAUSE ...
...IF THEY'RE SERIOUS, WOULDN'T THEY SAY IT OUT LOUD?
BLUSH
Y-
YOU'RE SO CRUDE. THEY WRITE THE LETTER BECAUSE THEY CAN'T SAY IT OUT LOUD.
FUJIO-SAN!
THAT'S IT!
...
FUME
To Mr. Cool, Tajima—♥
I like you because you're so cool!
I put my picture here.
If you feel like it, send me a text!
I'm enclosing my card.♥

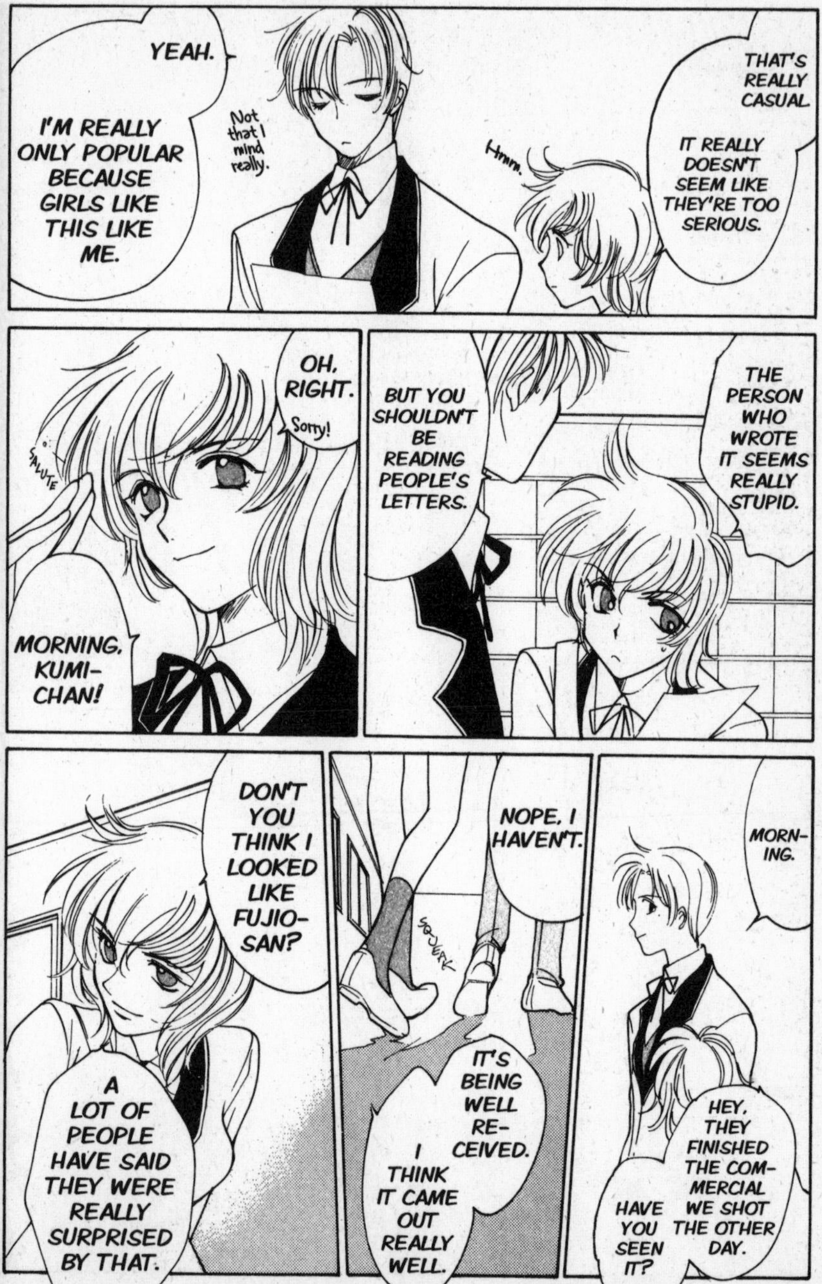
THAT'S REALLY CASUAL
IT REALLY DOESN'T SEEM LIKE THEY'RE TOO SERIOUS.
Hmm.
YEAH.
Not that I mind really.
I'M REALLY ONLY POPULAR BECAUSE GIRLS LIKE THIS LIKE ME.
THE PERSON WHO WROTE IT SEEMS REALLY STUPID.
BUT YOU SHOULDN'T BE READING PEOPLE'S LETTERS.
OH, RIGHT.
Sorry!
SALUTE
MORNING, KUMI-CHAN!
MORNING.
HEY, THEY FINISHED THE COMMERCIAL WE SHOT THE OTHER DAY.
HAVE YOU SEEN IT?
NOPE, I HAVEN'T.
SQUEAK
IT'S BEING WELL RE-CEIVED.
I THINK IT CAME OUT REALLY WELL.
DON'T YOU THINK I LOOKED LIKE FUJIO-SAN?
A LOT OF PEOPLE HAVE SAID THEY WERE REALLY SURPRISED BY THAT.

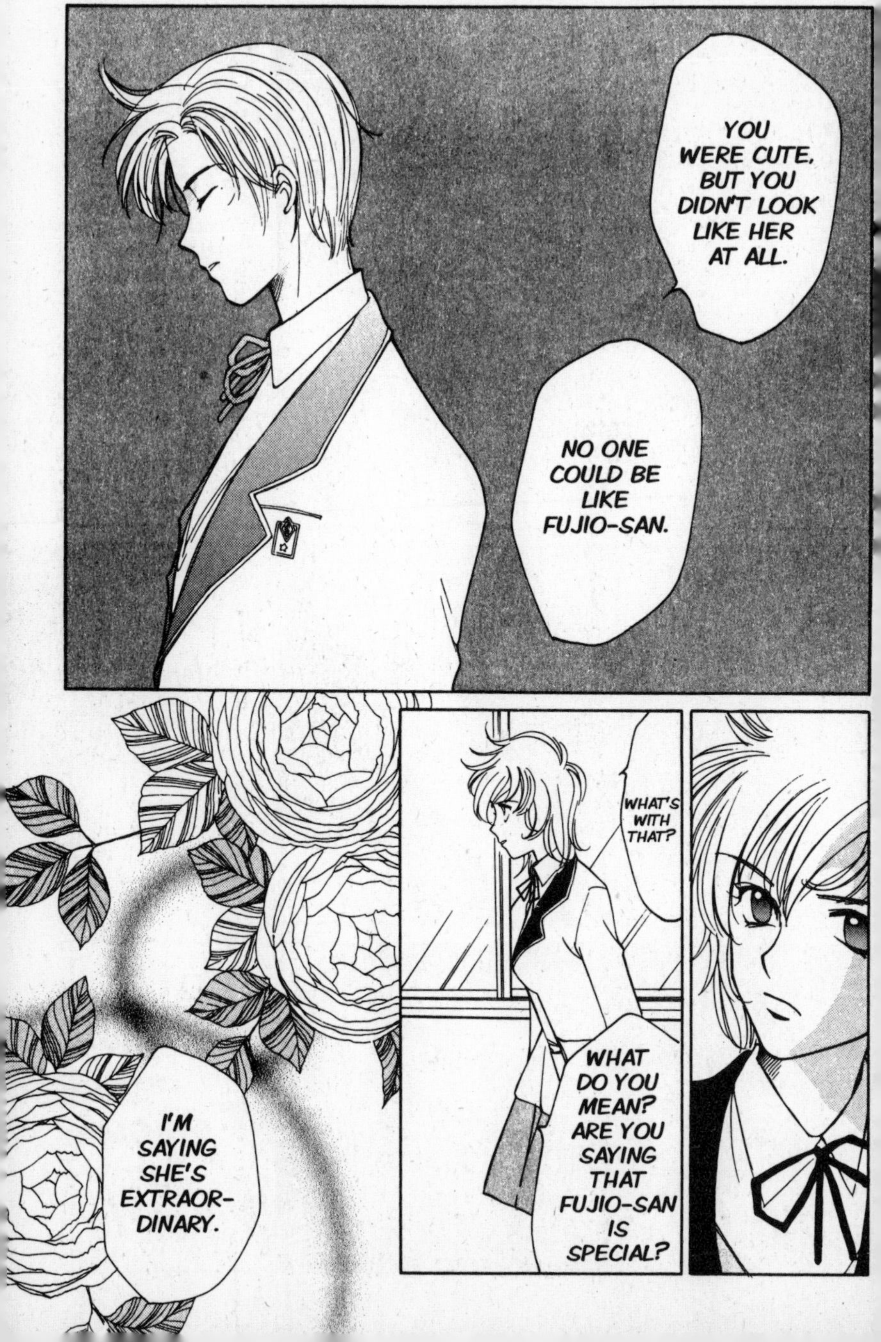
YOU WERE CUTE, BUT YOU DIDN'T LOOK LIKE HER AT ALL.
NO ONE COULD BE LIKE FUJIO-SAN.
WHAT'S WITH THAT?
WHAT DO YOU MEAN? ARE YOU SAYING THAT FUJIO-SAN IS SPECIAL?
I'M SAYING SHE'S EXTRAOR-DINARY.

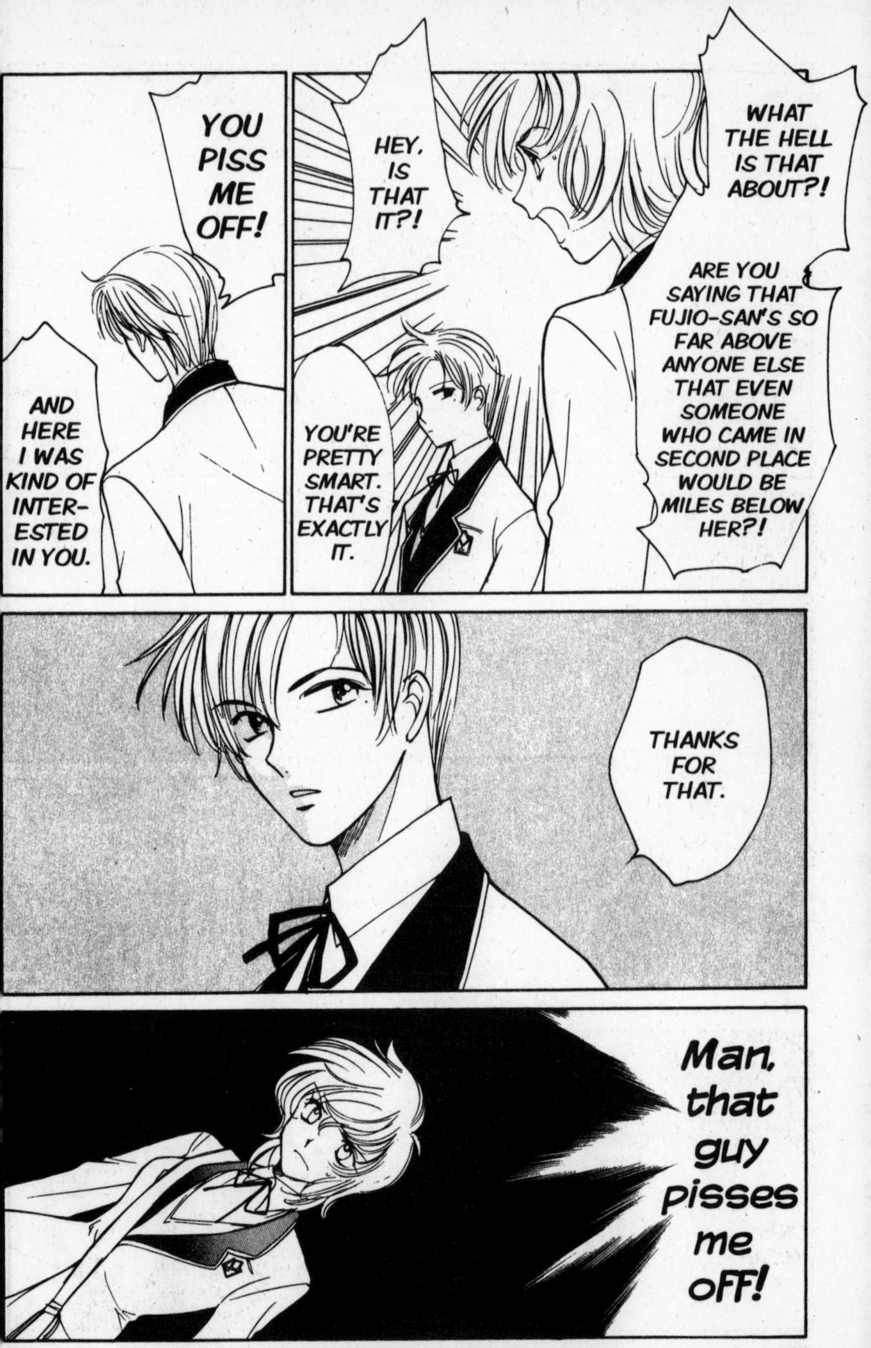
WHAT THE HELL IS THAT ABOUT?!
ARE YOU SAYING THAT FUJIO-SAN'S SO FAR ABOVE ANYONE ELSE THAT EVEN SOMEONE WHO CAME IN SECOND PLACE WOULD BE MILES BELOW HER?!
HEY, IS THAT IT?!
YOU'RE PRETTY SMART. THAT'S EXACTLY IT.
YOU PISS ME OFF!
AND HERE I WAS KIND OF INTER-ESTED IN YOU.
THANKS FOR THAT.
Man, that guy pisses me off!

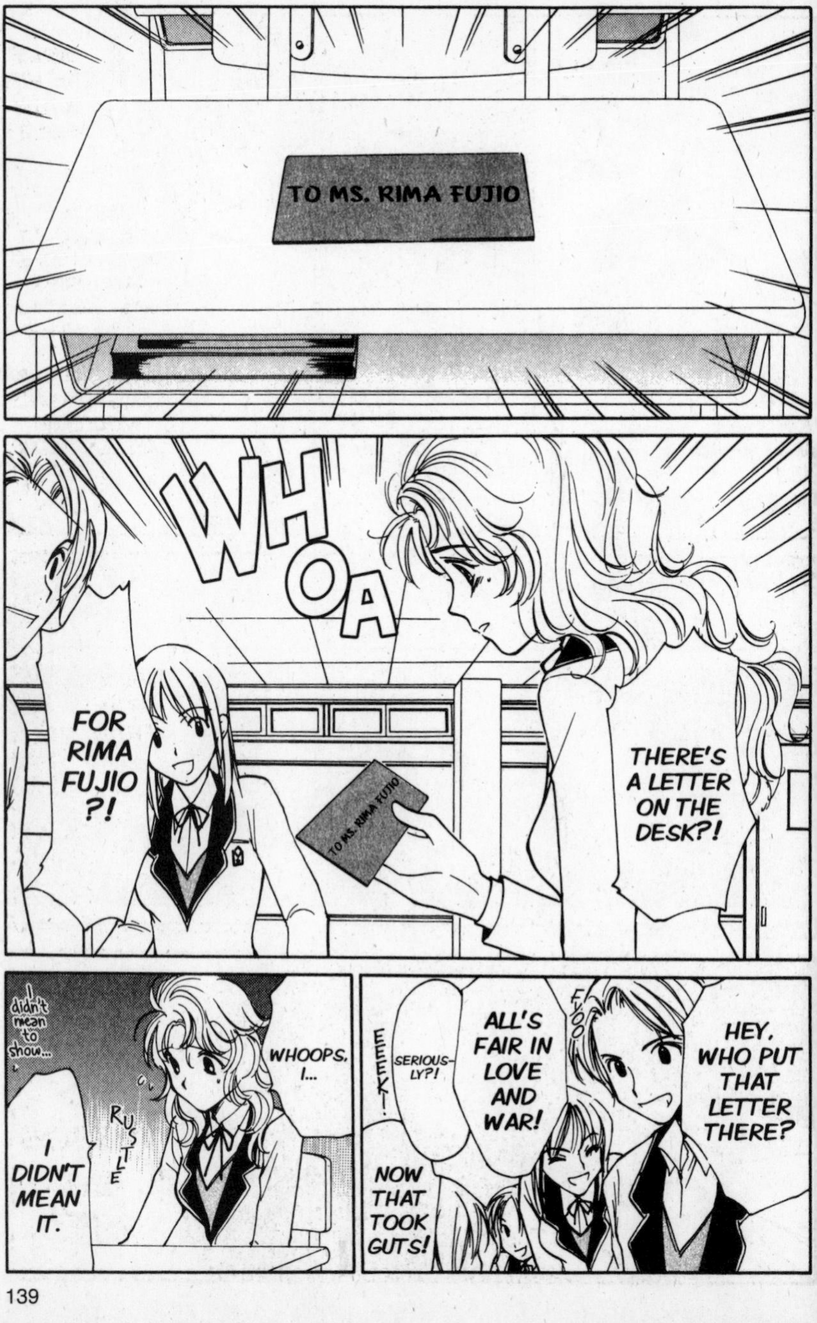
TO MS. RIMA FUJIO
WHOA
THERE'S A LETTER ON THE DESK?!
FOR RIMA FUJIO?!
TO MS. RIMA FUJIO
HEY, WHO PUT THAT LETTER THERE?
FYOO
ALL'S FAIR IN LOVE AND WAR!
SERIOUS-LY?!
EEEK!
NOW THAT TOOK GUTS!
WHOOPS, I...
I didn't mean to show...
RUSTLE
I DIDN'T MEAN IT.

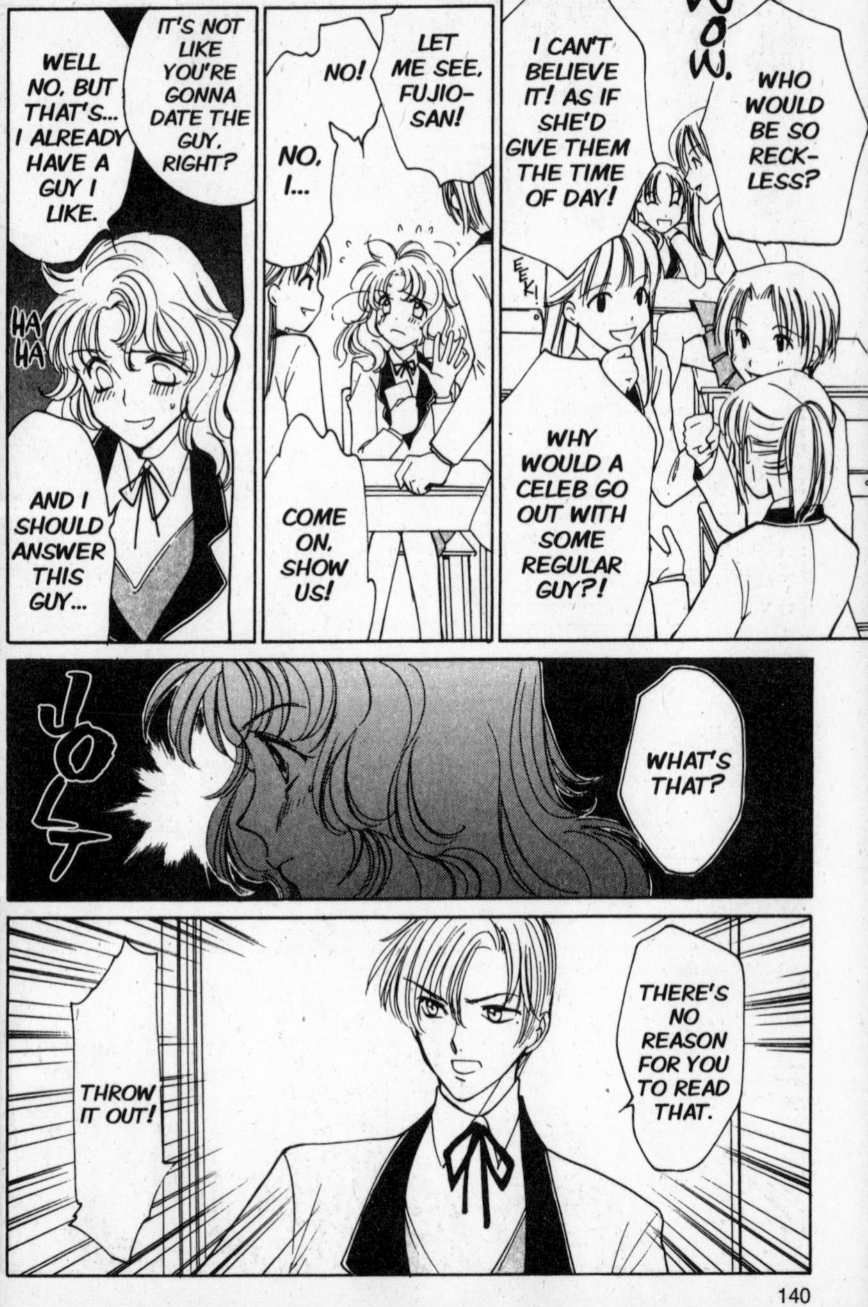
WOW.
WHO WOULD BE SO RECKLESS?
I CAN'T BELIEVE IT! AS IF SHE'D GIVE THEM THE TIME OF DAY!
EEK!
WHY WOULD A CELEB GO OUT WITH SOME REGULAR GUY?!
LET ME SEE, FUJIO-SAN!
NO!
NO, I...
COME ON, SHOW US!
IT'S NOT LIKE YOU'RE GONNA DATE THE GUY, RIGHT?
WELL NO, BUT THAT'S... I ALREADY HAVE A GUY I LIKE.
HA HA
AND I SHOULD ANSWER THIS GUY...
WHAT'S THAT?
JOLT
THERE'S NO REASON FOR YOU TO READ THAT.
THROW IT OUT!

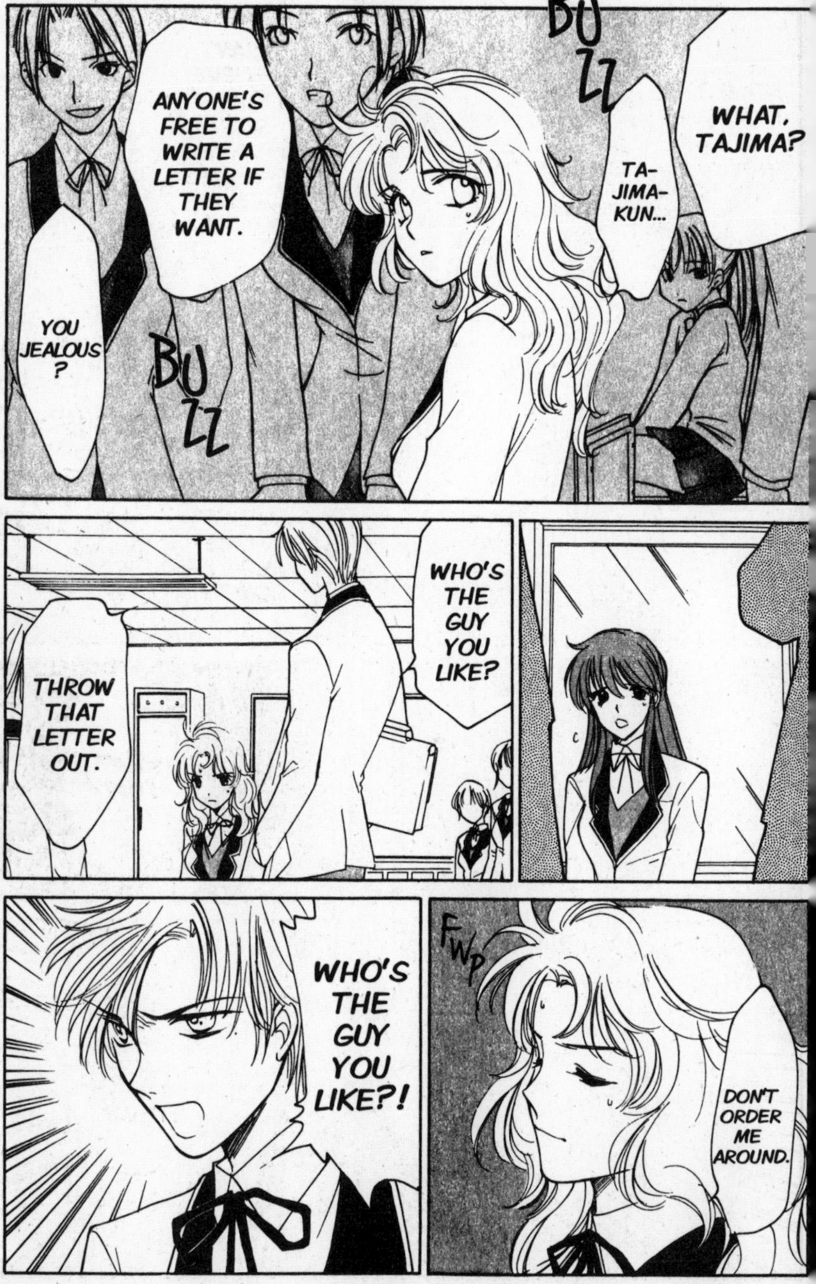

BUZZ
WHAT, TAJIMA?
TA-JIMA-KUN...
ANYONE'S FREE TO WRITE A LETTER IF THEY WANT.
BUZZ
YOU JEALOUS?
WHO'S THE GUY YOU LIKE?
THROW THAT LETTER OUT.
FWP
DON'T ORDER ME AROUND.
WHO'S THE GUY YOU LIKE?!

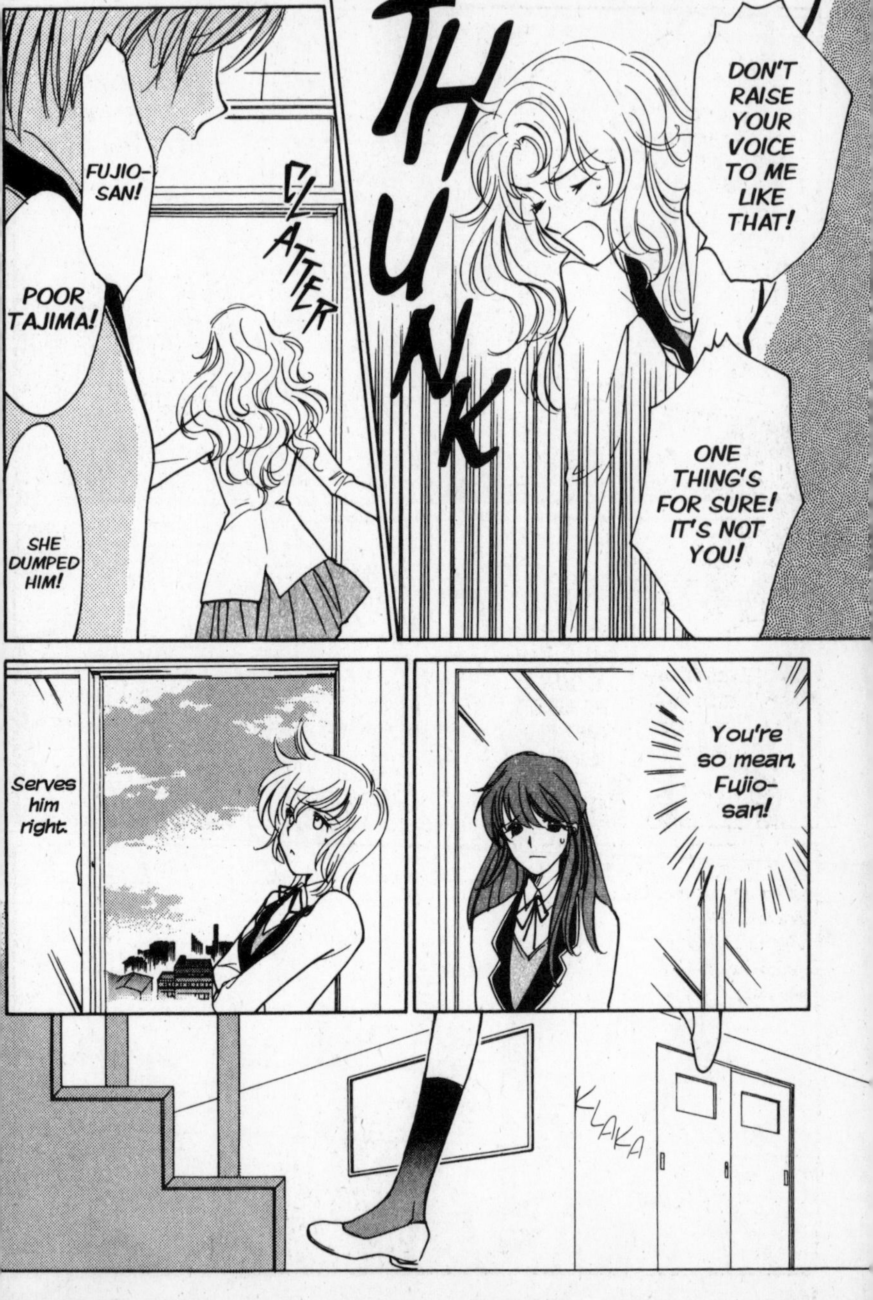
THUNK
DON'T RAISE YOUR VOICE TO ME LIKE THAT!
ONE THING'S FOR SURE! IT'S NOT YOU!
FUJIO-SAN!
CLATTER
POOR TAJIMA!
SHE DUMPED HIM!
You're so mean, Fujio-san!
Serves him right.
KLAKA

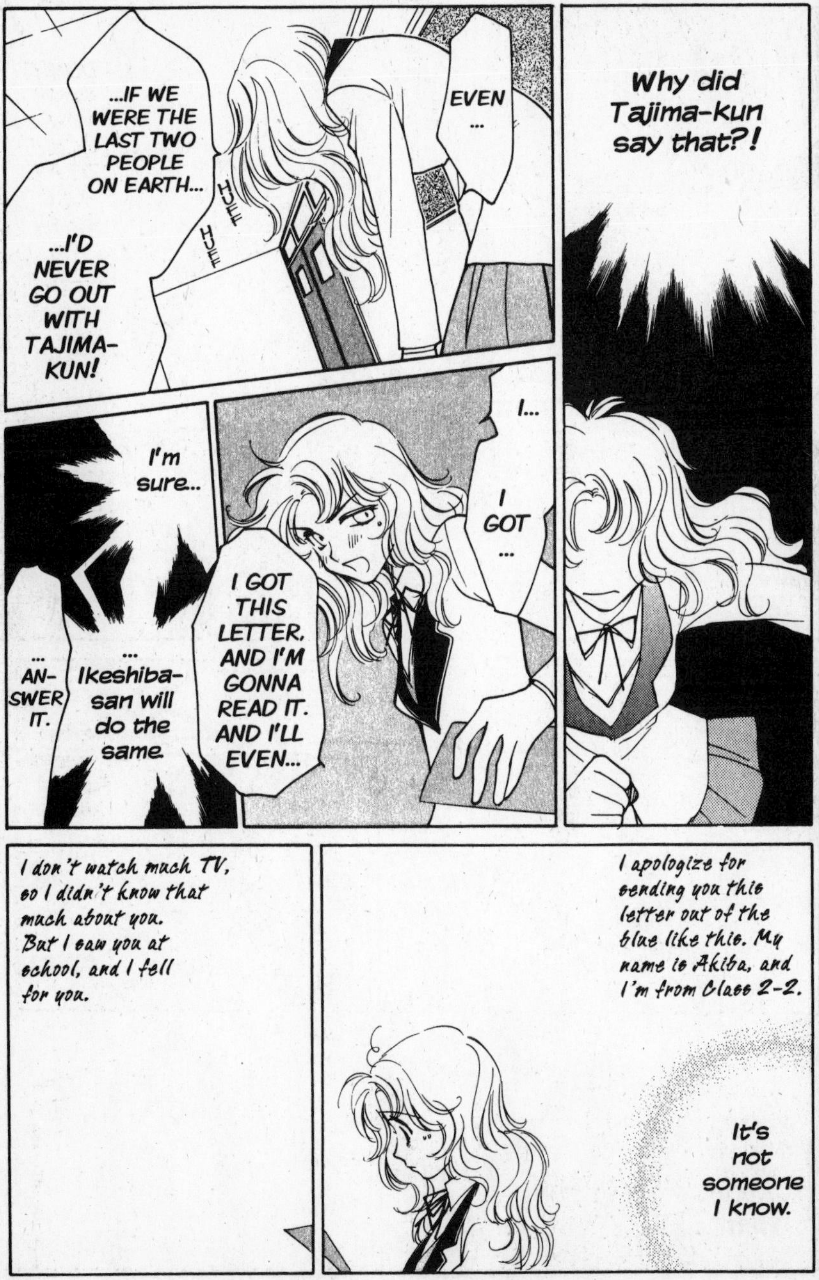

Why did Tajima-kun say that?!
EVEN ...
...IF WE WERE THE LAST TWO PEOPLE ON EARTH...
HUFF
HUFF
...I'D NEVER GO OUT WITH TAJIMA-KUN!
I...
I GOT ...
I GOT THIS LETTER. AND I'M GONNA READ IT. AND I'LL EVEN...
I'm sure...
... Ikeshiba-san will do the same.
... AN-SWER IT.
I apologize for sending you this letter out of the blue like this. My name is Akiba, and I'm from Class 2-2.
It's not someone I know.
I don't watch much TV, so I didn't know that much about you. But I saw you at school, and I fell for you.

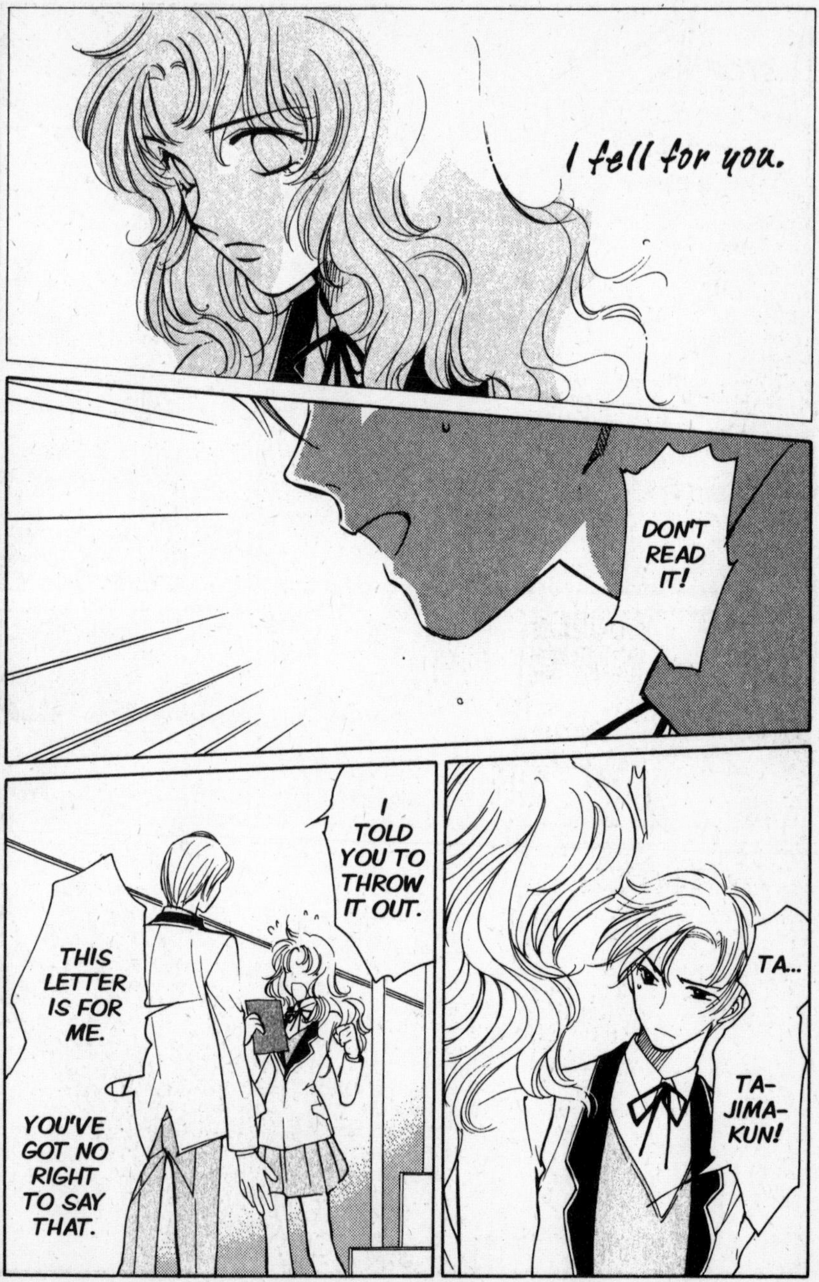
I fell for you.
DON'T READ IT!
TA...
TA-JIMA-KUN!
I TOLD YOU TO THROW IT OUT.
THIS LETTER IS FOR ME.
YOU'VE GOT NO RIGHT TO SAY THAT.

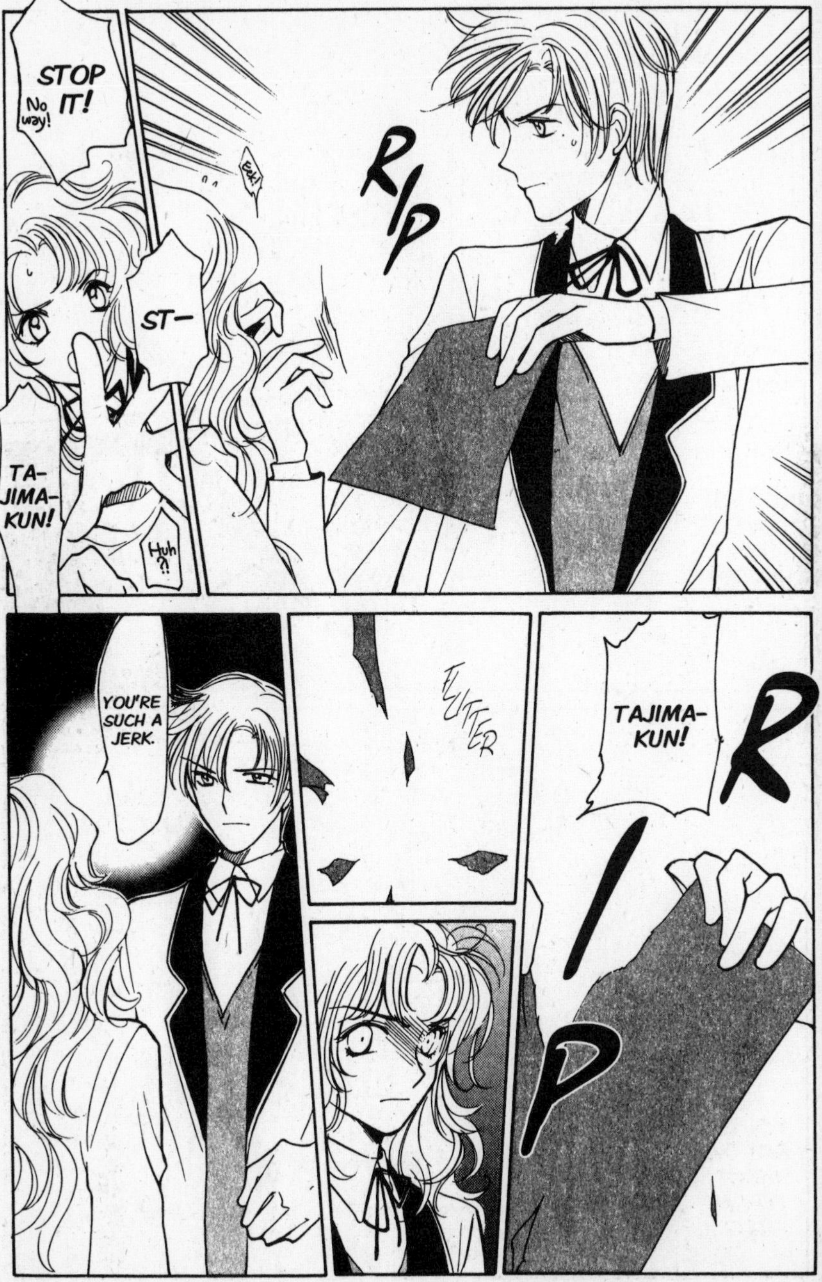
RIP
STOP IT!
No way!
Eek!
ST—
TA-JIMA-KUN!
Huh?!
TAJIMA-KUN!
RIP
FLUTTER
YOU'RE SUCH A JERK.

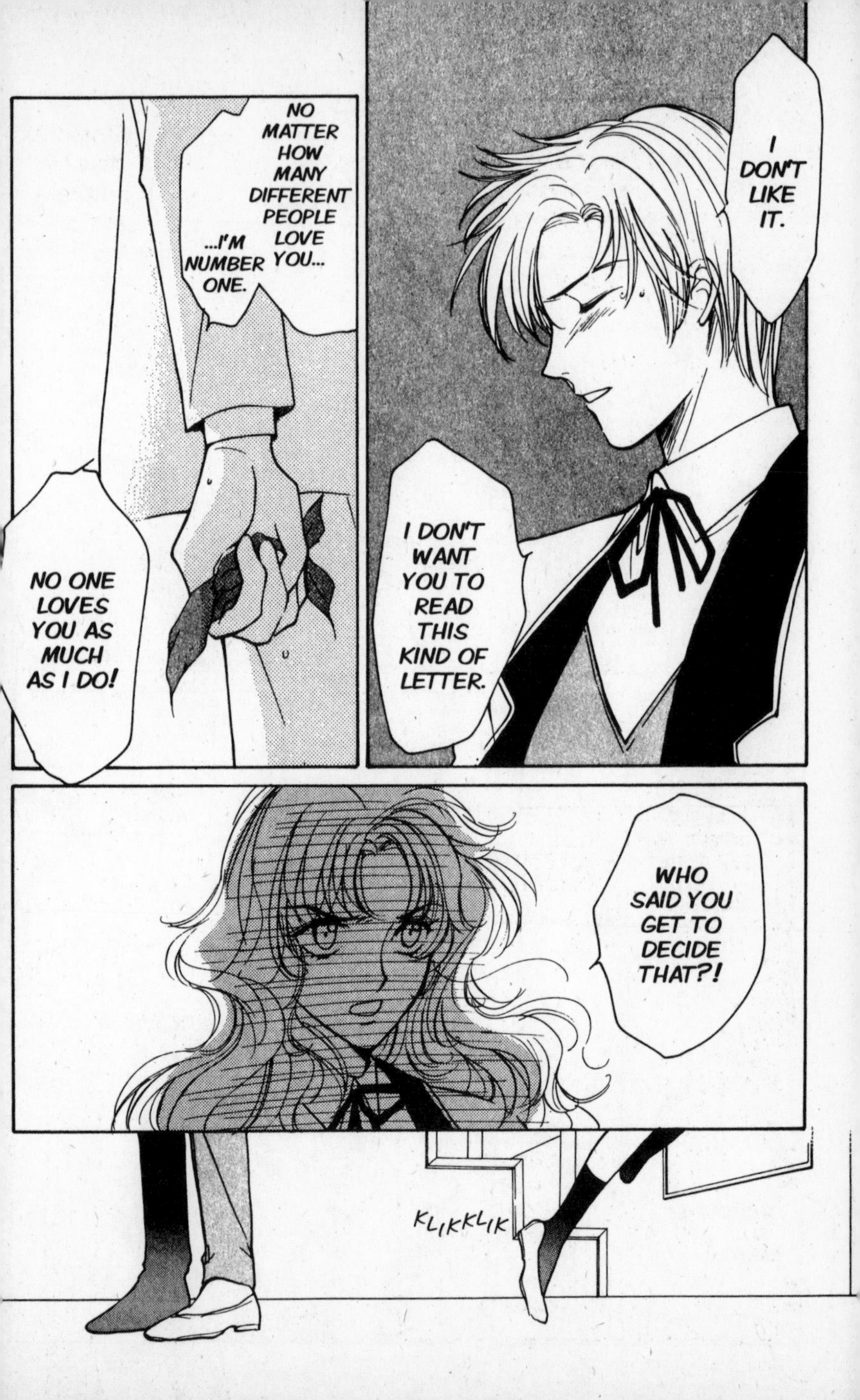
I DON'T LIKE IT.
I DON'T WANT YOU TO READ THIS KIND OF LETTER.
NO MATTER HOW MANY DIFFERENT PEOPLE LOVE YOU...
...I'M NUMBER ONE.
NO ONE LOVES YOU AS MUCH AS I DO!
WHO SAID YOU GET TO DECIDE THAT?!
KLIKKLIK

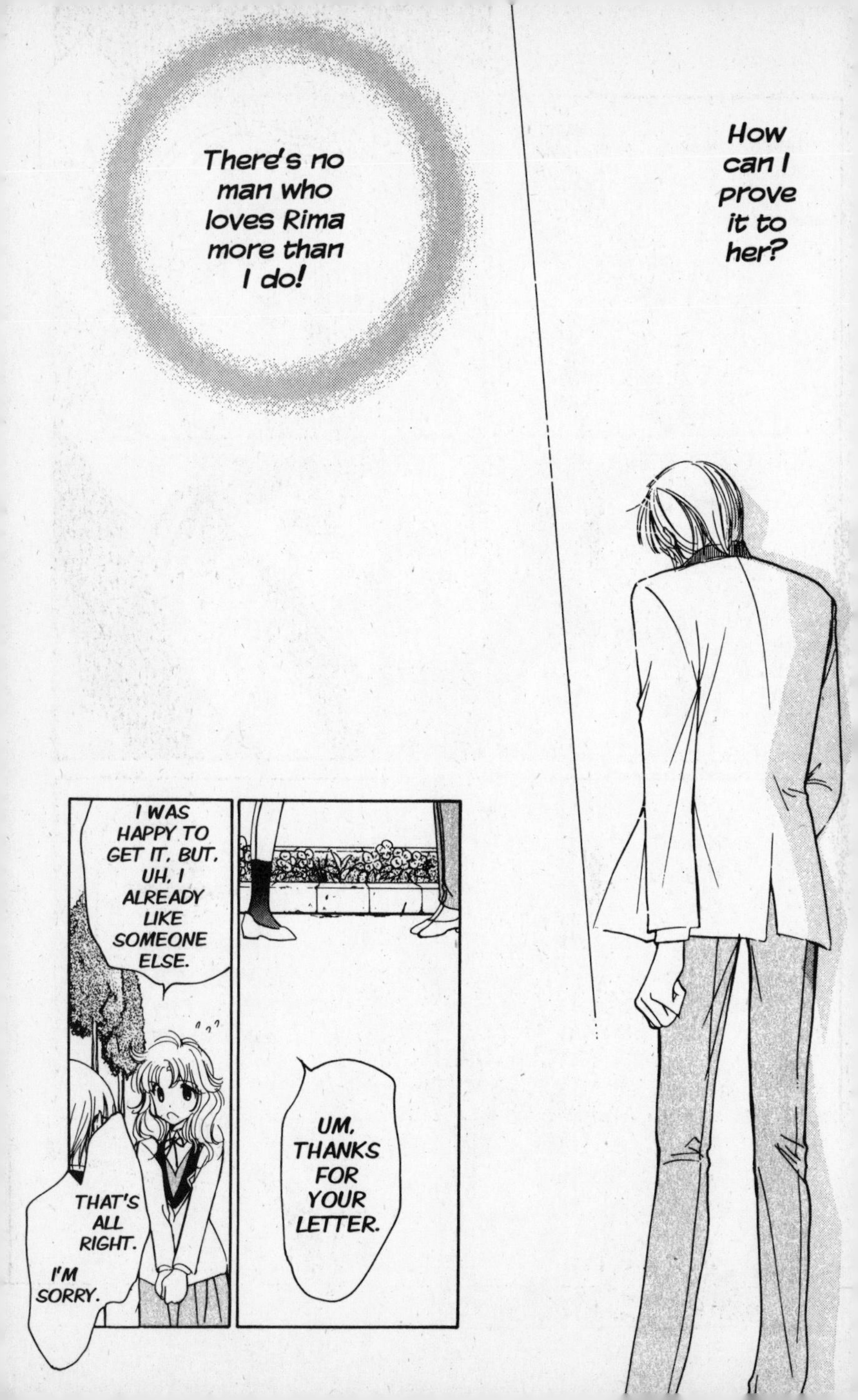
How can I prove it to her?
There's no man who loves Rima more than I do!
UM, THANKS FOR YOUR LETTER.
I WAS HAPPY TO GET IT, BUT, UH, I ALREADY LIKE SOMEONE ELSE.
THAT'S ALL RIGHT.
I'M SORRY.

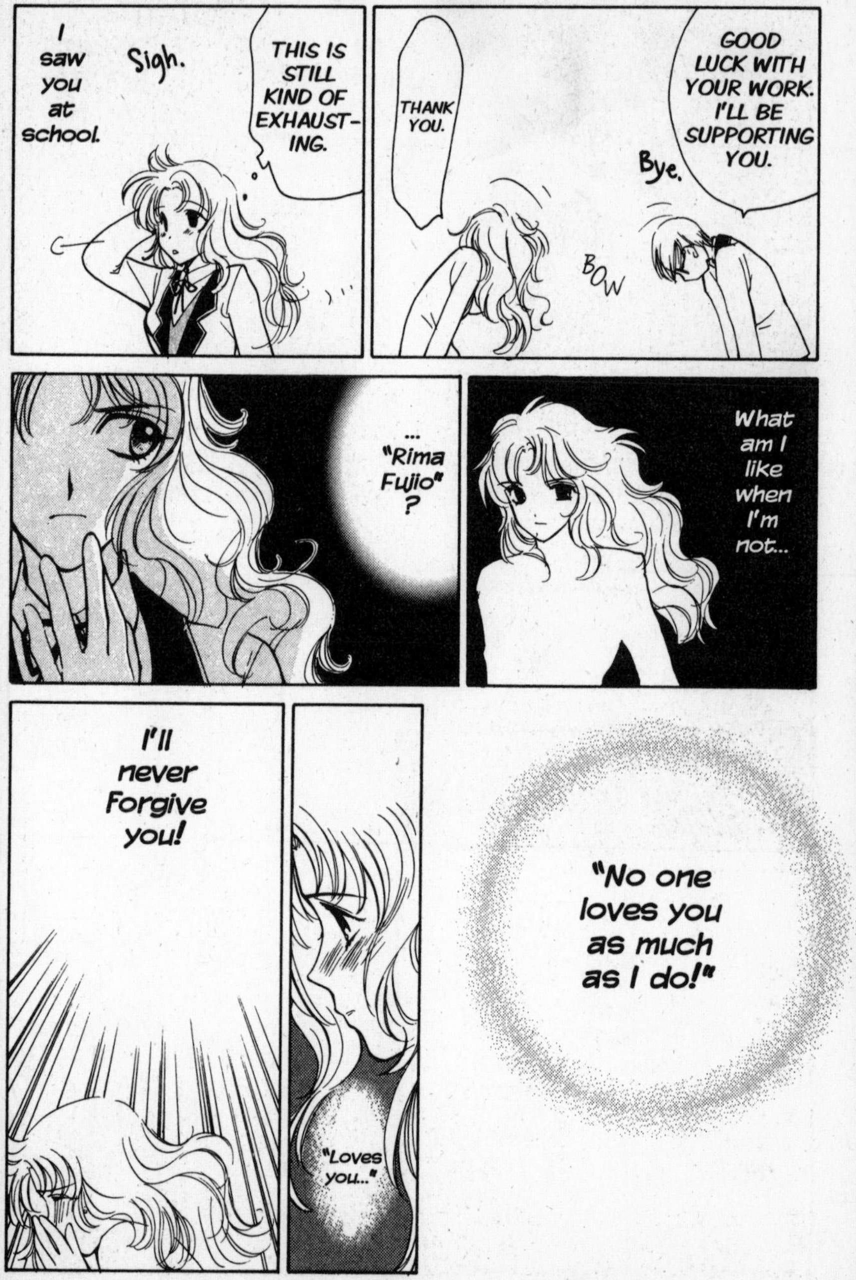
GOOD LUCK WITH YOUR WORK. I'LL BE SUPPORTING YOU.
Bye.
BOW
THANK YOU.
THIS IS STILL KIND OF EXHAUST-ING.
Sigh.
I saw you at school.
What am I like when I'm not...
... "Rima Fujio"?
"No one loves you as much as I do!"
"Loves you..."
I'll never Forgive you!

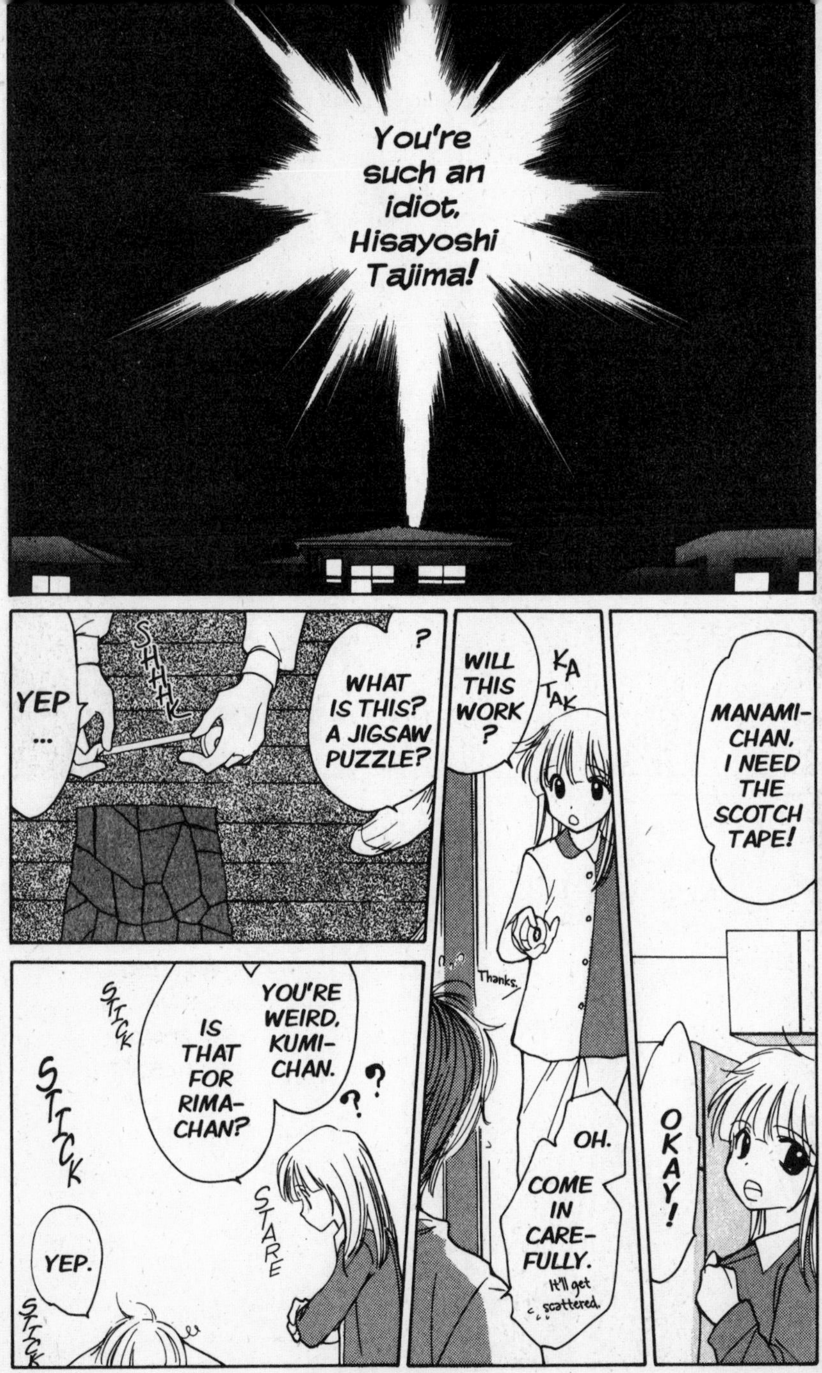
You're such an idiot, Hisayoshi Tajima!
MANAMI-CHAN, I NEED THE SCOTCH TAPE!
OKAY!
KA TAK
WILL THIS WORK?
Thanks.
OH. COME IN CAREFULLY.
It'll get scattered.
?
WHAT IS THIS? A JIGSAW PUZZLE?
SHHHK
YEP...
YOU'RE WEIRD, KUMI-CHAN.
IS THAT FOR RIMA-CHAN?
??
STICK
STICK
STARE
YEP.
STICK

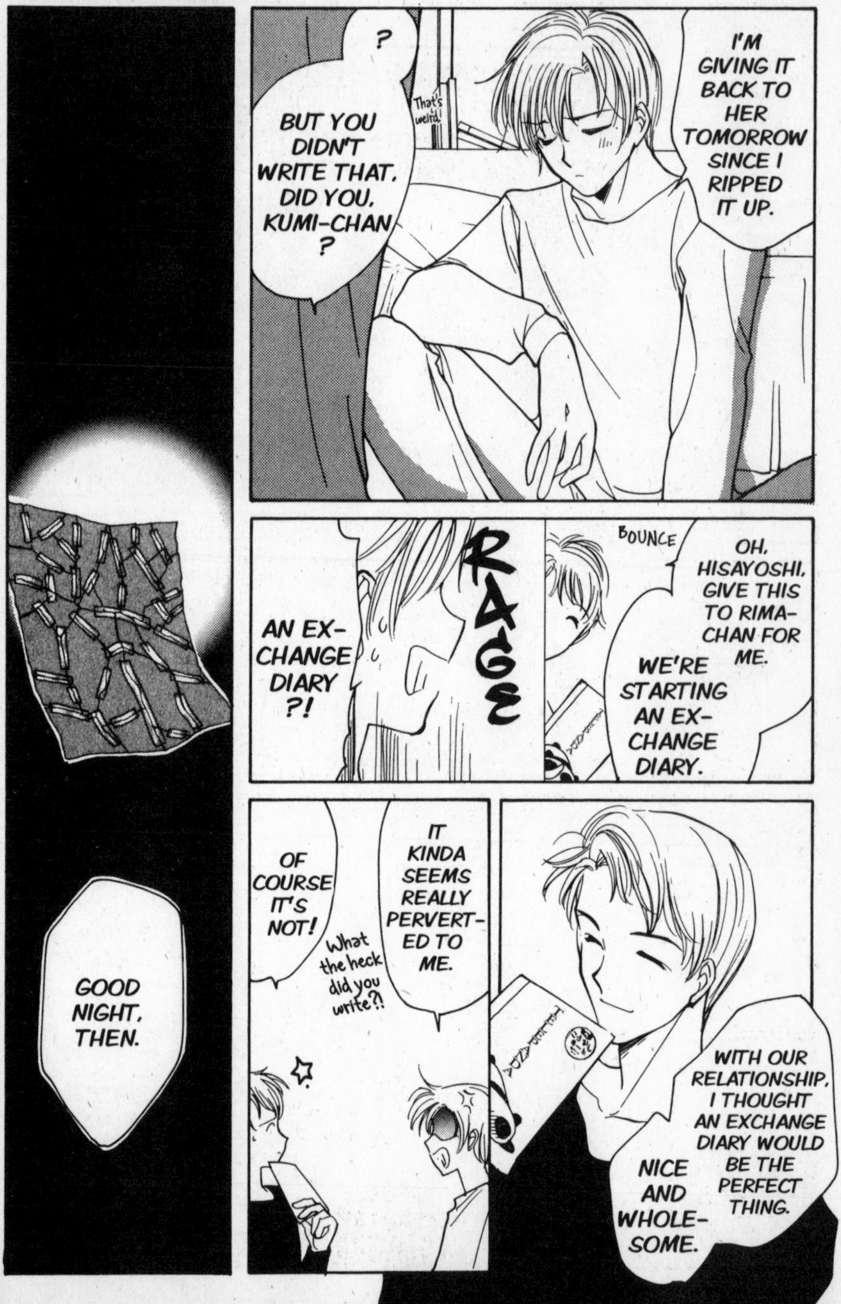
I'M GIVING IT BACK TO HER TOMORROW SINCE I RIPPED IT UP.
That's weird.
? BUT YOU DIDN'T WRITE THAT, DID YOU, KUMI-CHAN?
BOUNCE
OH, HISAYOSHI, GIVE THIS TO RIMA-CHAN FOR ME.
WE'RE STARTING AN EX-CHANGE DIARY.
RAGE
AN EX-CHANGE DIARY?!
WITH OUR RELATIONSHIP, I THOUGHT AN EXCHANGE DIARY WOULD BE THE PERFECT THING.
NICE AND WHOLE-SOME.
IT KINDA SEEMS REALLY PERVERT-ED TO ME.
OF COURSE IT'S NOT!
What the heck did you write?!
GOOD NIGHT, THEN.

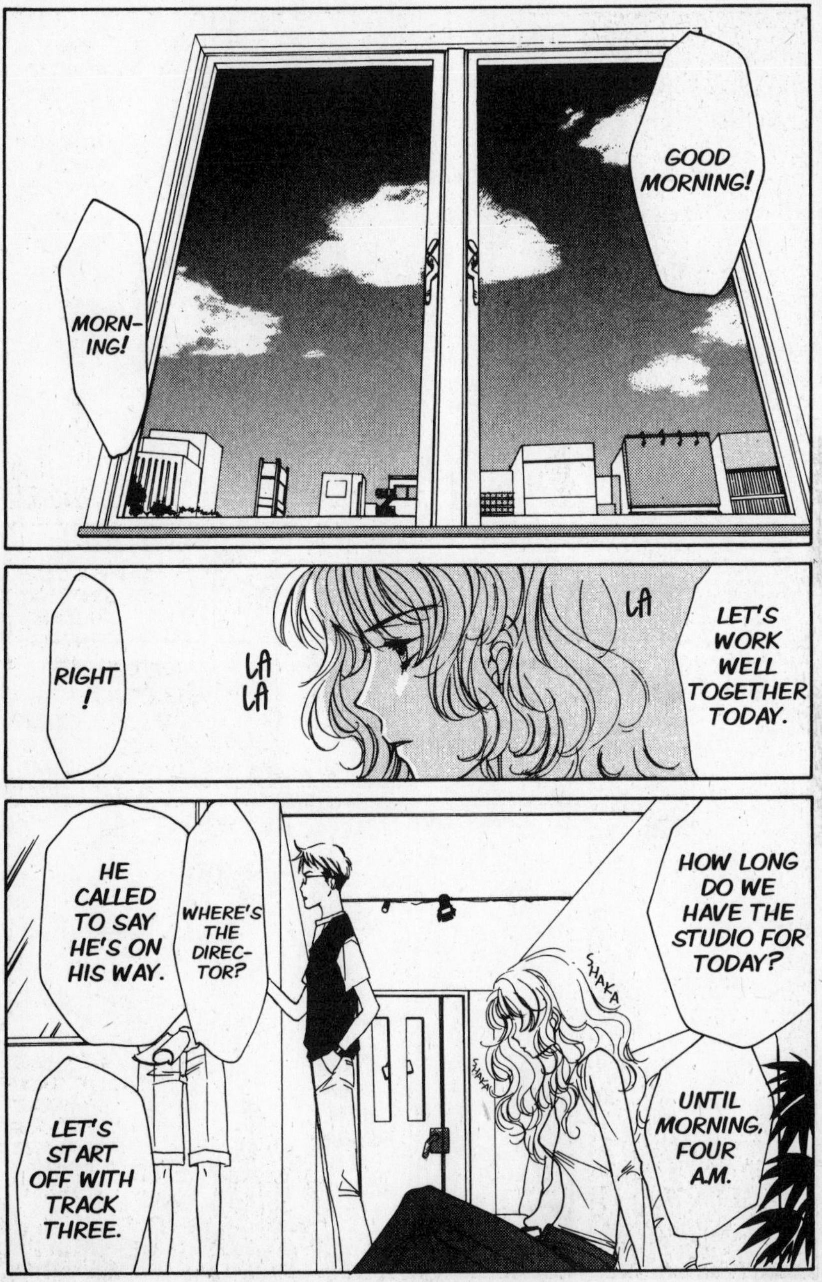
GOOD MORNING!
MORNING!
LET'S WORK WELL TOGETHER TODAY.
LA
LA LA
RIGHT!
HOW LONG DO WE HAVE THE STUDIO FOR TODAY?
SHAKA
SHAKA
UNTIL MORNING. FOUR A.M.
WHERE'S THE DIRECTOR?
HE CALLED TO SAY HE'S ON HIS WAY.
LET'S START OFF WITH TRACK THREE.

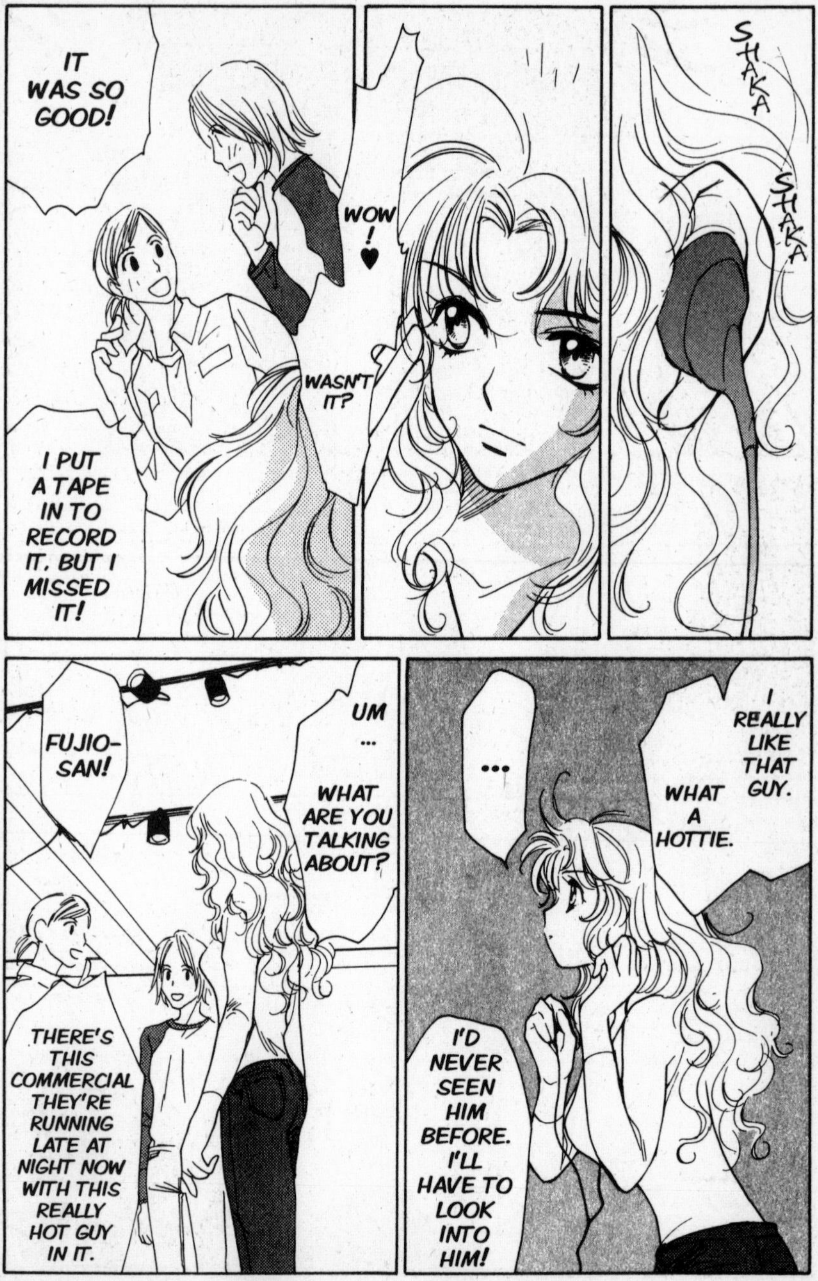
SHAKA
SHAKA
WOW! ♥
WASN'T IT?
IT WAS SO GOOD!
I PUT A TAPE IN TO RECORD IT, BUT I MISSED IT!
I REALLY LIKE THAT GUY.
WHAT A HOTTIE.
...
I'D NEVER SEEN HIM BEFORE. I'LL HAVE TO LOOK INTO HIM!
UM ...
WHAT ARE YOU TALKING ABOUT?
FUJIO-SAN!
THERE'S THIS COMMERCIAL THEY'RE RUNNING LATE AT NIGHT NOW WITH THIS REALLY HOT GUY IN IT.

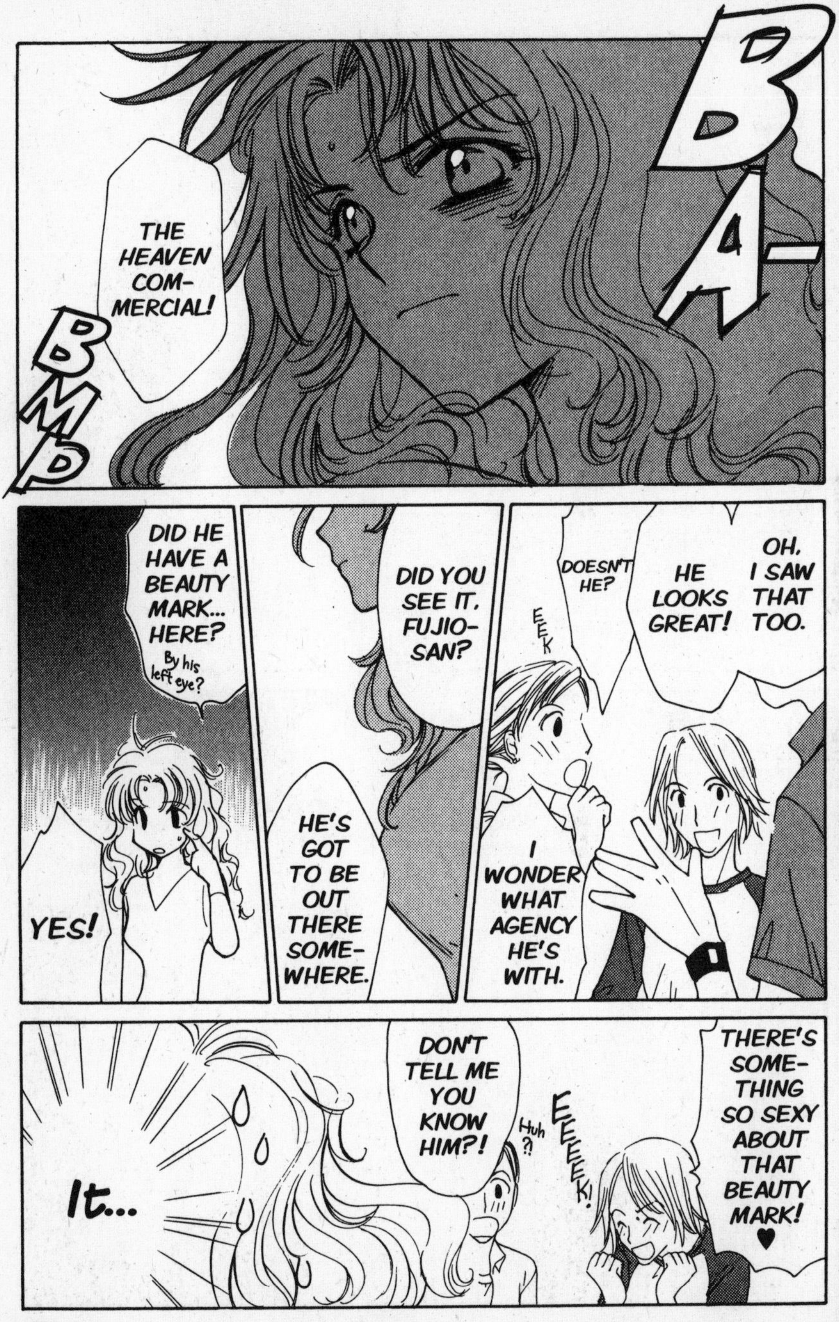
BA-N
THE HEAVEN COMMERCIAL!
BMP
OH, I SAW THAT TOO.
HE LOOKS GREAT!
DOESN'T HE?
EEK
I WONDER WHAT AGENCY HE'S WITH.
DID YOU SEE IT, FUJIO-SAN?
HE'S GOT TO BE OUT THERE SOMEWHERE.
DID HE HAVE A BEAUTY MARK... HERE?
By his left eye?
YES!
THERE'S SOMETHING SO SEXY ABOUT THAT BEAUTY MARK! ♥
EEEEEK!
Huh ?!
DON'T TELL ME YOU KNOW HIM?!
It...

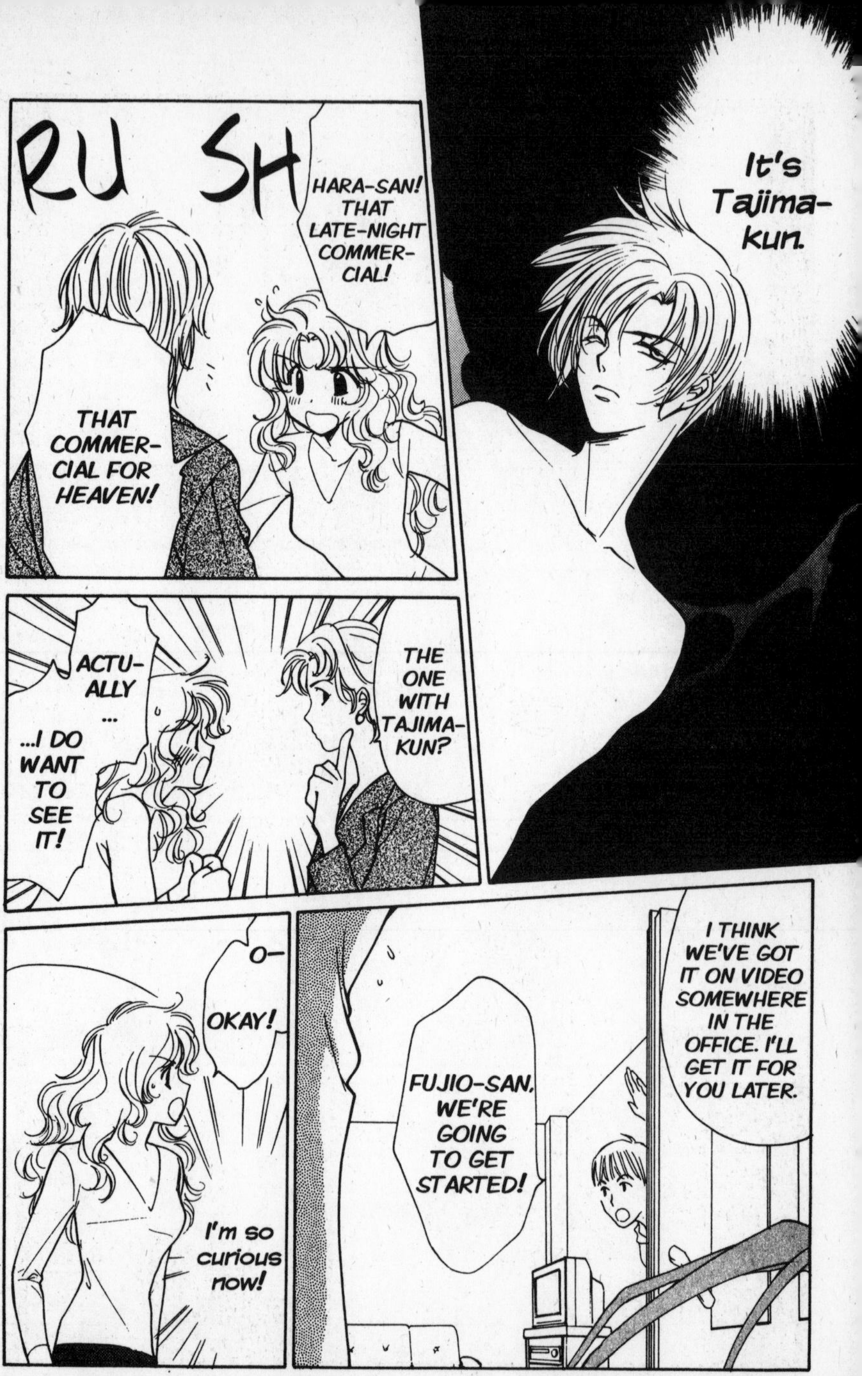
It's Tajima-kun.
RUSH
HARA-SAN! THAT LATE-NIGHT COMMERCIAL!
THAT COMMERCIAL FOR HEAVEN!
THE ONE WITH TAJIMA-KUN?
ACTUALLY...
...I DO WANT TO SEE IT!
I THINK WE'VE GOT IT ON VIDEO SOMEWHERE IN THE OFFICE. I'LL GET IT FOR YOU LATER.
FUJIO-SAN, WE'RE GOING TO GET STARTED!
O-OKAY!
I'm so curious now!

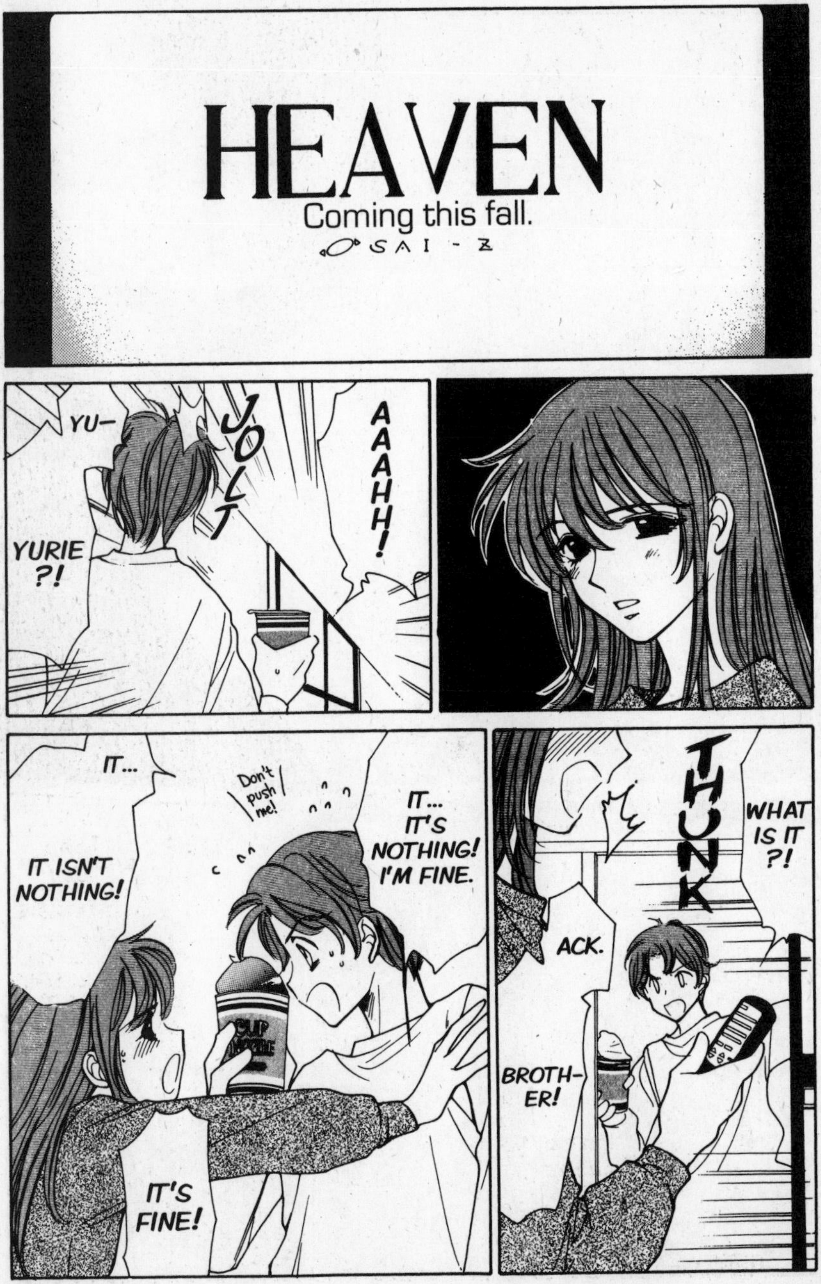
HEAVEN
Coming this fall.
AAAAHH!
JOLT
YU–
YURIE ?!
THUNK
WHAT IS IT ?!
ACK.
BROTH-ER!
IT... IT'S NOTHING! I'M FINE.
Don't push me!
IT...
IT ISN'T NOTHING!
IT'S FINE!

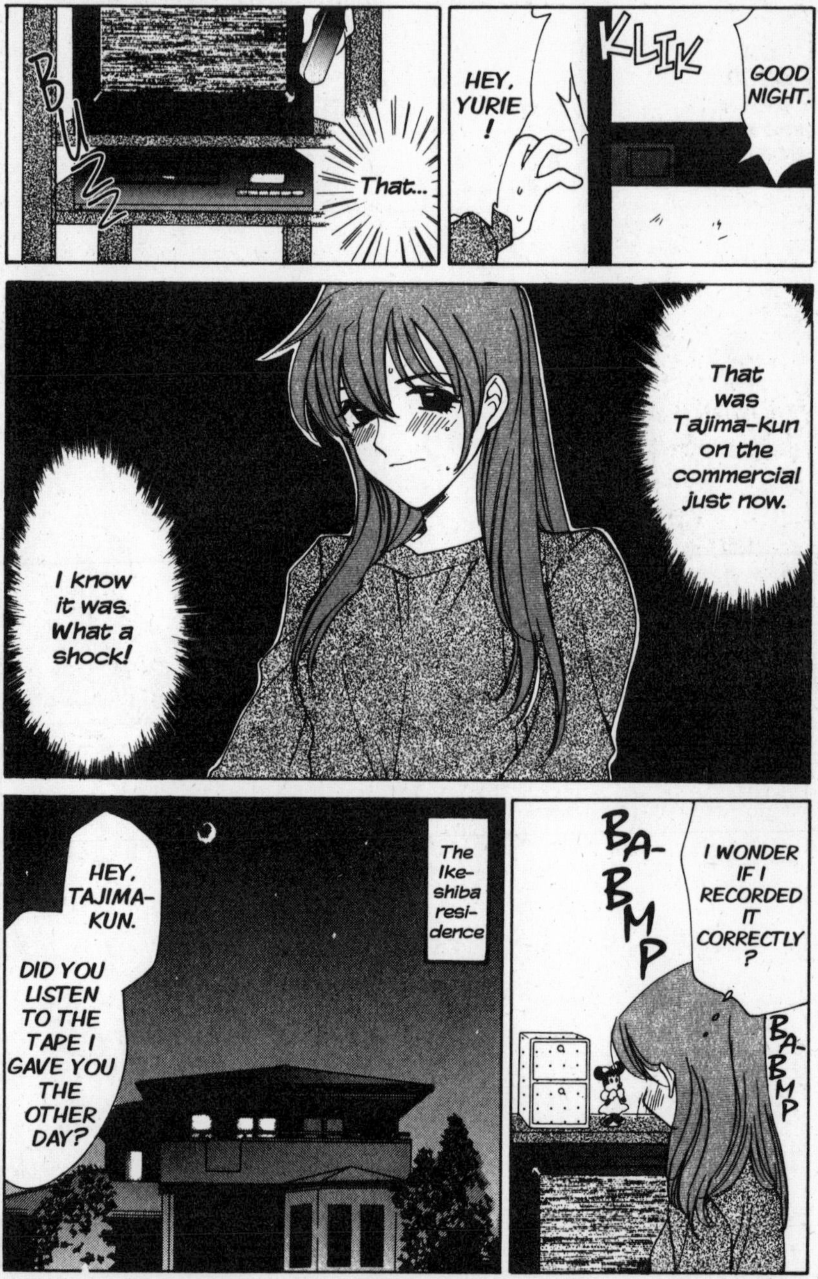
GOOD NIGHT.
KLIK
HEY, YURIE!
BUZZ
That...
That was Tajima-kun on the commercial just now.
I know it was. What a shock!
I WONDER IF I RECORDED IT CORRECTLY?
BA-BMP
BA-BMP
The Ike-shiba residence
HEY, TAJIMA-KUN.
DID YOU LISTEN TO THE TAPE I GAVE YOU THE OTHER DAY?

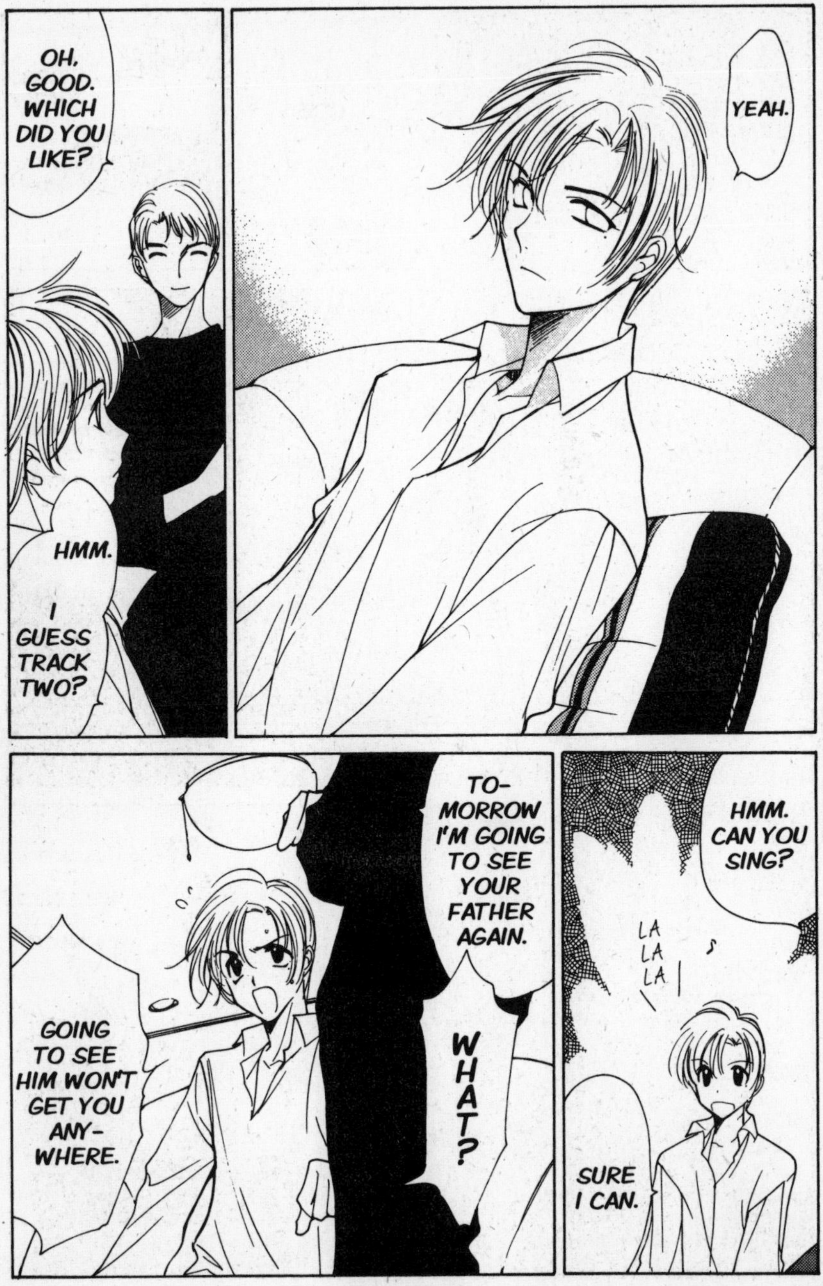
YEAH.
OH, GOOD. WHICH DID YOU LIKE?
HMM.
I GUESS TRACK TWO?
HMM. CAN YOU SING?
LA LA LA
SURE I CAN.
TO-MORROW I'M GOING TO SEE YOUR FATHER AGAIN.
WHAT?
GOING TO SEE HIM WON'T GET YOU ANY-WHERE.

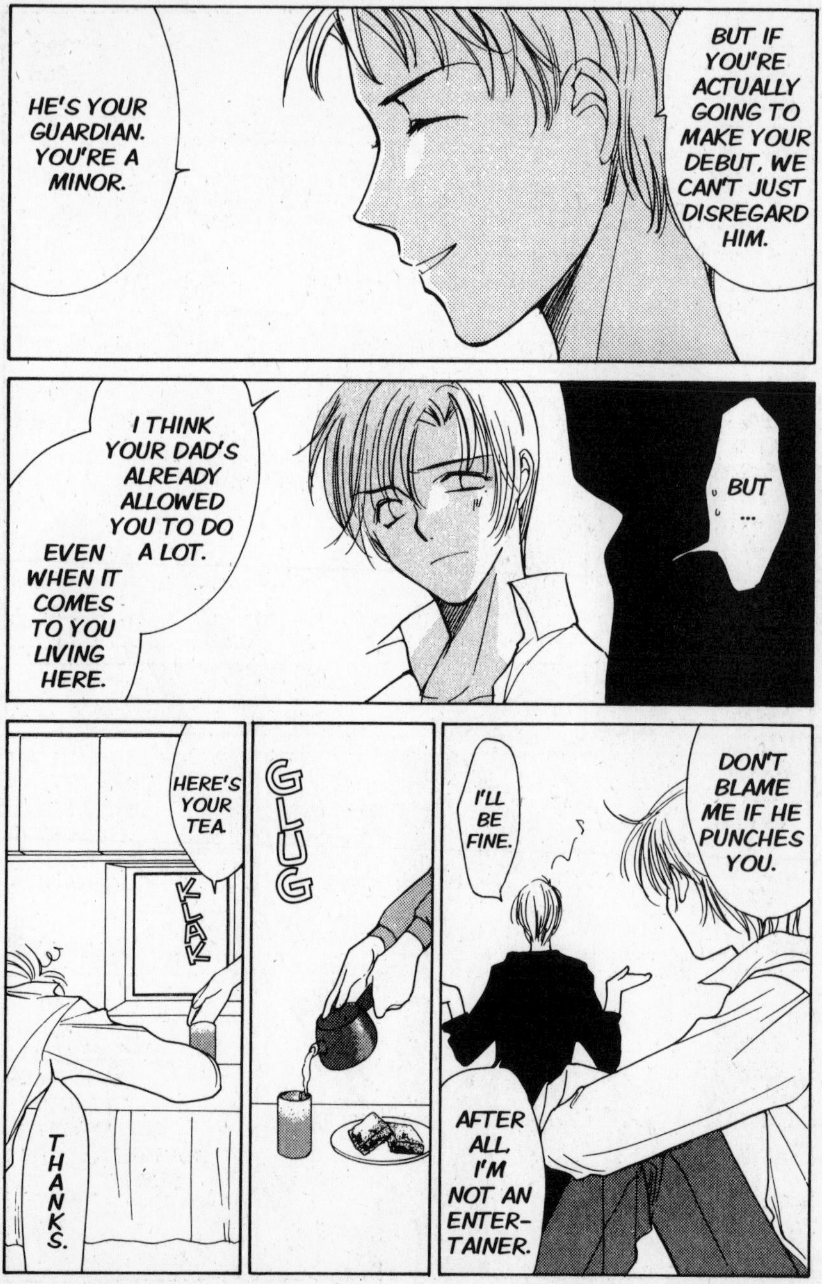
BUT IF YOU'RE ACTUALLY GOING TO MAKE YOUR DEBUT, WE CAN'T JUST DISREGARD HIM.
HE'S YOUR GUARDIAN. YOU'RE A MINOR.
BUT ...
I THINK YOUR DAD'S ALREADY ALLOWED YOU TO DO A LOT.
EVEN WHEN IT COMES TO YOU LIVING HERE.
DON'T BLAME ME IF HE PUNCHES YOU.
I'LL BE FINE.
AFTER ALL, I'M NOT AN ENTER-TAINER.
GLUG
HERE'S YOUR TEA.
KLAK
THANKS.

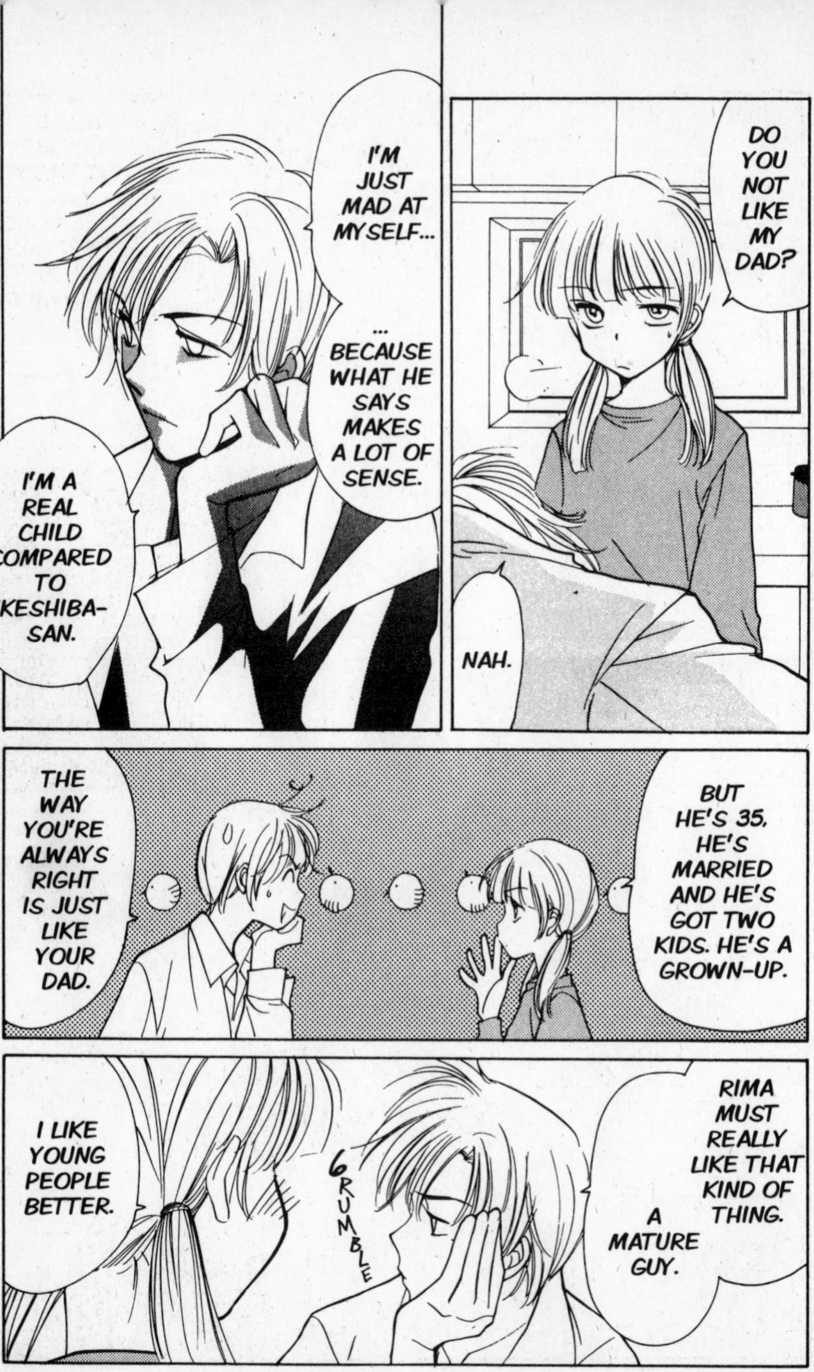
DO YOU NOT LIKE MY DAD?
NAH.
I'M JUST MAD AT MYSELF...
... BECAUSE WHAT HE SAYS MAKES A LOT OF SENSE.
I'M A REAL CHILD COMPARED TO IKESHIBA-SAN.
BUT HE'S 35. HE'S MARRIED AND HE'S GOT TWO KIDS. HE'S A GROWN-UP.
THE WAY YOU'RE ALWAYS RIGHT IS JUST LIKE YOUR DAD.
RIMA MUST REALLY LIKE THAT KIND OF THING.
A MATURE GUY.
RUMBLE
I LIKE YOUNG PEOPLE BETTER.

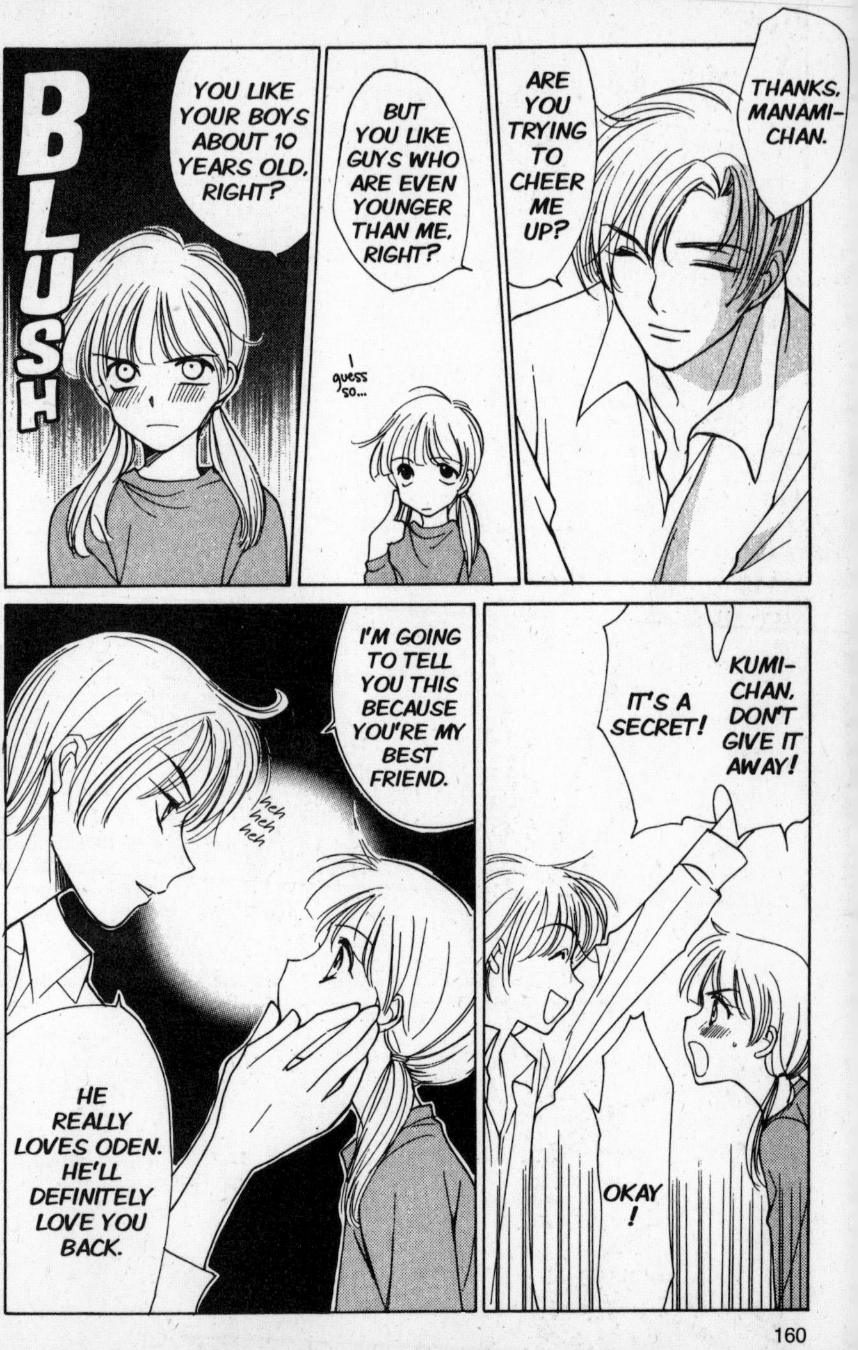
THANKS, MANAMI-CHAN.
ARE YOU TRYING TO CHEER ME UP?
BUT YOU LIKE GUYS WHO ARE EVEN YOUNGER THAN ME, RIGHT?
I guess so...
YOU LIKE YOUR BOYS ABOUT 10 YEARS OLD, RIGHT?
BLUSH
KUMI-CHAN, DON'T GIVE IT AWAY!
IT'S A SECRET!
OKAY!
I'M GOING TO TELL YOU THIS BECAUSE YOU'RE MY BEST FRIEND.
heh heh heh
HE REALLY LOVES ODEN. HE'LL DEFINITELY LOVE YOU BACK.

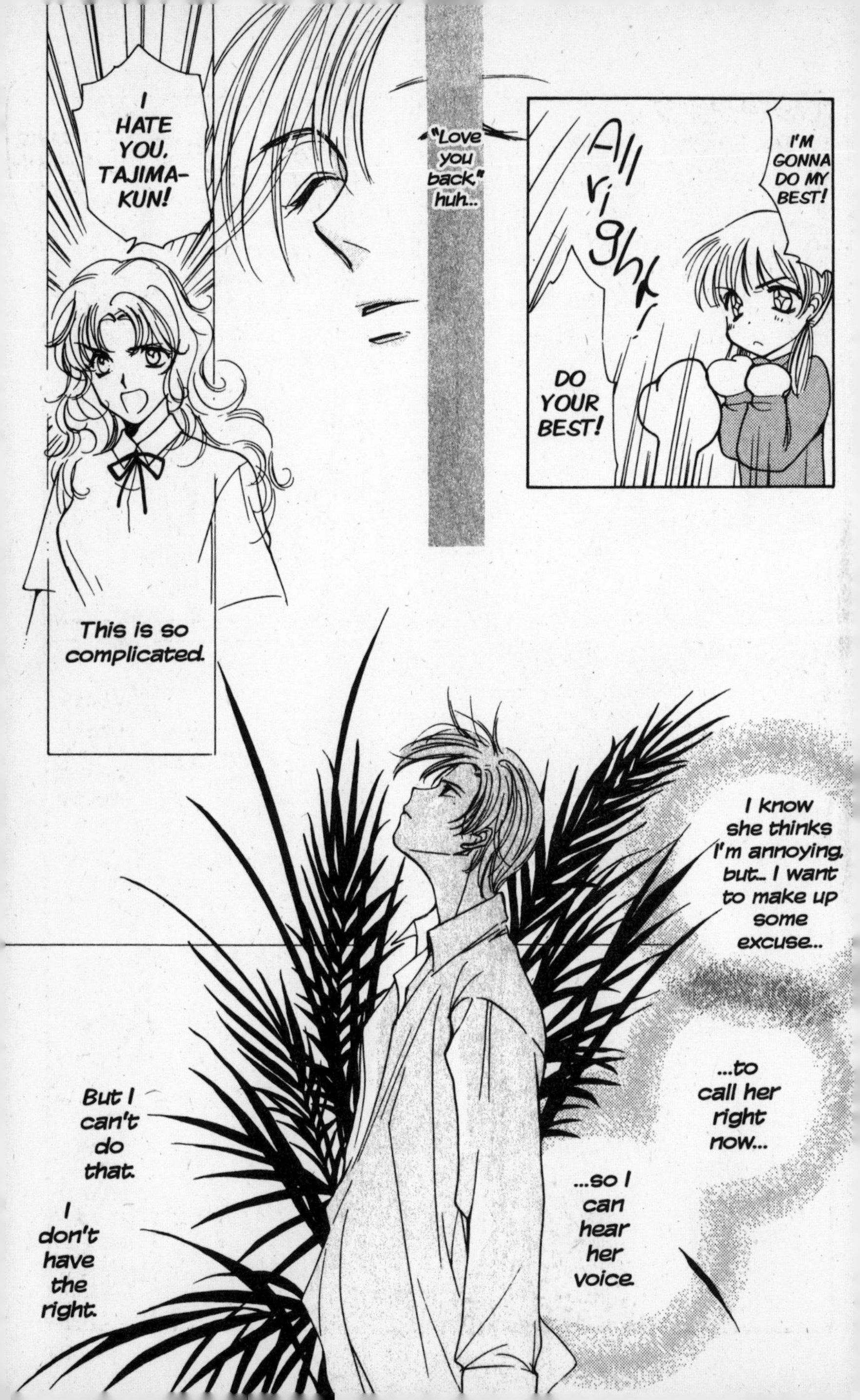
I'M GONNA DO MY BEST!
All right!
DO YOUR BEST!
"Love you back," huh...
I HATE YOU, TAJIMA-KUN!
This is so complicated.
I know she thinks I'm annoying, but... I want to make up some excuse...
...to call her right now...
...so I can hear her voice.
But I can't do that.
I don't have the right.

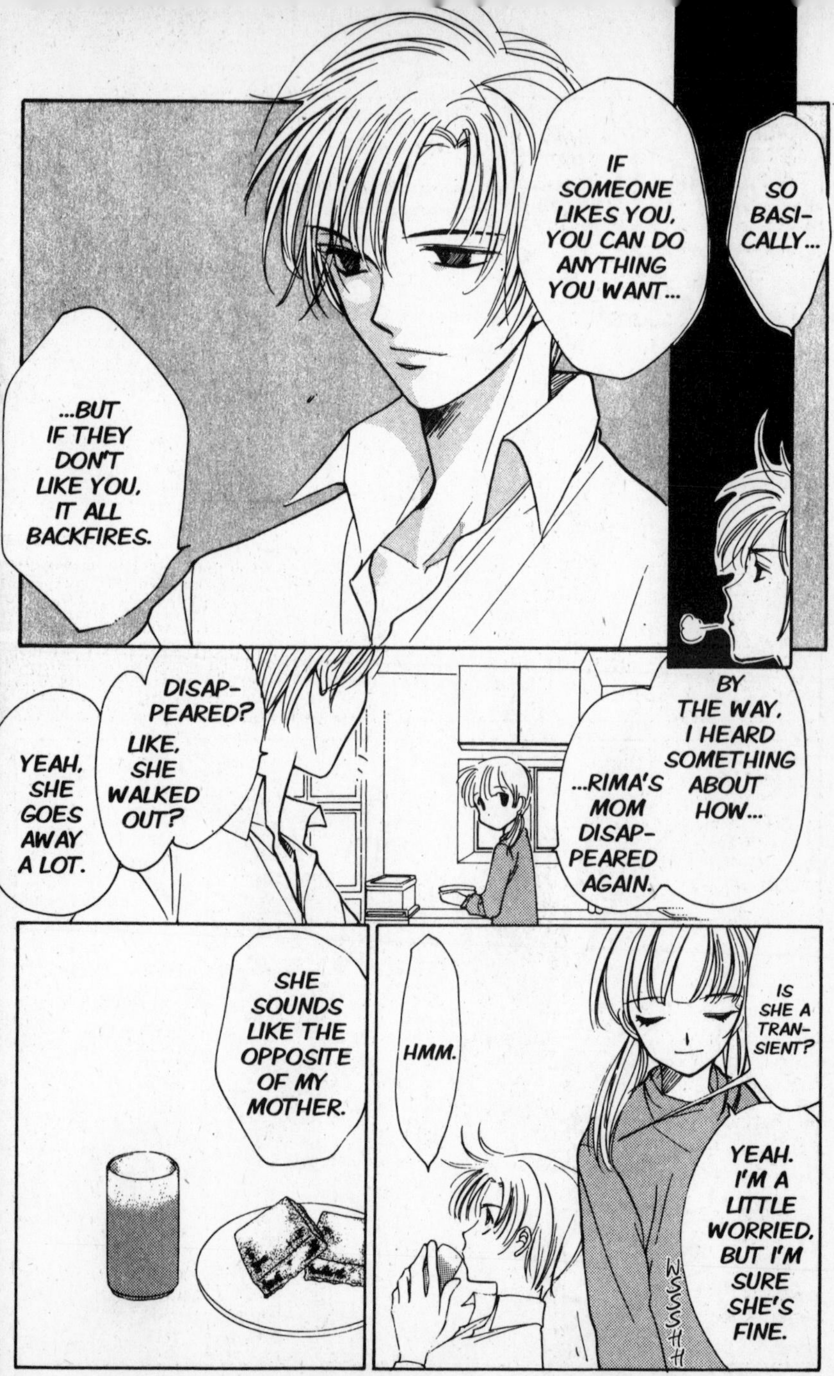
SO BASICALLY...
IF SOMEONE LIKES YOU, YOU CAN DO ANYTHING YOU WANT...
...BUT IF THEY DON'T LIKE YOU, IT ALL BACKFIRES.
BY THE WAY, I HEARD SOMETHING ABOUT HOW...
...RIMA'S MOM DISAPPEARED AGAIN.
DISAPPEARED?
LIKE, SHE WALKED OUT?
YEAH, SHE GOES AWAY A LOT.
IS SHE A TRANSIENT?
YEAH. I'M A LITTLE WORRIED, BUT I'M SURE SHE'S FINE.
WSSSHH
HMM.
SHE SOUNDS LIKE THE OPPOSITE OF MY MOTHER.

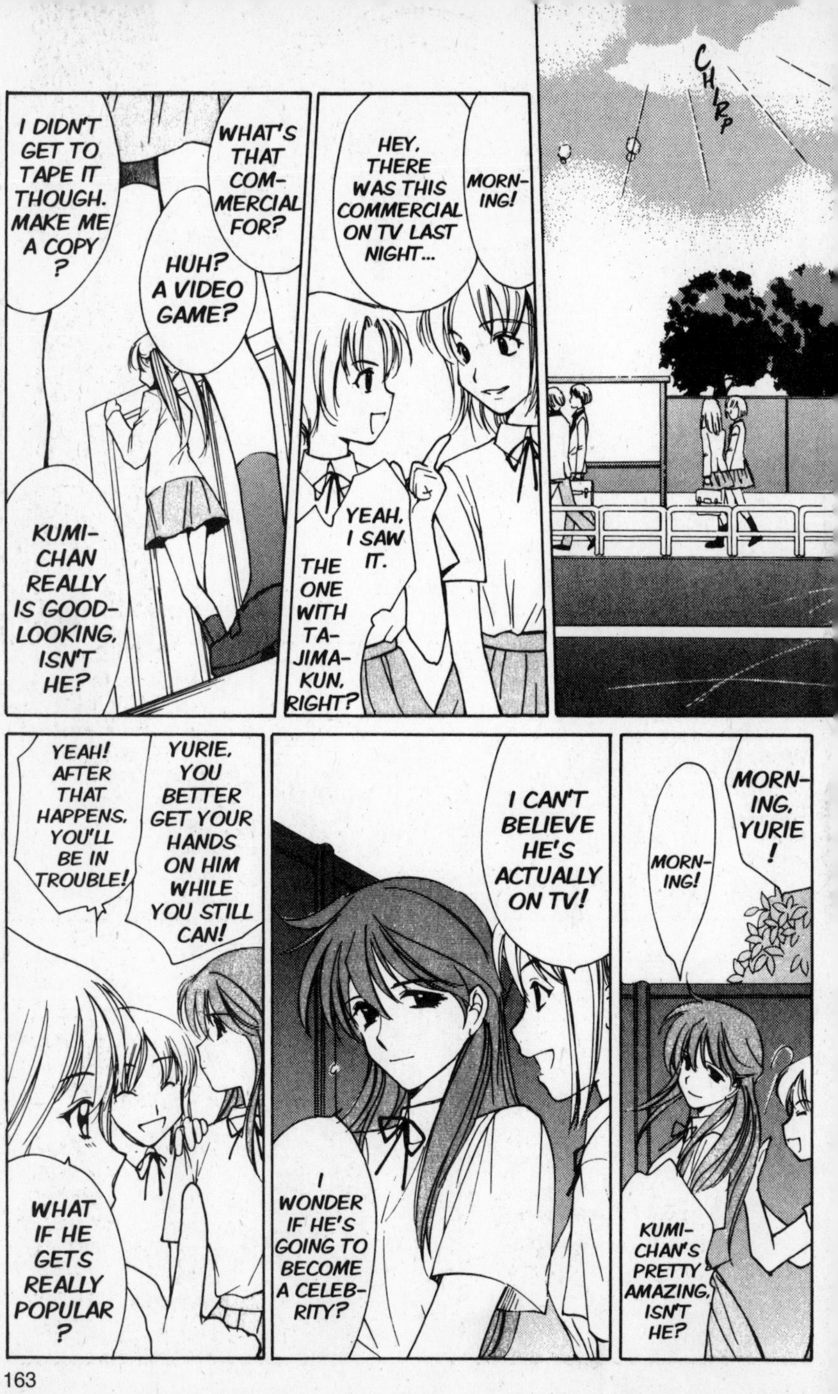
CHIRP
MORNING!
HEY, THERE WAS THIS COMMERCIAL ON TV LAST NIGHT...
YEAH, I SAW IT.
THE ONE WITH TAJIMA-KUN, RIGHT?
WHAT'S THAT COMMERCIAL FOR?
I DIDN'T GET TO TAPE IT THOUGH. MAKE ME A COPY?
HUH? A VIDEO GAME?
KUMI-CHAN REALLY IS GOOD-LOOKING, ISN'T HE?
MORNING, YURIE!
MORNING!
KUMI-CHAN'S PRETTY AMAZING, ISN'T HE?
I CAN'T BELIEVE HE'S ACTUALLY ON TV!
I WONDER IF HE'S GOING TO BECOME A CELEBRITY?
YURIE, YOU BETTER GET YOUR HANDS ON HIM WHILE YOU STILL CAN!
YEAH! AFTER THAT HAPPENS, YOU'LL BE IN TROUBLE!
WHAT IF HE GETS REALLY POPULAR?

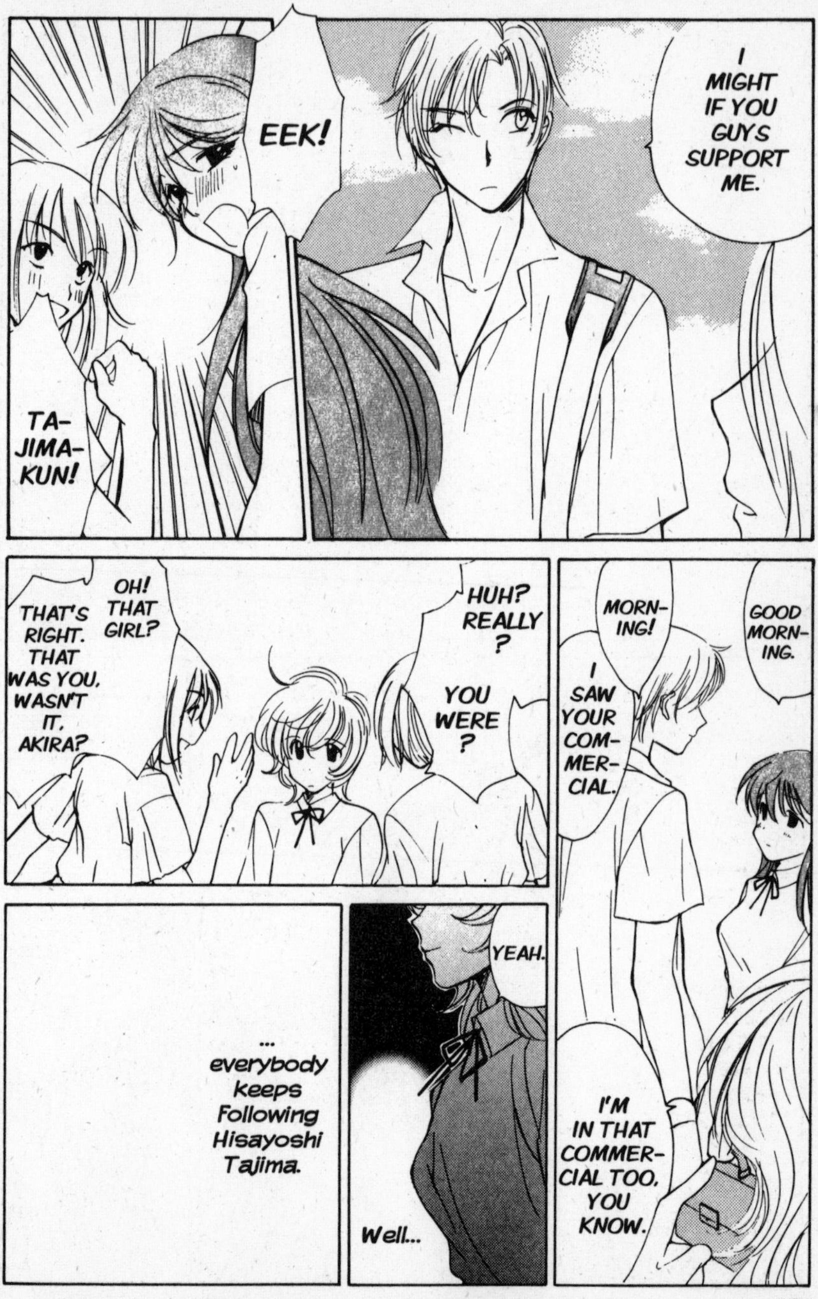

I MIGHT IF YOU GUYS SUPPORT ME.
EEK!
TA-JIMA-KUN!
GOOD MORNING.
MORN-ING!
I SAW YOUR COMMER-CIAL.
I'M IN THAT COMMER-CIAL TOO, YOU KNOW.
HUH? REALLY?
YOU WERE?
OH! THAT GIRL?
THAT'S RIGHT. THAT WAS YOU, WASN'T IT, AKIRA?
YEAH.
Well...
... everybody keeps Following Hisayoshi Tajima.

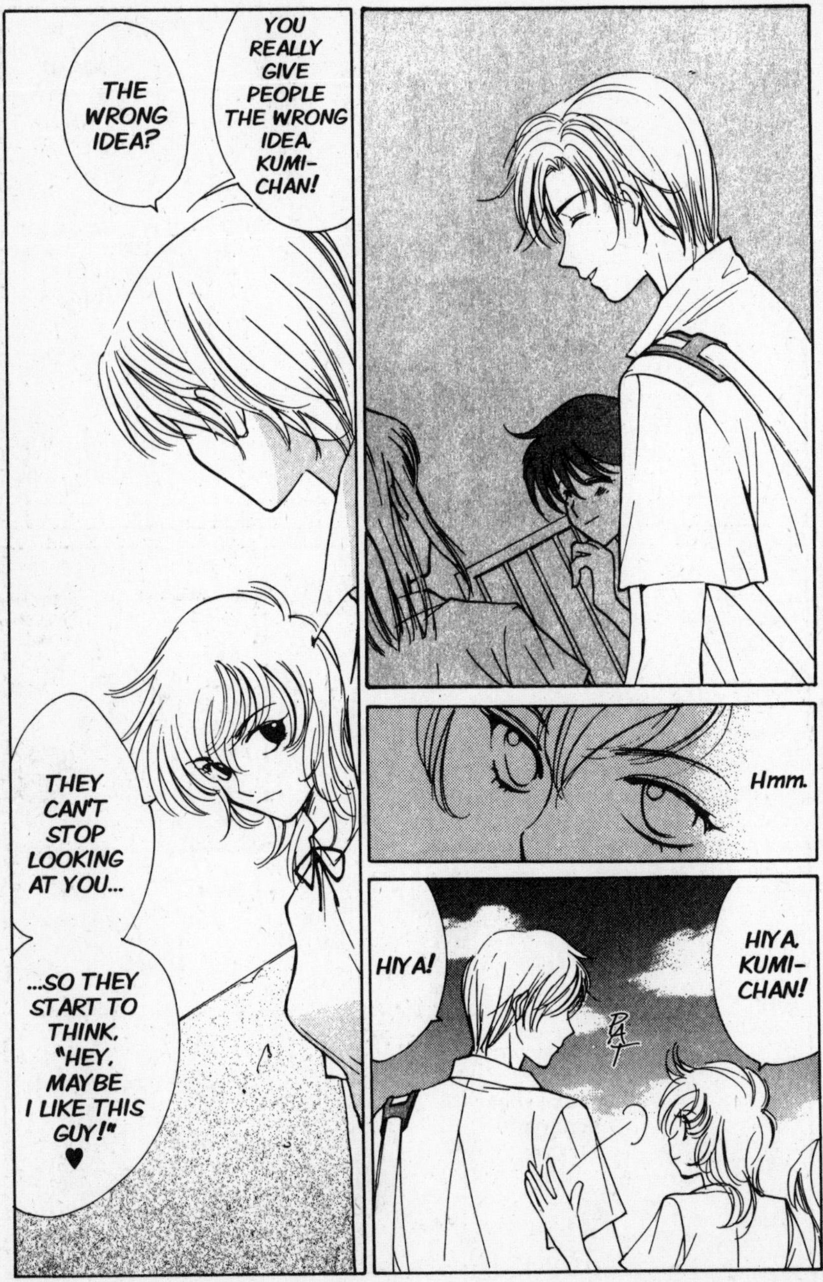
Hmm.
HIYA, KUMI-CHAN!
PAT
HIYA!
YOU REALLY GIVE PEOPLE THE WRONG IDEA, KUMI-CHAN!
THE WRONG IDEA?
THEY CAN'T STOP LOOKING AT YOU...
...SO THEY START TO THINK, "HEY, MAYBE I LIKE THIS GUY!" ♥

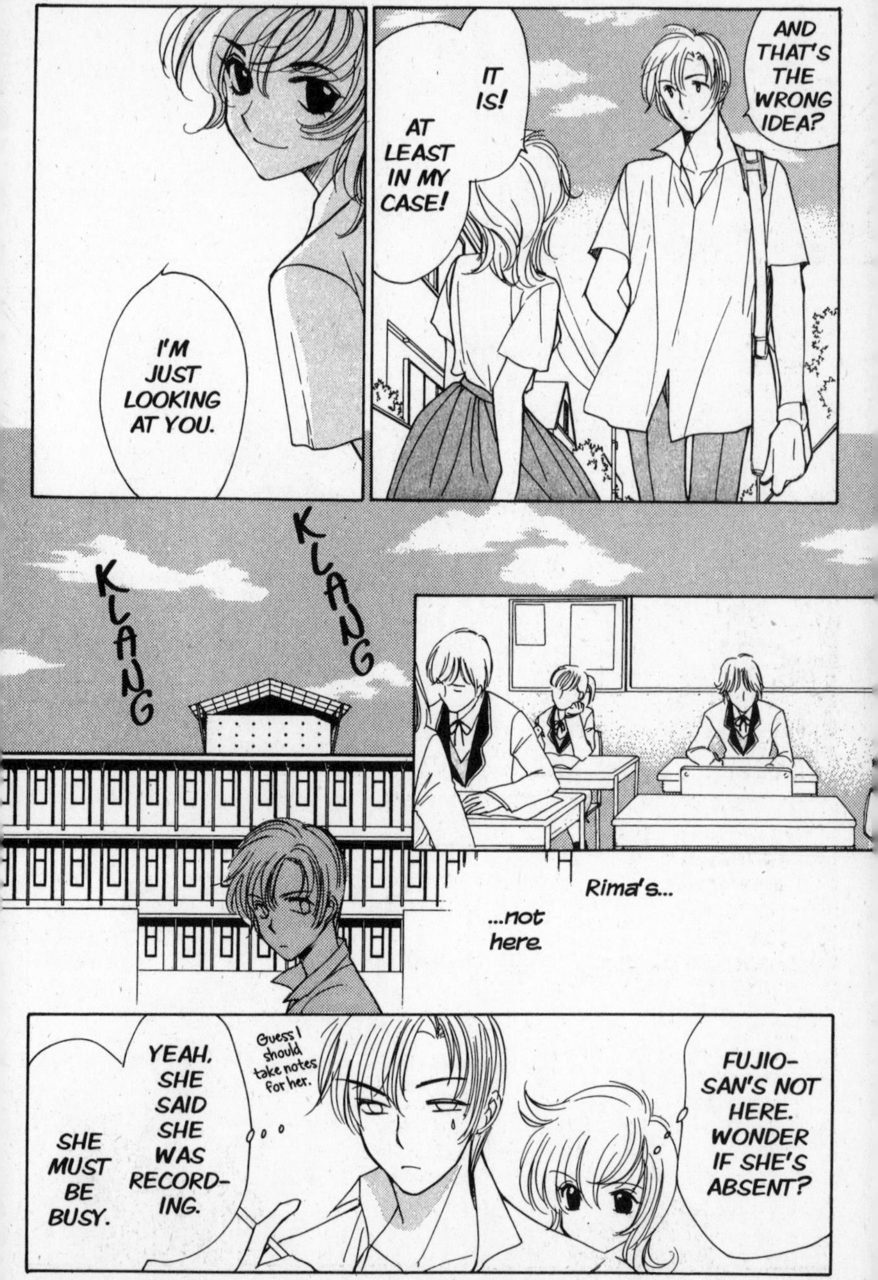
AND THAT'S THE WRONG IDEA?
IT IS! AT LEAST IN MY CASE!
I'M JUST LOOKING AT YOU.
KLANG
KLANG
Rima's...
...not here.
FUJIO-SAN'S NOT HERE. WONDER IF SHE'S ABSENT?
Guess I should take notes for her.
YEAH, SHE SAID SHE WAS RECORDING.
SHE MUST BE BUSY.

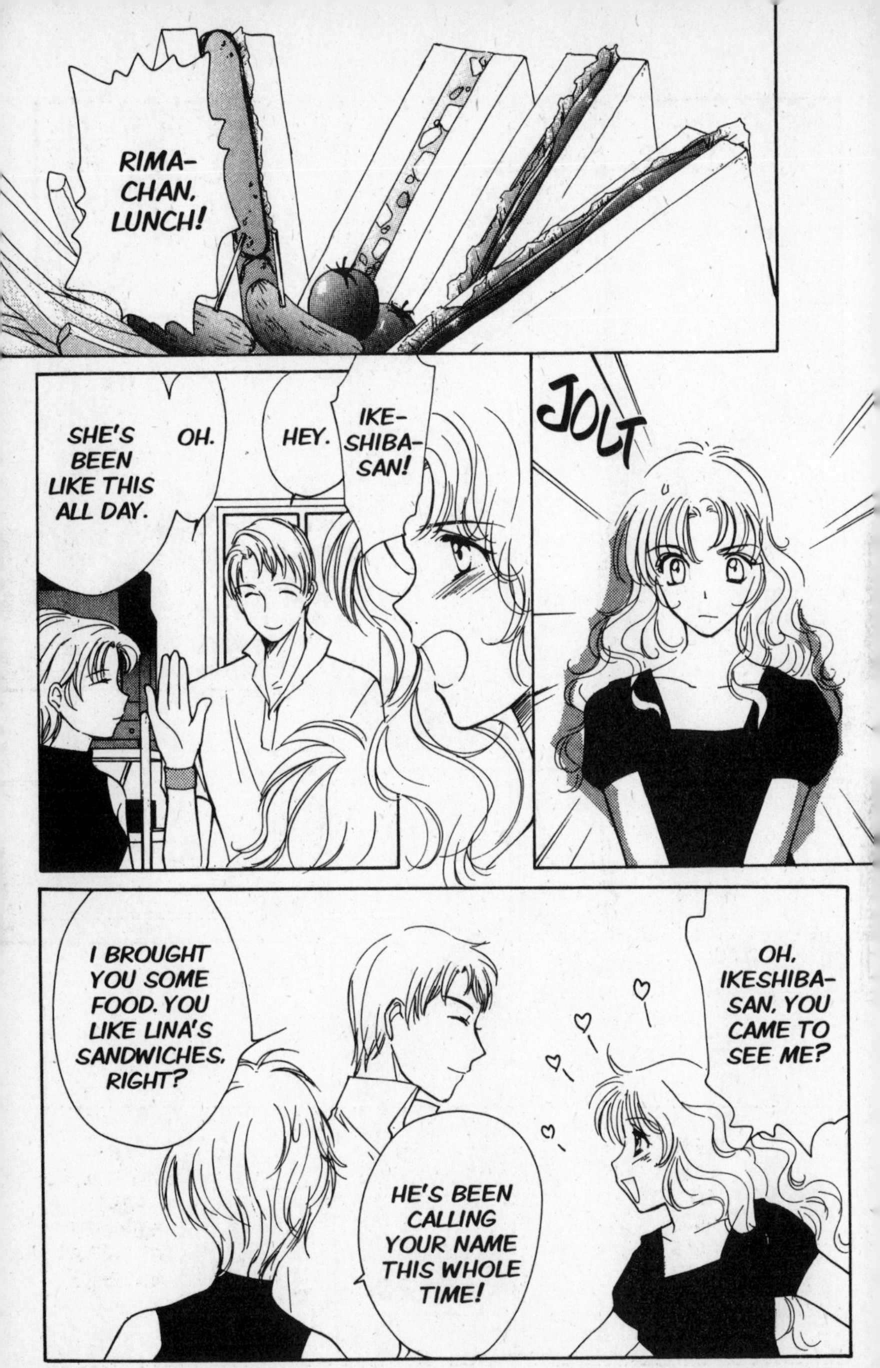
RIMA-CHAN, LUNCH!
JOLT
IKE-SHIBA-SAN!
HEY.
OH.
SHE'S BEEN LIKE THIS ALL DAY.
OH, IKESHIBA-SAN, YOU CAME TO SEE ME?
I BROUGHT YOU SOME FOOD. YOU LIKE LINA'S SANDWICHES, RIGHT?
HE'S BEEN CALLING YOUR NAME THIS WHOLE TIME!

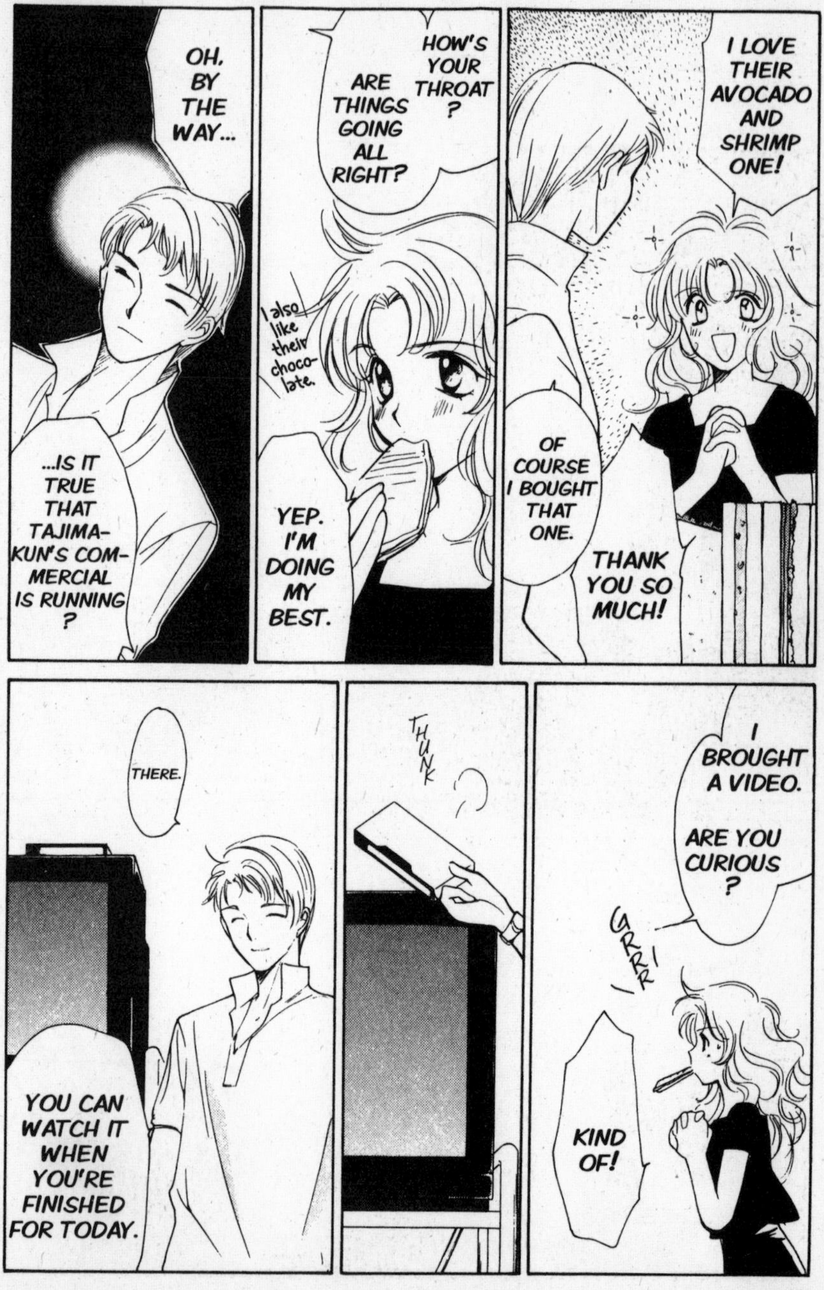
I LOVE THEIR AVOCADO AND SHRIMP ONE!
OF COURSE I BOUGHT THAT ONE.
THANK YOU SO MUCH!
HOW'S YOUR THROAT?
ARE THINGS GOING ALL RIGHT?
I also like their chocolate.
YEP. I'M DOING MY BEST.
OH, BY THE WAY...
...IS IT TRUE THAT TAJIMA-KUN'S COMMERCIAL IS RUNNING?
I BROUGHT A VIDEO.
ARE YOU CURIOUS?
GRRR
KIND OF!
THUNK
THERE.
YOU CAN WATCH IT WHEN YOU'RE FINISHED FOR TODAY.

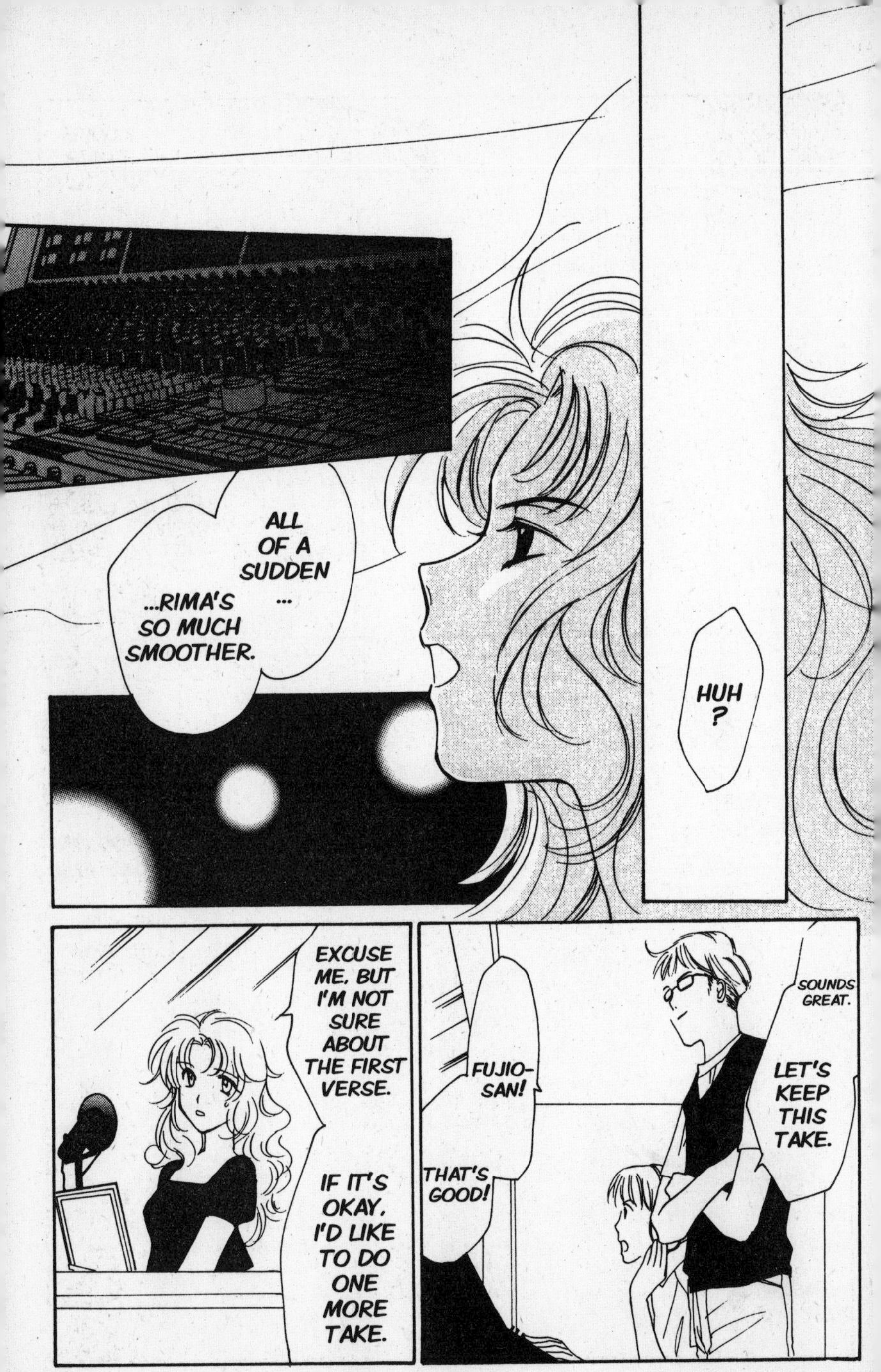
HUH?
ALL OF A SUDDEN ...
...RIMA'S SO MUCH SMOOTHER.
SOUNDS GREAT.
LET'S KEEP THIS TAKE.
FUJIO-SAN!
THAT'S GOOD!
EXCUSE ME, BUT I'M NOT SURE ABOUT THE FIRST VERSE.
IF IT'S OKAY, I'D LIKE TO DO ONE MORE TAKE.

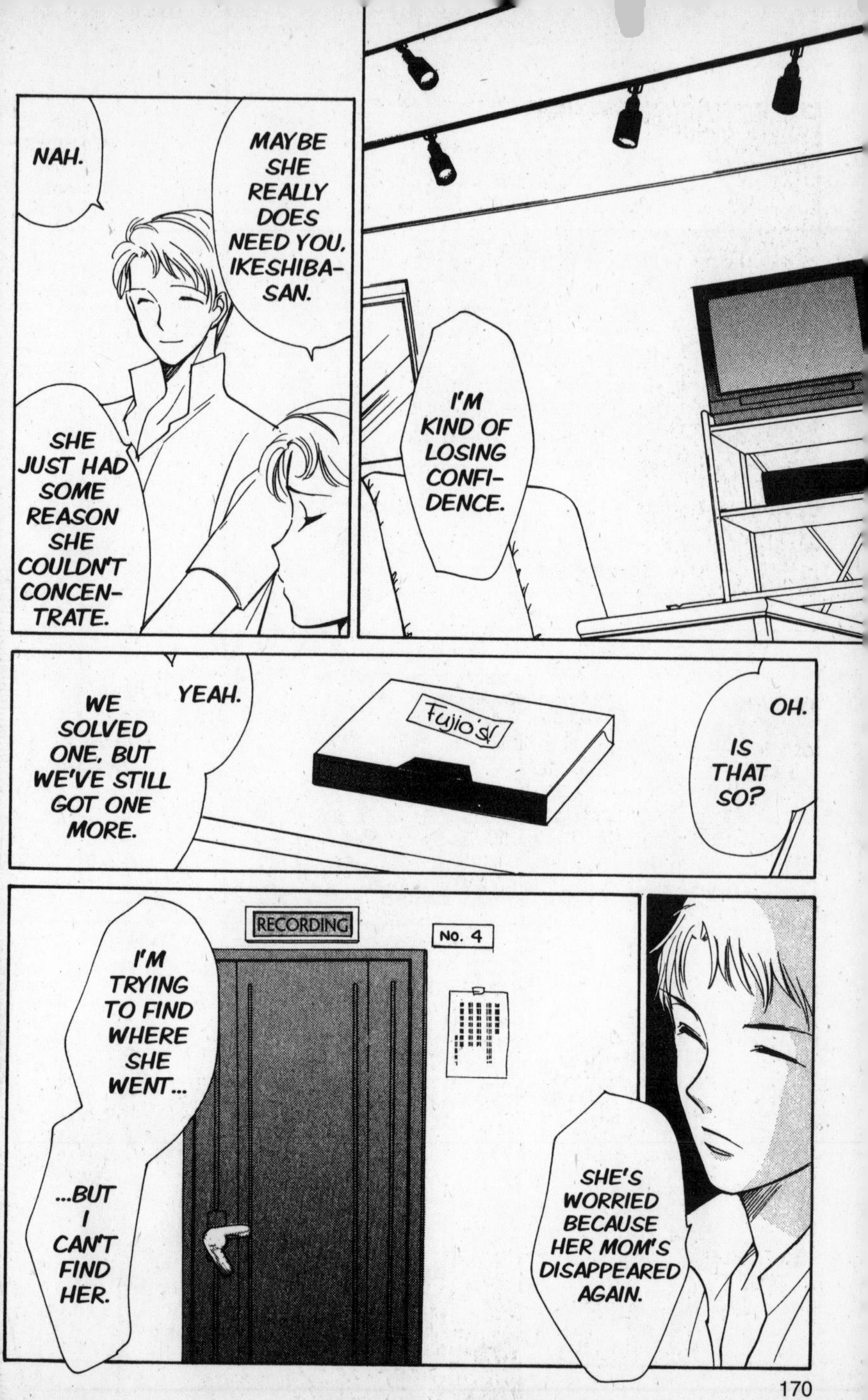
I'M KIND OF LOSING CONFIDENCE.
MAYBE SHE REALLY DOES NEED YOU, IKESHIBA-SAN.
NAH.
SHE JUST HAD SOME REASON SHE COULDN'T CONCENTRATE.
OH. IS THAT SO?
Fujio's!
YEAH.
WE SOLVED ONE, BUT WE'VE STILL GOT ONE MORE.
SHE'S WORRIED BECAUSE HER MOM'S DISAPPEARED AGAIN.
RECORDING
NO. 4
I'M TRYING TO FIND WHERE SHE WENT...
...BUT I CAN'T FIND HER.

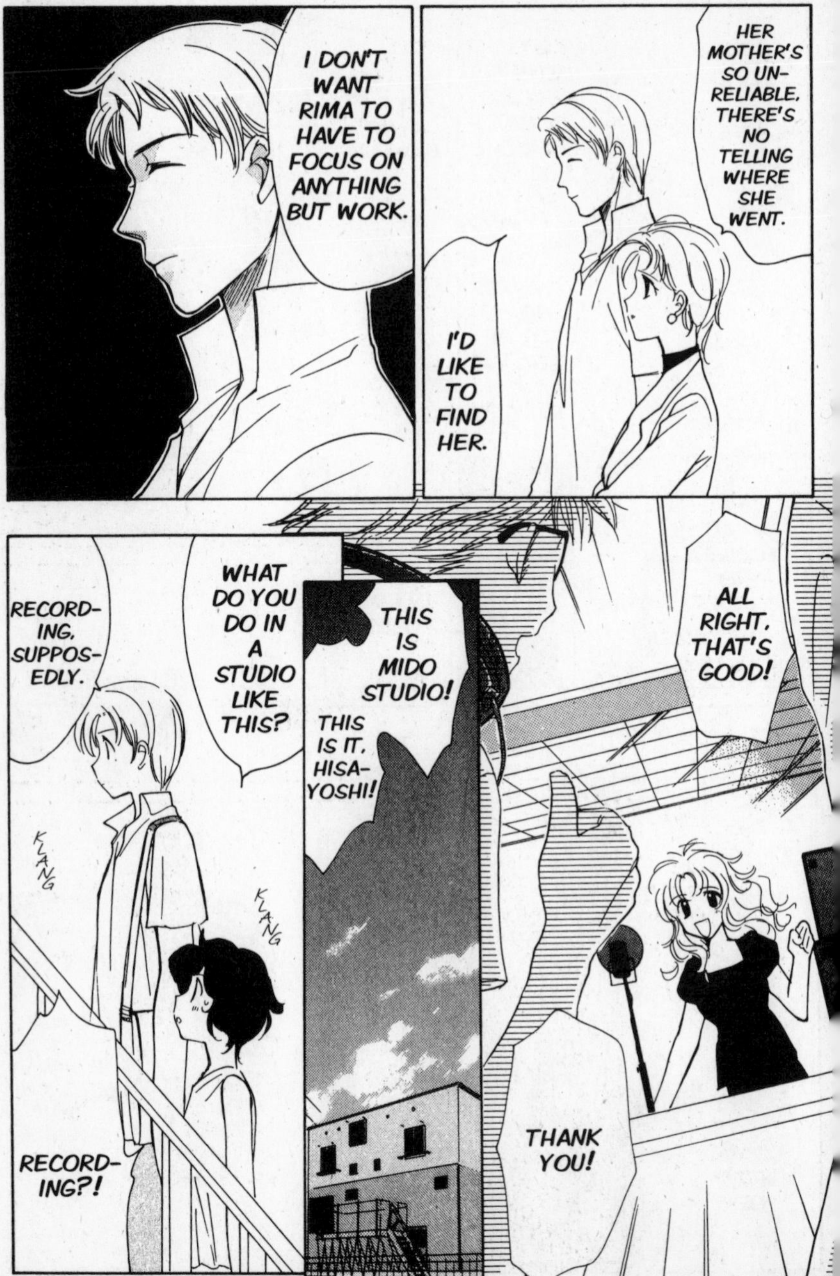
HER MOTHER'S SO UN-RELIABLE, THERE'S NO TELLING WHERE SHE WENT.
I'D LIKE TO FIND HER.
I DON'T WANT RIMA TO HAVE TO FOCUS ON ANYTHING BUT WORK.
ALL RIGHT, THAT'S GOOD!
THANK YOU!
THIS IS MIDO STUDIO!
THIS IS IT, HISA-YOSHI!
WHAT DO YOU DO IN A STUDIO LIKE THIS?
RECORD-ING, SUPPOS-EDLY.
KLANG
KLANG
RECORD-ING?!

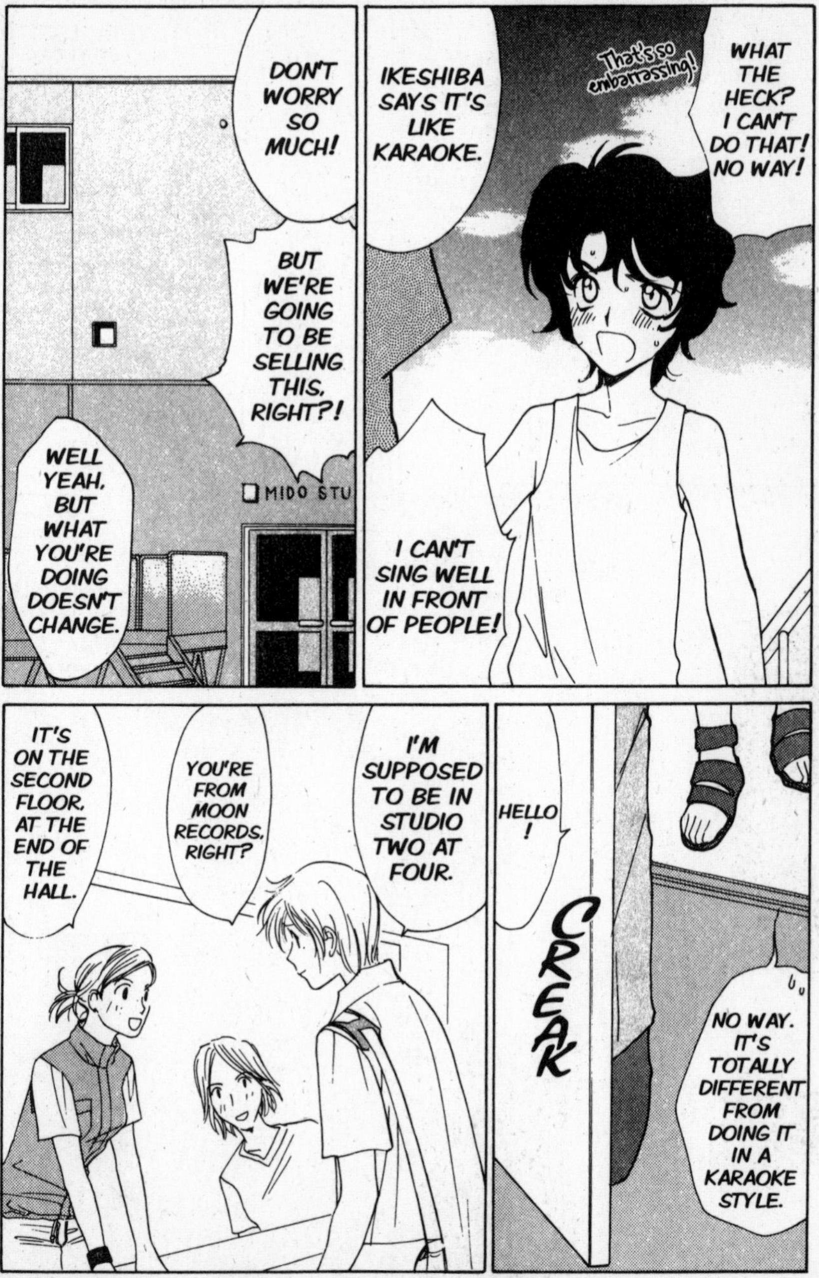
That's so embarrassing!
WHAT THE HECK? I CAN'T DO THAT! NO WAY!
IKESHIBA SAYS IT'S LIKE KARAOKE.
I CAN'T SING WELL IN FRONT OF PEOPLE!
DON'T WORRY SO MUCH!
BUT WE'RE GOING TO BE SELLING THIS, RIGHT?!
WELL YEAH, BUT WHAT YOU'RE DOING DOESN'T CHANGE.
MIDO STU
NO WAY. IT'S TOTALLY DIFFERENT FROM DOING IT IN A KARAOKE STYLE.
CREAK
HELLO!
I'M SUPPOSED TO BE IN STUDIO TWO AT FOUR.
YOU'RE FROM MOON RECORDS, RIGHT?
IT'S ON THE SECOND FLOOR, AT THE END OF THE HALL.

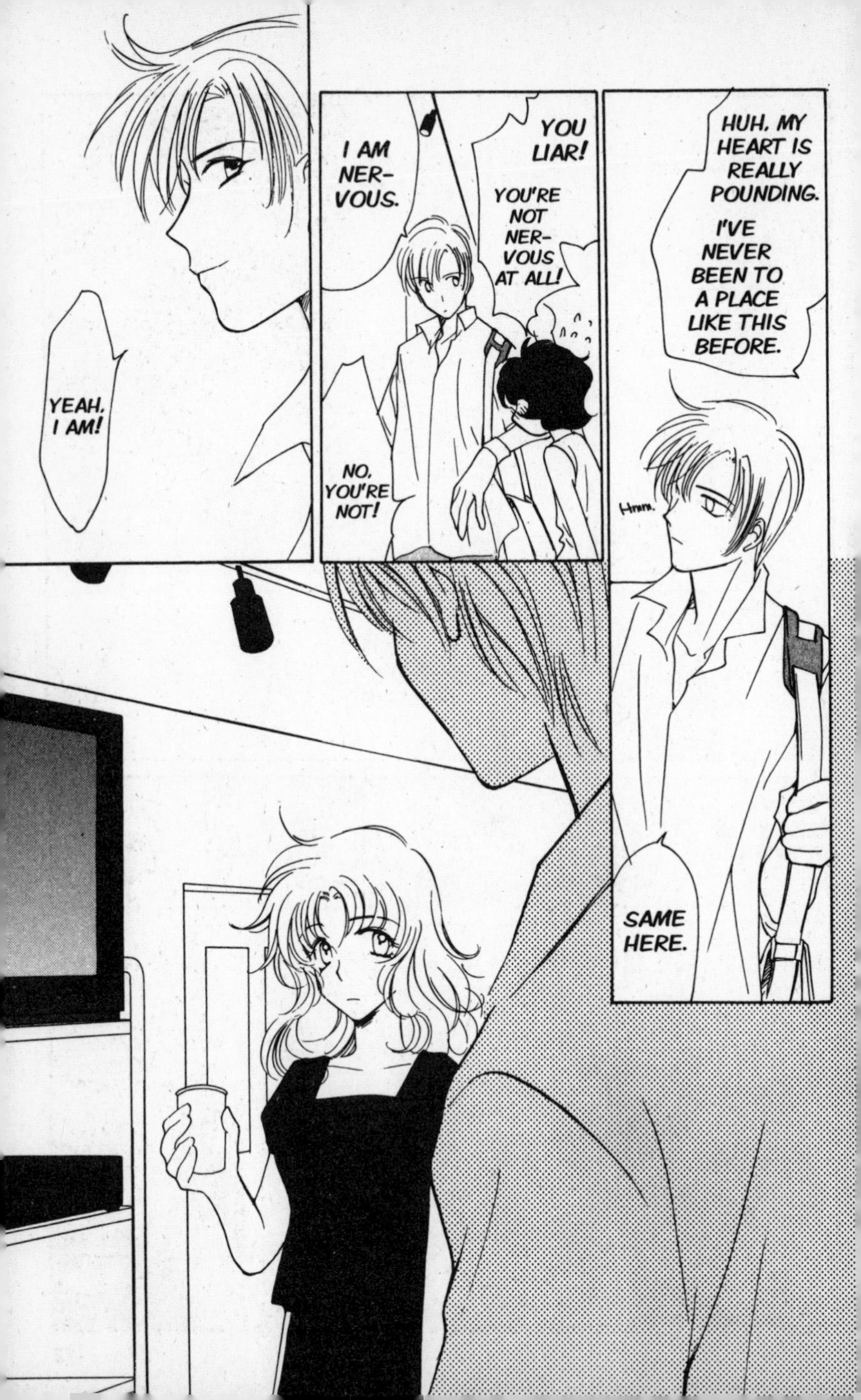
HUH, MY HEART IS REALLY POUNDING.
I'VE NEVER BEEN TO A PLACE LIKE THIS BEFORE.
Hmm.
SAME HERE.
YOU LIAR!
YOU'RE NOT NERVOUS AT ALL!
I AM NERVOUS.
NO, YOU'RE NOT!
YEAH, I AM!

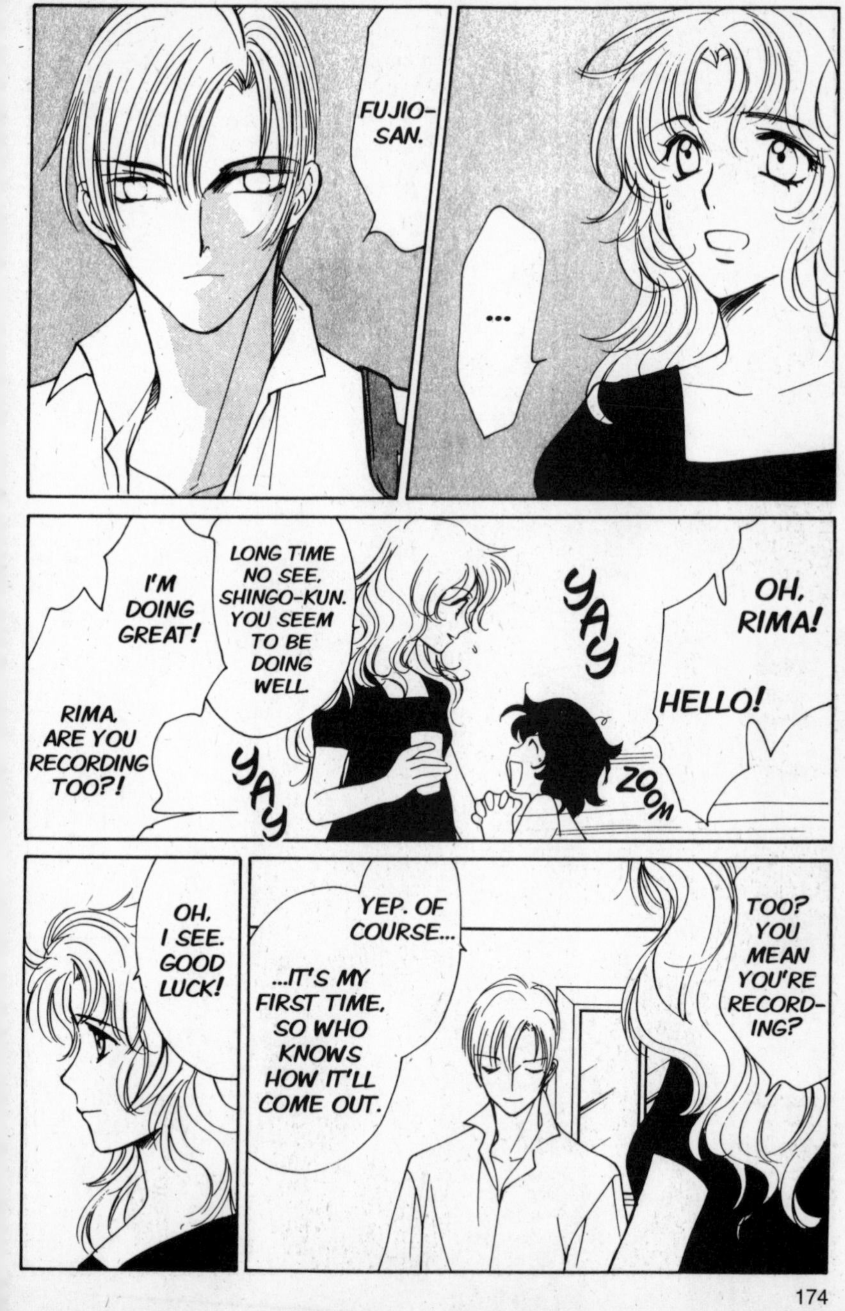
...
FUJIO-SAN.
OH, RIMA!
HELLO!
YAY
ZOOM
LONG TIME NO SEE, SHINGO-KUN. YOU SEEM TO BE DOING WELL.
I'M DOING GREAT!
RIMA, ARE YOU RECORDING TOO?!
YAY
TOO? YOU MEAN YOU'RE RECORDING?
YEP. OF COURSE...
...IT'S MY FIRST TIME, SO WHO KNOWS HOW IT'LL COME OUT.
OH, I SEE. GOOD LUCK!

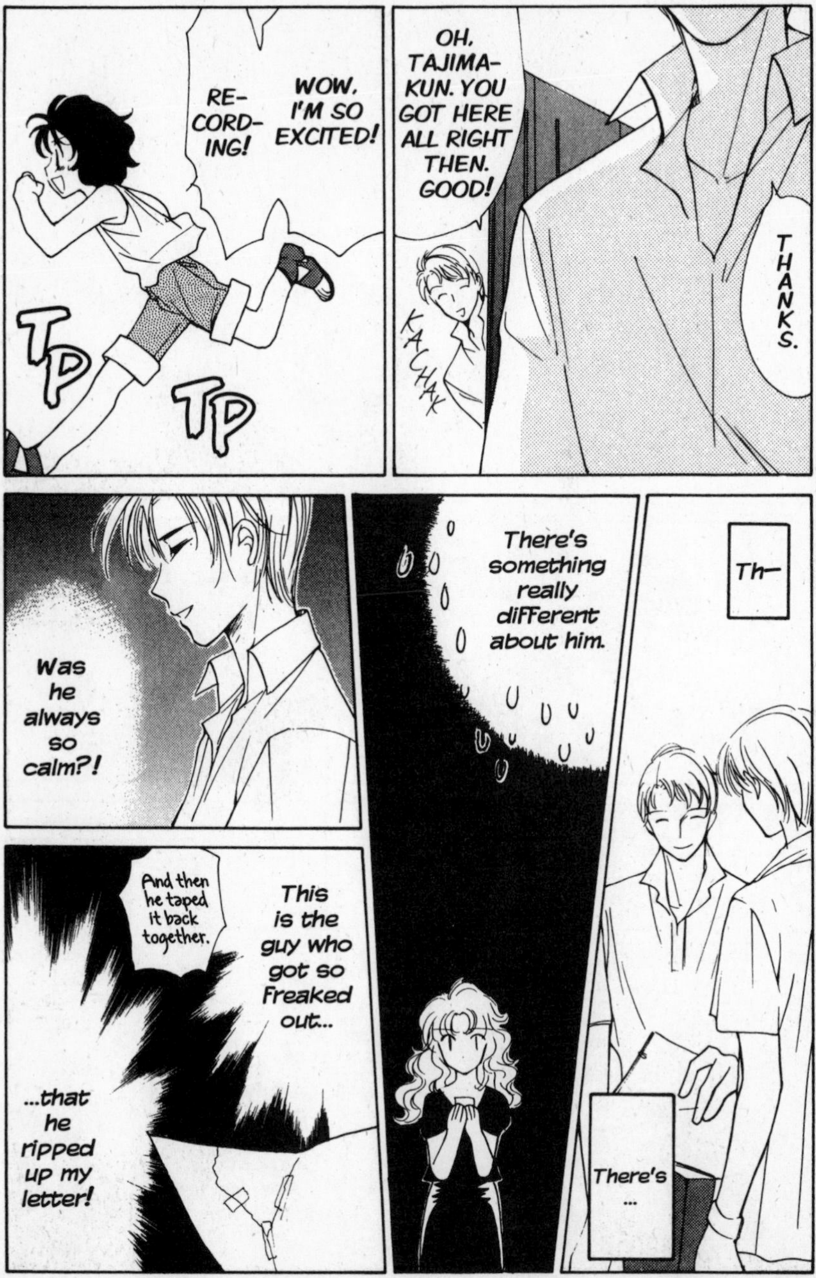
OH, TAJIMA-KUN. YOU GOT HERE ALL RIGHT THEN. GOOD!
KACHAK
THANKS.
WOW, I'M SO EXCITED!
RE-CORD-ING!
TP
TP
Th—
There's ...
There's something really different about him.
Was he always so calm?!
This is the guy who got so freaked out...
...that he ripped up my letter!
And then he taped it back together.

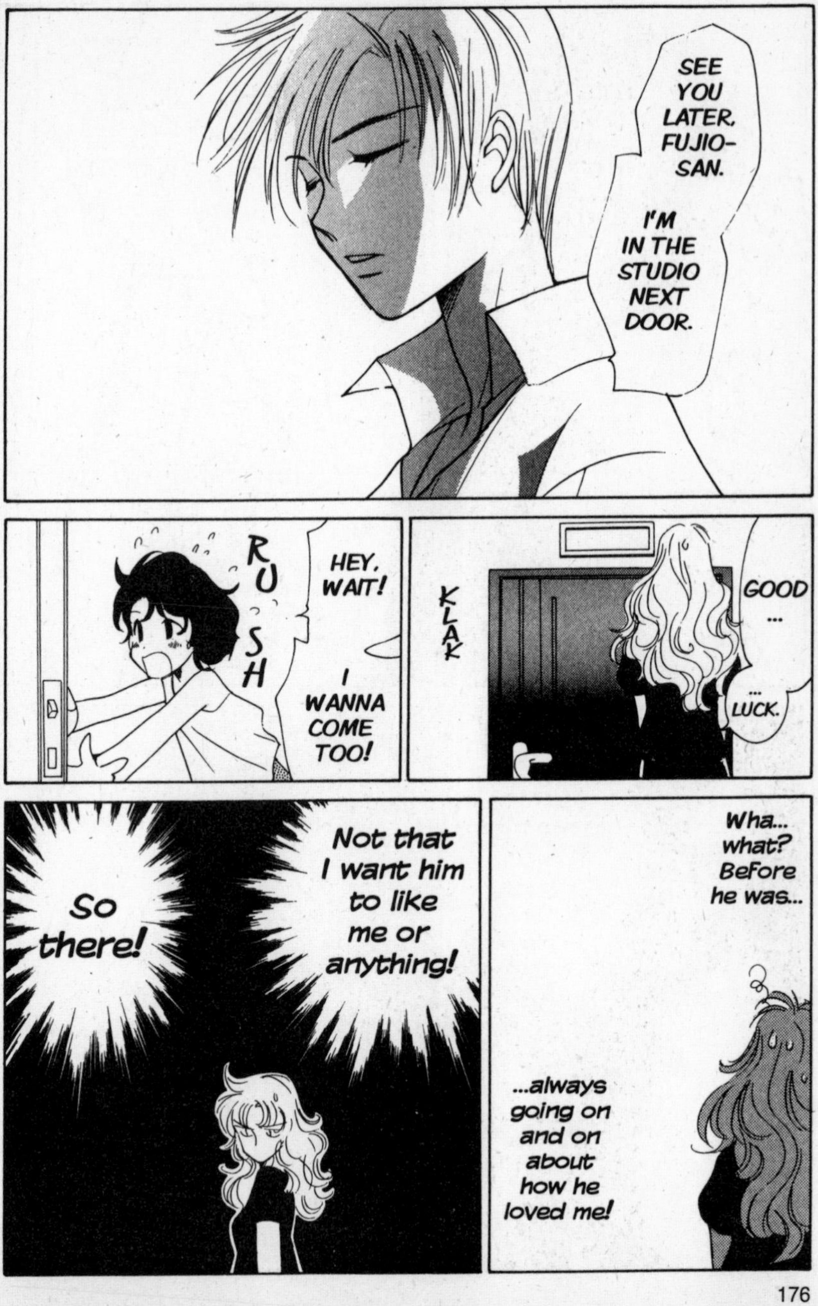
SEE YOU LATER, FUJIO-SAN.
I'M IN THE STUDIO NEXT DOOR.
GOOD ...
... LUCK.
KLAK
HEY, WAIT!
I WANNA COME TOO!
RUSH
Wha... what? Before he was...
...always going on and on about how he loved me!
Not that I want him to like me or anything!
So there!

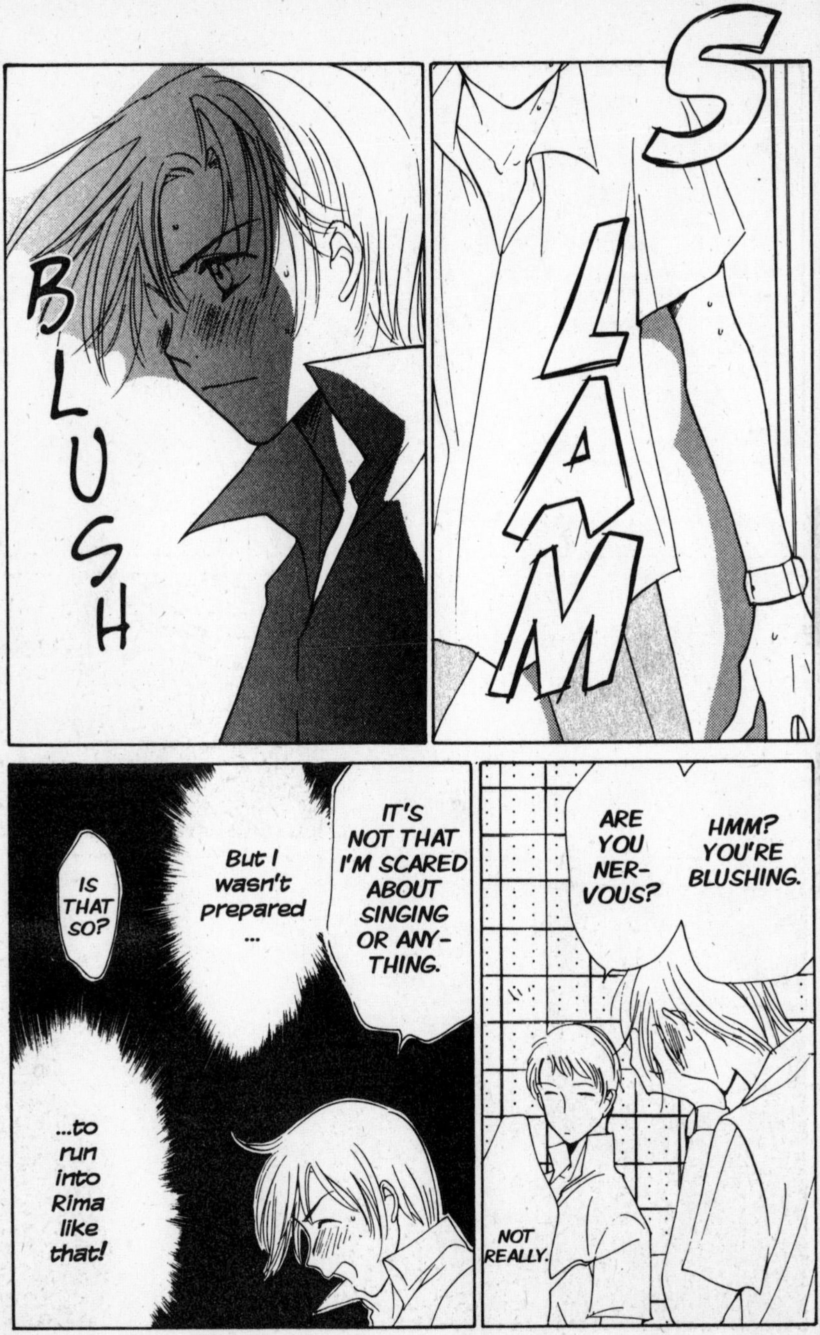
SLAM
BLUSH
HMM? YOU'RE BLUSHING.
ARE YOU NERVOUS?
NOT REALLY.
IT'S NOT THAT I'M SCARED ABOUT SINGING OR ANYTHING.
But I wasn't prepared ...
IS THAT SO?
...to run into Rima like that!

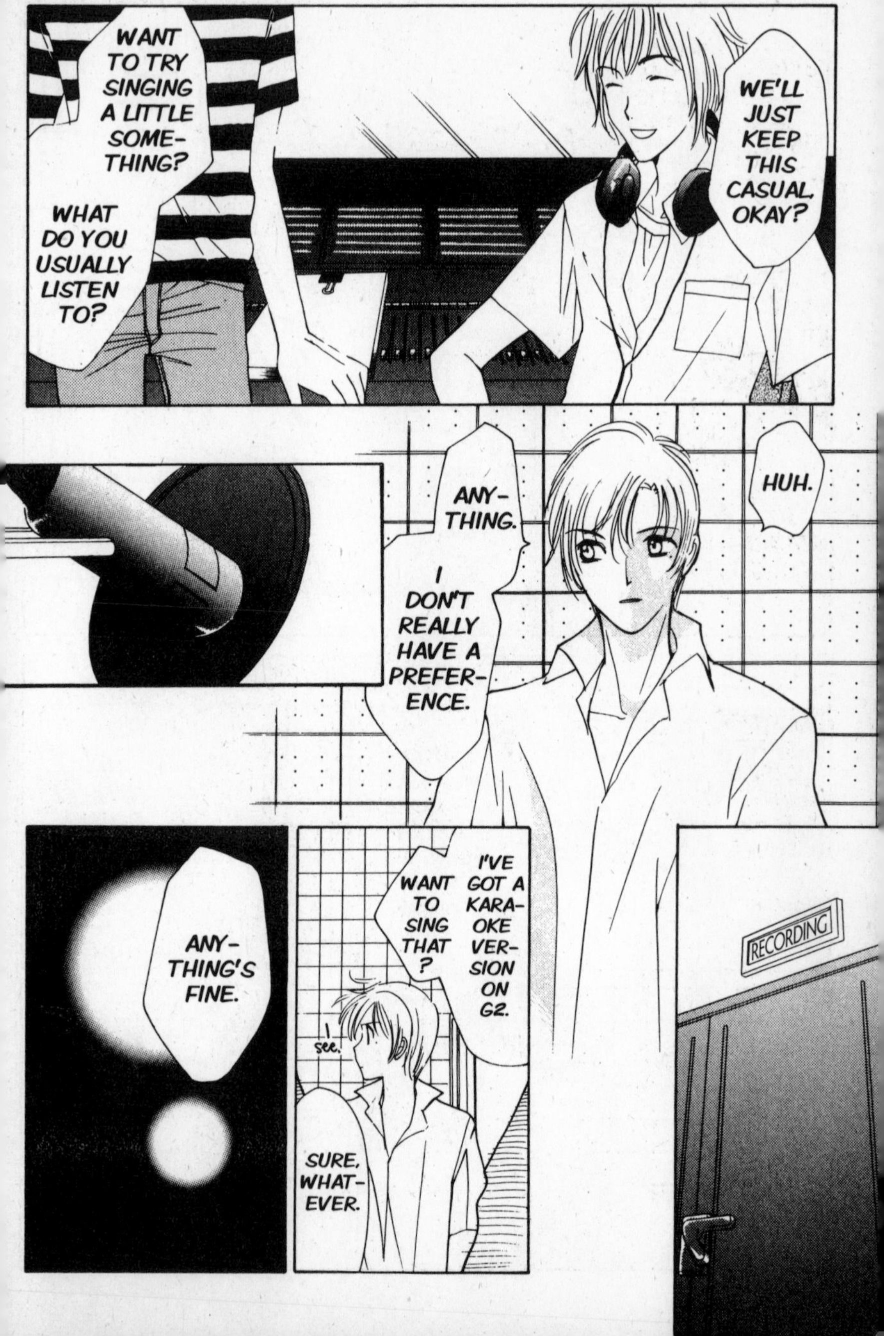
WE'LL JUST KEEP THIS CASUAL, OKAY?
WANT TO TRY SINGING A LITTLE SOMETHING?
WHAT DO YOU USUALLY LISTEN TO?
HUH.
ANYTHING.
I DON'T REALLY HAVE A PREFERENCE.
RECORDING
I'VE GOT A KARAOKE VERSION ON G2.
WANT TO SING THAT?
I see.
SURE, WHATEVER.
ANYTHING'S FINE.

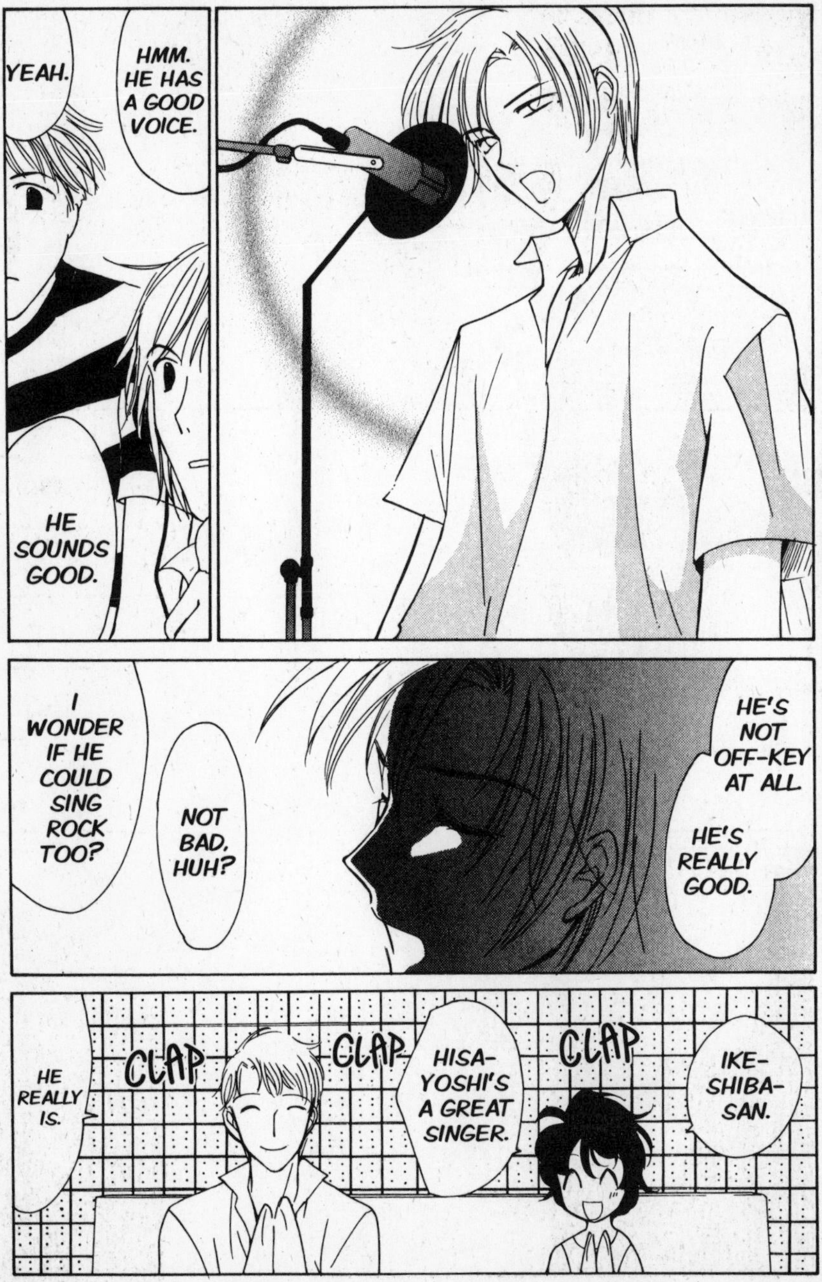
HMM. HE HAS A GOOD VOICE.
YEAH.
HE SOUNDS GOOD.
HE'S NOT OFF-KEY AT ALL
HE'S REALLY GOOD.
NOT BAD, HUH?
I WONDER IF HE COULD SING ROCK TOO?
IKE-SHIBA-SAN.
CLAP
HISA-YOSHI'S A GREAT SINGER.
CLAP
CLAP
HE REALLY IS.

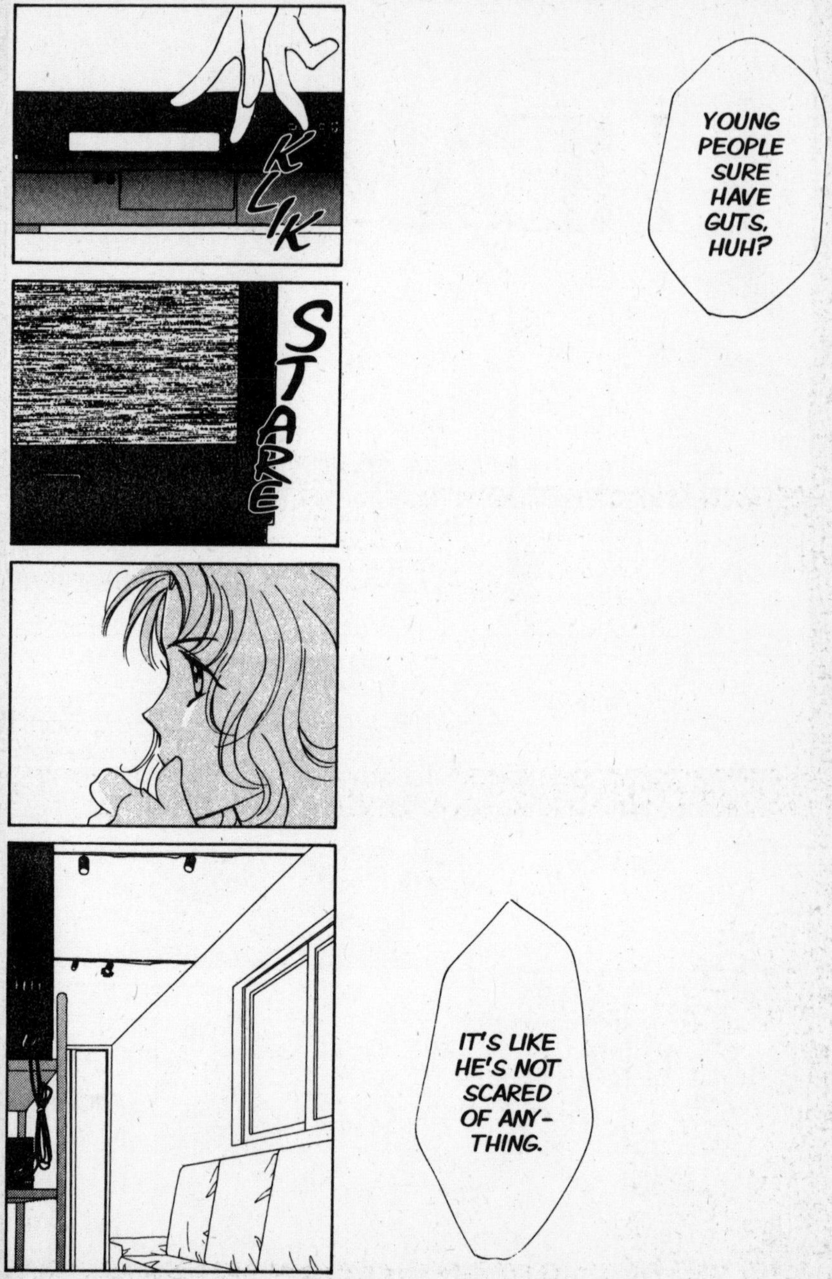
YOUNG PEOPLE SURE HAVE GUTS, HUH?
KLIK
STARE
IT'S LIKE HE'S NOT SCARED OF ANY-THING.

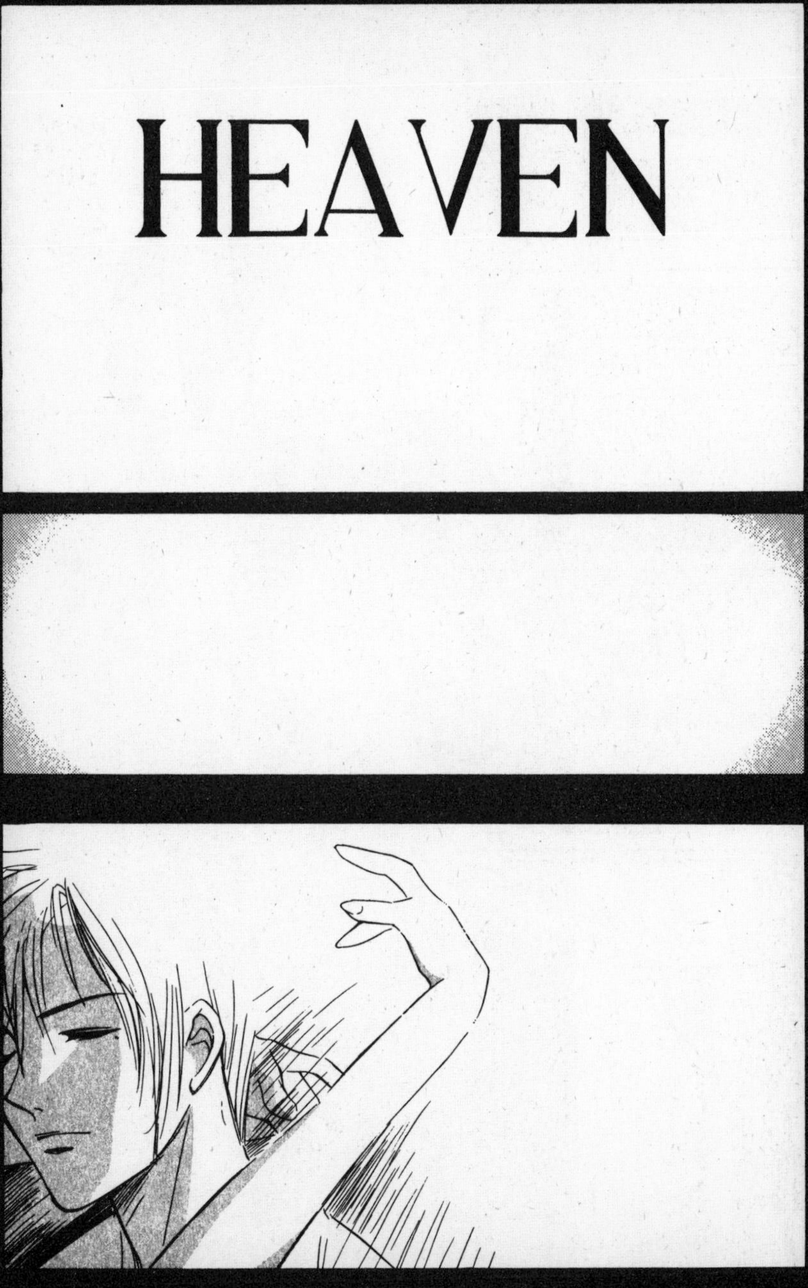
HEAVEN

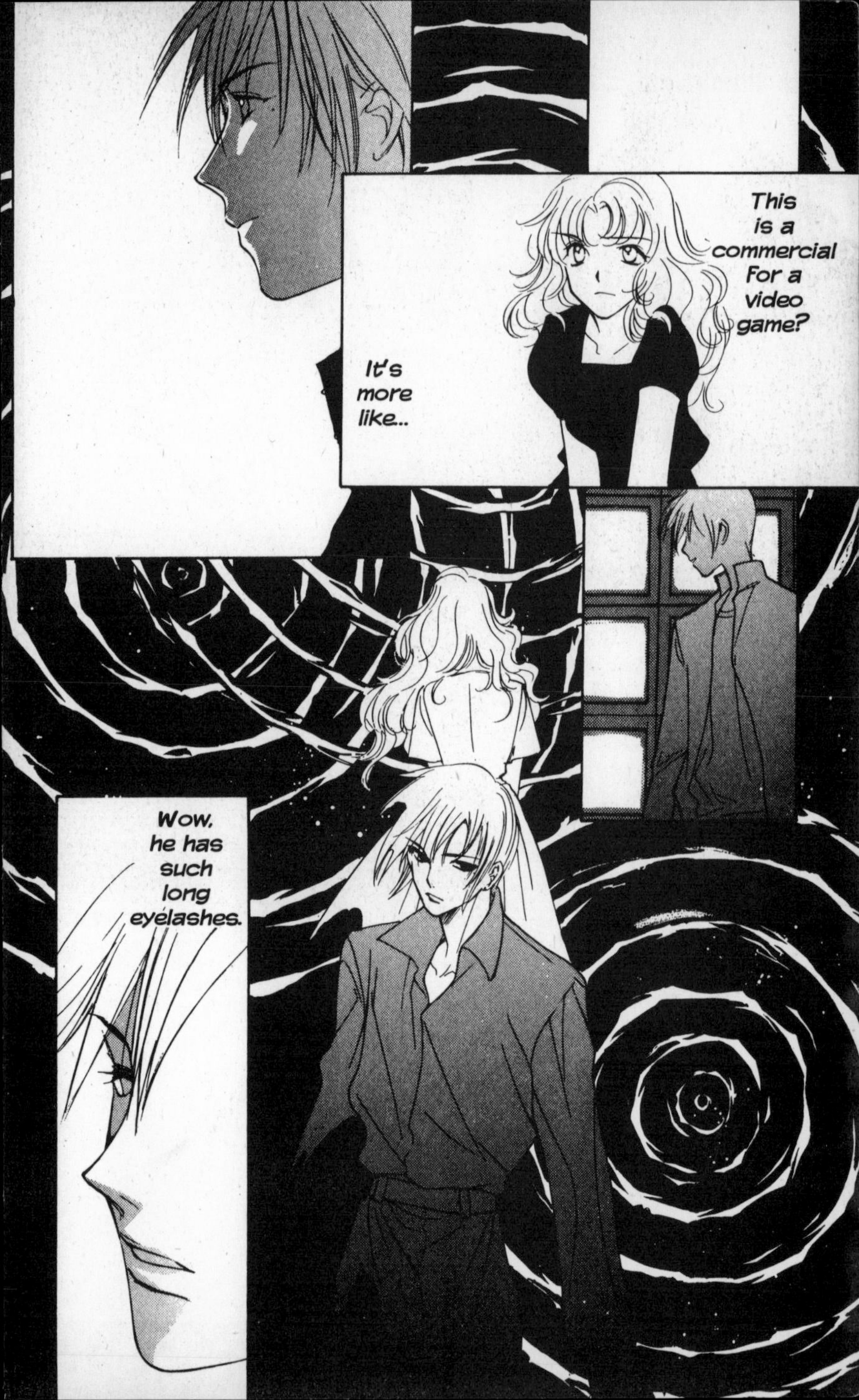
This is a commercial For a video game?
It's more like...
Wow, he has such long eyelashes.

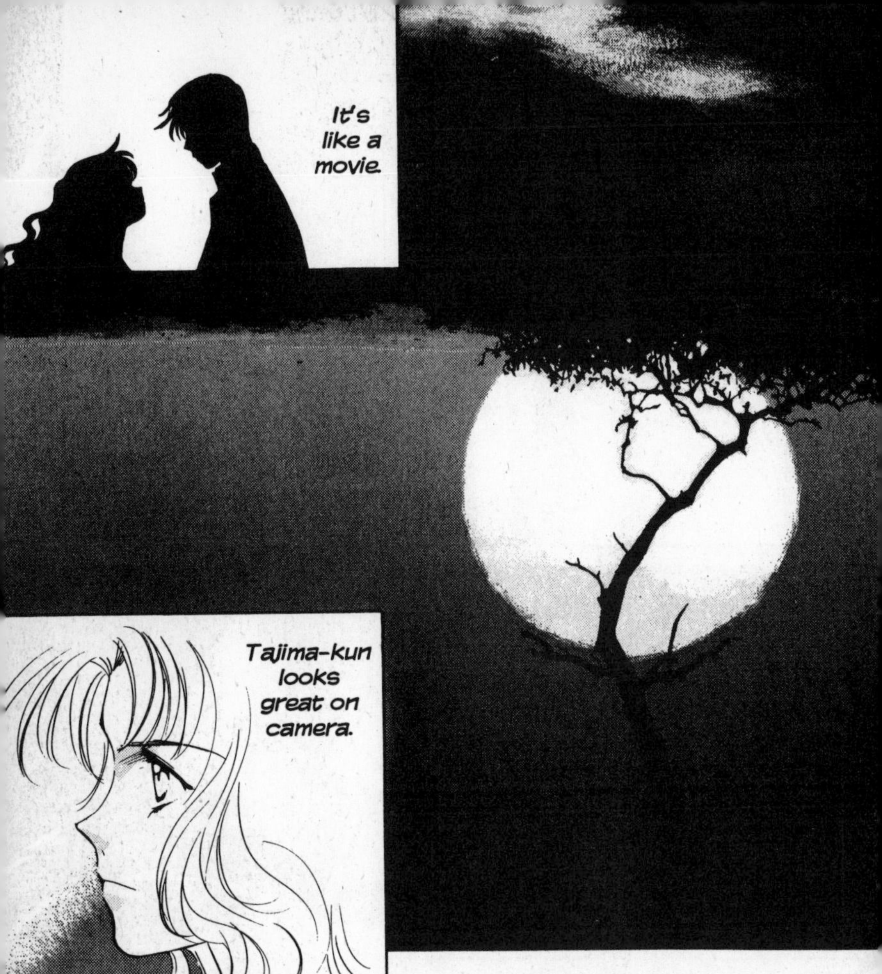
It's like a movie.
Tajima-kun looks great on camera.

HEAVEN

Coming this fall.

SAI-Z

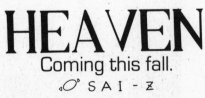

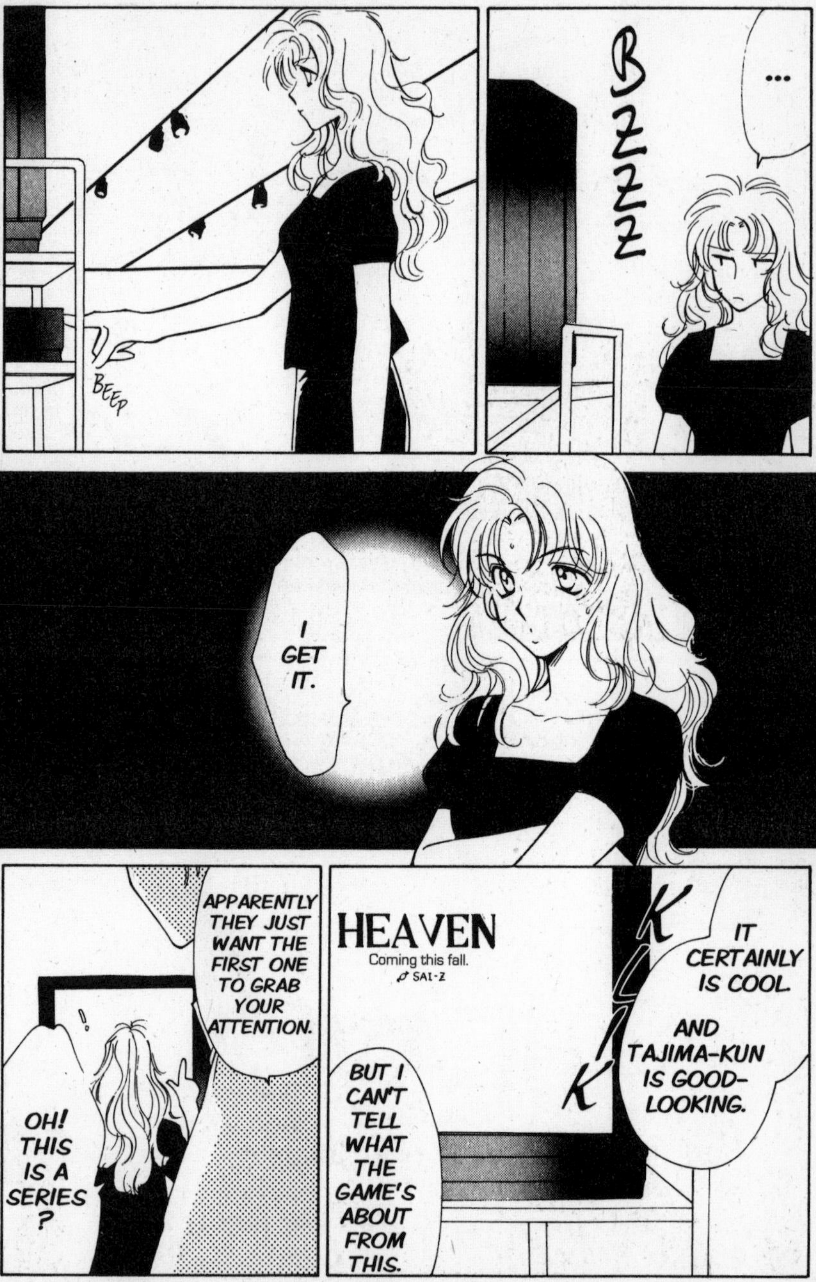
...
BZZZZ
BEEP
I GET IT.
IT CERTAINLY IS COOL.
AND TAJIMA-KUN IS GOOD-LOOKING.
KLIK
HEAVEN
Coming this fall.
SAI-Z
BUT I CAN'T TELL WHAT THE GAME'S ABOUT FROM THIS.
APPARENTLY THEY JUST WANT THE FIRST ONE TO GRAB YOUR ATTENTION.
!
OH! THIS IS A SERIES?

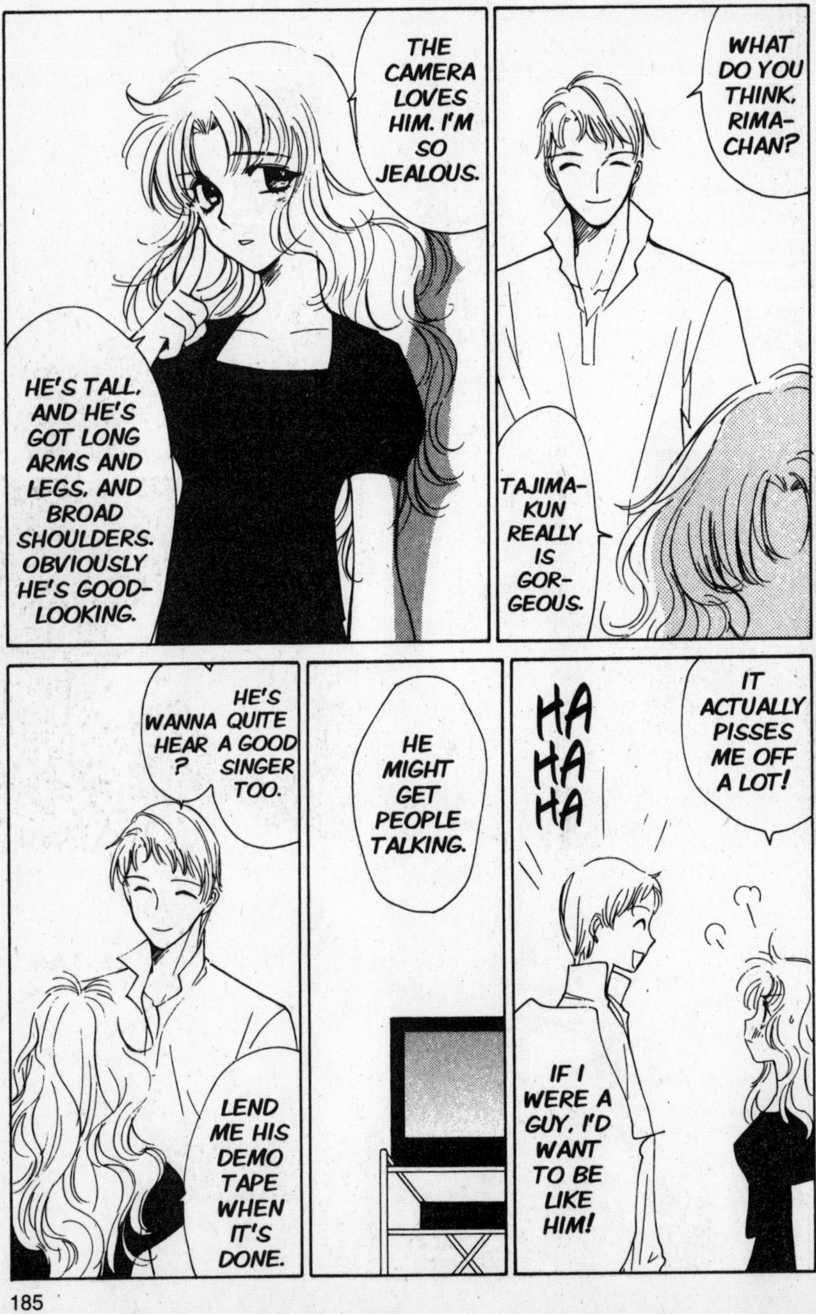
WHAT DO YOU THINK, RIMA-CHAN?
TAJIMA-KUN REALLY IS GORGEOUS.
THE CAMERA LOVES HIM. I'M SO JEALOUS.
HE'S TALL, AND HE'S GOT LONG ARMS AND LEGS, AND BROAD SHOULDERS. OBVIOUSLY HE'S GOOD-LOOKING.
IT ACTUALLY PISSES ME OFF A LOT!
HA HA HA
IF I WERE A GUY, I'D WANT TO BE LIKE HIM!
HE MIGHT GET PEOPLE TALKING.
HE'S QUITE A GOOD SINGER TOO.
WANNA HEAR?
LEND ME HIS DEMO TAPE WHEN IT'S DONE.

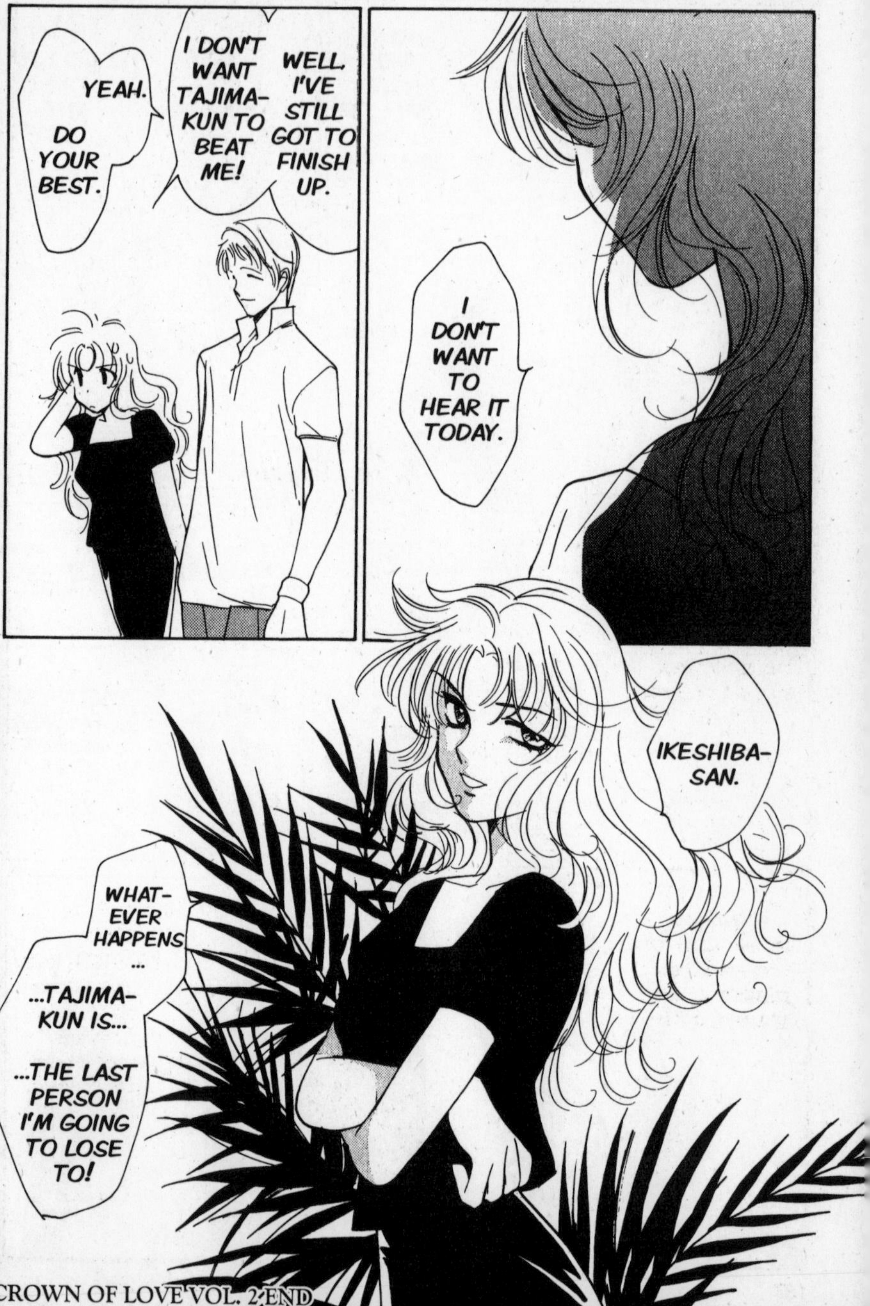
I DON'T WANT TO HEAR IT TODAY.
WELL, I'VE STILL GOT TO FINISH UP.
I DON'T WANT TAJIMA-KUN TO BEAT ME!
YEAH.
DO YOUR BEST.
IKESHIBA-SAN.
WHAT-EVER HAPPENS...
...TAJIMA-KUN IS...
...THE LAST PERSON I'M GOING TO LOSE TO!

CROWN OF LOVE VOL. 2 END

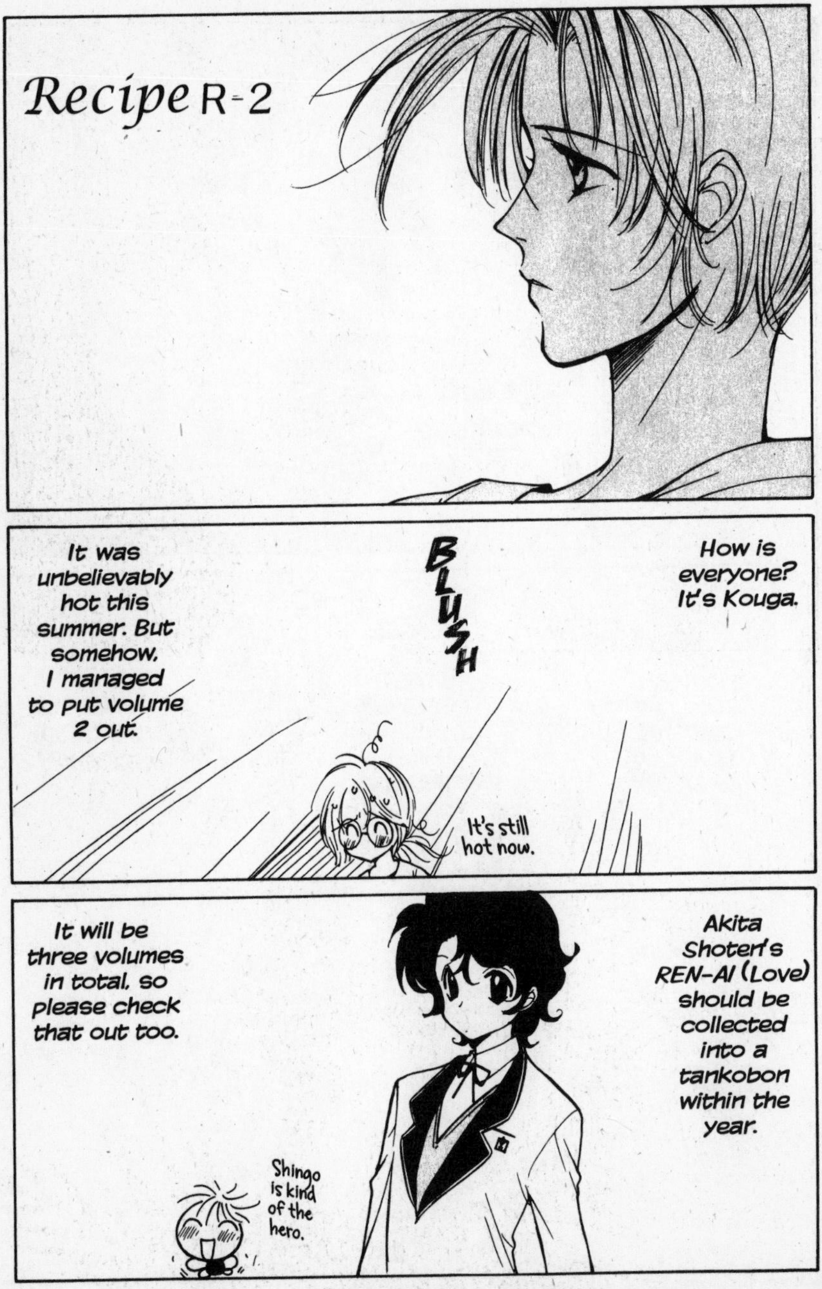
Recipe R-2
How is everyone? It's Kouga.
BLUSH
It was unbelievably hot this summer. But somehow, I managed to put volume 2 out.
It's still hot now.
Akita Shoten's REN-AI (Love) should be collected into a tankobon within the year.
It will be three volumes in total, so please check that out too.
Shingo is kind of the hero.

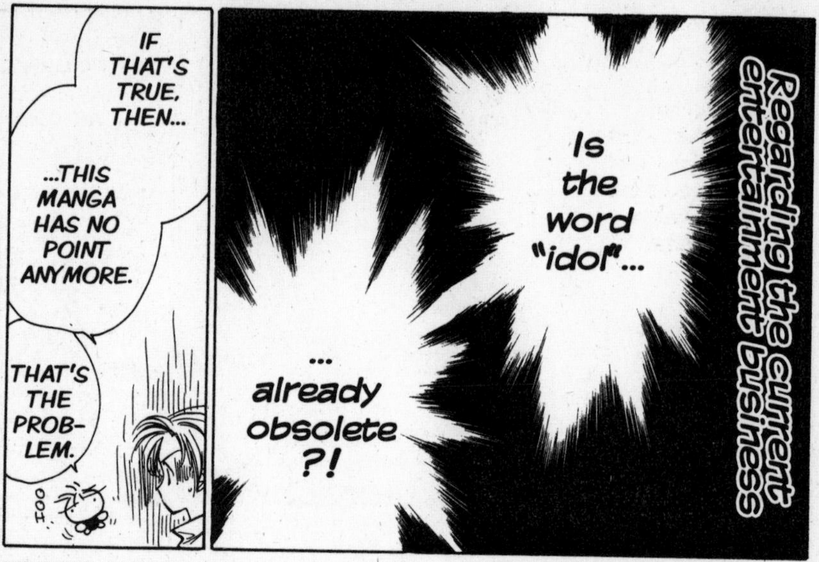
Regarding the current entertainment business
Is the word "idol"...
...already obsolete?!
IF THAT'S TRUE, THEN...
...THIS MANGA HAS NO POINT ANYMORE.
THAT'S THE PROBLEM.
OOH.

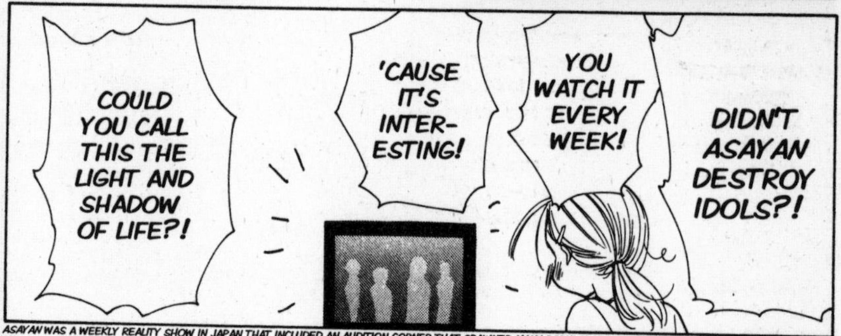
DIDN'T ASAYAN DESTROY IDOLS?!
YOU WATCH IT EVERY WEEK!
'CAUSE IT'S INTERESTING!
COULD YOU CALL THIS THE LIGHT AND SHADOW OF LIFE?!

ASAYAN WAS A WEEKLY REALITY SHOW IN JAPAN THAT INCLUDED AN AUDITION CORNER THAT SPAWNED MANY POPULAR IDOLS LIKE AMI SUZUKI AND MORNING MUSUME.

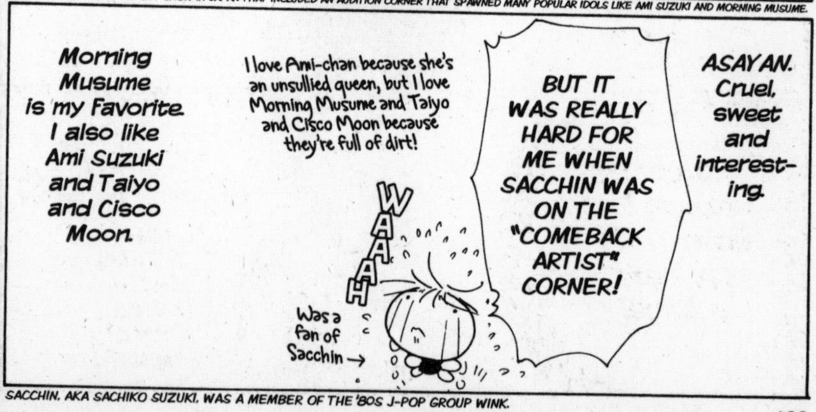
ASAYAN. Cruel, sweet and interesting.
BUT IT WAS REALLY HARD FOR ME WHEN SACCHIN WAS ON THE "COMEBACK ARTIST" CORNER!
WAAAAH
Was a fan of Sacchin →
I love Ami-chan because she's an unsullied queen, but I love Morning Musume and Taiyo and Cisco Moon because they're full of dirt!
Morning Musume is my Favorite. I also like Ami Suzuki and Taiyo and Cisco Moon.

SACCHIN, AKA SACHIKO SUZUKI, WAS A MEMBER OF THE '80S J-POP GROUP WINK.

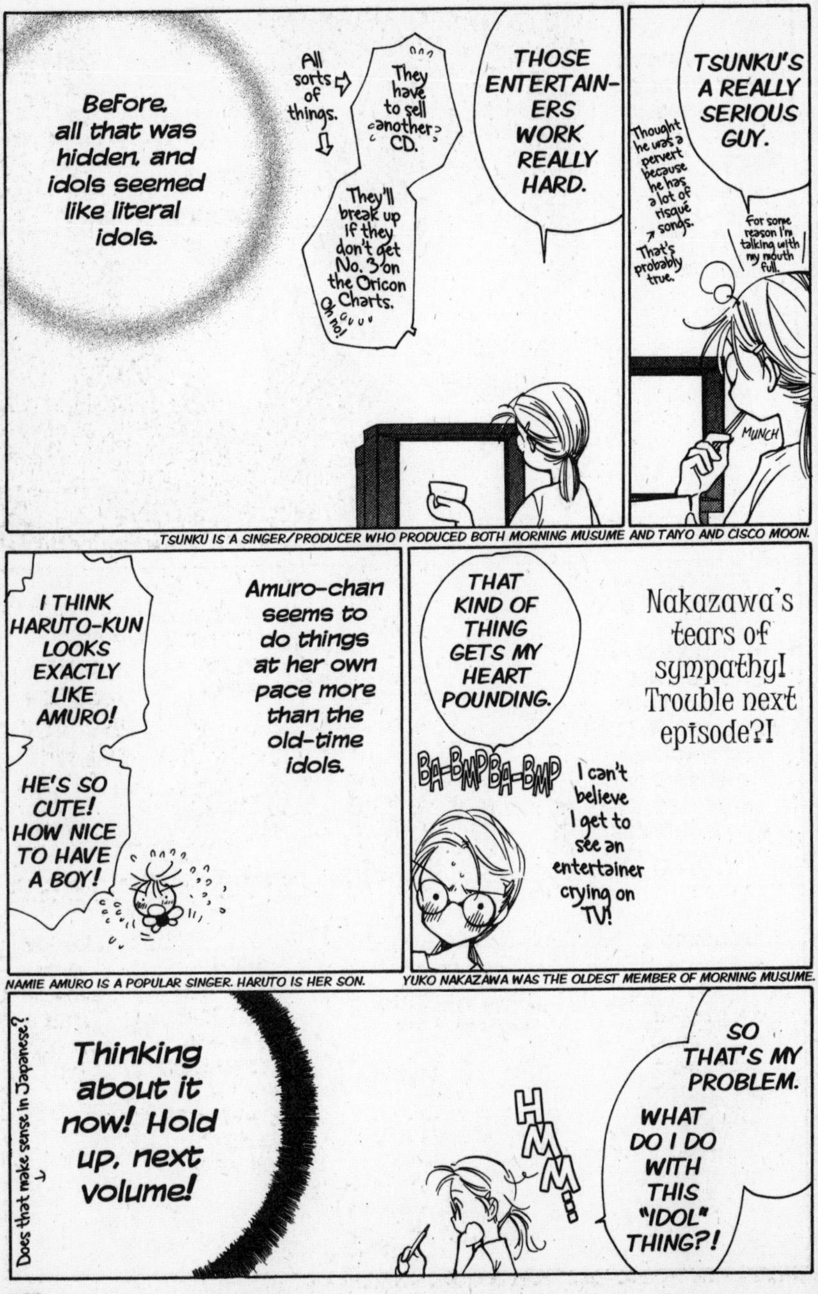
TSUNKU'S A REALLY SERIOUS GUY.
For some reason I'm talking with my mouth full.
Thought he was a pervert because he has a lot of risqué songs.
That's probably true.
MUNCH
THOSE ENTERTAINERS WORK REALLY HARD.
They have to sell another CD.
They'll break up if they don't get No. 3 on the Oricon Charts.
Oh no!
All sorts of things.
Before, all that was hidden, and idols seemed like literal idols.
Nakazawa's tears of sympathy! Trouble next episode?!
THAT KIND OF THING GETS MY HEART POUNDING.
I can't believe I get to see an entertainer crying on TV!
BA-BMP BA-BMP
Amuro-chan seems to do things at her own pace more than the old-time idols.
I THINK HARUTO-KUN LOOKS EXACTLY LIKE AMURO!
HE'S SO CUTE! HOW NICE TO HAVE A BOY!
SO THAT'S MY PROBLEM.
WHAT DO I DO WITH THIS "IDOL" THING?!
HMM...
Thinking about it now! Hold up, next volume!
Does that make sense in Japanese?

TSUNKU IS A SINGER/PRODUCER WHO PRODUCED BOTH MORNING MUSUME AND TAIYO AND CISCO MOON.

YUKO NAKAZAWA WAS THE OLDEST MEMBER OF MORNING MUSUME.

NAMIE AMURO IS A POPULAR SINGER. HARUTO IS HER SON.

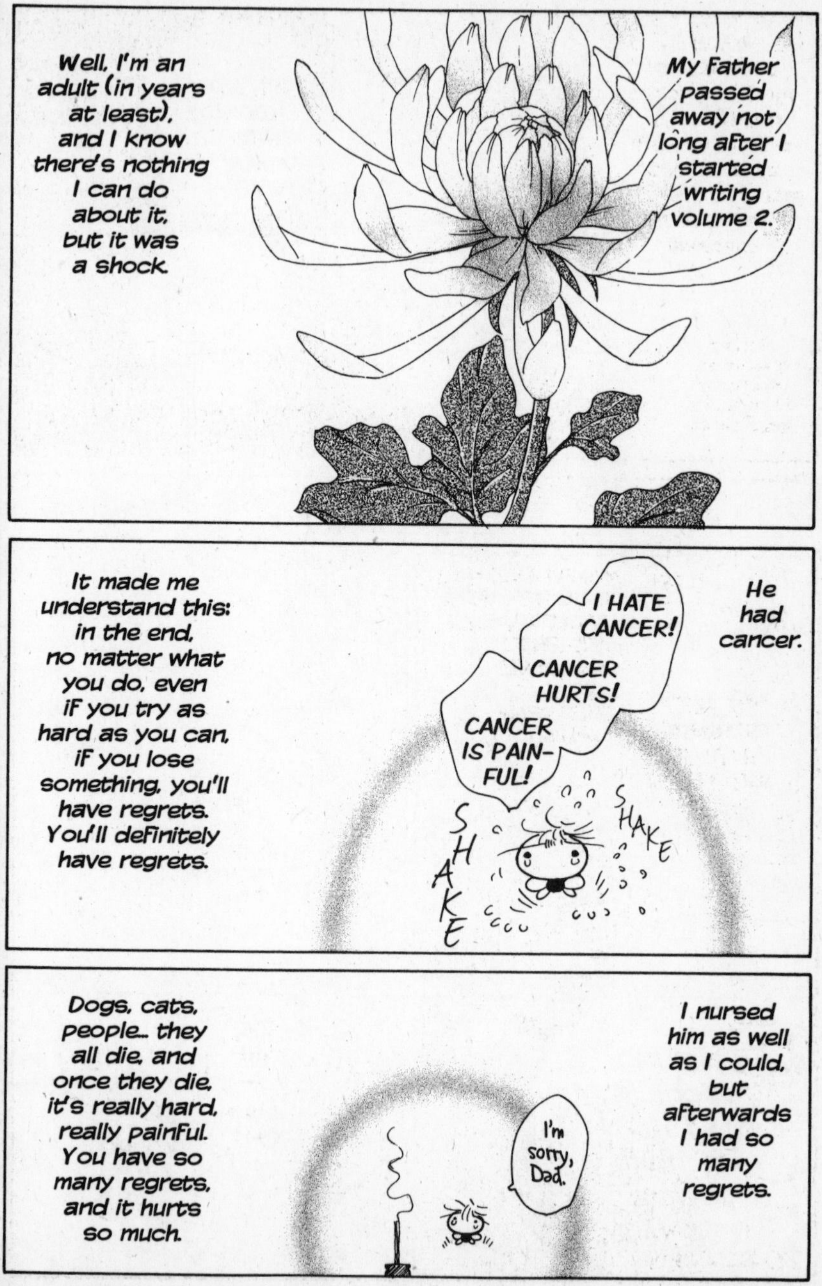
My Father passed away not long after I started writing volume 2.
Well, I'm an adult (in years at least), and I know there's nothing I can do about it, but it was a shock.
He had cancer.
I HATE CANCER!
CANCER HURTS!
CANCER IS PAIN-FUL!
SHAKE
SHAKE
It made me understand this: in the end, no matter what you do, even if you try as hard as you can, if you lose something, you'll have regrets. You'll definitely have regrets.
I nursed him as well as I could, but afterwards I had so many regrets.
I'm sorry, Dad.
Dogs, cats, people... they all die, and once they die, it's really hard, really painful. You have so many regrets, and it hurts so much.

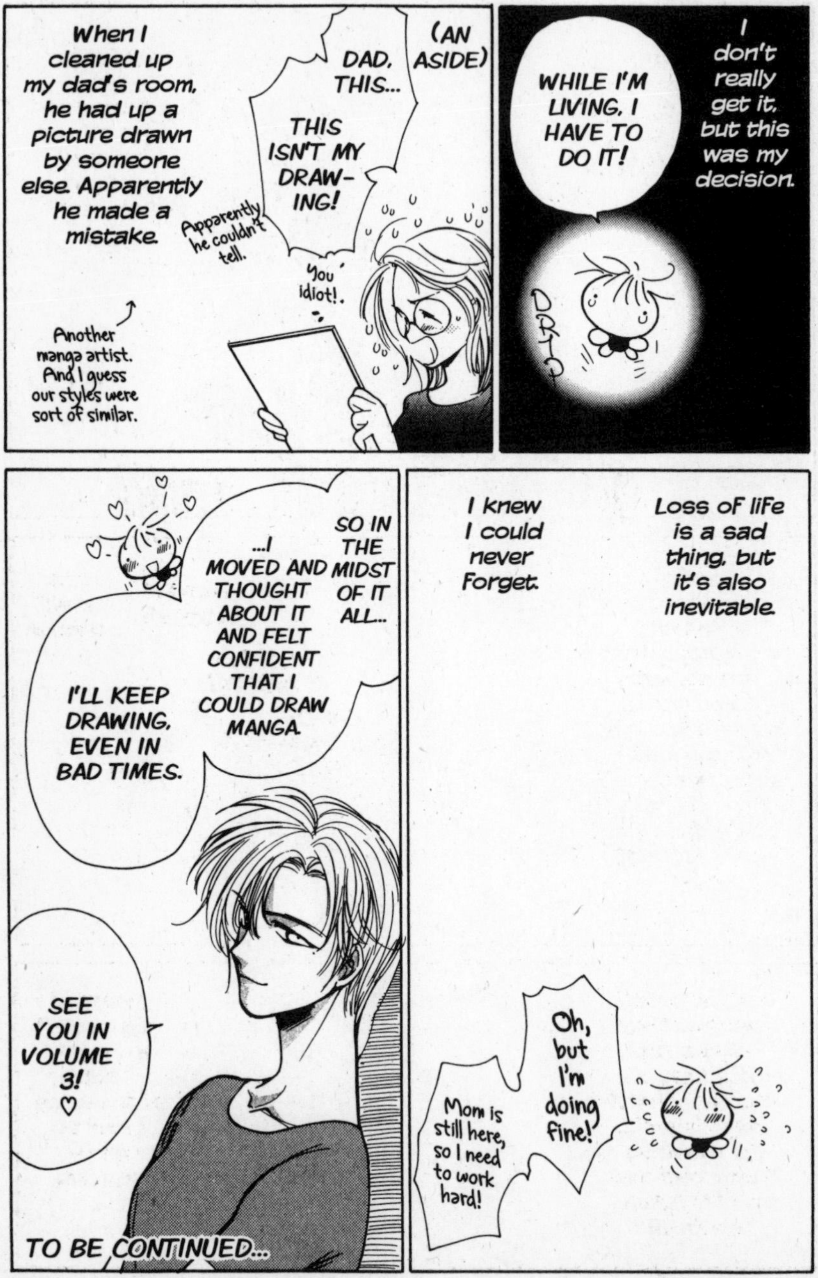
I don't really get it, but this was my decision.
WHILE I'M LIVING, I HAVE TO DO IT!
(AN ASIDE)
DAD, THIS...
THIS ISN'T MY DRAWING!
When I cleaned up my dad's room, he had up a picture drawn by someone else. Apparently he made a mistake.
Apparently he couldn't tell.
You idiot!
Another manga artist. And I guess our styles were sort of similar.
Loss of life is a sad thing, but it's also inevitable.
I knew I could never forget.
Oh, but I'm doing fine!
Mom is still here, so I need to work hard!
SO IN THE MIDST OF IT ALL...
...I MOVED AND THOUGHT ABOUT IT AND FELT CONFIDENT THAT I COULD DRAW MANGA.
I'LL KEEP DRAWING, EVEN IN BAD TIMES.
SEE YOU IN VOLUME 3! ♡
TO BE CONTINUED...

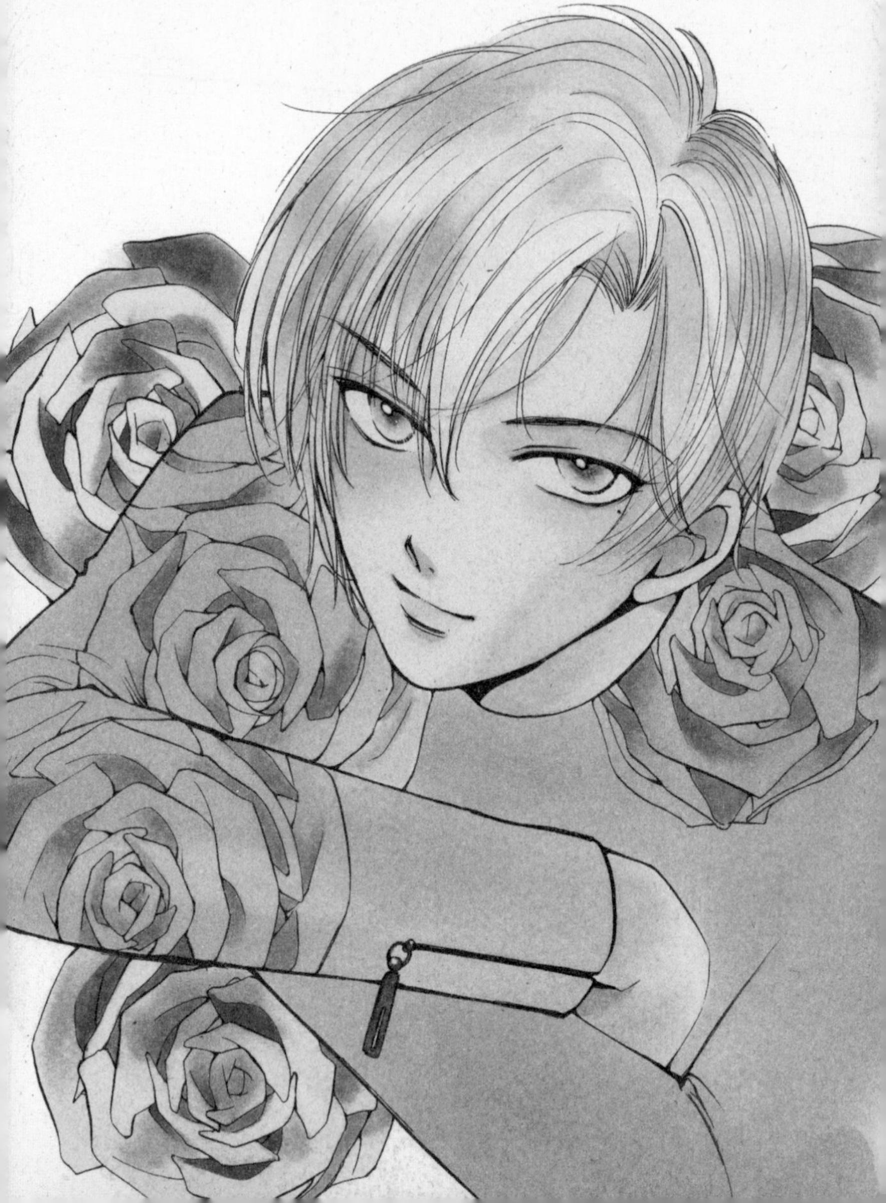

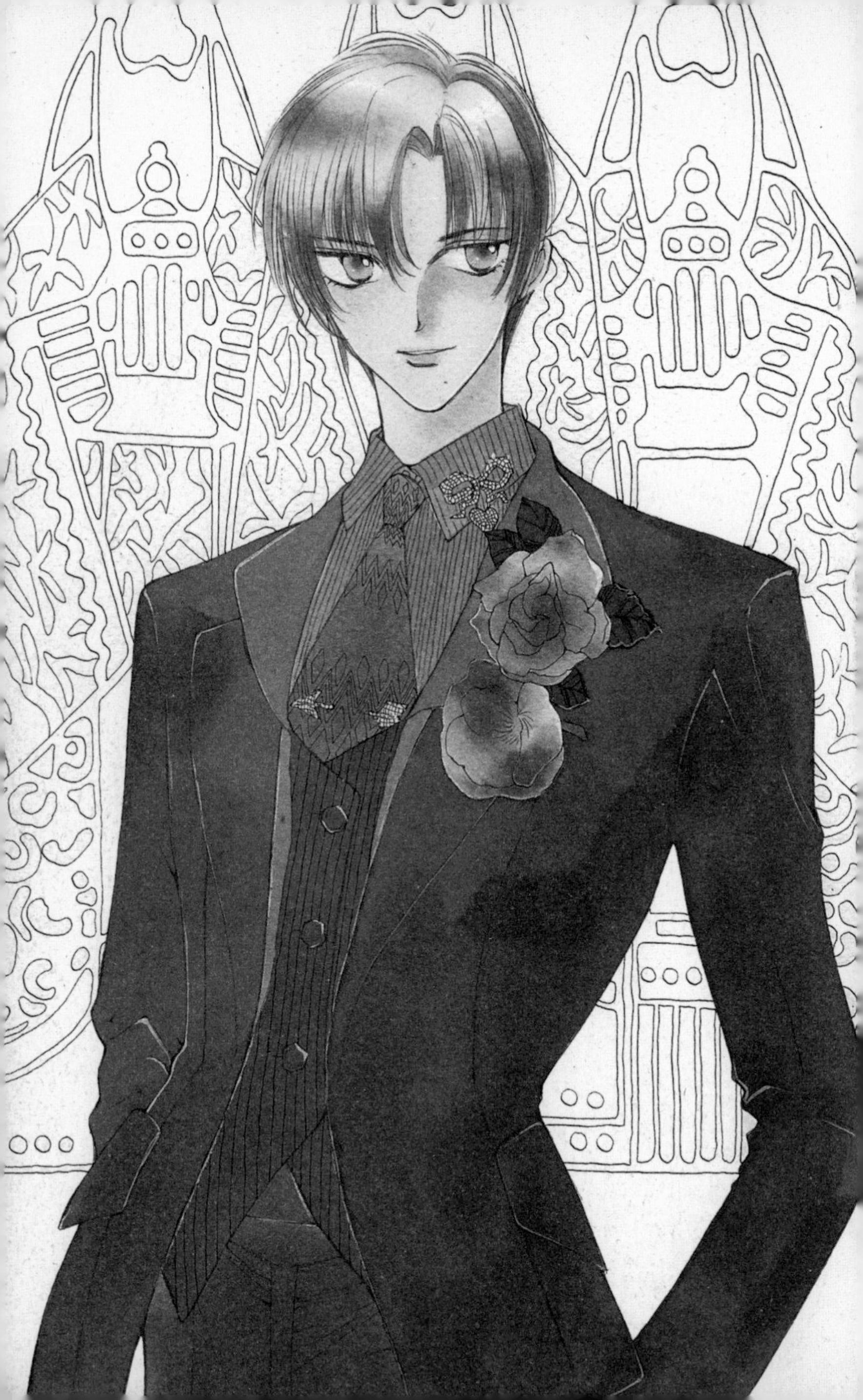

CROWN OF LOVE

Vol. 2
Shojo Beat Edition

STORY & ART BY YUN KOUGA

Translation **HC Language Solutions, Inc.**
Touch-up Art & Lettering **Annaliese Christman**
Design **Frances O. Liddell**
Editors **Yuki Murashige & Carrie Shepherd**

VP, Production **Alvin Lu**
VP, Sales & Product Marketing **Gonzalo Ferreyra**
VP, Creative **Linda Espinosa**
Publisher **Hyoe Narita**

Published by VIZ Media, LLC
P.O. Box 77010
San Francisco, CA 94107

10 9 8 7 6 5 4 3 2 1
First printing, May 2010

www.viz.com

www.shojobeat.com

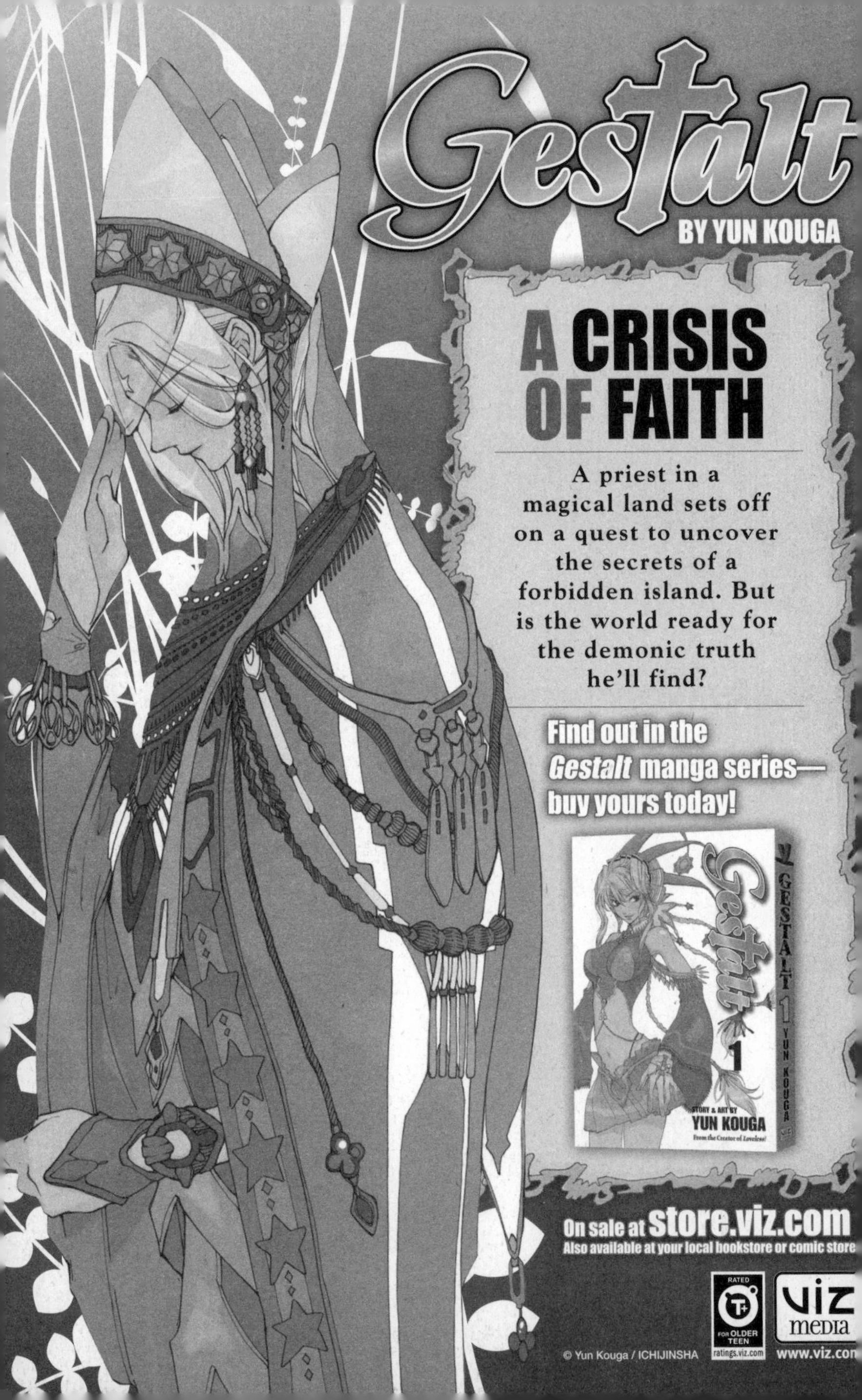
Gestalt
BY YUN KOUGA
A CRISIS OF FAITH
A priest in a magical land sets off on a quest to uncover the secrets of a forbidden island. But is the world ready for the demonic truth he'll find?
Find out in the *Gestalt* manga series—buy yours today!
Gestalt
GESTALT 1 YUN KOUGA
1
STORY & ART BY
YUN KOUGA
From the Creator of *Loveless*!
On sale at store.viz.com
Also available at your local bookstore or comic store
RATED T+ FOR OLDER TEEN
ratings.viz.com
VIZ media
www.viz.com
© Yun Kouga / ICHIJINSHA

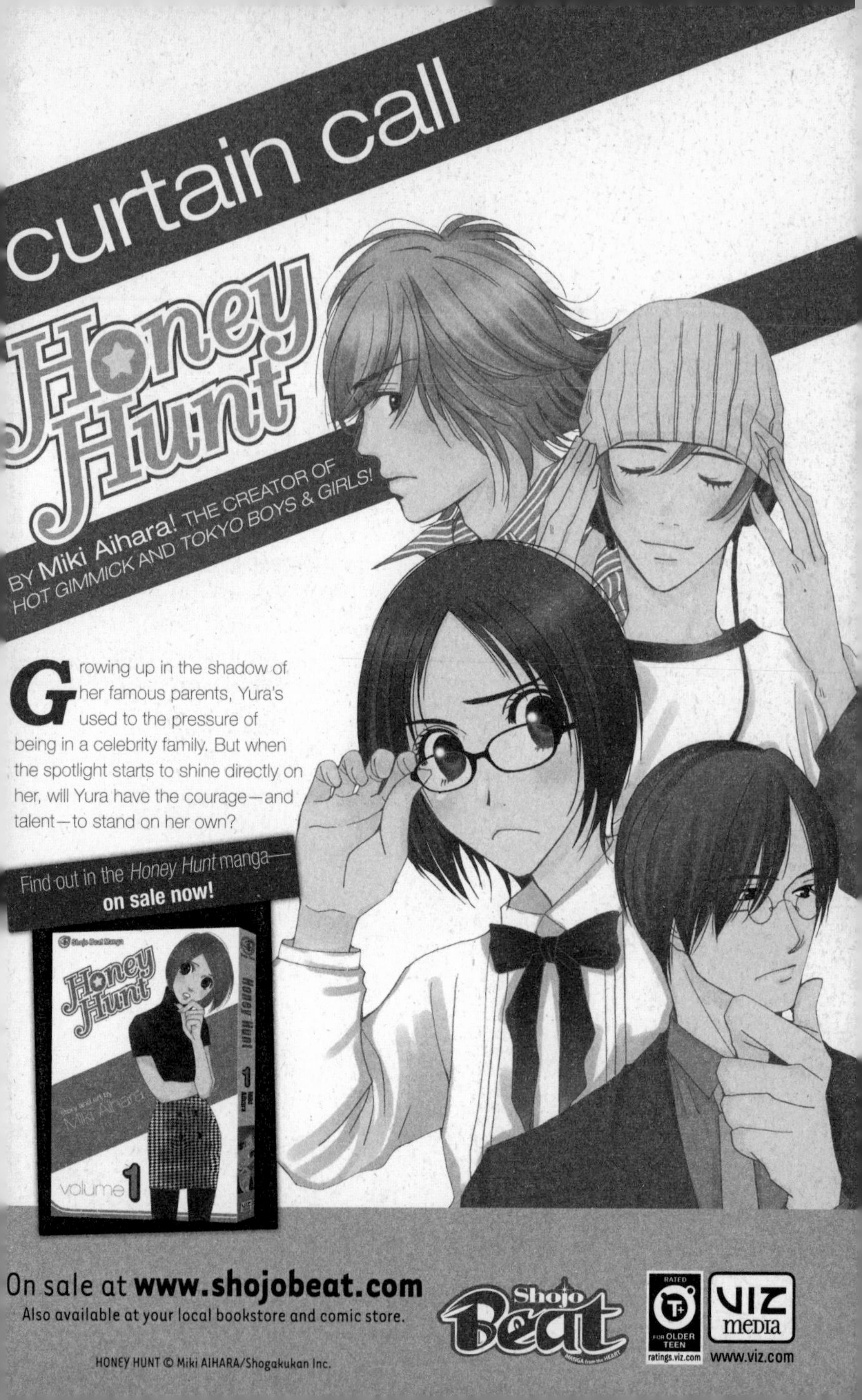
curtain call
Honey Hunt
BY Miki Aihara! THE CREATOR OF HOT GIMMICK AND TOKYO BOYS & GIRLS!
Growing up in the shadow of her famous parents, Yura's used to the pressure of being in a celebrity family. But when the spotlight starts to shine directly on her, will Yura have the courage—and talent—to stand on her own?
Find out in the *Honey Hunt* manga—
on sale now!
Honey Hunt
volume 1
On sale at **www.shojobeat.com**
Also available at your local bookstore and comic store.
Shojo Beat
RATED T+ FOR OLDER TEEN
ratings.viz.com
VIZ media
www.viz.com
HONEY HUNT © Miki AIHARA/Shogakukan Inc.

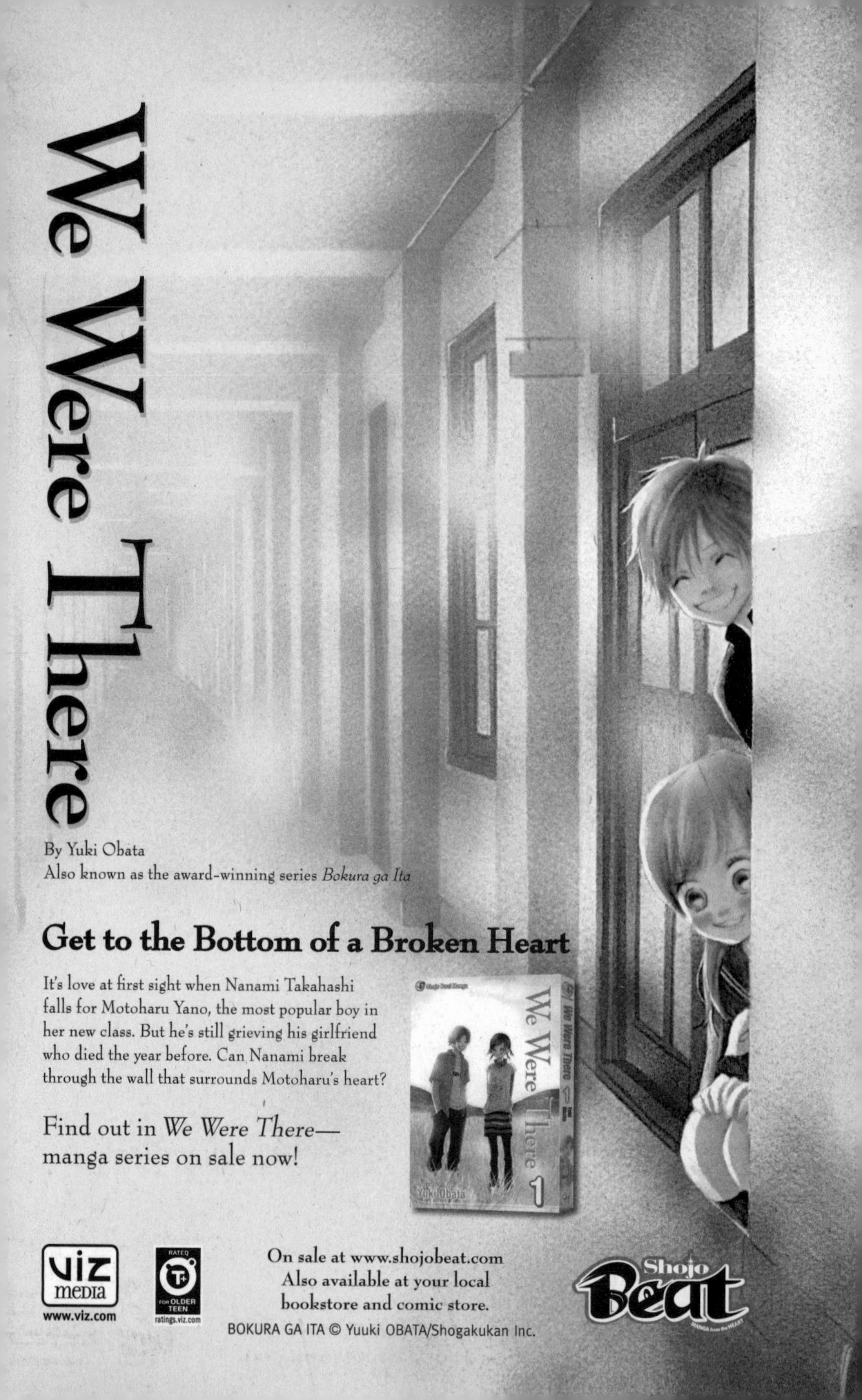

We Were There
By Yuki Obata
Also known as the award-winning series *Bokura ga Ita*
Get to the Bottom of a Broken Heart
It's love at first sight when Nanami Takahashi falls for Motoharu Yano, the most popular boy in her new class. But he's still grieving his girlfriend who died the year before. Can Nanami break through the wall that surrounds Motoharu's heart?
Find out in *We Were There*—manga series on sale now!
We Were There
Yuki Obata
1
viz media
www.viz.com
RATED T+ FOR OLDER TEEN
ratings.viz.com
On sale at www.shojobeat.com
Also available at your local bookstore and comic store.
BOKURA GA ITA © Yuuki OBATA/Shogakukan Inc.
Shojo Beat